Charles A Page, James Roberts Gilmore

Letters of a War Correspondent

Charles A Page, James Roberts Gilmore
Letters of a War Correspondent
ISBN/EAN: 9783337016920
Printed in Europe, USA, Canada, Australia, Japan
Cover: Foto ©ninafisch / pixelio.de

More available books at **www.hansebooks.com**

OF
A WAR CORRESPONDENT.

BY

CHARLES A. PAGE,

SPECIAL CORRESPONDENT OF THE NEW YORK "TRIBUNE"
DURING THE CIVIL WAR.

With Portraits and Maps.

EDITED, WITH NOTES, BY JAMES R. GILMORE,

AUTHOR OF

"PERSONAL RECOLLECTIONS OF ABRAHAM LINCOLN,"
"THE LIFE OF GARFIELD," ETC.

BOSTON:
L. C. PAGE AND COMPANY
(INCORPORATED).
1899.

Copyright, 1898,
BY L. C. PAGE AND COMPANY
(INCORPORATED)

𝔘𝔫𝔦𝔳𝔢𝔯𝔰𝔦𝔱𝔶 𝔓𝔯𝔢𝔰𝔰:
JOHN WILSON AND SON, CAMBRIDGE, U.S.A.

BIOGRAPHICAL INTRODUCTION.

THE correspondence of a first-class newspaper during our civil war is, in many respects, more valuable and instructive than the most impartial history of that important period. The historian relates facts and opinions as he has distilled them from the reports of others; the correspondent gives us his own impressions of events as they actually passed before his eyes. He is in the thick of the fight, where sabres clash, and minie-balls whistle, or he is perched in a friendly tree, or on some commanding hill, whence he views all the movements of the hostile battalions; and hence, if he be cool, truthful, and intrepid, we gather from him a living photograph of the tremendous conflict.

No more graphic, faithful, or venturous correspondent than Charles A. Page looked on at our civil war, and none more truthfully or graphically described its momentous events. "If Page says that it is so," was a common remark of Horace Greeley's in the "Tribune" editorial rooms; and the subsequent motto of the "Sun," "If you see it in the 'Sun,' it is so," was merely Charles A. Dana's appropriation of this familiar saying of Mr. Greeley. He once met Mr. Page on a railway train and said to him: "We are greatly pleased with your work; you are quick and graphic, and give us the news early, and we must have it early; but, Mr. Page, you are the most expensive young man the 'Tribune' has ever employed." To this Mr. Page replied: "Early news is expensive news, Mr. Greeley; if I have the watermelons and whiskey ready when the officers come along from the fight, I get the news without asking questions."

But watermelons and whiskey in war times are cash commodities, and so are steamboats and railway trains when they are chartered to convey a single passenger. Mr. Page did this on several occasions, and once he turned loose a valuable saddle-horse to catch a train. The passengers were noisy, and he could not think or write in the din, but getting to the office without sleep, he sat down and wrote out a five-column report of the Battle of the Wilderness in five hours, while the printers were putting it into type. The result was that the "Tribune" sold an extra edition of fifteen thousand copies four hours before any other journal had the news. Then Mr. Page went to sleep, and he did not wake for twenty-four long hours. He performed a like feat on a similar occasion after a horseback ride of seventy-five miles.

The old adage has it that "it is the early bird that catches the worm." Mr. Page was always early, first on the ground, and however great the obstacles, they never deterred him. He was one of the three correspondents who were the first to enter Richmond after the capture of that city, and the two who entered with him — Whitelaw Reid and Mr. R. T. Colburn — only got there by placing themselves under his wing, and submitting to his guidance. As soon as the War Department at Washington had tidings of the event, it cancelled all newspaper passes, and issued strict orders that no correspondent should be permitted to reach the army front. Mr. Page knew of this, but calling to mind that he had among his papers an outlawed pass from General Grant that might serve in the emergency, he, with his two friends, went boldly on board the Government steamer. Charles A. Dana, then Assistant War Secretary, hearing of their departure, sent telegram after telegram in pursuit of them; but by shifting from one steamer to another, and other expedients, they dodged the telegrams and got promptly into Richmond. Meeting Mr. Dana at a social gathering soon after his return to Washington, Mr. Page rallied him upon the incident, reminding him that his official orders were not always effective.

"Well, I did my best," said Mr. Dana.

"You were not aware," said Mr. Page, "that I am on familiar terms with most of the army officers, who, when they are directed to stop me, have a convenient way of ignoring my acquaintance."

But Mr. Page was not merely an alert gatherer of news; he was a graphic and skilful writer, an accomplished word-painter, who so vividly described the clash of the contending forces that his reader became, like him, a spectator looking on at the terrific conflict. Some of his battle-pictures are scarcely equalled by those of the most famous war-correspondents of this country or England.

Mr. Page was of pure New England origin, his ancestry on both father's and mother's side going far back to early colonial times. In 1834 his parents moved from New Hampshire to Illinois and settled on a farm near Dixon, in Lee County, about a hundred miles west of Chicago, which city had been settled only three years previously, and had then an estimated population of less than 1,000. The entire State was sparsely occupied, and Mr. Page's nearest neighbors were four, ten, and twenty miles distant. The buffalo and wild turkey still tenanted the prairies, and some few of the Indian tribes yet lingered around their old homes, though the peace which ended the Black Hawk War, in 1832, had banished their nation beyond the Mississippi. The spot was on the very confines of civilization; but there Mr. Page "drove his stakes," and built for his family the log cabin so universal in the backwoods. In this rude dwelling, four years later, on May 22, 1838, Charles A. Page was born, and in that neighborhood he passed the first eighteen years of his life in the usual employments of a farmer's son.

When he was about three years old his father built a log school-house on a corner of his farm, and with the aid of three or four neighbors, opened there a school for the instruction of the young people of the vicinity during the winter seasons. Here the common branches — "reading, 'riting and 'rithmetic" — were taught to students of all ages from three years to twenty-five, and of every stature from thirty-six inches to six feet. Special attention was paid to the spelling lesson. It was the closing exercise of each day, and then all the scholars were ranged in a row, their toes precisely upon a chalk mark, and if a scholar misspelled a word, the first one below him spelling it correctly was advanced over him to the head of the class. Charles Page was one of the youngest boys at the school, and small for his age, but he was a good speller. It is related to me by a surviving brother that he was one day standing in the class directly below a scholar over six feet high, when the tall fellow misspelled a word, and in passing above him the smaller boy dodged between the tall fellow's legs.

This was the only school that Mr. Page attended until he was eighteen years of age, but he was an omnivorous reader of books. He read all he could buy or borrow, and when he could neither buy nor borrow any more, he read over again what he had read before. He read them everywhere — at his meals, in going and coming from his farmwork; and while his horses were taking their needed rest at the plough, he would be found engrossed in a book at the plough-handle. The result was that, though lacking set instruction, he acquired a wide range of knowledge, and at the age of eighteen was fitted for admission at Cornell College, Mount Vernon, Iowa.

He studied there three years, graduating at the age of twenty-one, and then for two years edited "The Mount Vernon News," a weekly newspaper published at the seat of his Alma Mater. He visited Washington to be present at President Lincoln's first inauguration, and having been a zealous Republican, it was in accord with political practice that he sought reward for his party services by the appointment of postmaster at the little village of Mount Vernon. He was then but twenty-three — too young, it was thought by his townsmen, to fill so important a position, and he was awarded in lieu of it a clerkship in the Fifth Auditor's office of the Treasury Department, where his duties would be the adjustment of the accounts of consuls and foreign ministers.

Very soon the war broke out, and his previous editorial experience having given him a taste for journalistic work, he speedily became attached to the "New York Tribune," as a war correspondent, not, however, relinquishing his post in the Department; but it was understood that when "his desk was up," as the phrase was, he was absent with the army in his capacity of reporter.

The war over, he was, in 1865, appointed by President Johnson United States consul at Zurich, in Switzerland, — a district famous for its fine milch cows and its abundant herbage. Seeing this, Mr. Page conceived the organization of a condensed-milk company to sell this product in Great Britain and the United States. The result was the widely known Anglo-Swiss Milk Company, organized in 1866, which has now thirteen places of business in five different countries, and employs a capital of four millions of dollars.

Mr. Page died in London in May, 1873, at the early age of thirty-five — "fifty years too early," adds his brother, in his summing up of his very brief, but highly honorable career.

JAMES R. GILMORE.

LAKE GEORGE, N. Y.,
August, 1898.

CONTENTS.

	Page
Battle of Gaines' Mill	3
The Work of Evacuation	16
Battle of White Oak Swamp	20
Second Battle of Bull Run	23
The Escape of Lee from Gettysburg	35
The Grand Army	43
The Battle of the Wilderness	46
Spottsylvania	64
Cold Harbor	77
The Battles of Cold Harbor	86
Questions answered	104
The Movement to the James	107
The Movement beyond the James	109
The last grand Movement	116
Our Cavalry Operations during the Week	120
Around Petersburg	125
Where Lee's Troops are	131
Operations on Wednesday and Thursday of last Week	136
Operations on Friday	141
Going to the Front	155
An Artillery Duel	174
In Front of Petersburg	183
The Mine Explosion	194
A Letter from the Honorable Ben Wood	197
The Norfolk and Portsmouth Election	199
The Feeling over the Mine Disaster	207
Tobacco for Soldiers	210
The Wooing and Wedding of John Kick	214
Operations north of the James	218
Reply to Edmund K. Snead	225
The Colored Troops	231
On the Weldon Road	233
The new Position	237
From the Army of the James	246

EVENTS OF THE AUTUMN	259
A GLANCE AT THE SITUATION	283
FIVE FORKS	288
THE PETERSBURG BATTLE	297
INCIDENTS OF THE OCCUPATION	308
RICHMOND	313
THE OBSEQUIES OF ABRAHAM LINCOLN	354
THE GREAT REVIEW	391

LIST OF PORTRAITS AND MAPS.

PORTRAIT OF CHARLES A. PAGE	*Frontispiece*
BATTLEFIELDS OF THE GREAT CIVIL WAR	*Facing page* 2
THE SEAT OF MILITARY OPERATIONS IN AUGUST AND SEPTEMBER, 1862	" " 22
THE SEAT OF WAR FROM HARPER'S FERRY TO SUFFOLK, VA.	" " 42
PORTRAIT OF ULYSSES S. GRANT	64
PORTRAIT OF BENJAMIN F. BUTLER	165
PORTRAIT OF EDWIN M. STANTON	261
PORTRAIT OF JEFFERSON DAVIS	318
PORTRAIT OF ABRAHAM LINCOLN	354

Part First.

ARMY OF THE POTOMAC.

From June, 1862, to July, 1863.

THE letters of Mr. Page from the Army of the Potomac, while it was under the command of Generals McClellan and Meade, give no connected account of army operations, but are a series of detached pictures of battles and army scenes, so graphic and lifelike as to rank among the best that were written during that momentous period. They are here reproduced precisely as they appeared at the time in the columns of the New York "Tribune;" and this remark applies to all of his letters that are inserted in this volume.

LETTERS

OF

A WAR CORRESPONDENT.

BATTLE OF GAINES' MILL.

I.

ATTACK ON PORTER'S CORPS. — GOOD ARTILLERY SERVICE AGAINST SUPERIOR NUMBERS. — EVERY ASSAULT GALLANTLY REPELLED. — OUR LOSS FROM 300 TO 400. — ORDER TO FALL BACK. — DESTRUCTION OF $100,000 WORTH OF STORES. — DESCRIPTION OF THE FIGHTING. — THE PENNSYLVANIA RESERVE. — A PANIC.

SAVAGE'S STATION, Saturday, June 28, 1862.

THE events of the last two days, recounted in detail, with full lists of the casualties, would require a triple sheet of the "Tribune." Set forth with the ordinary discursiveness of army correspondents, McClellan might push forward to Richmond or be pushed back to Yorktown, before the task were completed by one pen. I shrink from even so much as I mark out for this letter. At no time in the history of the campaign have events so tread upon each other, and at this hour they seem to thicken in a whirl of the immediate future. God grant that these last two days of June, which loom up so portentous, may hasten our advent into Richmond more than the last forty-eight hours seem to have done!

Day before yesterday Porter's corps was strongly attacked in his position at the extreme right, near Mechanicsville, at a late hour in the afternoon. Not being on the ground, I am unable to give a detailed account; but the general features are given me by the brigade commanders.

McCall's Division bore the brunt of the encounter, though Morrell was severely engaged. Our superiority in artillery compensated in a measure for their superiority in numbers.

During long hours of the declining day and through half the night, anxious thousands of brave hearts who fight under Hooker and Keyes and Heintzelman and Sumner listened to that tremendous cannonading, and wondered how it fared with their brethren in arms.

Every attack was magnificently repelled, every inch of ground retained. Our loss was 300 to 400. It was the opinion of our generals that the position could have been maintained yesterday, but authentic information having reached General McClellan that the enemy had been re-enforced by Stonewall Jackson, our whole force was ordered to the Chickahominy, and the movement commenced during the night. The Eighth Illinois Cavalry, Colonel Farnsworth, formed the vigilant rear-guard. The enemy followed closely, took numbers of prisoners, including Company K, of the Pennsylvania Bucktails, and forced our quartermasters to burn at least $100,000 worth of stores. Captain Hooker, one of the best officers of the Eighth Illinois, was mortally wounded and left on the field. But the concentration of forces designed was effected with less loss than was doubtless expected when the order was given. Early in the forenoon of yesterday the pursued columns had taken position on the east bank of the Chickahominy and awaited the pursuers. They had not to wait long.

At this juncture your correspondent reached the field, and henceforth the narrative is that of an eye-witness.

The battle was fought in dense woods. Our forces were posted on the south side of a belt of forest on a line nearly two miles long, the general course of which was nearly parallel with the Chickahominy. The woods vary in depth from forty to one hundred rods; a small stream flows the entire length, and the ascent on either side is quite sharp. Cultivated fields cover the brow and crest of the hills on either side, and in the right rear of our position extend half a mile to the bottom-land of the Chickahominy. On the left the fringe of woods reaches to this bottom-land. At eleven A. M., when I reached the field, our pickets occupied the top of the hill across the ravine along its whole winding length. They reported a battery of the enemy at Gaines House, a mile north in his left rear, and numbers of Rebels in distinct view. This battery soon exchanged shots with guns on our right. Half an hour later they saluted our left with an occasional shell from a position so far westerly as to enfilade our line. Meanwhile an occasional report from a sharpshooter's rifle warned of the enemy's approach. The fire of our batteries on the right gradually grew more rapid, but the day wore away until it was three P. M., and there had been few casualties. *Would the enemy make a serious demonstration?* A volley from one company of a regiment on the left, directed at as many of the enemy who appeared on the crest of the opposite hill, causing them to hurry back, did not answer the question conclusively, for it was followed by dead silence. Twenty minutes later the answer came, and it was unmistakable — it was a tornado of musketry.

Butterfield's Brigade was on our extreme left, Martindale's at his right, Griffin's next, and at our extreme right Sykes' Division of regulars. McCall's Division formed the second line, and were held in reserve.

The ball opened with the centre, but only a moment, and the tornado swept right and left as if one current of electricity had discharged every man's musket. Our men disappeared, sending back cheerful shouts as they rushed into that dense wood where now corpses are thick as the trees. A spatter of Rebel lead lifted little puffs of dust on the hill from which, with straining eyes, I in vain sought to penetrate those dark recesses. A dull, heavy undercurrent of murmur as of the swarming of bees, the sharp ring of a random Minie overhead, the incessant roar of musketry, and now the wounded and the dead being borne out of those jaws of death tell how fierce is the fight. There are cheers and yells, for our men *cheer*, while they, like other savages, *yell*. But we drive them. As yet their superior numbers, enabling them to oppose always with fresh troops, do not tell. The fire slackens from left to right.

A tawny sergeant, whose moustache would vie with a Turkish pasha's tails — I see the fierce light in his eyes now — inquires of me where he shall carry the wounded man he bears on his back, and says, "The sinners are skedaddling!"

The battle had now raged three-fourths of an hour; Slocum's Division, which had already marched to the Chickahominy, was ordered up and McCall had not been engaged. The situation appeared promising. But only a small portion of the enemy's force had been beaten, and he was not disposed to cry quits. For the next hour the terrific firing would break out now at one point, anon at another, indicating that fresh columns were being continually pushed against our decimated lines. During this time every man of McCall's Pennsylvania Reserve was brought into action. Some time earlier his regiments had rushed at double-quick to the supporting positions assigned them, and had thrown themselves flat upon the ground till the order should come, "Up and at them!" At intervals, as some point in the line seemed weak, they went sternly into that wooded valley and shadow of death. Up to this time not a regiment had behaved unseemly. When relieved by new men, to be sure, they would straggle out like a dispersing mob, but they did not fail to "fall in" on the hill at the order. Sometimes a wounded man would be surrounded by a suspicious number of friends, but the skulkers bore no proportion to the true men.

Still at this hour, between half-past five and six, the situation was not hopeful. Beat back as many Rebel regiments as you would, fresh ones were poured into their places. The evidence is conclusive that no repelled assault — and there were a score of such — was renewed by the same column. Our coolest officers began to perceive that the enemy's force was overwhelming — probably 75,000, and 25,000 larger than had been anticipated or provided for.

At this time, Slocum's Division (late Franklin's) was brought into action. There were no more reserves, save cavalry. Every available regiment was fighting or had become exhausted in strength and in cartridges.

I saw Slocum's men go into the fight, and they did it handsomely, the brigades being conducted to their positions amid a murderous fire, by Lieut. Fred. Mead of his staff, who, sick for a month, left his couch for the battle-field. But I confess, from this time on, so great was the confusion that I know nothing circumstantial of the movements and fighting of the several brigades and regiments of any of the divisions, notwithstanding I was coaxed some distance into the woods by Mr. Crountze of "The World," who seemed bent on securing a place among the martyrs.

My note-book says that, at six o'clock, the enemy commenced a determined attack on our extreme left, evidently with a design of flanking us. It was an awful firing that resounded from that smoke-clouded valley, — not heavier than some in the earlier part of the engagement, but more steady and determined. I am told that some men on the other side and farther up the river saw more than a dozen Rebel regiments march in at that point, and, remaining only a few minutes, file out a little distance up the ravine. It was only by overbearing exhausted men with fresh ones that the enemy succeeded in turning that flank, as at length he did succeed, only too well. And he accomplished it in three-quarters of an hour. At the expiration of that time our officers judiciously ordered their men to fall back; the order was not obeyed so judiciously, for they ran back, broken, disordered, routed. Simultaneously the wounded and skulkers about the buildings used as hospitals caught a panic, whether from a few riderless horses plunging madly across the field, or from instantaneously scenting the rout, does not appear. A motley mob started pell-mell for the bridges. They were overtaken by many just from the woods, and it seemed as if Bull Run were to be repeated.

As the infantry betook themselves from the point of attack, some twenty guns, fortunately posted in the morning for such an emergency, and which had not yet made a sign, opened a terrific fire of canister at short range. The enemy recoiled. The bridge of Lodi was not half so terrible. Until night set in, until the Valley of the Chickahominy was canopied with sulphur, until their ammunition was exhausted — and many of them went upon the field with over two-hundred rounds — did those guns hold the raging enemy at bay.

Meanwhile, the panic extended. Scores of gallant officers endeavored to rally and re-form the stragglers, but in vain, while many officers forgot the pride of their shoulder-straps and the honor of their manhood, and herded with sneaks and cowards. O that I had known the names of those officers I saw, the brave and the cowardly, that here, now, I might reward and punish by directing upon each individual the respect or the contempt of a whole people!

That scene was not one to be forgotten. Scores of riderless, terrified horses dashing in every direction; thick-flying bullets singing by, admonishing of danger; every minute a man struck down; wagons and ambulances and cannon blockading the way; wounded men limping and groaning and bleeding amid the throng; officers and civilians denouncing and reasoning and entreating, and being insensibly borne along with the mass; the sublime cannonading; the clouds of battle-smoke, and the sun just disappearing, large and blood-red — I cannot picture it, but I see it, and always shall.

Among those most earnest in withstaying the frightened host was ex-Governor Wood of Illinois. A large, handsome old man, with a flowing white beard and the voice of a Stentor. I should not have been astonished had those poor, bewildered men taken him for some old patriarch risen from the dead and calling to them; *had* one risen from the dead they would not have heeded him. I thought, too, of the old regicide who left his concealment to head the simple Puritan villagers against the savages, and then vanished as quickly, leaving his appearance as the tradition of a heavenly visitant.

About this time a new battery and two fresh regiments of Meagher's Brigade were brought up, headed by that officer. The mob parted, and they passed rapidly through, cheering as they went. The answering cheers were sickly.

I do not wish to be harsh with these men. Many of them had fought and marched all the previous day and night. The day was excessively hot. The men were exhausted. I do not think they left the field with an average of two cartridges to the man. If there was a single regiment that did not go into the battle with spirit and maintain it with credit, I do not know it. Besides, he must be a brave and a strong man who whips three of equal training. This much in extenuation. Add to it the statement of several generals that men never fought better. Still, I cannot refrain from expressing the one thought that possessed me at the time,—the fact that 10,000 men were in full retreat.

Some time after the main body had passed on, when that stream had become decently small, in company with Governor Wood, I rode to find the Illinois Cavalry, and came upon them stretched across the plain halting every unwounded man. They had cooped up several thousands, but the task of re-forming them was found impossible by even such officers as their Colonel and Major Clendenning, and they were at length permitted to continue rearward.

I crossed the Chickahominy at eleven P. M., at which time comparative order had been restored. The enemy were in possession of our hospitals and the battle-field, but we still showed a determined front. It was not known by the brigadier-generals whether we should try to hold the position the next day, or cross the river during the night.

At six o'clock this morning I rode to the bridge, with the intention of re-crossing, but was some distance off when I heard the explosion that destroyed it, the force having passed over mainly after midnight. It is impossible at this day to estimate our loss. But few of the dead were brought from the field, and not one-half the wounded. Hundreds of the latter were brought as far as the river, but could not be brought over before the destruction of the bridges. Basing my opinion on the number who were brought over (about 800), and the proportion that number must bear to the remainder, I estimate, the entire wounded at 3500 and the killed at 800. How many prisoners and what amount of stores are lost, it is even still more difficult to estimate. I judge but few stores and several thousand prisoners. The loss in officers is particularly severe. Colonels

Gove of the Twenty-Second Massachusetts; Black, Sixty-Second Pennsylvania; McLean, Eighty-Third Pennsylvania; Major Naghle, Eighty-Third Pennsylvania; Colonel Tucker, Second New Jersey; Lieutenant-Colonel Heth, Fifth Maine, are among the killed. Colonel Howland, Sixteenth New York, slightly wounded; Lieutenant-Colonel Marsh, Sixteenth New York, severely wounded; Colonel Simpson, Fourth New Jersey, wounded and a prisoner; Colonel Pratt, Thirty-First New York, wounded.

In the early part of the day one of our men captured a Rebel knapsack, hung to which was half a skull, used evidently as a drinking-vessel. An inscription upon it stated that it came from Bull Run. During the stampede, for a moment the attention of hundreds was attracted to a horse galloping around carrying a man's leg in the stirrup, — the left leg, booted and spurred. It was a splendid horse, gayly caparisoned.

Instances of extraordinary gallantry are not wanting. General Butterfield led his men like another Ney, and with that marshal's good fortune escaped without a scratch. A shattered scabbard, clothes torn with bullets, and a hat wrenched from his head and demolished by the fragment of a shell — the general might predicate a fatalistic belief in his "star."

This was also one of several instances where officers left sick-beds rather than their commands should go to the field without them.

The French princes — the Prince de Joinville and the two young men — rode upon the field in hot haste during the engagement, and were ubiquitous as they certainly were daring and efficient, especially in rallying and re-forming the men as they came out of the woods.

The circumstances under which Lieut. J. Howe of the Third New Jersey met his death show him a hero. After the panic he had gone down upon the plain, found a portion of Company H of his regiment, and with them as a nucleus, was rallying to his colors a provisional regiment from the mass of stragglers. He had gathered several hundred, was addressing them in stirring words and pointing to the flag, when a conical rifled shot struck him in the breast, passing through his body and into the ground at the feet of the men. It was the only cannon-shot that fell in that vicinity.

Summing up, we had about 30,000 men engaged, the Rebels double at least that number with Stonewall Jackson in command. As a great battle, this of Gaines' Mill (it will perpetuate the name of a rank traitor) ranks, I judge, only second to Shiloh and Fair Oaks; how disastrous, or whether disastrous, remains to be seen. If I have guessed out the correct theory of the campaign it will neither change nor hinder future operations already determined upon.

The sad feature is that our wounded are to-night subjected to, not only the neglect of those of Fair Oaks, but perhaps to the additional barbarity of those at Bull Run.

II.

The Battle of Gaines' Mill. — A Desperate Encounter. — Killed and Wounded, Forty-Five Hundred — Thirty Thousand against Seventy-Five Thousand. — The Heroism of the Union Troops. — The Fighting by the Regulars. — The Casualties at the Battle of White Oak Swamp.

White Oak Swamp, with the Army before Richmond.
Sunday, June 29, 1862.

THE battle of day before yesterday, — I call it the battle of Gaines' Mill, — now that forty-eight hours have passed, is found to be one of even greater magnitude than we thought when we saw the angry red sun go down on our beaten — if not beaten, say shattered — columns. The numbers engaged were as I then estimated 30,000 upon our side. Upon the enemy's, fully 75,000. We have brought across the Chickahominy 1,000 wounded. The killed and wounded left upon the field cannot be less than 4,500, and still there are 3,000 to be classed as missing. Some of these last will come in, but as many others will straggle into the hands of the enemy. Not far from twenty guns were left on the field. Each of these estimates is something less than my fears.

And the terrible fighting, — the tornadoes of musketry, and the volleys of thunderbolts from hundreds of cannon, —

"The scream of shot and burst of shell
And bellowing of the mortars," —

these have not been paralleled by this army, despite Williamsburg and Fair Oaks. The swollen list of martyrs is the terribly sad evidence.

The movements of the last hour of battle, by sifting and comparing the statements of those engaged, are assuming a more definite shape in my mind. Our line was broken at the left of Martindale's position, not because our men there fought less bravely than elsewhere, but because the enemy made that the point of his last desperate repeated efforts. They were simply overpowered, — mortal men could do no more. The Twelfth and Eighty-Third Pennsylvania of Butterfield's Brigade, posted at his right, withstood a part of these assaults, and gave way only on finding their flank turned. The Twelfth forever erased the discreditable record of Bull Run. It actually faced about at the quick eye which dictated the prompt command of its officers, and fought into the Rebel flank as they pushed through the line. It was then and there that Major Barnum, Lieutenant-Colonel Richardson, and Lieutenant-Colonel Rice were heroes. Captain Rucker, of the Twelfth, came last from the woods, bringing but fourteen men of his company. Captain Hoyt, of the brigade staff, repeatedly rode through every regiment, waving them on with a regimental flag he had seized from a fallen man. Simultaneously, and from the same superhuman impulse, General Butterfield was doing the same thing with other tattered colors.

At another time, learning that the colors of a regiment, by a misapprehension of an order to bury them in the cover of trees lest they serve as a target, were upon the ground, the same general rode to the front, raised them from the dust, flaunted them before his men, and stirred them with hot words. That banner was not again trailed.

Among the incidents of the attempt to stay the falling back was a charge of the Fifth Cavalry (regulars) from a flat at the left, around the base of a hill, full into a withering fire. But one-third of them came back. Here Captain Whiting was killed.

Among those most efficient in rallying the men, and forming provisional companies and regiments when the rout became general, were General Butterfield and staff, General Martindale, and the French princes. Colonel Berdan was frantic in his valorous efforts, actually discharging his pistols to stop the runaways. The lines these and other officers brought up in the gathering darkness must have been taken by the enemy for reenforcements — hence he desisted. The artillery men did their whole duty — they peopled Hades.

Those who lost their guns stood by them until half the company's men and horses were struck down, and the ammunition expended, and in several instances dragged them some distance by hand. Had they not been sold as dearly as they were, had they been brought off when it was possible, the main body of the corps must have surrendered.

The reader may not be able to reconcile the fact that we were defeated with my almost indiscriminate award of praise, and accounts of hard fighting. Let him bear in mind that we should have held the ground had not our ammunition given out; that the numbers opposed were in vast excess of ours; that the enemy were desperate; and finally, that they were led by Stonewall Jackson, who is just now, and with reason, their favorite leader.

I have said nothing of the generalship displayed on the field. Whether the field was judiciously chosen, I have said nothing. Whether there was any necessity for allowing a battle to come on with such fearful disparity of forces, I have said nothing. These are questions that should be held in abeyance. Were I to listen to the complaints and accept the opinions of several prominent officers engaged, I must answer them in the negative. Were I to put on record the assertions of others who have some claim to speak *ex cathedra*, I should say each of the above points were made with more than ordinary generalship. For the present let the whole matter rest.

If my letter of yesterday is safely transmitted, you will notice that I give more prominence to the fighting on the left of the field. Naturally, I have written first and most of what I actually saw, and if I have seemed to bring myself in the foreground of the narrative, it is because I could be certain of only those movements that came under my eye, and could easiest recount them by making the account one of personal observation.

On the right, as stated in yesterday's letter, General Sykes' Division, consisting of two brigades of regulars and Warren's Brigade of Fifth and Tenth New York and First Connecticut, were in the first line.

Take the day together, the action was less severe here than at the left. I think I am warranted in saying this, and also in saying that the regulars did not fight as well as many volunteer regiments, if as well as the average,—not certainly to compare with the Twelfth New York, the Eighty-Third Pennsylvania, the Second Maine, and the Twenty-Second Massachusetts. In one item they excelled the volunteers,—they could be re-formed, when they had fallen back completely out of fire, with less difficulty.

It is the first battle in which the regulars have taken any considerable part, and fighting side by side with volunteers they have not shamed the latter.

I must advert once more to the terrible scenes with which the day closed, in order to again note the superhuman exertions made by officers to rally the stampeders. I add to those I mentioned yesterday, as deserving the same encomiums, Colonel Roberts, Second Maine; Major Von Vegesack, Butterfield's staff; Major Welch, Sixteenth Michigan; and several officers of the Ninth Massachusetts whose names I failed to learn. Of course there were hundreds of others of like gallantry, some in every regiment, but no one man can speak from personal observation of a tithe of the gallant efforts to stay that fell disaster.

THE WORK OF EVACUATION.

THE REMOVAL OF STORES FROM WHITE HOUSE. — SAVAGE'S AND DISPATCH STATIONS. — APPEARANCE OF THE REBELS. — A CHECK.

LANDING ON JAMES RIVER, 17 MILES BELOW RICHMOND.
Monday, June 30, 1862, 12 M.

THERE has been a series of battles — fiercely contested, exhaustive battles, — from Thursday, June 26, at Beaver Dam, near Mechanicsville, up to this hour, when I hear artillery and musketry and shelling from Galena, and wounded men are being borne by. The army was put in motion for this point on Saturday morning, General Keyes's Corps taking the front, next to which followed Porter's thinned ranks and the enormous trains of baggage. Heintzelman's, Sumner's, and Franklin's Corps were left to face the enemy and protect the retreat. The railroad was at once given up. Troops of the enemy's cavalry appeared simultaneously, early on Saturday morning, at half a dozen points between White House and Savage's Station.

Early on Friday morning, before the battle of Gaines' Mill, General Stoneman left Porter, taking with him the Second and Sixth (regular) Cavalry, the Seventeenth New York, Colonel Lansing, and the Eighteenth Massachusetts and some artillery, and marched towards Old Church and White House. I have no word of his movements, but I presume he guarded the railroad until the stores at the different stations could be destroyed, and the scattered detachments along the road could beat a timely retreat, either to White House or to Savage's, and then fell back upon Yorktown. Colonel Farnsworth of the Eighth Illinois Cavalry sent two companies of his regiment, under Captain Farnsworth, to Dispatch Station, six miles from Savage's. The captain emptied the hospital, then burned all the stores at the station, and protected the hospital train into our lines, not, however, without brisk skirmishing and the loss of several of his command. On Saturday the baggage trains of the whole army were started. Keyes moved his divisions to White Oak Swamp, six miles south of Savage's. Porter's Division straggled some distance after him. At midnight the stores had been removed from Savage's, or heaped up for burning. More than 800 wounded were there. Becoming aware that the place was not to be held, perhaps a third of the more able wandered, lame and bleeding, out into the darkness, and followed the wagons. Surgeons volunteered to remain with the others, Dr. Page of Heintzelman's Division in charge.

At daybreak on Sunday morning the works in front were evacuated, the troops falling back in line on the railroad, two miles back. By eight o'clock the enemy appeared, and engaged portions of Smith's, Richardson's, and Sedgwick's divisions. He was repulsed by an hour's heavy fighting. The affair fought near Fair Oaks, in which our loss was several hundred, may be known as the battle of Peach Orchard. Again the line faced about, and took a position near Savage's. Late in the afternoon the enemy came up, and a similar struggle, with a similar result, brought on night. In these engagements the artillery was of the utmost service, raking the enemy with canister, repelling him, aided by but few volleys of musketry, and making his loss ten times our own.

The action at Savage's, the more severe of the two, was splendidly fought by both sides, and the final repulse of the infuriated hordes of the enemy was complete and destructive. General Heintzelman commanded on the field.

In the early part of the same day Keyes came upon the enemy in front, a small distance beyond White Oak Swamp — squads of cavalry in every road. Half a regiment came charging full into Couch's Division, pursuing a dozen of his scouts, evidently entirely unsuspicious of our approach in force. They swept furiously on, yelling and brandishing their swords, when, quick as powder-flash, they were treated to a tremendous surprise. Masked batteries turned upon the Rebels slaughter as free as when they quenched the genius of a Winthrop, and that dashing band came square up to five guns — a slight earthquake, and there were thirty empty saddles. The pursued became the pursuers. Sixty-one prisoners were taken, nine of the enemy killed, including a major and two captains, and twenty wounded. We did not lose a man. This nice little job was executed by Captain Flood's Company D, First Pennsylvania Artillery.

From ten o'clock until five, the front of the columns halted. Generals McClellan, Keyes, Porter, Peck, Morrell, Butterfield, and others, were in anxious consultation. Had the enemy penetrated our design in season to intercept with any considerable force? He was close and strong upon our rear: was he close and strong in front? Would the rear-guard fight him back? We could hear tough old Heintzelman at work. God give him victory! was the spoken or unspoken prayer of all hearts. Were Heintzelman beaten it was utter ruin; if there were even one Rebel division in front, the march to the James would be disputed and delayed. It was an absolute necessity that the way be unimpeded. There were twenty-five miles of trains cooped up between the advance and rear guards.

Huddled among the wagons were ten thousand stragglers — for the credit of the nation be it said that four-fifths of them were wounded, sick, or utterly exhausted, and could not have stirred but for dread of the tobacco warehouses of the South. The confusion of this herd of men and mules, wagons and wounded, men on horse, men on foot, men by the roadside, men perched on wagons, men searching for water, men famishing for food, men lame and bleeding, men with ghostly eyes, looking out between bloody bandages that hid the face — turn to some vivid account of the most pitiful part of Napoleon's retreat from Russia, and fill out the picture — the grim, gaunt, bloody picture of war in its most terrible features.

It was determined to move on during the night. The distance to Turkey-Island Bridge, the point on James River which was to be reached, by the direct road was six miles. But those vast numbers could not move over one narrow road in days; hence every by-road, no matter how circuitous, had been searched out by questioning prisoners, and by cavalry excursions. Every one was filled by one of the advancing columns. The whole front was in motion by seven P. M., General Keyes in command of the advance.

I rode with General Howe's Brigade of Couch's Division, taking a wagon track through dense woods and precipitous ravines, winding sinuously far around to the left, and striking the river some distance below Turkey Island. Commencing at dusk, the march continued until daylight. The night was dark and fearful. Heavy thunder rolled in turn along each point of the horizon, and dark clouds spread the entire canopy. We were forbidden to speak aloud, or, lest the light of a cigar should present a target for an ambushed rifle, we were cautioned not to smoke. Ten miles of weary marching, with frequent halts, as some one of the hundred vehicles of the artillery train in our centre, by a slight deviation crashed against a tree, wore away the hours to dawn, when we debouched into a magnificent wheat field, and the smoke stack of the Galena was in sight. Xenophon's remnant of the ten thousand, shouting, "The sea! The sea!" were not more glad than we.

Wakened from my couch of newly cut wheat by sharp spears of eight-o'clock sunlight stabbing my eyes, I rode to this place, and have since been industriously trying to ascertain the situation. I learn that twenty-five miles of wagon trains were moving last night, and that not a single disaster occurred to them. The entire siege train, one only of the heavy guns excepted, is brought safely off. The rear-guard hold White Oak Swamp, with prospect of heavy work to-day.

A word as to the destruction of stores during the last two days.

Porter's entire train was brought over the Chickahominy before the battle of Friday, hence nothing was lost there. At Savage's, when that place was abandoned, seventeen hundred cubic feet of ammunition, and enormous heaps of quartermaster's and sutler's stores, officers' baggage and soldiers' knapsacks, were destroyed, and at every halting-place since, the fagot has been busy with whatever could be transported no further. I can form no estimate of the entire value, but it is immense. One thing is certain, but little has fallen into the enemy's hands.

I close to ride back to the rear — now our front.

BATTLE OF WHITE OAK SWAMP.

THE PENNSYLVANIA RESERVE. — EXCELLENT BEHAVIOR OF THE MEN GENERALLY.

TURKEY BRIDGE, JAMES RIVER.
Nine A. M., Tuesday, July 1, 1862.

ANOTHER tremendous battle, more terrible carnage, yesterday. From Wednesday to Monday has this army been fighting, — a six days' battle, or, if you please, forty battles.

Early yesterday morning the enemy appeared in force at White Oak Swamp, the position we had assumed during the night previous. In this retreat — why hesitate to use that word? — he has not in a single instance long hesitated to attack; he did not now. By noon the action had commenced, — the battle of White Oak Swamp. Musketry had not ceased when I left the field at ten P. M. It will scarcely rank in magnitude with Gaines' Mill, and yet we did not suffer more, nor cause to suffer more, at Fair Oaks.

It is impossible for me to give a circumstantial account of this battle, raging as it did ten hours, and extending along a line of two and a half miles, and fought on ground such that not one-tenth of the field was in view from any one point cf vision. At least three-fifths of what remains of McClellan's army was engaged or in immediate reserve. Heintzelman's, Sumner's, and Franklin's corps were thus, and a portion of each of Keyes's and Porter's. More could scarcely have been brought into an action had the fate of the country depended on the one effort. Not so many can be brought into line to-day. And yet we only barely held our ground — perhaps not quite.

I shall have to hurry on to the results. Our loss of yesterday may be estimated at 6,000. Many of these are prisoners. The Pennsylvania Reserve were again in the thickest. This morning they do not muster 3,000 men. Add to these 1,000, who are straggling and will yet come in, and the number is less than half that they began with at Beaver Dam. They lost severely there, they were more than decimated the next day at Gaines' Mill, and yesterday they shrank to this small measure. Their leader, General McCall, is severely wounded and in the enemy's hands. Our brigade commander, Gen. J. J. Reynolds, is a prisoner at Richmond, another, Gen. Geo. G. Meade, lies in a tent near us seriously wounded. Officers of lower grade we have lost in about the same proportion. Of the Bucktail Regiment, not a hundred respond to the roll-call.

And so with other divisions. For the losses of the last six days cannot be less than fifteen thousand. It is only hoped that they will not reach twenty thousand.

Our generals behaved like Napoleon's under his own eagle eye. General McCall was severely wounded in the shoulder, but refused to leave the field or to dismount. At night, when the enemy had been driven back, his horse was found dead, and this is all that is known of his fate. That Generals Richardson and Dana, always well up in the mêlée, escaped unhurt, seems miraculous. The same may be said of scores. General Burns and General Brooks were each slightly wounded, but neither so disabled as to leave the field. Colonel Wyman, Sixteenth Massachusetts, was killed late in the day, under what circumstances I cannot say, but in a brave fight it may be warranted, for such was the place he always sought. Colonel Hinks, Nineteenth Massachusetts, fought his regiment until he had fewer officers than companies, made two bayonet charges, and fought his men until at length he fell wounded.

Let it be recorded here that a regiment always fights precisely like its officers. This fact recurs to me as I speak of the Nineteenth, since that furnishes one of the most notable instances bearing on the assertion.

The varying fortunes of the field are shown by the fact that each side took guns and large numbers of prisoners. Among those taken from the enemy are Colonel Lamar of Georgia, ex-M. C., the noted Secessionist of long standing, and Colonel Pendleton, of a Louisiana regiment, formerly of Cincinnati. A whole brigade was captured by Heintzelman, — a small brigade, 1,600 strong. Perhaps 3,000 were taken during the day.

That the enemy's loss of the last week is in excess of our own is as nearly certain as anything can be of which there is no direct proof. He has lost fewer by capture than we, but his killed and wounded must fully balance the account. By fighting the enemy in chosen positions, where the artillery could play havoc with all who should attempt to approach, we piled his dead in windrows. Our superiority in artillery has saved the army from utter annihilation. And yet the most tenacious struggles have been over these very guns. The enemy never fails to attempt their capture, — evidently having a wholesome sense of their value.

Yesterday the gunboats participated to the extent of silencing a Rebel battery which had succeeded in getting into play upon our baggage trains.

The salvation of this decimated, exhausted, and depressed army is a question of supplies and re-enforcements, immediate and heavy. If these weary thousands could get twenty-four hours' rest their safety would be assured, but if left alone, any cessation of attack and repulse until the final catastrophe will not be permitted.

THE SEAT OF MILITARY OPERATIONS IN AUGUST AND SEPTEMBER, 1862.

Map 24. Cm. Military operations in August and September, 1862.

SECOND BATTLE OF BULL RUN.

THE GREAT FIGHT OF FRIDAY. — BULL RUN REGAINED. — THE STRUGGLE OF SATURDAY. — SIGEL THE HERO OF THE DAY. — REBELS REENFORCED ON FRIDAY BY LONGSTREET. — LEE'S FORCES ARRIVE ON SATURDAY. — THE RENEWAL OF THE CONFLICT. — POPE RETIRES UNMOLESTED AFTER A TWO HOURS' FIGHT. — HIS FORCE IN STRENGTH AT CENTREVILLE. — SIXTY THOUSAND RE-ENFORCEMENTS GONE TO HIM.

CENTREVILLE, VA., 5 A. M. Sunday, Aug. 31, 1862.

THE battles of yesterday and the day before on the already classic ground of Bull Run will rank with Napoleon's bloodiest. And more than one general fought in them to whom, ere this hour, *he* would have given a marshal's baton, while he would have made proud a hundred privates with the ribbon of the Legion of Honor.

Let me first detail the movements by which the two days' struggle was brought on.

While at Warrenton early on Wednesday, I learned that Jackson was in our rear, and that we should once more try to trap him. Sigel and McDowell marched that morning up the turnpike from Warrenton toward Centreville, where the enemy was supposed to be. This road passes through Bull Run battlefield, five miles west of Centreville. Hooker, Porter, and Reno moved from our left (now, as we faced about toward Washington, become our right) toward the same point, via Manassas Junction. Sigel, in advance of McDowell, reached Gainesville, four miles from the Bull Run field, that night, and came upon the enemy's cavalry and stragglers. Resting a few hours, by three o'clock he was moving. The enemy did not appear in front, and leaving McDowell to take care of that road, Sigel turned to the right to connect with Hooker at Manassas Junction. Hooker had fought near there on Wednesday (of which I will speak in a moment), and it was possible he needed help.

When within two miles of the Junction, Sigel learned that the enemy was on the Warrenton road, and turning short to the left, he marched to the south side of the Bull Run field. It was then six P. M. McDowell, who, as before stated, had remained on that road between the enemy and Warrenton, had been throwing shell some hours, and now we could hear musketry. Gaining .the heights where Hunter fought a year ago, and approaching the turnpike, we could locate the scene of the engagement by the line of musketry flashes. It was King's Division repelling the enemy in his attempt to escape toward Warrenton. The affair lasted two hours, and King held the field. We had come upon the enemy's left flank. Schenck's Division became partially engaged, gave the enemy's cavalry a few shell, then the whole corps rested for the night. At the very time King was fighting on the Warrenton road, Ricketts was engaged fighting Rebel re-enforcements coming up through Thoroughfare Gap, five miles farther west. He was compelled, having suffered a loss of 250, to withdraw and join King, after the latter had finished his day's work. Reynolds's Division (Pennsylvania Reserves), then temporarily with McDowell's Corps, was in the same vicinity.

The situation, then, Friday morning was this: Sigel's Corps (divisions of Schurz, Milroy, Steinwehr, and Schenck) on the Bull Run field, fronting to the west, was close against the enemy. McDowell's Corps nearly connected with Sigel on the latter's left, but was not within fighting distance of the enemy. Heintzelman's Corps (divisions of Hooker and Kearney, and Reno's Corps) were at Centreville moving down the turnpike, which would lead them upon Sigel's right. Porter was far back — seven or eight miles — in Sigel's rear. These corps — Sigel's, Reno's, Heintzelman's, McDowell's, and Porter's — were all that were engaged at any time during the two days, Friday and Saturday. They came upon the field in the order I have named them.

Fortunately I had been with Sigel during his two days' march to find the enemy, and was with him now that it fell to him to open the main struggle. His corps had held the advance under heavy artillery fire on the Rappahannock the four previous days, had now marched two days, a part of the time in line of battle, and taking but four hours' rest moved into a battle, — not a skirmish, not an affair, not an action, not an engagement, but a great battle; for such are the names given to fights in the order of their magnitude.

Long before daylight Sigel had visited every position of his line, had seen to the placing of every battery, and with the daylight his artillery sounded. The "Jessie Scouts" (transferred by Fremont to Sigel) reported the enemy as massed in and beyond a stretch of woods a mile long, west of and running nearly parallel with the road. Their line, however, extended on their right to the road, where they had guns on commanding heights on their left to Bull Run stream, with a battery or two across upon the north side. Sigel's line was opposite, on the south side of the road.

The first hour it was all artillery. Sigel was advancing battery after battery to this and that eminence, supporting each with a brigade, hearing the reports of scouts, sending cavalry now far to the right, now far to the left, gradually advancing his divisions in cover of hills upon which he had placed guns — in a word, feeling for the enemy, rapidly advancing, but cautiously, every step. The enemy disdained to make any sign — but not long. His artillery was compelled to answer ours, and, pressing on, we unearthed his infantry. There was a light rattle, then a roar of musketry. Milroy, in the advance, had come square upon Rebels in masses. Our line of battle was formed, Schurz having the right, Schenck the left, Milroy the advance centre, Steinwehr the reserve centre.

Just at this opening of the battle I saw, from the hill from which Schurz was going into action, a column bearing down upon our right, and at first supposed them to be Rebels. Unaccountably, they carried high over their heads sundry white flags and appeared to march stragglingly, and it was soon seen they were unarmed.

They proved to be six hundred and thirty-four prisoners taken by Jackson when he appeared at Manassas three days before, now released on parole. The enemy could not feed them, and would themselves starve unless re-enforcements should push to them with supplies.

A little after Milroy, Schurz became engaged. They drove the enemy a mile or more, and rested from outright fatigue. During this time Schenck had been engaged on the left, but not heavily. Tough old Heintzelman arrived at this juncture from Centreville with his whole corps. Schurz was withdrawn for Kearney and Hooker to take his place. Reno arrived soon after from the same direction. Stevens's division of his corps marched to the left to support Schenck, and the attack was once more along the whole line. I should have stated that some time before the cessation, Milroy, after two hours of musketry in tornadoes, was driven back, much cut to pieces, and replaced by Steinwehr, who was assisted by Schenck at his left.

It was now one o'clock. Sigel's Corps only had been engaged, and we had on the whole gained ground — at the right nearly a mile. It was reasonable to suppose that with the assistance of Reno and Heintzelman, and most of the day before us, we should utterly demolish the enemy. It has since appeared that simultaneously with our re-enforcements he received larger ones. Longstreet's whole command, whose passage through Thoroughfare Gap Ricketts had disputed the day before, had now joined Jackson and Ewell, whom we had been fighting hitherto. Longstreet would naturally join Jackson at his right; it was upon our left and occasionally our centre that we were most severely pressed the remainder of the day.

Up to this time Sigel had command of the field. He had made the dispositions before the fight, and conducted it successfully six hours. Pope arrived from Centreville about noon and assumed command, but wisely and generously deferred to Sigel the rest of the day, as being best acquainted with the position.

At two o'clock the fight was raging along the whole line terrifically, musketry like Gaines' Mill, and artillery like Malvern Hill. There was not ten minutes' cessation at any one time for the next three hours. We advanced not a step; we retired not a step. The enginery of war, men, guns, and "villanous saltpetre," seemed equal, each side to the other. At five o'clock Schenck was ordered back from the left, and the artillery of that wing fell back to the next eminence.

During the three hours, scarcely a regiment of the three corps on the field that had not been into the thickest. Promptly and skillfully, as a command would become exhausted, it would be replaced by another, but only for a brief rest, then to up and at it. These splendid "passages of lines," as such movements are technically called, seem to me a feature that ought not to pass uncommended. Gaines' Mill would have been a victory had such movements been made promptly and orderly.

The withdrawal of the left was not a giving up of the battle. Troops were rushed to the right, and a redoubled onset made there. Again the enemy was forced back. His left was swept upon his centre — we took him "endways," in flank. While the infantry fought those, our artillery, eleven batteries in line, played stunningly, each gun pointed well to the left, that no unlucky shell might harm a friend.

We could move the Rebels no further than their centre. Musketry in rolls, in crashes, sounded out of the spot of woods where our advance was stayed; how tenaciously the enemy held their ground, I cannot hope to adequately express. How Schurz fought — ask any eye-witness of the conduct of his men, led by the orator fighter.

It was six o'clock. The enemy not only held his centre, but advanced upon our left. It was critical.

Opportunely, McDowell's Corps appeared, coming to our relief. Two brigades (Hatch's and Doubleday's) immediately met the enemy's advance upon our left, and although suffering terribly, stayed him until dark.

The day's work was ended. We held more ground than in the morning, but not so much as at noon.

Waking in my fence-corner sleeping apartment at daylight Saturday morning, I first walked to the summit of the hill to ascertain the position of affairs. Everything indicated a renewal of the battle. Already columns were marching in every direction, men at the left being brought to the right, and *vice versa*, being brought from front to rear, and from rear to front, generals with staffs and body-guards riding over the field, each, of course, with a purpose; but to an eye-witness seeming, with the other movements, like "confusion worse confounded." Every few minutes a shell from our battery farthest to the left, replied to as often by guns whose smoke clouded in the far western horizon, made me question whether the enemy had not retreated. While my horse was eating my hay-bed I had speech with several major-generals' staff officers, and they participated in the fear that the enemy had sprung from under our finger.

The day wore away until noon, with a continuance of desultory shelling ("bumi'n," the butternut prisoners call it), General Pope on horse the whole time, giving orders, rapid and imperative, each carried instantly by a galloping aid, receiving reports from all parts of the field, and never detaining the messenger long for his reply, from each eminence sweeping the position with his glass — he was evidently ascertaining the position of the enemy, and determined to fight if he stood or if he ran.

The division commanders were seeing that their men were provided with rations, made a difficult matter by the forced cross-marchings of the week, which prevented quartermasters from knowing where to conduct trains. For once red tape was summarily cut, and rations issued to every unsupplied regiment from whatever stores were at hand. I heard Sigel exclaim that crackers were "worth as much as muskets."

Porter's Corps had arrived on the ground at nine o'clock from Manassas, making five corps ready for action. The number of men comprised in these I should estimate at 60,000. Hooker's Division had but 2,441 men in the ranks, so terribly has it shrunk by battle and disease.

In the order of battle for the day Heintzelman commanded the right, Porter centre, McDowell the left, and Sigel, whose corps had borne the brunt the day before, the reserve. At ten Heintzelman advanced skirmishers into the wood on the right of the battle-field of the day before, and found it only held by a few troublesome bushwhackers. Driving them back, large numbers of wounded were got off, and passed to the rear.

SECOND BATTLE OF BULL RUN. 29

I rode in with these skirmishers as far as I deemed prudent. At any rate I got upon ground where the corpses attested the fighting of the day before. First I came upon bodies in blue. These were our fallen. Then there were those in blue mingled with others in gray and nondescript. That ground had been fought over. A little further they were all blue and nondescript. And there the bodies were the thickest. Upon ground that I judged to be not over half an acre, I counted seventy-nine bodies, dead and wounded. Advancing farther still, I saw a Union soldier seized, not ten rods from me, and carried off by bushwhackers. I retired (in good order), satisfied that the enemy's loss exceeded our own.

At two o'clock, by the movements of the troops from right to left, I inferred that the positions of the enemy had been found in that direction. By this time our line was different from that of the day before. Our right was farther advanced, our left withdrawn so that we fronted almost to the south. At Bull Run a year ago we faced exactly south.

At three o'clock General Stevens attacked at the right, and soon after General Butterfield at the left. The enemy's shells seemed equally distributed along the whole line, and at each point of attack he met us with musketry.

I was at General Sigel's headquarters. That general was certain the enemy intended to turn one or the other of our flanks, and said we must ascertain which, or the result was at the best doubtful; for his scouts had just reported that Lee, with the entire remainder of the Rebel army, had come up and assumed command. The scouts were correct. On Saturday we fought the whole Rebel army.

Posting myself in the centre, within view of both portions of the field where infantry were engaged, I could not determine which had the best of it. Evidently but few troops were engaged, and I surmised that we were fighting merely to learn where lay the enemy's main force. At length our force at the right was driven back, and I thought General Pope had been out-generalled, when he moved men at an earlier part of the day from right to left.

A quarter of an hour later I wished he had moved a still greater proportion to the left. I have heard the musketry of the best contested battles fought in Virginia, and I say unhesitatingly that the fire which broke out at the left and up to the centre was by far the heaviest of any. Talk of volleys, and rolls, and crashes! It was all these, continually accumulating, piling upon each other in mighty, swelling volumes, the wrestle of rushing tornadoes such as chaos may have known.

From my position it seemed that artillery played from each of the cardinal points upon the devoted centre, where I knew men were struggling. I could not see them struggling, — the smoke of gunpowder prevented that; but I knew they were there, and I trembled for the result. A few minutes later Schurz, who was in reserve, was ordered to the left. Before he could get fairly into position, McDowell and Porter were irretrievably broken. Their soldiers fought like brave men; if moments be reckoned by their intensity, they fought long, as they surely did fight well. I doubt not they piled the ground with Rebel slain as Halleck sings of Moslem slain by Bozzaris' band. I believe there cannot be a man who heard or participated in that awful tragedy but counts the hour between half-past four and half-past five o'clock the severest fighting he ever knew. It was all at one point. Along the right half of the line the combatants seemed to desist in amazement at the struggle there. By half-past five it was apparent that we were beaten, — out-flanked by a concentration upon the left. Wagoners and stragglers about the hospitals scented the retreat, and soon trains of the former and streams of the latter could be seen making for the Bull Run bridges and fords. McDowell and Porter's Corps retired in comparative order. I use this term, not as a mild but false paraphrase for driven back, but because it covers the actual fact in the case.

I do not think there was a brigade that could not, as it came from the field, show its distinct regiments, or rather a nucleus of each regiment, to whose standard, ere it had marched a mile, its scattered men gathered.

Still there were several thousands hurrying pell-mell in advance of them toward Centreville, crowding the stone bridge and wading the stream. A dozen long wagon trains centred there, but there was little confusion among them, no desertion of wagons, but simply a jam where each desired and pushed to be first. They were thus cool, notwithstanding a few shells burst among them. All this time the right was firm, and only at the calm discretion of its generals.

Unaccountably to me at the time, as soon as we fell back from the left the musketry almost entirely ceased. We were pursued by shells only. It is probable that the enemy dared not advance lest Heintzelman and Sigel should fall upon his flank as he should pass by them. Sigel had not had his fight out, nor had Heintzelman, and the enemy was hardly in condition for another battle immediately. It is possible also that Banks' Corps was nearing the field; he was known to be at Manassas early in the day, and they may have seen his advance and been afraid. It was all done in two hours. Another corps upon the field would have frustrated that rush of overpowering numbers upon one point. Those numbers were so overpowering that they succeeded before men could be moved against them from any other part of the field. Franklin lay at Centreville; Sumner at Arlington Heights. Why had they not been sent to Pope five days before, as they were ordered and as he expected?

I forded Bull Run in the dusk of the evening and sat some time looking at the crossing of men and trains. While conversing with General Butterfield, who had withdrawn his men only when ordered, although he had made the attack at that point and was in advance, a shell struck the ground some twenty feet from us, and in its ricochet passed over our heads. I instinctively dodged and my horse sprang forward. The general did not move a muscle until he smiled as he remarked that his horse was too accustomed to those things to be disturbed by them. A moment after, another shell knocked a wagon to pieces close by. The fragments were taken out of the road and the trains moved on undisturbed. I recalled the scenes at this crossing of the same place a year ago after that battle, and knew that this was no panic.

Riding on towards Centreville, which is six miles from the field, about midway I met Franklin's Corps, which, having learned the position of affairs, that the whole army was retiring to Centreville, was on the point of retracing its steps; I marched with it to Centreville. Richardson's Division and Kimball's Brigade of Sumner's Corps arrived here during the night, from Alexandria, and this morning Sedgwick's Division, being the balance of the same corps, is coming in from Arlington Heights.

Altogether the position appears favorable. These two corps comprise not less than 30,000 veteran soldiers under the best of the peninsula generals. Besides these there is Banks' Corps, 10,000 strong, which must be somewhere in the neighborhood; for I do not credit the rumor that he is cut off, though he may have been forced to destroy his trains. This last conjecture is strengthened by heavy explosions having been heard in the direction of Manassas Junction last night. It is estimated this morning that at least 50,000 men of those engaged Friday and Saturday are still in their ranks. Add to all these bodies 25,000 newly volunteered men which have been ordered here from Washington, and there is a total of over 100,000 ready, within twenty-four hours, to meet the enemy, — that number exclusive of Banks. The army engaged yesterday is understood to be concentrating here, though much of it camped but little this side of Bull Run, and has not yet come up.

A few incidents, and I must go to bed — in a clover field. Among the last episodes on Friday was a charge of the Harris Cavalry, simultaneously with the advance of Hatch and Doubleday where our left was being sharply pressed. Led by Lieutenant-Colonel Kilpatrick, 500 men charged straight up the road into the very teeth of the enemy's position. How they struggled was seen by no one, for no eye could penetrate the gathering darkness, thicker for clouds of dust and smoke. But one-fourth of them were of the unreturning brave, and the contest was of but twenty minutes duration. The regiment was engaged again on Saturday, with considerable loss.

At one time in the early part of Friday, Hampton's Pittsburgh Battery, attached to Schurz's Division, by some changing of commands was left unsupported just as it was charged upon. Grape at short range twice repelled the assailants, but three cannoneers and as many horses were disabled. The third time the Rebels were seen advancing, Captain Hampton gave the order to limber up. The disabled gun remained with the enemy. General Sigel highly commended the battery.

While stretched upon the ground behind the crest of a hill, and watching Rebel shells pass over me, I noticed that a part of them went pitching through the air "eend over eend," snorting and tumbling but never exploding, while others I could scarcely see, but they seemed to go small end first, and the sound was a whistle not so ragged as that of the others. Afterwards I found that the former were pieces of railroad iron. The enemy must be short of decent projectiles is the logical deduction. I may remark here that I discovered my position to be unsafe some time before I discovered a safe way of getting out of it.

General Sigel's Chief of Ordnance is Capt. Ulric Dahlgren, son of the commodore of that name. I hope he came safely out of yesterday's battle, for a more gallant officer or one more capable for that position is not in the service. General Sigel, who believes that artillery should be made to fight battles, and himself knows how to use it, seemed to rely upon his youthful aids more than upon all others. He spoke on Friday night of two batteries that held a forlorn hope, if the term may be applied to a dangerous and important position, as having fought their pieces with cool audacity. They were Captain Hampton's, mentioned above, and Captain Roemer's. Hooker and Kearney's Division fought bitterly and lost heavily on Friday, but were scarcely engaged on Saturday.

The loss of Colonel Brown, of the Twentieth Indiana, whose name you will see among the killed, will be felt not more by his friends at home than by his soldiers and commanders in the army.

General Stevens, better known as ex-Governor of Washington Territory and chairman of the Breckinridge National Committee, led his division with consummate skill and coolness, had a horse killed under him, and won golden opinions. I have in my mind a hundred and more who deserve notice, but I must forbear and sleep.

THE ESCAPE OF LEE FROM GETTYSBURG

THE ESCAPE OF LEE. — HOW IT WAS EFFECTED. — WHAT HE LEFT BEHIND. — A COUNCIL OF WAR. — WHY NO ATTACK WAS MADE.

WILLIAMSPORT, MD., Tuesday noon, July 14.

YOU have been informed, by telegraph, of the time and manner of Lee's escape. The last six hours have demonstrated the fact that for the Rebel army to recross the Potomac, intact since Gettysburg, is nothing less than an escape. It is now palpable that from that hour, Friday night, July 3d, when Lee began to fall back, he has bent every energy to the one end of placing the Potomac between his own army and a better one. He has not for a moment ceased to elude battles. He dared not hazard another. He has improved the first practicable opportunity of recrossing the river which limits his master's pseudo empire.

Always opposing to our advancing columns a heavy rearguard, for the last five days he held each parallel ridge as though he would retreat no further, but there, once for all, accept battle. But not so. Each succeeding morning he held another line, apparently in better position and in more force than before. Half of our army was led to believe that of all things he most desired battle. Officers high in command reasoned that he could not afford to go back bleeding from defeat, but, nerved and stung by disaster, would risk everything in the "do or die" of another struggle.

And was it an unreasonable hope that, in a position of his own choosing, his battered army fighting with safety — ay, and Washington and peace — hanging upon the result, he had more than half the chances? The crafty Rebel leader did not think so. He remembered Gettysburg, and knew that to meet the

Army of the Potomac again would be to meet it at Philippi. And so all those days we were closing in upon him he chafed and swore because the loyal Potomac remained bank full — because the pontoon train sent from Richmond when the first was destroyed was long on the way.

Yesterday noon that train arrived at Falling Waters. Yesterday morning the first wagon forded at Williamsport. Last night he made the transit with his whole army, mainly at the former place, though most of his cavalry, a portion of his train, and one division of Ewell's Corps, forded at the latter place. This division during yesterday was pressed hard against us on the enemy's left, opposite our right at Hagerstown. Unable to march to Falling Waters in season to escape, it was pushed into the water here, a swollen torrent, whose terrible current, running to their chins, washed away several hundreds who were too weak or short to stem it. Several prisoners with whom I have talked, half-grown boys and sick men, were permitted by their officers to remain behind, since to attempt to cross was death. Twenty-five or thirty wagons, with horses still attached, are stranded on a bar a hundred rods below the ford.

Up to this hour 500 prisoners have been taken on the road from Hagerstown here. As many more will be picked up in the vicinity during the day. I understand a brigade, probably not more than 1,600 strong, has been taken near Falling Waters. The entire number that will fall into our hands during the day may be estimated at 2,500.

It is possible a few wagons have been taken on the left. With the captured brigade are said to be two guns. Except these trivial losses the enemy gets off unhurt.

I understand that in the actual crossing he was wholly unmolested; that except by our cavalry, he has been utterly unmolested on his retreat; that our army was in admirable position yesterday within a mile of the Rebel's ostensible line — but did not attack.

On Sunday night a council of corps commanders and chiefs of departments was held at headquarters. The question to be decided was, "Shall the position of the enemy be assaulted to-morrow?" There were twelve officers present, of whom five gave their opinions in the affirmative and seven in the negative. The former were: General Meade, General Howard, commanding Eleventh Corps; General G. K. Warren, Chief of Engineers; General Wadsworth, commanding First Corps; and General Pleasanton, commanding Cavalry Corps. Of these, General Howard was apparently the most thoroughly convinced of the necessity of immediate attack; at least he was the most strenuous in debate. Those opposed were the oldest corps commanders, and their weight carried a decision in the negative. It was conceded by all that if an attack were ventured upon it should be upon the Rebel left. Now it happens that Generals Howard and Wadsworth must have led the advance, had it been permitted. Hence their votes were a request to be allowed to fight. Moreover, from their position we must suppose them best acquainted with the probabilities of success. Besides, General Kilpatrick, who had recently fought all over the ground where the fight would have been, who himself had the extreme right at Hagerstown, was confident that, his cavalry assisting, and assisted by one good corps, he could force the Rebel flank. So urgent were he and General Howard that on Monday morning they telegraphed for permission to make a reconnoissance in force in that direction. Permission was not granted, and the sole operation of the day was a small reconnoissance, just at night, by two brigades, one of cavalry and one of militia, which was pushed out half a mile or so, but was unable to determine the vital question whether the force in front was an army, or a rear-guard making believe an army. The event has shown that this day, Monday, was our golden opportunity. Had the attack been made we should have caught the Rebels in the midst of a general breaking up, with only a thin line to oppose us, with the roads full of trains, with a thousand wagons yet quietly parked at Williamsport; their army, its artillery, its trains, its vast spoils, would have been our prey.

That no attack was made can be accounted for only on the ground of imperfect information, or of no knowledge whatever in relation to the enemy. It may have been known that up to

Sunday night the enemy had no means of crossing, and have been thought impossible that he could obtain means so soon and to such an extent as to get away the next night. Again, the army may have been ordered in no case to uncover Washington, while the generals may have thought that the only practicable advance was from the position of the right with our whole force, thus forming the army between Lee and Pittsburgh. There is color to this view, in the fact that the ridges between the Shearns run parallel with our line, while, advancing from the other direction, they would be perpendicular to it, thus affording better ground for offensive operations.

This nick of time for an attack comprised not more than ten practicable hours; it is not wonderful, therefore, that it was not seized, — not an impeachment of generalship that it was not seized. It would have been surprising had it been hit upon.

The effective force was probably not far from 60,000 out of 100,000 Lee led into Maryland. It goes back not so demoralized as some have fondly believed, but certainly acknowledging a terrible whipping, I judge from the testimony of citizens and prisoners. A certain "Herald" correspondent who reports himself as having been three days a prisoner with Stewart's Cavalry, and as having been treated with the "most distinguished consideration," tells another story, avers that they are in splendid condition, and do not consider themselves beaten at Gettysburg; but I prefer to take the evidence of the greater number of witnesses — and the least questionable. One of the prisoners I have conversed with this morning is a nephew of U. S. District-Attorney Price of Baltimore, a citizen of Hagerstown, and for two years a sergeant in the First Maryland Cavalry (Confederate). He was "convinced that Secesh was played out. For nearly a year the Yankee cavalry had been too much for theirs, and now our infantry had begun to outfight theirs. He was sick of the business, and remained behind with the purpose of getting out of it. Half their army shared his feelings." All this from a young man of good education, who "enlisted in the Rebel Army for the sake of the principle."

As I close my letter, at one P. M., but two cavalry-men of all the Rebel "Army of Northern Virginia" are visible across the Potomac. Kilpatrick's guns occasionally drop a shell into the woods beyond, but elicit no response. The different corps of the Army of the Potomac will to-night line the banks of the river of its name.

Part Second.

THE GRAND CAMPAIGN.

May to December, 1864.

GENERAL GRANT was given supreme command of the armies of the United States, then operating against the Southern Confederacy, on the 9th of March, 1864, and at once proceeded to organize a plan of campaign for the various Union armies then occupying the revolted States, making his first headquarters at Culpeper Court-House, Virginia, a few miles south of the headquarters of the Army of the Potomac. His general plan was to concentrate all the force possible against the Confederate armies in the field, and to wear them out by simple attrition, — the capture of Richmond and other local strongholds being to him a secondary object. His principal objective was the army of General Lee, the destruction of which, and the consequent fall of Richmond, would insure the collapse of the Confederacy. By the early part of May, 1864, he had collected on the Rapidan an army of 116,000 men and with this force he began the operations which are detailed in the following letters.

THE GRAND ARMY.

ITS TRIALS AND TRIUMPHS. — SPLENDID CONDITION OF THE FORCES. — GENERAL MEADE AND HIS CORPS COMMANDERS. — THE TRIBUNE BRIGADE.

ARMY OF THE POTOMAC, May 3, 1864.

TO make bricks without straw, to write a letter which shall contain nothing, to shun everything of importance simply because it is important, to work nothings into substantial shape, confining one's self to the nothings because they are nothings — such is the military necessity to which I respectfully bow. The things that I see I may not relate, those imparted to me I may not repeat, those I infer I may not hint, much less enlarge upon.

There is left me one resource. Those things which in the shock and swift succession of events, seem to have already "gone glimmering through the dream of things that were," — though they shall live more than "a schoolboy's tale," more than "the wonder of an hour," — to these I may recur.

It has been my fortune to know this army from its organization. I saw it dig — dig intrenchments and dig graves — upon the Peninsula. I saw it during the classic Seven Days, when each intervening night it stole away from a victory; at the second Bull Run, when it faltered as a high-bred race-horse carrying too much weight (I smile as I think that the cumbering jockey did not get a sword the other day); I have known how it stood at Antietam, how it was hurled back from Fredericksburg, how it almost made Chancellorsville glorious, how it saved a nation at Gettysburg. And now, joining the veteran legions on the eve of another campaign, I have given four days of spur and rein and most industrious curiosity, to acquaint myself thoroughly with their present might and hope.

Never before has this Army of the Potomac been so peculiarly and emphatically the "Grand Army," as it is to-day. It is a compact, self-reliant, veteran host, conscious that it is able to deliver mightier blows than ever before, knowing that there will be blows to take as well as blows to give, and prepared in every drop and fibre for both. We have all hoped and felt that this must be so — it is so.

Ah, the blows to take! Well, it must be. This campaign into which the Army of the Potomac is just now to be launched probably holds the pivotal battle that shall be an era for all time. And Arbela and Marathon and Waterloo, those mountainous facts where have rooted the destinies of nations and of civilization, were not made altogether of blows given, nor shall the bloody conclusion we are now to try be other than they. It must be met. But think how gallantly it will be met! I see the long, glittering lines, panoplied in steely splendor and marching in bannered magnificence, — and now there is the flash and smoke and thunder of battle. It must be met. God save the right!

The press generally of late habitually speaks as though General Grant had superseded General Meade in the command of this army. This is not the case. General Meade commands the entire army as much as General Sedgwick does his corps, or any colonel his regiment.

It is true that the presence of the Commander-in-Chief relieves him of the responsibility of planning the campaign, but as to the discipline and organization of the army he is still responsible and paramount. General Grant has not interfered with machinery that he finds in admirable working order, and in no instance does he issue an order except through General Meade. The army has very thorough and unwavering confidence in the latter, though by no means unwilling that he shall be supplemented with the prestige of Grant.

If the army is fortunate in the commander-in-chief and in the commanding-general, it is not less so in the corps commanders. It is a great tribute to General Sedgwick that he has been longer in this army with high command than any other officer, and has had the unshaken confidence of every commanding-general. His record would make a French soldier marshal of the empire.

General Warren was the first officer of the regular army to ask and obtain permission to accept command in the volunteer service. He is now "major-general commanding" the same corps in which he first served as lieutenant-colonel. General Hancock takes the field for the first time since his wound at Gettysburg. You may look to hear from him at the next Gettysburg.

It has been charged that General Meade, from the time he was placed in command, has been in intimate correspondence with General McClellan; in short, that the latter has counselled, devised, commanded. Now, I am able to contradict this by authority. During the time mentioned, General McClellan has twice written to General Meade, — once congratulating the latter on his accession to the command, and again transmitting a copy of his report. To each of these General Meade replied in brief terms. And this is all the correspondence that has passed between the two.

General Meade remarked to a correspondent yesterday that he thought there would soon be a movement of this Army of the Potomac, for he noticed that The Tribune Brigade seemed to be reaching the front. The Second Brigade is well organized, is in high spirits, and awaiting developments. It is supplied with ten days' rations. Its quartermaster arrived last night with ten pounds of bologna and four pounds of killikinnick. The one drawback to its efficiency is that, like the cavalry, it has a large proportion of dismounted men. It should be understood that this is a brigade of veterans, re-enlisted for the war.

THE BATTLE OF THE WILDERNESS.

I.

THE BATTLE OF THURSDAY. — BURNSIDE MOVING UP. — FINDING THE ENEMY. — THE SECOND CORPS ENGAGED. — AN OBSTINATE INFANTRY FIGHT. — LEE AT HIS OLD TRICKS. — GRANT FOILS HIM THIS TIME. — OUR LOSS THREE THOUSAND TO FOUR THOUSAND.

WILDERNESS TAVERN, HEART OF THE WILDERNESS.
8 A. M., Thursday, May 5, 1864.

LATE on Tuesday the whole army became aware that it would be moved within a few hours. During the night and the first daylight of the next morning everything was put in motion. Gregg's Division of Cavalry crossed Ely's Ford, without opposition, at daybreak. Wilson's Division (late Kilpatrick's) crossed Germania Ford. Hancock's Second Corps followed Gregg, and Warren's Fifth Corps followed Wilson. Long before night Hancock had posted his corps and established headquarters at Chancellorsville, while Warren had pushed on to Wilderness Tavern and occupied the ridges facing Mine Run and the enemy. By sunset Sedgwick, with the Sixth Corps, had crossed Germania Ford, and last night encamped along the road in rear of Warren. Sheridan, with the Cavalry Corps, thoroughly scoured the country in all directions. He intercepted despatches from the Rebel General Rhodes to Ewell, stating that Meade had effected a crossing, and asking instructions. Another intercepted despatch apprised us that Stuart was having a cavalry review at Hamilton's Cross-Roads. Sheridan was anxious to assist at the spectacle, but it was not thought expedient.

General Grant left Culpeper and General Meade Brandy early yesterday morning, and early in the afternoon pitched headquarters just this side of Germania Ford.

BATTLE OF THE WILDERNESS.

At daybreak this morning Sheridan moved with all his force with two purposes, — to find and fight Stuart, and to push a reconnoissance far to our left on the enemy's right flank. The order of march to-day, as fixed since midnight, is for Warren to advance to Parker's Tavern, five miles toward Mine Run, for Hancock to take a road leading him from Chancellorsville, that will enable him to establish a line on the left of Warren, connecting with the latter, while Sedgwick is to move up and assume Warren's present position.

It is possible, however, that Lee may cause a change in the programme. General Griffin reports the enemy menacing his position on the ridge south of this point, and not a mile away. Warren orders him not to move off toward Parker's Tavern until Sedgwick can come up and relieve him. General Meade rode up ten minutes ago and said to Warren, "If the enemy comes near you, pitch right in with all you've got!" The dispositions necessary to sustain an attack, if such be Lee's purpose, have caused a halt of the columns, and now we are listening for the first gun. If the enemy does not choose to precipitate the battle here, our army before night will hold the position contemplated by the morning order. On the other hand, we can well afford to fight him now. It is six miles back to the Rapidan; if we are attacked it will be with the hope of breaking through the moving columns by a vigorous assault upon the flank. Generals Grant and Meade and Warren and Sedgwick will see to it that what the enemy supposes to be a weak flank he shall find to his cost is nothing less nor else than a formidable front.

I have never seen the army move with more exact order, with a less number of stragglers, and with so little apparent fatigue to the men. All had a full ration of sleep last night — which is a better augury of victory than a re-enforcement of thousands. The roads are in excellent condition, the weather delightful, and so warm that whole divisions abandoned their overcoats and extra blankets on the march. At one point I noticed some hundreds of overcoats had been thrown into a stream to improve the crossing. Overcoats and blankets are decidedly better for the purpose than rails.

I understand that Burnside marched last night to join this army, and will reach Germania to-day. It is understood that General Butler is making a simultaneous "Onward to Richmond," and will first occupy City Point, James River. That these two movements are being made is generally known in the army, and has a most inspiring effect.

Rest your confidence, not only in what may be predicted upon the records of its generals as to how this army will be handled, but in this : *the rank and file will fight this fight with more than the élan of the French, with more than the pluck of the British.* They feel it in their bones, — that *something* allied to these, but better than either or both.

WILDERNESS BATTLE-FIELD,
Thursday, May 5, 2 P. M.

How perfect have been the combinations, how completely on time they have been executed, how well in hand the army has been every hour and is now, how masterly and successful thus far has been the movement, — all this is so clearly apparent that I can but notice it here, even while a spirited battle is being fought only half a mile from where I write.

Let me here pay a tribute to the first soldier killed in this campaign. Let Charles Wilson, of Franklin, Mass., private in Co. I, Eighteenth Mass., Col. Jos. Hayes commanding, be remembered as the first man to give his life in this (God willing) last grand campaign of the war.

Immediately after "writing up" this morning, I rode out to Griffin's lines, then reported to be menaced by the enemy. His division was in line of battle at right angles with and on either side of the Old Turnpike. The enemy had evidently despatched a force from his lair on Mine Run to worry and delay our march by threatening in flank. General Griffin had sent the Eighteenth Massachusetts and Eighty-third Pennsylvania, under Colonel Hayes of the former, to feel well out on the turnpike. It was here that Charles Wilson fell, the Rebel skirmish line opposing a vigilant front. Finally, after some little firing, General Warren, who had come up in person, ordered an advance down the road in force. Ayres' Brigade moved on upon the right of the road, and Bartlett's upon the left, with each flank well supported.

Field officers were obliged to dismount, so dense was the growth of dwarf pines. An advance of less than half a mile, and a smart fusillade opened the action. The two brigades carried the first eminence, and were pushing up a second, when, owing to a failure of the commands right and left to connect and form a continuous line, the Rebels flanked them on both sides. Colonel Hayes, Eighteenth Massachusetts, finding himself in command of several regiments and the enemy all around him, formed a line facing to the rear and fought in both directions. At length he gave the order to fall back, and the movement was being executed when he was hit on the scalp and fell. The brigade bugler brought him safely off. Meanwhile fresh troops were put in, and the Rebels slowly driven along, the whole front then fighting. In this action our loss is probably 300 or 400. At this hour the enemy has ceased to make demonstrations, and we are waiting for Hancock to join on our left. General Grant is smoking a wooden pipe, his face as peaceful as a summer evening, his general demeanor indescribably imperturbable. I know, however, that there is great anxiety that Hancock should fall into position, for it is believed that the entire Rebel force is massing upon us.

WILDERNESS BATTLE-FIELD,
9 P. M., Thursday, May 5.

Heavy fighting since three o'clock, mostly at the extreme left, under Hancock. Getty's Division, Sixth Corps, was at the right of the Orange Plank road, fronting toward Mine Run, where Carr's Division, Second Corps, joined him on his left. The other divisions of Hancock's Corps were pushing up; in the twinkling of an eye the Rebels were upon him in great force, with the evident purpose of turning our left. The ground was fearfully overgrown with shrub trees, thick as one sees shoots from the same root. In a few minutes urgent requests came back for re-enforcements. The enemy was repeating his tactics at Chancellorsville of falling with tremendous force and superhuman *vim* upon one wing. This time he was not repulsed, but foiled. The battle raged for three hours precisely where it began, along a line of not more than half a mile. Fast as our men came up they were sent in — still no ground gained, none lost. It was all musketry, roll surging upon roll, — not the least cessation. We were fighting 20,000 men, and such was the nature of the country but two guns could be planted bearing upon the enemy. Hayes's Brigade of Birney's Division became warmly engaged soon after the ball opened. A little while and he asked for re-enforcements. Hancock sends back word: "I will send a brigade within twenty minutes. Tell Gen. Alex. Hayes to hold his ground. He can do it. I know him to be a powerful man." Within that time General Hayes was killed and his body brought to the rear. The work was at close range. No room in that jungle for manœuvring; no possibility of a bayonet charge; no help from artillery; no help from cavalry; nothing but close, square, severe, face-to-face volleys of fatal musketry. The wounded stream out, and fresh troops pour in. Stretchers pass out with ghastly burdens, and go back reeking with blood for more. Word is brought that the ammunition is failing. Sixty rounds fired in one steady, stand-up fight, and that fight not fought out. Boxes of cartridges are placed on the returning stretchers, and the struggle shall not cease for want of ball and powder. Do the volleys grow nearer, or do our fears make them seem so? It must be so, for a second line is rapidly formed just where we stand, and the bullets slip singing by as they have not done before, while now and then a limb drops from the tree-tops. The bullets are flying high. General Hancock rides along the new line, is recognized by the men, and cheered with a will and a tiger. But we stay them. The Second Corps is all up, and it must be that troops will come up from Warren or Sedgwick, or else they will divert the enemy's attention by an attack upon another quarter. Yes, we hold them, and the fresh men going in will drive them. I ride back to General Headquarters, and learn that an advance has been ordered an hour ago along the whole line. General Meade is in front with Warren, and Grant is even now listen-

BATTLE OF THE WILDERNESS.

ing for Wadsworth's Division or Warren's Corps to open on Hill's flank, for it is Hill's Corps that is battling with Hancock. The latter reports that he shall be able to maintain his ground. The severe fighting for the day is over, and it is sunset.

I write now at 10 P. M. Since dark there has been brisk firing at intervals at different points along the line. The enemy has been splendidly foiled to-day in his intention of beating us before we should be ready to fight. To-morrow we shall be altogether ready. Our line to-night extends, perhaps, six miles from northeast to southwest, the right being a little advanced.

General Burnside has come up 25,000 strong, and will probably be the reserve to-morrow. Our loss to-day may be estimated at 3,000 to 4,000. The main battle, probably a decisive one, must be to-morrow. To-day we have fought because the enemy chose that we should. To-morrow, because we choose that he shall.

II.

FRIDAY'S BATTLE.— FOURTEEN HOURS OF FIGHTING.— DESPERATE ATTEMPT BY LEE TO BREAK UP SEDGWICK'S DIVISION.— HEROIC RESISTANCE OF OUR MEN.— DEATH OF GENERAL WADSWORTH.— VARYING SUCCESSES, BUT FINAL REPULSE OF THE REBELS.

FIELD OF THE BATTLE OF THE WILDERNESS,
Friday, May 6, 11 P. M.

FOURTEEN hours of severe fighting to-day, and still nothing decisive. The position this morning was that of last night, substantially. General Sedgwick, with two of his divisions, Ricketts' and Wright's, has fought upon the right; General Hancock, with the four divisions of his corps, viz., Birney's Carr's, Barlow's, and Gibbons', with Getty's Division of the Sixth Corps, has fought upon the left; and General Warren, with his full corps and Stevenson's Division of the Ninth Corps (Burnside's), has fought in the centre. Burnside's Corps has constituted the reserve, and has marched and countermarched incessantly, and gone in by brigades at the centre and on the left.

Sedgwick was to advance at five A. M., but Ewell, who commands opposite him, attacked at four forty-five. Sedgwick says Ewell's watch must be fifteen minutes ahead of his. This action on our right was spirited and well fought. At the expiration of an hour the Rebels were handsomely borne back, the firing ceased, and each side held the ground they had bivouacked upon. Our loss was severe, and the enemy's could not have been less.

General Sedgwick's staff were brilliant and ubiquitous throughout, while the old general was the man of Antietam and Fredericksburg repeating himself. This action barely over, and suddenly we heard from the extreme left that peculiar monotonous swell and volume of sound which tells of large numbers engaged, — so many that single shots and even volleys of long lines are not distinct, but are merged in the mighty noise of a great battle. Hancock was engaged.

BATTLE OF THE WILDERNESS.

The details of his two hours' steady struggle I do not know, but I know that he did his work cleanly and completely. Longstreet had joined the Rebel right, and this was a second determined attempt to turn our left, and a second utter discomfiture.

Only ten o'clock, and Lee had tried each wing and had met in each case more than he could overcome; and we asked ourselves what next. All his movements were silent and invisible, and unknown until he developed them in the event. We can deliver blows over in the direction whence blows are dealt us, — against an enemy advancing in bold sight, but not against one who has mysteriously gathered and poised himself for a deadly spring.

But the suspense is not long. Both combatants are too eager to compel the issue for either to delay another and still another encounter. Shots begin to ring all along the six miles of front.

At eleven o'clock the enemy press close upon Warren and Sedgwick, and train a number of guns exactly upon the latter's headquarters. A man and three horses are killed within twenty feet of the general, and in the very centre of his grouped staff. Finding the enemy disposed to renew the engagement of the early morning, Sedgwick accepts the challenge, and advances his whole line. The men go in with more dash and hold on more sturdily than in the morning. Ewell is driven back to his second line where his guns are in position, and there makes a stand.

At this juncture, Warren, who connects with Sedgwick's left, is extremely anxious to go in with all his might, but the enemy's position in his front seems too formidable.

I see a troop of horsemen riding rapidly up to the perilous edge of battle, and recognize Warren and his white horse, as Jehu was recognized by the prophet of old, for they came furiously. With him are Generals Griffin and Hunt, and officers of General Grant's and Meade's staffs.

Halting at the first line they dismount and walk more than half a mile in front of the men, who are flat upon their breasts, and firing rapidly. We hold the woods on one side of an open space, perhaps one-fourth of a mile across, and the Rebels lie along the trend of the woods upon the other side. Their intrenchments are plainly visible, and the open mouths of their artillery peer over.

No; it will not do to charge across. It were stark madness. The sharpshooters may continue to reply to this, but no man shall start across the plain and live. Warren had perhaps hoped that his own judgment would be overruled by the officers with him, but all declare that no advance can be made here. But more to the left, where Wadsworth's and Robinson's Divisions of Warren's Corps lap up to Hancock, the prospect is better, and there an assault is ordered.

It is noon, and Sedgwick's second fight is over, and he again rests on the line of his last night's bivouac. Wadsworth advances and finds the enemy — A. P. Hill's Corps — strong and prepared. The divisions on his right and left become engaged with him, and the work is warm. Here, as elsewhere, the contest is in a tangled jungle, and the soldiers push aside the bushes and find mortal enemies bursting through the adjoining growth of bushes, and face to face with them.

Half or three-fourths of an hour of alternating success and repulse, and General Wadsworth orders a charge to recover his command from a slight wavering. He is cheered loudly by his men, who loved the gray haired chieftain. One horse is shot under him. He mounts a second and spurs to the front, hat in hand, and we should have won then, but his men saw him fall. He was shot through the head, killed instantly, and his body fell into the hands of the enemy.[1]

His command fell back to their original position with comparative order. Wadsworth's death is a heavy loss; scarcely an officer in the army but could have been better spared, and none would have been more deeply regretted. Yesterday and to-day he had displayed such marked ability and gallantry as

[1] Though at first unconscious, and supposed to be dead, he lingered, it is said, on the ground for two days, by his heroic bearing continually inspiring his troops to renew the contest, when but for him they would have yielded.

BATTLE OF THE WILDERNESS. 55

to compel his recognition on all hands as an able soldier, who, now that he is gone, can hardly be replaced. He was a true man, a beloved, a high-toned gentleman, to be respected, an unshrinking patriot to be emulated, an accomplished soldier, dead on the field of honor, to be mourned.

But this battle does not pause for a hero slain. From noon until five o'clock, a number of sharp assaults at various points were made and invariably repulsed, whether made by us or by the enemy. Each one of these affairs were material for a long letter, but I find it simply impossible at this time to ascertain and write out correctly the facts in detail.

Prisoners came in at the rate of 100 an hour. The day was excessively hot, and the men were much exhausted. We had neither gained nor lost ground, but continued this thing long enough, and we hoped to finally wear them out. At half-past five o'clock Hancock was preparing for a grand movement of our entire left. He did not make it, for the enemy anticipated him, and he had to repel perhaps the most wicked assault thus far encountered, — brief in duration, but terrific in power and superhuman momentum.

The first few minutes we were staggered. Stragglers for the first time in all this fighting streamed to the rear in large numbers, choking the roads and causing a panic by their stampede and incoherent tales of frightful disaster. It was even reported at general headquarters that the enemy had burst entirely through, and supports were hurried up. Grant and Meade seated their backs against the same tree, quietly listened to the officer who brought the report, and consulted a moment in low tones. The orders for sending re-enforcements were given, and for a little time not a word was spoken in the group of more than twenty officers. They but looked into each others' faces.

At length Grant says, with laconic emphasis, "I don't believe it." He was right. Long before that Hancock had recovered from the first shock, held his own awhile, and now was gaining ground. In forty minutes from this attack the enemy was completely beaten back with tremendous slaughter, and the loss of some hundreds of prisoners.

It was now nearly sunset. From one end of the line to the other not a shot could be heard. The day's work seemed over. Our line of to-night would be that of last night. The auguries were good. In two days' fighting we had lost heavily, but not more than the enemy. Our assaults had been futile, but the enemy's had been equally so; and it is by these massed assaults that he has ever achieved his victories.

The inference was clear that we had overmatched him fighting at his best and strongest.

Men separated in the heat of the day, now chancing to meet, congratulated each other. The Rebels can't endure another such day, and we can, was the expressed conviction on all hands; and this statement epitomizes the situation at sunset.

The sun went down red. The smoke of the battle of more than 200,000 men destroying each other with villanous saltpetre through all the long hours of a long day filled the valleys, and rested upon the hills of all this Wilderness, hung in lurid haze all around the horizon, and built a dense canopy overhead, beneath which this grand army of Freedom was preparing to rest against the morrow. Generals Grant and Meade had retired to their tents. Quiet reigned, but during the reign of quiet the enemy was forging a thunderbolt.

Darkness and smoke were mingling in grim twilight and fast deepening into thick gloom, when we were startled out of repose back into fierce excitement. The forged thunderbolt was sped, and by a master. A wild Rebel yell away to the right. We knew they had massed and were charging. We waited for the volley with which we knew Sedgwick would meet the onset. We thought it but a night attack to ascertain if we had changed our position. We were mistaken — it was more. They meant to break through, and they did. On Sedgwick's extreme right lay the Second Brigade, Third Division of his corps, under General Seymour, who had been assigned to it but two days before. The brigade is new to the Sixth Corps, and is known as the Milroy Brigade; connecting on the left of Seymour by Shaler's and then Neill's brigades, the latter being a brigade of Getty's Division that had not been sent to Hancock. These troops were at work intrenching when fallen upon. The enemy came down like a torrent rolling and dashing in living waves, and flooding up against the whole Sixth Corps. The main line stood like a rock, but not so the extreme right. That flank was instantly and utterly turned. The Rebel line was the longer, and surged around Seymour's Brigade, tided over it and through it, beat against Shaler, and bore away his right regiments. All this done in less than ten minutes, perhaps not five. Seymour's men, seeing their pickets running back, and hearing the shouts of the Rebels, who charged with all their chivalry, were smitten with panic, and, standing on no order of going, went at once, and in an incredibly short time made their way through a mile and a half of woods to the plank-road in the rear. They reported, in the frantic manner usual with stampeded men, the entire corps broken. Grant, as in Hancock's case, did n't believe it. But when three of Sedgwick's staff rode in to army headquarters separately and stated how they had ridden from Sedgwick to keep Seymour's men to their work, had been borne back by the panic, and had last seen Sedgwick and Wright hard to the front working like Trojans to hold the wavering line, the situation appeared more critical. No word came in from Sedgwick. It began to be feared that he and Wright, disdaining to fly, were prisoners.

Artillery moved quietly to commanding positions, to be prepared for the worst, and cool heads felt that were the whole Sixth Corps broken, the army, as an army, would still be invincible. Warren's Corps is instantly, but in perfect composure, disposed to meet the situation. Grant and Meade and Warren are in Grant's tent, to and from which officers come and go with a certain earnest air that bespeaks urgent and important cares. So during an hour. No firing has been heard the last three-quarters of an hour. The Rebels must have ceased to advance; but how far have they penetrated, and what is the present situation?

The Sixth Corps' flag comes in. Where is the Sixth Corps' chieftain? My watch says ten o'clock at night. A despatch received. John Sedgwick safe. Wright safe. The Sixth Corps holds a strong line ; only Seymour's and a part of Shaler's brigade have been broken. The enemy can do nothing more. The Sixth Corps proper has not lost its pristine glory. Compelled to withdraw, under orders, after the defection of its right, it is still invincible, — is now, and ever shall be. I may not refrain from mentioning for gallantry Sedgwick's staff and Wright's.

Riding in the thickest, with rare presence of mind and rare judgment, they won and deserved John Sedgwick's emphatic commendation. Generals Seymour and Shaler were captured. It should be stated that both are awarded by their division and corps commanders every credit for doing all men could to recover their troops from panic, communicated to the latter's brigade, not beginning there.

III.

SATURDAY'S REPORT. — FLIGHT OF THE REBELS. — RUMOR THAT GENERAL WADSWORTH IS A PRISONER. — ESTIMATE OF LOSSES.

WILDERNESS, 5 P. M., Saturday, May 7, 1864.

UP to this hour there has been but little fighting to-day. Our position this morning was unchanged from yesterday's, excepting that the right had been bent back. Sedgwick's affair last night has in no wise disconcerted the plans of our leaders, depressed their hope, or impaired the efficiency of the army. It was but a disastrous episode.

This became clearly apparent when the morning disclosed the fact that nowhere on the line was the enemy pressed up against us; that he had during the night withdrawn from the battlefield, leaving us free to occupy nearly all the ground where lay the slain. He had retreated, however, only to another line, where he evidently challenged an attack. He has played upon us all of to-day with long-range guns and has kept a bold skirmish line in his front. Large parties have been seen all day at work intrenching just in Warren's front; 2,000 or 3,000 men have been digging all day upon a half-mile line, from which several solid shot have been thrown nearly to army headquarters. Lee's success on our right must have been so greatly overbalanced by his repulse on our left an hour before that he did not dare risk another day on the same ground. He concedes by this quasi withdrawal that he cannot longer stand the battle though he felt able to precipitate it.

Very great relief is felt this afternoon on account of a report of prisoners that General Wadsworth is in the enemy's hands, severely wounded. The cheering statement is quite circumstantial, and is generally credited. On the same authority Longstreet is wounded and Jenkins killed.

During the day I have ridden along several miles of front over the ground most stubbornly contested yesterday,— how stubbornly is attested by the trees hewed and trimmed and perforated by bullets, and by the thick-strewn dead. It is like other fields of this war; certainly none have presented a more terrible scene; nearly all the wounded had been removed, but none of the dead buried.

Far down the plank road where Hancock fought, beyond the thickest Rebel dead, lay a boy severely wounded, perhaps not less a soldier that he was but a boy. He had fallen the day before when we were farthest advanced, and had remained unmolested within the Rebel lines. They had not removed him, and he was alone with the dead when I rode up. The poor fellow was crawling about gathering violets. Faint with loss of blood, unable to stand, he could not resist the tempting flowers, and had already made a beautiful bouquet. Having caused a stretcher to be sent for, I saw him taken up tenderly and borne away, wearing a brave, sweet, touching smile.

About two o'clock the Rebels made a demonstration upon our right flank, penetrating nearly to the plank road, and threatening communication with Germania. However, we had cleared the road of everything valuable, had removed the pontoons, and probably did not care to prevent the Rebels from occupying.

I am not permitted to speculate in regard to Grant's plans and probable movements. He will, however, make a vigorous assault yet to-night. Lee's generalship has been magnificent. His main force was at Orange Court-House. He moved simultaneously with Grant, and as rapidly.

Wednesday night he held the Mine Run line. Grant had put his army over the Rapidan, and Fifth Corps Headquarters that night were where Army Headquarters have been since. Lee menaced our line of march, and Warren steps out and fights him. Next Lee hurries everything to his right to penetrate between Warren and Hancock, who was marching from Chancellorsville.

Foiled in the attempt he adopts the system of masked massed assaults. Beaten through two days at his own game, he last night retires, intrenches, and invites attack where the ground is unknown to us, familiar to him. That Grant and Meade, working in thorough concord and concert, have met and thwarted him at every turn is sufficient comment upon their generalship. This fact must be ominous to Lee of the fate in store for him before this campaign shall close.

I have yet said nothing as to the extent of our loss, or how it compares with the enemy's. Eight thousand of our wounded have already been cared for in the hospitals. It is thought that say 1,000 remain on the field. Estimating the killed at 1,500, and prisoners at 2,000, I cannot reduce the total to less than 12,000. Included are seven general officers, viz.: Hayes, killed; Wadsworth, killed or a prisoner; Shaler and Seymour, prisoners; Getty and Webb — these last two did most admirably — wounded. The ambulance and hospital arrangements have been perfect. It is certain that in no previous battle have the wounded been so speedily and well cared for.

The enemy's loss, judging from the appearance of the battle-field, and from the manner of fighting and the nature of the ground, cannot be less than ours — is, indeed, undoubtedly greater. The whole army believes that it has inflicted more than it has suffered. Our wounded, to the number of 3,000, are now being placed in ambulances and empty wagons, and the train, accompanied by 3,000 to 4,000 wounded able to walk and a strong escort, will start for Ely's Ford by sunset.

It is a remarkable circumstance that during three days of battles the artillery reserve has remained quietly parked three miles to the rear. The artillery attached to the corps has been ten times more than could be brought into action.

The cavalry has had considerable fighting, and has done important service. It has hung upon our left, has kept Stuart at bay, has attacked him when it has been possible to reach him. Sheridan's business was to protect our immense stores, which were mainly in the rear toward Chancellorsville, — to prevent Stuart from raiding around us toward Fredericksburg; in short, to take care of that enterprising rider, and thrash him if he could be brought to an encounter.

The imperative part of this business has been well and vigilantly attended to.

Wilson's Division rode into and drove a portion of the enemy's cavalry on Thursday, on the road to Robertson's tavern. Our loss was some 300,— the Fifth N. Y. suffering the most.

Sheridan seems to have taken the cavalry reins with a master's hand, and to be fast gaining the confidence of the Cavalry Corps. I suspect a general cavalry fight may be contested far down on the enemy's right before many days, for I know the destruction of Stuart's power for mischief is considered important to the carrying out of the campaign in the shape contemplated. By an arrival from Washington this afternoon, we learn of Butler's landing on James River. The news will at once be disseminated throughout the army, to give to this movement the impulse and inspiration springing from the knowledge of another onward to Richmond. The Hon. E. B. Washburne joined Headquarters at Culpeper, and has since ridden with the staff, — a species of " Congressional interference " to which the army does not object.

It is now nearly sunset, Saturday, May 7. There is quite vigorous firing, and some artillery, at different points on the line, induced by an advance on our part. I think it will not assume the proportions of a general engagement. It is proposed, doubtless, to learn something of the Rebel position, and it may be for another object. Perhaps the main one is to inform the enemy that we are here in full force as night sets in. I doubt if we shall be when the sun rises, and under this convinced impression that there is to be no more heavy work on this ground, I shall leave immediately for Washington.

WASHINGTON, Monday, May 9, 1864.

C. A. Page, our army correspondent, brings to me the foregoing despatches. The brave man was repeatedly fired upon by guerillas while on his way. S. WILKINSON.[1]

[1] Speaking of this battle of the Wilderness in his "Memoirs," General Grant says: "More desperate fighting has not been witnessed on this continent than that of the 5th and 6th of May. Our victory consisted in having successfully crossed a formidable stream, almost in the face of an enemy, and in getting the army together as a unit."

RAPPAHANNOCK STATION,
Monday, May 9, 10 A. M.

The long train of wounded, containing over 8,000, which had been ordered to come to this point for railroad transportation, has been turned back at Ely's Ford and the pontoons taken up. It will probably be sent back via Fredericksburg and Belleplain. It must have proved too hazardous to despatch them this way.

Grant probably marched in the evening of Saturday to turn the enemy's right, compel him to move out and fight on equal ground, or see our army pass by unmolested on its way to Richmond. I have news from Grant up to sunset Saturday, up to which time we had gained decided advantages. There was but little fighting on Saturday.

SPOTTSYLVANIA.

MAY 9TH TO 21ST.

I.

"MY object in moving to Spottsylvania," says General Grant, "was twofold: first, I did not want Lee to get back to Richmond in time to attempt to crush Butler before I could get there; second, I wanted to get between his army and Richmond if possible; and if not, to draw him into the open field. But Lee, by accident, beat us [in getting] to Spottsylvania." By noon of the 9th inst. both armies were in position, each one engaged in intrenching and manœuvring, but not joining in any general collision until the 12th.

On the morning of that day there was a severe struggle, of which General Grant gives the following account in his "Memoirs": "The morning opened foggy, delaying the start more than a half-hour. The ground over which Hancock had to pass to reach the enemy was ascending and heavily wooded to within two or three hundred yards of the enemy's intrenchments. . . . But notwithstanding these difficulties, the troops pushed on in quick time without firing a gun, and when within four or five hundred yards of the enemy's line broke out in loud cheers, and with a rush went up to and over the breastworks. Barlow and Birney entered almost simultaneously. Here a desperate hand-to-hand conflict took place. The men of the two sides were too close together to fire, but used their guns as clubs. The hand conflict was soon over. Hancock's Corps captured some four thousand prisoners, among them a division and a brigade commander; twenty or more guns, with their horses, caissons, and ammunition; several thousand stands of arms, and many colors. . . .

SPOTTSYLVANIA.

"This victory was important, and one that Lee could not afford to leave us in full possession of. . . . He massed heavily from his left flank on the broken point of his line. Five times during the day he assaulted furiously, but without dislodging our troops from their new position. His losses must have been fearful. Sometimes the belligerents would be separated by but a few feet. In one place a tree, eighteen inches in diameter, was cut entirely down by musket-balls. All the trees between the lines were very much cut to pieces by artillery and musketry. It was three o'clock next morning before the fighting ceased. Some of our troops had then been twenty hours under fire. . . . Our losses were heavy." His losses (as subsequently stated by himself) in the Wilderness and at Spottsylvania, of killed, wounded, and missing, the latter mostly prisoners, were 27,549, — nearly one-fourth of the 116,000 with which he went into the Wilderness. Therefore his celebrated despatch of May 11th, in which he said, "Our losses have been heavy as well as those of the enemy. I think the loss of the enemy must be greater. We have taken over 5,000 prisoners by battle, whilst he has taken from us but few, except stragglers. I PROPOSE TO FIGHT IT OUT ON THIS LINE IF IT TAKES ALL SUMMER," was properly characterized by Horace Greeley as pithy but rather roseate. Moreover, Lee had made him miss a chance to get between the Confederate army and Richmond.

On the 17th Mr. Page, having returned from Washington, writes as follows to the "Tribune."

II.

GOOD WEATHER. — GREAT EVENTS AT HAND. — SEVERITY OF LATE BATTLES. — GENERAL WRIGHT. — SPLENDID ACHIEVEMENT OF GENERAL BARLOW'S DIVISION, &C.

HEADQUARTERS ARMY OF POTOMAC,
One Mile North of Spottsylvania Court-House,
4 P. M., May 17, 1864.

THE sun shines brightly to-day; the ground is fast drying. Grand events are on the tapis. As illustrating the severity of our work, I note that Getty's Division Sixth Corps reports but 4,100 muskets, and it marched with 8,400, and only 580 are "missing," the others all killed and wounded; and this one instance is but an illustration for the whole. But I know that the loss inflicted equals or exceeds the loss suffered, and I trust to the unconquerable endurance and tenacity of the rank and file.

General Wright is the natural successor of the lamented Sedgwick, and none other would have been so well received by the corps. In social, personal temperament, and in military qualities he seems to bear a marked resemblance to Sedgwick himself. His instant promotion to a major-generalship's assignment to the corps is, indeed, peculiarly happy and auspicious, regarded as a recognition of the wishes of the thousands he is to lead.

In the endeavor to be first in point of time, it is inevitable that glaring inaccuracies of statement and misawards of credit should be made in the first accounts of battles that reach the public. It has thus happened that Hancock's splendid success of Thursday, with its trophies of prisoners and guns, should be wrongly attributed. Let me make the correction on authority, and in the light of four subsequent days. The main assault was made, and the chief success gained, by General Barlow's Division.

This is from Hancock's own lips, and will appear in his report. Not that there need be any detraction from Birney's work. His division was out next, not attacking so soon and going in on the flank. While it participates in the honor, to General Barlow's Division attaches the highest credit. Besides, the formation of their commands for the charge was left to the division commanders, and Barlow formed his front twenty men deep, and the momentum thus gained was irresistible. The other divisions, as usual, attacked in thinner lines, and were unable to push so far.

I have written this on request and as a matter of justice, and have backing for the statement.

Doctor Morton of Boston, one of the first discoverers, if not indeed the first discoverer, of the anæsthetic properties of ether, has been with the army the last week, working and observing in his capacity with all his might. During this time he has, with his own hands, administered ether in over 2,000 cases. The Medical Director, when asked yesterday in what operations he required ether to be used, replied, "In every case."

I believe the division of labor in the manufacture of any given article has now reached the point where twenty-five different men help make a pin. Science is scarcely behind art in this particular, as the following incident will show.

Day before yesterday some three hundred rebel wounded fell into our hands. Of these, twenty-one required capital operations. They were placed in a row, a slip of paper pinned to each man's coat collar telling the nature of the operation that had been decided upon. Doctor Morton first passes along, and with a towel saturated with ether puts every man beyond consciousness and pain.

The operating surgeon follows and rapidly and skilfully amputates a leg or an arm, as the case may be, till the twenty-one have been subjected to the knife and saw without one twinge of pain. A second surgeon ties up the arteries; a third dresses the wounds. The men are taken to tents near by and wake up to find themselves cut in two without torture, while a windrow of lopped-off members attest the work. The last man had been operated upon before the first wakened. Nothing could be more dramatic, and nothing could more perfectly demonstrate the value of anæsthetics. Besides, men fight better when they know that torture does not follow a wound, and numberless lives are saved that the shock of the knife would lose to their friends and the country. Honor, then, to Morton and Jackson, the men who so opportunely for this war placed in our hands an agent that relieves the soldier from untold misery, and his friends from untold anguish.

III.

THE ADVANCE ON WEDNESDAY. — TWO LINES OF THE ENEMY'S WORKS CARRIED. — THE THIRD TOO FORMIDABLE FOR ASSAULT. — OUR LOSS ONE THOUSAND.

HEADQUARTERS ARMY OF THE POTOMAC,
6 P. M., May 18, 1864.

EARLY yesterday it was determined to attack this morning. At first the decision was to try a movement upon the left, with the view of turning the enemy's right; but late in the afternoon, it being apparent that the enemy must have seen us moving troops to mass upon the left, and the line of attack not proving as favorable there as had been expected, the plan of attack was recast, and the Second and Sixth Corps were moved during the night to the extreme right. The assault was to be at sunrise, Wright at the right, Hancock joining with his left, and Burnside and Warren still farther to the left, in the order they are named. The struggle actually began soon after daybreak. It has proved abortive. The losses of the day I estimate at 1,000, and we hold no more ground than in the morning. The day's work has been unsuccessful.

The Second Corps, having less distance to pass, and being first placed on the road, were soonest in position, and opened the ball. The divisions of Barlow and Gibbon, with the Corcoran Legion, just brought up from Washington, moved upon the enemy's works immediately, while the Sixth Corps, Neill's and Ricketts' Divisions, did the same a moment later a little farther to the right. Each of the four divisions easily carried the first two lines of works and each of the four division commanders halted his men on approaching the third line, and refrained from attempting to carry it. Three days of rest had enabled the enemy to construct an impenetrable abatis fifteen to twenty rods wide, with strong works in its rear, and the division generals instantly and simultaneously saw that they could not carry the obstacles that confronted them. Meanwhile they were subjected to a fatal artillery fire; the loss was becoming severe, and there was no opportunity of inflicting a compensating loss. The whole line withdrew, and so ended a movement which seemed to promise large success. During these two or three hours, Burnside at the centre and Warren at the left were subjected to severe shelling, and plied their own guns in return. Burnside was compelled to withdraw his headquarters behind the cover of an eminence, so thick and fatal fell the shot and shell. By ten o'clock the affair was over. New plans were formed at once, and movements made accordingly, whereof it is not proper yet to speak.

The Corcoran Legion suffered most severely. By far the largest loss was inflicted by the enemy's artillery, which he has had ample time to place in position. I have never before seen such terrible wounds as those of to-day, and have never heard of so many hair-breadth escapes. Horses seemed to be particularly unlucky, and men particularly lucky.

Four days these armies have been manœuvring, — little fighting, but a contest of generalship. The enemy is quiet, and hits back only when hit. He is sullen, and purely on the defensive. Nevertheless, I am convinced there are more things in Grant's philosophy than he dreams of. Await the development of these things and possess your souls in patience.

IV.

FIGHT OF THURSDAY. — DASH OF EWELL'S CORPS. — NEARLY A MILE OF BATTLE. — THE ENEMY'S PICKET LINE CAPTURED. — PLUCKY FIGHTING BY THE NEW TROOPS. — CONGRATULATORY ORDER BY GENERAL MEADE. — LEE TELLS HIS MEN THEY ARE "NEAR OUR RICH STORES AND IMMENSE BAGGAGE."

HEADQUARTERS ARMY OF THE POTOMAC,
Friday Evening, May 20, 1864.

OUR extreme right had been considerably withdrawn last night; it rested say two miles rearward of the battlefield of Wednesday, and seemed to barely cover the Fredericksburg Pike.

This extreme right of the line (understand that the entire line is fully six miles long) was held by Tyler's Division, consisting of six heavy artillery regiments, lately brought to the front from the forts about Washington, and their great guns exchanged for muskets, and Kitching's Brigade, being the Sixth and Fifteenth New York Artillery, taken from the reserve artillery, and likewise given muskets.

In the course of the afternoon skirmishing became quite warm, but the firing was not such as to attract the attention of the various headquarters until about five o'clock. At that hour the volleys became continuous and so heavy that at the extreme left, where I happened to be, it was apparent that a well contested action was being waged.

It appears that having forced back the skirmish line in some confusion upon their supports, Ewell's entire corps burst upon the troops above mentioned. Instantly that able general developed a brisk skirmish into a determined assault. The object is palpable. He meant if possible to turn our right and get at our baggage train, perhaps cut and permanently hold our communications. Failing in this, he might reasonably expect to gain the advantages and information to obtain which a reconnoissance in force is the last resort. He was beautifully foiled. He gained certainly one bit of information which may be of service, though not particularly agreeable to him, viz.: that this army knows how to take care of itself, let the emergency be never so instant and critical.

Colonel Tannott's Brigade, First Maine Heavy Artillery, and First Massachusetts Heavy Artillery, received the assault, and then, as a wider front of Rebels appeared, the whole division became engaged, and not long after Kitching's Brigade found the enemy coming upon them, and there was nearly a mile of battle.

I asked a veteran officer of the First Massachusetts how his men fought. His reply was, "Well, after a few minutes they got a little mixed, and did n't fight very tactically, but they fought confounded plucky — just as well as I ever saw the old Second."

He had served in the Second Division of the Second Corps, and must have seen some of the best work of the war.

Finding his men gradually yielding ground, Colonel Tannott ordered a counter charge, and drove the Rebels across a small field. He could not dislodge them from the adjacent woods, and was finally himself driven back to the cover of the woods on his own side of the open space.

Meanwhile General Hunt had ridden rapidly from headquarters, and succeeded in planting Hart's battery at the left of the line of action, and just in time to repulse an assault upon that quarter. A little later he had placed another battery in effective position, and Colonel Tidball's Fourth New York Artillery was brought up, but not then put in.

Until sunset, a period of an hour and a half, charges and counter charges swayed the action back and forth, deflecting the line, bearing it back here and pushing it forward there, but never once breaking it, and scarcely changing the mean position. It was not yet decisive, but the enemy was checked, and heavy re-enforcements were coming up. It must have been during this time that a few hundred of the enemy penetrated the woods widely around our right, and burst out of the woods, upon the

Fredericksburg Pike, almost directly in the rear of the main engagement.

During a few minutes they were in possession of a long empty train headed to the rear for supplies. They had captured a few teamsters and killed a few horses, when they were hustled back by an impromptu force, gathered in the vicinity by one or two energetic and quick-thoughted officers. This raid did not yield them a single hard tack, and lost them twenty prisoners. By dark the firing ceased.

Less than ten thousand new troops had repulsed the three divisions of Ewell's Corps, Rhodes', Early's, and what Hancock's charge of a week ago left of Johnson's.

Before the close of the action enough troops had come up to have repelled the two other corps of Lee's army. Birney's Division of the Second Corps, Crawford's of the Fifth, and Russell's of the Sixth, assumed the line before the firing had quite ceased, and held it during the night, with brisk skirmishing at intervals.

At three A. M. to-day these divisions advanced. The movement was so rapid and unexpected that the enemy's picket line was captured almost to a man, and, sweeping on, prisoners were gathered at every step, until over two miles had been gained and hundreds of prisoners taken.

Judging from what I saw in riding over the ground this morning before the dead were buried, I estimate our own killed at 150, the Rebel dead at 200.

I think the same proportion holds with the respective loss in wounded. Knowing our own to be fully 1,000, the enemy's would then be over 1,300, all of which he carried off, though leaving his dead on the field. Among those we have buried for him is a Colonel Boyd of the Forty-fifth North Carolina.

We already have between 500 and 600 prisoners corralled near Army Headquarters, and there are perhaps a hundred still to be brought in. Our loss in prisoners will not exceed 200.

Altogether, the result of this attack by Ewell is eminently encouraging to the army. It is accepted as a fit offset to our failure on nearly the same ground two days before. It demonstrates that the troops added to the army since the ten days' battle may be relied upon. A prompt and judicious recognition of this fact has been made by a General Order issued this morning, which reads as follows: —

HEADQUARTERS ARMY OF THE POTOMAC,
Friday, May 20, 1864, 8 A. M.

THE Major-General commanding desires to express his satisfaction with the good conduct of Tyler's Division, Kitching's Brigade of heavy artillery, in the affair of yesterday evening. The gallant manner in which these commands, the greater portion being for the first time under fire, met and checked a persistent corps of the enemy, led by one of its best generals, justifies the commendation in this special manner of troops who henceforward will be relied upon as were the tried veterans of the Second and Sixth Corps, at the same time engaged. By command of

Major-General MEADE.

SETH WILLIAMS, A. A. G.

Prisoners state that Lee came with them across the Ny, rode along their lines, and addressed each brigade, telling them they were to undertake a most important movement, which, if successful, would be a fatal blow to the Yankee invaders, and adjuring them to make it successful. He told them they were even then close to our rich stores and immense baggage, and that a determined assault would give them everything we possessed.

So many prisoners state the above, in substance, that it must have some foundation in truth.

On the 20th, Lee showing no disposition to come out from his intrenchments, Grant gave orders for a renewed left-flank movement with a view to another attempt to get between the Confederate army and Richmond. The armies were now operating in a highly cultivated country, where the roads were wide and good, but where Grant, being without guides or maps, had to pick his dangerous way by the help only of his engineers and staff officers. His course was south, and his troops took all roads leading in that direction, leaving the Sixth (Wright's) and Ninth (Burnside's) Corps at Spottsylvania in front of Lee, while Hancock and Warren, with the Second and Fifth Corps, should press forward, and get between Lee and Richmond. This gave Lee an excellent opportunity to fall upon either one of these bodies while out of supporting distance of the other, but he forbore it, though he had been but recently re-enforced by not less than 15,000 fresh troops under Pickett, Hoke, and Breckinridge. "He never again," says Grant, "had such an opportunity of dealing a heavy blow."

The Union movements were easily seen from the higher ground occupied by Lee, whose position covered the direct and best road to Richmond, compelling Grant to make a wide detour, and to move by narrow and much inferior roads.

On the evening of the 21st, the corps of Wright and Burnside moved out from their intrenchments near Spottsylvania Court-House, and followed Hancock and Warren, closely watched and almost constantly annoyed by the enemy. Very considerable engagements, in which most of the Union troops participated and heavy losses were suffered on both sides, occurred until the 26th, when Grant telegraphed to the War Department: "Lee's army is really whipped. The prisoners we now take show it, and the action of his army shows it unmistakably. A battle with them outside of intrenchments cannot be had. Our men feel that they have gained the *morale* of the enemy, and attack him with confidence. I may be mistaken, but I feel that our success over Lee's army is already assured. The promptness and rapidity with which you have forwarded re-enforcements has contributed largely to the feeling of confidence inspired in our men, and to break down that of the enemy."

His re-enforcements had amounted to 40,000 men, a number fully 10,000 in excess of his losses, so that on the 30th of May he was that much stronger than when he set out from the Rapidan. Lee's position at this time stretched from Atlee's

Station, on the Virginia Central R. R., to Cold Harbor; Grant's was directly opposite, the two lines being so closely together that either side could instantly detect any movement of the other. At this point we reach again the correspondence of Mr. Page.

COLD HARBOR.

I.

OUR PROGRESS TOWARD RICHMOND. — FURIOUS ATTACK BY THE
REBELS. — THEY ARE BEATEN BACK WITH HEAVY LOSS.

HEADQUARTERS ARMY OF THE POTOMAC,
TWELVE MILES NORTH OF RICHMOND,
Tuesday, 9 A. M., May 31, 1864.

THE army marched yesterday at daybreak, the right swinging from Hanover Court-House, and the left moving from Hanovertown on the Pamunkey.

Heavy reconnoissances, made the day before from each corps, had determined the position of the enemy.

An average march of four miles, occupying nearly all day, brought the different corps in connected line of battle close upon the enemy's intrenchments, Warren having the left, Hancock the centre, Wright the right, and Burnside the reserve, though the latter has this morning assumed a portion of the line.

Warren advanced upon a direct road leading from Howe's Store to Bethesda Church. Hancock moved upon a road leading from the former place to Shelton's Cross Roads, where it intersects the road to Richmond, via Mechanicsville. Wright swung to the left by cross-roads aiming to connect with Hancock. Warren and Hancock pressed the enemy's skirmishers from the first. The former crossed the Tolopatomoy without serious opposition and intrenched in three lines. A little after dark the enemy attacked his left, which lay upon the road, first falling upon Crawford's Division and forcing a part of it from the first line, but reaching the second line, or rather a line further to the left and so practically a second line, held by Kitching's Brigade, late heavy artillery, they met a terrible repulse. The line was concave toward the enemy, with a battery at each horn of the half-moon. Early's division rushed into this "jaws of death and mouth of hell," and speedily went back, all that was left of it. The repulse was complete; our own loss was trivial, the enemy's terrible. Crawford and Kitching lost perhaps 200 killed and wounded, and they have buried that number of the enemy's dead, taken over a hundred prisoners, exclusive of over a hundred Rebel wounded left on the ground. This affair was between eight and nine o'clock last night.

Meanwhile Hancock had been not less successful in gaining the position he wanted. By noon he had pushed back a heavy skirmish line so close to their own works that Barlow's Division planted Arnold's battery within 500 yards of a Rebel battery. An artillery duel of an hour silenced the Rebel guns first engaged, but disclosed others right and left. This cannonading was exceedingly rapid and at short range. That our casualties were few is due to the promptness and skill which threw up formidable earthworks, enabling a few men to hold a well-sheltered and easily defended line.

During the evening, while Warren repelled an assault, Hancock made one. Barlow's Division charged and carried a range of Rebel rifle-pits, thus advancing the left and centre of the corps line equally with the right, and cutting off an enfilading fire which might have troubled us. This advance was under cover of an artillery fire of a dozen guns and eight Cohorn mortars. The latter are considered very effective.

The Sixth and Ninth Corps were not engaged during the day. The march of the former had to be made warily, since it came in from so far to the right as to be exposed to an attack while isolated.

Longstreet holds the enemy's centre, Ewell his right, and Hill his left, or did last night.

This morning opens like a battle day, artillery sounding with the first daylight, occasional musketry at various points, and now (at ten o'clock) heavy, and still heavier volleys on Hancock's left.

II.

WHAT "SCYUGLE" MEANS. — THE VALUE OF STAFF OFFICERS. — A HERETIC WHO FIGHTS LIKE JOHN BROWN. — THE CAPTAIN WHO HAS BRAINS. — AN UNKNOWN HERO. — THE HARD FACTS OF A CAMPAIGN. — "FIGHTING IT OUT ON THIS LINE."

HEADQUARTERS SIXTH CORPS, ELEVEN MILES NORTH OF RICHMOND, noon, Tuesday, May 31, 1864.

WHILE artillery thunders all along the front, and the line closes hard up against the enemy, while the minutes are hours, for fatal musketry may break out at any moment and open the Battle of Richmond, to kill the time and relieve the terrible suspense that wears on a man more than work or danger, permit me to write a general gossipy letter, on all sorts of topics, — a letter that shall waive "the situation," and deal with things other than "the latest from the front." A Sixth Corps staff officer dismounted near me a moment ago. I inquired where he had been riding. He informed me that he had been sent out on a general " scyugle ;" that he had "scyugled " along the front, where the Johnnies " scyugled " a bullet through his clothes; that on his return he "scyugled" an ice-house; that he should "scyugle" his servant — who, by the way, had just "scyugled" three fat chickens — for a supply of ice; that after he had " scyugled " his dinner he proposed to "scyugle" a nap — and closed by asking how I "scyugled." The word originated at these headquarters, and is supposed to be derived from two Greek words. Army libraries do not contain "Liddell and Scott," or I should endeavor to ascertain what the two words are. The word "scyugle," it will be perceived, has any meaning any one chooses to attach to it, has not only a variety, but a contrariety of meanings. It is synonymous with "gobble" and with "skedaddle," is used for any other word and for want of any other word. To fully define it would require the thirty-nine volumes the German savant gave to a discussion of Greek particles.

"Scyugle" is respectfully commended to persons curious and learned in orthoepy. The general public is at the same time informed, with a smack of Delphic oracularity which it is hoped will be appreciated, that newspaper correspondents with the army, being "scyuglers," "scyugle"!

A good staff officer is a good thing. No ability on the part of a general can compensate the want of a good staff, while an incompetent general often wears the laurels that belong rightfully to some junior officer who rides with him. It is only lately that the importance of an efficient staff has been half appreciated in the army; by the country it is not yet understood. Know, then, that General Smith, Jones, or Brown commands this or that division or brigade well, because he has the good sense to defer to the opinions of Captain Brown, Jones, or Smith of his staff; know that Captain B., J., or S. is every whit as good an officer as General S., J., or B., and that the latter's brilliant reputation often rests on the former's brilliant brains. I know a lieutenant-colonel and chief of staff who, if required to assume command of this corps to-morrow, would acquit himself as well as the best of major-generals, and yet he is in no direct line of promotion, and his reputation, being an army growth, is confined mainly to the army. Politically he is a rank heretic, but — and the fact is an illustration of the larger fact involved in "He makes the wrath of men to praise Him" — my lieutenant-colonel fights as though he were John Brown himself!

Then there is a certain captain of engineers at Army Headquarters, who is, with scarcely an exception, the hardest-worked and most useful officer in this whole army. It is his business to ascertain — and he must do it mainly by personal observation — the topography of every new region the army occupies. He must make surveys, question contrabands, deserters, and prisoners in regard to roads, bridges, and fords, draw maps, and consult, oftener even than corps commanders, with the "major-general commanding." In a word, the army is often dependent upon the judgment of this one captain. A fortnight ago, at Spottsylvania, he partly discovered and partly made a road whereby four miles were saved in moving troops from right to left of the line. That night, amid the darkness and rain, he piloted over this road the Second and Sixth Corps, and the next morning by attack and surprise we captured 20 guns and 7,000 prisoners. But for the discovery of a blind bridle path, which fifty pioneers in two hours' time widened and improved to the capacity of a road fit for artillery, the attack which resulted so successfully would not have been thought practicable. Victor Hugo attributes the timely arrival of Blucher at Waterloo to the happy choice by a subordinate of the right road, which was but a half-defined path; so much do battles hinge on apparent trivialities. The officer I have been talking of — a modest man, who will be startled beyond composure should he ever see this — is Capt. W. H. Paine, of the Topographical Engineers.

Which one of the brilliant lecturers who delight the winter-night audiences of Northern cities recited, a few years ago, the apotheosis of "Pluck"? He should have waited for this war, and for this campaign of this war, for a better illustration of his theme. This is the twenty-ninth day of the campaign; every day has seen more or less marching, more or less fighting. 30,000 wounded have been sent back on honorable furlough, 5,000 dead have been buried in honorable though obscure graves. Sedgwick and Wadsworth, and many another whose memory we cannot afford to let die, have fallen. Still the army is "fighting it out on this line."

The roads are strewn with the carcasses of 6,000 horses. Actual marching has worn out 50,000 pairs of shoes. Two-thirds of the men, more than 100,000, have not changed a garment since they started, — have marched, and fought, and slept thirty days and thirty nights in heat and dust and rain, and have not changed a garment. They are "fighting it out on this line."

On the march there are fewer stragglers now, and fewer grumblers, than thirty days ago. Rising from the bivouac at all hours, resting when they may, perhaps counter-marched over the same ground without halt or purpose, they endure all things with a patience and a pluck and a certain easy nonchalance, as astounding as it is commendable.

> " Theirs not to reason why,
> Theirs but to do and die."

They propose, with Grant, "to fight it out on this line."

The rank and file have a pretty good appreciation of the strategy of the campaign. They understand that it has been a series of splendid flank movements, and "flanking" has become the current joke with which to account for everything from a night march to the capture of a sheep or a pig. A poor fellow, terribly wounded, yesterday, said he saw the shell coming, "but had n't time to flank it." And he enjoyed his joke with a smile and a chuckle, when his quick eye had sought and found appreciation among the bystanders. The shell had "flanked" him, by taking off an arm.

HEADQUARTERS SIXTH CORPS,
ELEVEN MILES NORTH OF RICHMOND.
May 31, 10 P. M., 1864.

The tremendous cannonading and smart fusillading noted in my despatch of this morning were Birney and Barlow carrying a line of rifle-pits in Hancock's front. They sent back over 100 prisoners within the next hour, and desisted from their advance, under orders, when they had accomplished precisely what was intended.

Wright, advancing at the same time, encountered an impassable marsh, which his left, under Ricketts, evaded by falling in behind Birney, and then sliding gradually out beyond the latter's right until he had his entire division in position. A dangerous movement, since it exposed his flank while in march, but successful, because done quietly and gradually.

Desultory artillery and continuous sharp-shooting filled up the day at the right. The peculiarity of this fighting has been the close proximity to each other of the opposing lines, and the skill and courage of the skirmishers on either side.

Of Warren's and Burnside's fighting at the left I have no particulars, but it was not unlike that on the right. I set down the casualties of the day at 300. It is evident that neither side cares to bring on a general engagement by attacking, and as evident that each would be happy to have the other do so.

Barlow captured a number of Breckinridge's renegade Kentucky Division. The old A. P. Hill Corps was upon the enemy's left, Longstreet's in his centre, and Ewell's on his right.

Capt. James H. Platt, acting chief quartermaster of the Sixth Corps, with five orderlies and a light wagon laden with valuables, was captured night before last. He was returning from the rear, where he had been hurrying up supplies. Following the sinuous marching of his corps he was probably not two miles from headquarters when taken. Captain Platt was a line officer of a regiment the first two years of the war — fought his company nearly all away, was then made assistant quartermaster, and was an efficient and favorite officer.

Supplies will arrive to-morrow via White House. The last received came by Port Royal and Dunkirk, a wagoning distance of 50 miles.

III.

BRIEF RECORD OF CAVALRY OPERATIONS SINCE THE GRAND RAID. — SPLENDID BEHAVIOR OF OUR MEN.

OLD-CHURCH TAVERN, FOUR MILES NORTH OF GAINES' MILL BATTLE-FIELD, Wednesday, June 1, 1864, 11 A. M.

THE Sixth Corps, marching from the right of our line on the Tolopatomoy at midnight, cut Smith's advance from White House at this point, about nine o'clock this morning. At the instant Major G. A. Forsyth of General Sheridan's staff reported to General Wright that Torbert's Division of cavalry was warmly engaged at Cold Harbor, Gaines' Mill, with Rebel infantry; that he was in search of General Smith to ask for infantry support. Sheridan had been ordered to hold the position, and could do so, but would like help from the infantry. Wright continued his march, and the head of his column must have reached the contested ground an hour or two ago.

I shall sketch the operations of the cavalry since its return from its grand raid. Wilson's Division was at once detached to protect the rear of the army, to guard the communications, and to scour the country to the right, when we should have assumed position. The work assigned to him (Wilson) was done vigilantly and successfully. Gregg's and Torbert's Divisions, under Sheridan in person, led the army's advance.

Thursday, May 26, they crossed the Pamunkey at Hanovertown, Custer's Brigade leading, — that officer swimming his horse over the stream, and with his orderlies nabbing the Rebel pickets, all in Custer's usual style, peculiar to himself. A smart brush with, or rather race after, the enemy, a number of prisoners for trophies, and the command bivouacked.

The following morning, May 27, the enemy had been reenforced, and disputed every inch. Torbert's Division alone fought him all day, drove him from the field, captured 79 prisoners, and lost 69 killed and wounded.

On Friday, May 27, the same division and Davies's Brigade of Gregg's Division, advanced four miles, to Howe's Store, engaged the enemy, who appeared in larger force than hitherto, and made one of the hardest cavalry fights of the campaign. The Rebel cavalry have learned better than to fight as cavalry. They dismount, take to the woods, and use Springfield muskets, or a very superior rifle made at Fayetteville, N. C.

Davies's Brigade especially distinguished itself. Davies lost one staff officer and three orderlies, and had two horses killed, and has since been unable to draw his sword, — the scabbard having become so badly indented by bullet blows. Our loss was 340 killed and wounded, 30 of the number being officers. The enemy left 127 dead upon the field, and a number of wounded. It was a clean victory for our folks.

Sunday, May 29, the cavalry rested. Monday, 30th, Torbert swept a large force from Old Church Tavern and neighborhood, with a loss of 60. Tuesday, 31st, he attacked and drove the enemy from Cold Harbor, driving Fitzhugh Lee's Division and Rosser's Brigade of cavalry, and Clingman's Brigade of Hoke's Division of infantry. Torbert's loss about 80. He buried 43 Rebel dead and took 67 prisoners. Adjutant Murphy, Sixth Pennsylvania cavalry, killed; Captain McKee, First U. S. cavalry, severely wounded.

There are just two officers whose splendid daring and other officer-like qualities have shone forth so brightly, who have received such conspicuous mention from men in authority, that I cannot refrain from writing their names: Captain Wadsworth of Torbert's staff, son of the late General Wadsworth, and Major George A. Forsyth of Sheridan's staff, a graduate of the Eighth Illinois cavalry.

THE BATTLES OF COLD HARBOR.

I.

Cold Harbor Battle-Field,
Thursday, June 2, 10 A. M.

NOT a general engagement, but a very severe action, was fought here between five P. M. and ten P. M. yesterday. Our force was the Sixth Corps (Wright's) and the Eighteenth Corps (Baldy Smith's). The enemy marshalled against these the Longstreet Corps and the troops with which Beauregard has been fighting Butler, — Beauregard commanding on the field.

It resulted in our gaining considerable ground, taking over 600 prisoners, occupying a portion of their main works, and securing the position desired for the whole army.

Our loss is, in the Sixth Corps, 960 wounded and a few less than 200 killed; in the Eighteenth Corps about 650 wounded and 125 killed. The enemy, owing to reasons which will appear hereafter, suffered much more severely.

The Sixth Corps, marching from the right of our line on the Tolopatomoy at midnight the night before, toward White House, having moved 10 miles at eight o'clock yesterday morning, struck the head of Smith's Corps, marching from White House, at Old Church Hotel. The Sixth, without halting, turned square to the right, and marched four miles farther, to this place, followed by the Eighteenth Corps, turning, from its previous course, square to the left. The former at once went into position, relieving the cavalry which had held the ground all the morning, and only awaited the arrival of the Eighteenth to move forward in battle's "magnificently stern array."

This march of the Sixth Corps I consider one of the most remarkable of this campaign. On Monday they marched all day *without rations*. That night they formed line of battle, and what with the labor of intrenching and several hours of the night getting rations, they obtained no sleep. On Tuesday, they were engaged with the enemy more or less all day. This night, on thirty minutes' notice, they marched at midnight, marched till morning, marched till noon, marched till four o'clock, and then set to work with all their might intrenching. And the day was one of the sultriest I ever knew, and the roads ankle deep with dust, — impalpable Virginia dust, that hung so densely in the air that it became exceedingly palpable. And yet these Sixth Corps veterans, hungry for two days, sleepless for three days, fatigued with relentless marching by day and by night, all streaming with perspiration, grim and blear-eyed, their hair dusted to the whiteness of three-score years and ten, — these men, despite it all, grasped shovels and axes with brawny hands, and sprang to work with never-surpassed vigor, and an hour later exchanged tools for weapons, and fought with unequalled spirit and tenacity. Show me another record that matches this!

Smith formed on Wright's right, — the battle-field being substantially that of Gaines' Mill, fought June 27, 1862. There is this remarkable difference, however. We had the enemy's position of two years ago, they ours. Then they attacked, and, being successful, turned the right of our army. Now we attacked, and have turned the right of their army. Neill's Division (Second) held the extreme left, Russell's (First) the centre, and Ricketts' (Third), the right of the Sixth Corps's position. Devine's Division connected with Ricketts' right, Brooks' Division with his right, and Martindale's Division with the latter's right. The last three divisions constitute the Eighteenth Corps.

As usual, the battle was felt for by advancing skirmishers, and prepared for by planting artillery, while the lines of infantry extend between. About five P. M. the shots from the skirmish line indicated the near presence of the enemy, when Wright's artillery opened. The enemy's guns replied instantly. This determined to us his position, and an advance of the whole line was ordered. Meanwhile our superiority in artillery was being demonstrated. The Rebel batteries were either silenced by stress of ours, or by shortness of ammunition. They, however, threw shells enough to raise a good many clouds of dust, to lop down a great many trees, and to disturb a great many people.

The assault ordered was made at six o'clock, or a little before. It was successful. The spattering shots of the hour previous instantly became a tempest of musketry. Colonel Drake's Brigade, at the very left of the Eighteenth Corps, opened the storm, and then the volleys ring, crashing louder and still louder to the left. It is Ricketts and Russell. And now the whole line volleys and thunders. Everything has been formed into the column of attack excepting Martindale's Division at the extreme right, and Neill's on the extreme left, who must hold back and take care of the flanks.

Oh! what a ring of battle! How the shot and shell of our artillery vex the air with howl and shriek! Do you hear that cheer? *That's our men!* General Wright and staff, grouped a little — only a little — to the rear of the advancing line, look into each other's faces, and smile and nod their heads, and two or three, audibly, but more to themselves than to their

"Comrades, tried in battles many,"

say, "It's all right!" "That's good!"

Yes, it is "right," it is "good." But there is no cessation; therefore it is not yet decisive.

Will this "damnable iteration" of musketry *never* cease? — this demoniacal "shriek of shot and burst of shell, and bellowing of the mortar," *never* cease to split our ears?

I think how much the scene resembles Gaines' Mill two years ago. The same sun getting red in the west — it is at my right hand now, it was at my left hand then. The same clouds of dust and "white infernal powder-smoke" obscure the scene, till, with the gathering darkness, it resembles my boyish conception of the "Night's Plutonian shore." Finally, after an hour and a half of this, the noise of battling ceases.

I go to get my horse, which an orderly — a quaint Vermonter — has been grazing in the rank clover. "A pretty big fuss in there," remarks the Green Mountain boy. I assent. "I guess our folks wanted to go eout in that direction, and them Johnnies wanted to come this way, and they could n't agree which should git eout of the road." Again I assent. "If you'd 'a' been on your hoss a few minutes ago you'd 'a' been off on him neow." "How so?" "Well, neow, if one o' them shells didn't make *him* squat, an' *me tew!*"

Ricketts alone had been able to take and hold the enemy's last line of works. Other divisions had advanced as far, and occupied the Rebel rifle-pits, but none save Ricketts held on. Russell lost as many men, but he advanced over open ground half a mile, subject to a sweeping fire, and could not get enough men across to hold the pits against the Rebel ebb tide. He led his own old brigade in person on this charge, and received a slight wound in the arm.

The success of the Third Division (Ricketts' Sixth Corps) is the more gratifying, for hitherto it has not been considered the peer of its two companion divisions. Its 500 prisoners taken yesterday, and the following despatch from General Meade, sent late last night, make for it a proud record. The despatch was read this morning to the entire division, and is as follows:

June 1, 9 P. M.

To MAJOR GENERAL WRIGHT: Please give my thanks to Brigadier-General Ricketts and his gallant command for the very handsome manner in which they have conducted themselves to-day. The success attained by them is of great importance, and if followed up will materially advance our operations.

Respectfully yours,

GEO. G. MEADE, Major-General com'd'g.

Devine's Division, Eighteenth Corps, distinguished itself equally with Russell's and Ricketts'; it was engaged next in line to the latter, and it was impossible to distinguish between their musketry. Colonels Drake and Townsend of this division were killed on the charge; both were officers of conspicuous merit.

Brooks' Division advanced with the others, and carried the Rebel position, but was at length compelled to relinquish it from encountering an enfilading fire.

Martindale did not participate in the charge, but warmly engaged skirmishers, front and flank, and lost numbers.

II.

SECOND BATTLE OF COLD HARBOR. — A SHARP AND BLOODY CONFLICT. — OUR LOSS OVER 4,000. — A GENERAL ASSAULT ON LEE'S WORKS. — THE WHOLE LINE ADVANCED AND THE NEW POSITION HELD. — MANY REBEL WORKS TAKEN. — CAPTURE OF BOTTOM'S BRIDGE. — CASUALTIES.

HEADQUARTERS ARMY, COLD HARBOR,
Friday, June 3, 9 P. M.

THIS, the thirtieth day of the campaign, has witnessed still another general engagement, nearer to Richmond than any other, and scarcely less bloody than any other. It is the second battle of Cold Harbor, the first being that of day before yesterday. Our loss is between 4,000 and 5,000, distributed among the corps as follows: Eighteenth Corps, say 2,000; Second Corps, 1,400; Sixth Corps, 1,000; Fifth and Ninth Corps, say 600 to 1,000.

A general assault was ordered to be made at half-past four A. M., and was made promptly at the hour.

The relative positions of the corps, beginning at the left, were in this order: Second Corps, Hancock; Sixth Corps, Wright; Eighteenth Corps, Smith; Fifth Corps, Warren; Ninth Corps, Burnside.

Warren and Burnside did not participate in the assault. Brave as was the attack, and severe as has been the loss, the result is indecisive. Generally the line has been materially advanced. Everywhere we hold closer to the Rebel line. Baldy Smith carried and retains a distinct, well-intrenched position, and other corps are in possession of detached works and various positions more or less important, from which they drove the enemy.

Hancock charged with Barlow's and Gibbon's Divisions, holding Birney in reserve in the works from which he moved and protecting his left front. Barlow carried everything before him, capturing guns, prisoners, and colors; but whether unsupported by corresponding success on his right, or whether he finally met more than any one division could withstand, at length he was forced to relinquish nearly all these trophies, — intrenching some distance in advance of his original position, at the right nearest the Chickahominy, Burnside (Ninth Corps) on the left, and Wright (Sixth Corps) in the centre. Army Headquarters tonight will be at Cedar Grove. Sheridan is off with the divisions of Gregg and Torbert to find Hunter and pilot him in this direction. Wilson's Division will watch our rear and right flank.

General Getty has been placed in command at White House. His wound will not admit of field service for some weeks. His adjutant-general, Captain Hazard Stevens, also wounded in the Wilderness, has also returned to duty.

The heat and dust of to-day's marching are terrible.

Dirt, dust, pulverization of earth into infinitesimalities of concreted nastiness. Dirt, dust, soil, no longer soil but ashes. Powder, worse than that of guns, worse than any prescribed by physicians. Dirt, dust, ashes, powder.

Alluvium — crushed, ground, pulverized, and powdered. Fine dirt, knee-deep to wade through. Impalpable dust sky-high to breathe. A hundred thousand shirts, uncomfortable as the shirt of Nessus. A hundred thousand skins, uncomfortable as the skin of Hazael after the leprosy of Naaman cleaved unto him. Dirt, dust, ashes, as we go marching on.

Yesterday Hancock, assuming a portion of Wright's front, caused Neill's Division to be taken from the left to the right of the Sixth Corps, leaving Russell on the left and Ricketts in the centre. The whole division charged, excepting Russell's second and third brigades. Neill and Ricketts gained nearly half a mile, Russell less, owing to his coming upon open ground swept by musketry. Besides, it would not do to advance beyond Gibbon, who connected with his left.

During the afternoon when I visited the Sixth Corps, which had already constructed admirable works, an incautious head, exposed never so briefly above any point of the parapet, drew, in every instance, a shower of bullets from the Rebel line, not two hundred yards distant.

Devine's Division having been moved to the right of the Eighteenth Corps, Martindale's became the centre, and Brooks' the left. The Eighteenth probably achieved the most decisive success of the day, gaining more ground and holding it with great tenacity and loss. It should be stated, however, that five times as many straggled from it as did from all other corps combined. I account for the paradox by the assumption that the officers did their entire duty, and this view is confirmed by the great fatality among them.

After the morning assault and the almost simultaneous desistance from the same, the whole line set to intrenching, while the heavy guns never ceased to play, nor the skirmish lines their hot fusillade, till sunset. But there has been no line-of-battle firing. The position remained unchanged, except that Birney's Division was withdrawn from the left and sent to occupy the space between Smith and Warren, giving to the army a connected line of six miles. It is mainly parallel with the Chickahominy, although confusingly zigzag in particular direction, and extends through alternate fields and woodland. I judge the ground to be on the average higher than the enemy's, and to that extent we have the better position.

The prisoners taken are from the most diverse commands: from all the corps of Lee's army proper, from Breckenridge, and from three divisions of Beauregard,—showing that the enemy has used everything he can command.

Thirty-two pounders, probably brought from the defences of Richmond, opened upon us at daybreak, and dropped shells far to the rear, not only of troops, but of the different headquarters, of the trains and the hospitals ; indeed every corps headquarters has been under warm fire from morning to night. I suspect our artillery has been more troublesome to the Rebels. We have certainly had more pieces in position, and in better position, and they have been served with diligence and judgment.

One instance in illustration : Captain Stevens, Fifth Maine, disclosed to the Rebels at daylight two guns of his battery on the Gaines' Mill road at Wright's left, well covered by earthworks, and within 200 yards of their line. From there he has thrown grape and canister at their troops, excepting when either of two batteries nearly opposite would open upon him, when he would turn his attention and his guns to shelling them to silence. So close are these guns to the enemy that a cap lifted over the parapet upon a ramrod is instantaneously perforated, while a minie goes jeering by.

Imagine it — men work all day, and never once stand upright; load the pieces upon their hands and knees, extending the rammers out of the embrasures, while others ply shovels to replace the earth knocked away by hostile projectiles. Here, where the bushes have been allowed to stand in the embankment, if you will rise up cautiously and peer through, you shall see the shovelled earth as it is thrown up and falls upon their line 200 yards away. You must be wary, and you must promptly drop on your knees when you see a puff of smoke, for they suspect some one is looking through that clump of bushes. You will have sufficient time to drop down into safety, for the smoke will puff out white and distinct a quarter of a minute before the sound of the discharge reaches you or the ball whizzes by or thuds in the thrown-up dirt. Better take off your hat, for it can be seen more distinctly than your naked head; and don't betray any nervousness should the ball, which will surely come, shower dirt upon your head, else those old artillerymen will laugh at you. Now, if you want to get to the rear, stoop low and double-quick it till you get under cover of the woods. It's only eight or ten rods. Oh, there isn't any danger. They won't hurt you — more than a hundred men have run across there to-day. Every one has been fired at, and only three have been struck. You see they only get a glimpse of you, and can't get a good aim. They'll shoot over you, or behind you, or ahead of you. Those two guns alone would stop the advance of a brigade.

Since I began this letter the enemy have attacked Barlow and been repulsed. Sheridan is reported to hold Bottom's Bridge on the Chickahominy. This may induce the enemy to abandon his present position to-night and cross that classic stream.

Colonel James McMahon, One Hundred and Sixty-fourth New-York, Corcoran Legion, is supposed to be a prisoner, badly wounded. In the charge he was in advance of his regiment, had mounted the parapet simultaneously with the color-bearer, had taken the colors in his own hands, had rammed the staff into the earth, and was shouting to his men, only a few of whom were near, when he was seen to clap his hand to his side, to walk back a few steps, and then to sink upon the ground. In the accompanying list of casualties will be seen Colonel Frederick Wead, Ninety-eighth New-York, killed. Wounded quite severely last night, he could not be prevailed upon to leave the field. This morning in the charge he fell.

III.

AFFAIRS TO SUNDAY EVENING. — NO GENERAL ENGAGEMENT FOR TWO DAYS, BUT CONSTANT SKIRMISHING. — THE EXTENT OF OUR EARTHWORKS. — SILENCING A REBEL BATTERY. — A JOLLY BURIAL. — RESCUING A WOUNDED OFFICER. — A RICH HAUL. — YANKEE TRICKS.

HEADQUARTERS ARMY OF POTOMAC,
COLD HARBOR, June 5, 6 P. M.

NO general engagement yesterday and to-day; no line of battle assaults by either army; nevertheless there has been incessant firing day and night, now at one point, now at another, anon rippling from one end of the line to the other, and the casualties have not been inconsiderable. It could not have been otherwise with the lines so close to each other. I have never before seen such extensive works constructed with such magical rapidity, or that pressed so hard to the enemy's. Nor are they simply straight ditch and embankment. They are intricate, zigzagged lines within lines, lines protecting flank of lines, lines built to enfilade an opposing line, lines within which lies a battery which must keep silent. Some small battery that ranges into the trenches of other lines, may be half a mile away — a maze and labyrinth of works within works, and works without works, each laid out with some definite design either of defence or offence. Let the necessity of any one of these remain unperceived or neglected, and a battle might be lost and an army imperilled.

Half an hour ago a staff officer rode into Sixth 'Corps headquarters, from General Neill, commanding Second Division, and reported that the enemy had opened a battery from a position on the flank of one of his advanced lines, which dropped shells directly and surely into a trench where lay 1,000 men. General Wright replied: "My compliments to General Neill, and say to him that when I inspected the line two hours ago I suspected the enemy would plant a battery there, and I found a position on the front of the Eighteenth Corps where guns could be placed that would silence it. I stated the case to General Smith and he instantly ordered a battery there, and I think by this time it must be about ready to open. General Neill has only to keep his men steady a few minutes and he won't be troubled by any more shells from that quarter." The staff officer rode rapidly off, and the clatter of his horse's hoofs had not died away when four shots some distance to the right boomed in quick succession, and General Wright halted in his measured tread in front of his quarters, listened for another, and remarked, "There, that's from the right quarter, — that'll shut up the guns that are playing the deuce with Neill." And so it did.

The incident will serve to show the alert vigilance, the topographical eye, and the prompt decision which enables us to baffle such adroit generalship as — as that which manages the Rebels, who fairly swarm right over yonder, not half a mile from where I write, and who cause shells to drop even in this cloth city, yclept "Headquarters of the Army of the Potomac."

Neill was to have moved with the rest, but Rebels were discovered swarming in the woods on his flank. It was suspected that they were planting a battery there, and he had to drive them out. In doing so, I suspect he rendered a very important service.

From half-past seven to nine o'clock the front remained quiet. The enemy attempted to regain the things he had lost, by a system of hasty night attacks, — first at one point, and then at another. He kept these up till after eleven o'clock, sometimes as though scarcely in earnest, again with a certain apparently terrible fury, that in every case expended itself in a few minutes against a stern vigilance for which it is no match.

This morning there have been a few shots, large and small; but the day can hardly wear away without a renewal of the struggle.

The Second Corps (Hancock's) has moved down during the night, and Generals Grant and Meade, dusty as mummies with eight miles' riding on roads filled with tramping troops and grinding trains, are conversing with General Wright.

As illustrating the systematic perfection which the medical

and ambulance departments have attained, the fact may be worth stating that *all* of the Sixth Corps wounded up to ten o'clock in the evening had been carried on stretchers to ambulances, and in the ambulances to hospitals, two miles back, before one o'clock, only three hours later. Neither night nor the enemy's pesky night-fighting prevented the stretcher-bearers from searching for, finding, and bearing away the last man. There are none braver than these stretcher-bearers. One was killed and five wounded of those attached to the Sixth Corps yesterday, for they press to the very front for the wounded. Twenty-six of them have been killed and wounded in this corps during the campaign, and scarcely less than a hundred in the army altogether. There seems to be an abundance of good surgeons and nurses, and an abundance of all needed supplies at the hospitals. The Eighteenth Corps, however, owing to its late organization, had to borrow these to some extent.

Twelve hundred of the wounded will be sent to White House this afternoon. The prisoners will also be sent at the same time. Among them is a Colonel McDonald of the Fifty-first North Carolina.

Three miles to the right, where it has become necessary that Warren should stretch his decimated corps over a long line and hold it at all hazards, else the right flank might be turned, over forty solid shot and unexploded shells were picked up within a radius of 100 yards extended from a certain oak tree. Beneath that tree Warren had his headquarters during two field days, because that particular locality commanded the best view of the battle-line, and was easiest of access to division and brigade commanders.

When I saw them they were piled up in the manner represented by diagrams in the text-book in Algebra of my school days, where certain theorems for calculating the number in any given heap, without the labor of counting, were given, — known in schools as the " cannon-ball theorems." Two men were making an excavation close by, — a little too short for a grave, a little too square-cut for a rifle-pit. It proved, on inquiry, that arrangements were making for decent and safe interment of the innocent-looking but ugly-meant and ugly-meaning things. They were taken up tenderly and handled with care, not because they were fashioned so slenderly, though some were eight inches in length by two an a half in diameter; nor because they were young and fair, for nothing was known as to their age, and they were not fair; but because they were *percussion* shells, and might resent harsh treatment. Altogether, it was a jolly funeral. General Warren looked down into the grave and smiled, as an unrelenting man might smile upon the tomb of a mortal foe. Your humble servant assisted as pall-bearer. Several drums were heard, and several funeral notes, — bugle notes, halting a battery that was going into position hard by. Several soldiers discharged their Rebel shots toward the grave where the "varmints" were buried. We buried them brightly at height of noon, the sod with a shovel turning, and then sat down to a merry dinner. We thought as we narrowed their lowly beds, and scooped out the dirty hole, that the foe and the stranger would tread o'er their heads, — and perhaps get blown sky-high.

Hard tack, roast beef, sweet potatoes (two hundred bushels were found buried in a garden, where a family pretending to be destitute were receiving army rations), and good coffee, the soldiers' *vade mecum*, make not a bad dinner, and are relished, spite of the fact that yesterday, on this same ground, crockery and tin ware had scarcely been removed from the rubber blanket which suffices for both table and table-cloth, when a shell plunged through it into the ground. A percussion shell too, only it did not happen to "percuss" — I use an army slang.

An old artillery man once explained to me the distinction between a shell and a soldier. The one "percusses," the other "cusses."

All day yesterday a wounded officer of a New Hampshire regiment lay some twenty yards in front of General Marston's works, unable to crawl in, and the Rebel sharpshooters would suffer none to go out for him. He had fallen the day before in the morning assault, and the lines as finally established left him midway between friend and enemy. One man had been severely wounded in attempting to reach him. Hard bread was shied out to him in abundance, but a dozen canteens were thrown away before one lodged within his grasp.

Finally, night setting in, opens a chance to get him off. A zigzag is started from the main works; men work with zeal and well-directed muscle, but noiselessly as though they were the original managing directors of "Oft in the *Stilly Night.*" Three hours of such work and the wounded man is reached; is pulled into the trench; is carried triumphantly back its tacking course, and then is received behind cover with great cheers. The cheers cause a volley, but the volley is harmless, and the man is saved. I am chagrined that I have been unable to ascertain this officer's name.

A "Fresnel Lens," such as are placed in the largest light-houses, was found buried near a house in Wright's front last night. This lens is manufactured only in Paris, and costs from $2,000 to $3,000. How it came to be in this vicinity is a mystery. The most probable hypothesis is that it is a part of the plunder of some one of the light-houses which the Rebels have despoiled. The facetious explanation is that it must have been sent by some ignorant official to *Cold Harbor*, he supposing that place to be a port of entry, and that it fell into the hands of some citizen of the locality. The joke is apparent when it is remembered that "Cold Harbor" is not a harbor, and is fifteen miles from navigable water. The lens has been started to Washington in a quartermaster's wagon.

The richest find, however, is that of a man in the Ninth Corps, who, digging for sweet potatoes, found over $4,000 in silver. He very generously divided it with his company, and that company has since been "matching" quarters and half-dollars as though they were pennies.

I stated in a late letter how Barlow's Division swept the ground before them on Friday morning; how the enemy's reserve came up before theirs did, and forced out of their grasp position, prisoners, Rebel guns, and Rebel flags; and how they at last intrenched in advance of the line of the night before. In those intrenchments they have now burrowed two days, no man standing erect save at his peril, all living on hard bread and water; for it is impossible in those narrow trenches to prepare meat and coffee. Naturally the time hangs a little heavily when, as sometimes happens, nothing that may be shot at is seen for an hour or two. During one of these intervals this morning one man conceived a brilliant scheme, which, unfolded to his comrades, was instantly adopted. Every man loads his piece and points it over the parapet or through one of the many small portholes made by placing ammunition boxes in the wall. Then the author of the plan begins to shout orders as though commanding at least a brigade:—

"Colonel, connect your line with the forty-seventh! Give way to the right! Close ranks! Right dress! Fix bayonets! Double quick! *Ch-a-a-rge!*"

Instantly 500 men rise into plain sight behind the Rebel works, expecting to see an advancing line. Not so, but 500 men from safe cover fire upon them on the instant. The volley, which must have inflicted considerable loss, is followed up with cheers and jeers, laughter, and much chaffing, as: "What do y' think o' Yankee tricks?" "That's the way John Brown's soul marches on." "No use o' baitin' hooks when you're fishin' for gudgeons."

The trick has been repeated several times during the day, with ingenious variations, always to crowded houses, and always eliciting much applause from the performers.

"The Richmond Examiner" of the 3d devotes a column to "The Demoralization of Grant's Army." The article is false in premises, in logic, in conclusion, and is great only in impudence. This army is conscious of growing numbers, and of a perfect state of *moralization.*

The Richmond and York River Railroad is being rebuilt,— that part of it which we most need. The first ten miles from White House will require but few repairs. Quite distant and heavy cannonading yesterday afternoon and evening from lower down the Chickahominy indicates that the cavalry is operating in that quarter. I suspect Sheridan has been told to take and hold the bridge till a corps of infantry can be sent there.

Re-enforcements continue to arrive. The slightly wounded of

the battle of the Wilderness are beginning to return. Daily mail communication has been established with Washington, under the efficient supervision of Colonel Markland, special agent of the Post-Office Department.

HEADQUARTERS ARMY OF THE POTOMAC,
Monday, June 6, 8 A. M.

No battle yesterday, but constant firing across from one line of works to the other as soon as any portion of a man's body could be seen. The casualties during the day, all from sharpshooters and intermittent artillery, are not less than 400. To these must be added between 100 and 200 during the night.

A little after eight o'clock a furious blast rang a fierce discordant metre from the left, where lay Hancock's Corps. Judging by the powder burned, it was more than a usually desperate night assault. Soon the following despatch is received:

HALF-PAST 8 O'CLOCK P. M.— They at first attacked Wright, but are now rushing down upon me. Apparently no damage.

HANCOCK.

Tremendous discharges of musketry, and the awful blasts of Cohorn mortars continued fifteen or twenty minutes longer, and then like a tornado breaking into fitful squalls and then clearing into fine weather, this tempest of war broke into detached volleys, and finally ceased altogether.

It seems to have been brought on by the enemy, as is always the case with these night affairs. He discovered men planting fascines for a new line, and at once assaulted to stop the work; whereupon both sides opened fire right and left. The assault was repulsed easily enough, but neither party seemed inclined to first stop firing, hence its duration.

An hour later the Eighteenth Corps made some lively shooting, but there was nothing in the nature of an attack.

During the night the Fifth Corps (Warren's) has been withdrawn from the right, and marched around to the extreme left. There will be other changes of position to-night.

From "The Richmond Examiner" of the 3d it is learned that ex-South-Carolina-Congressman Lawrence M. Keitt was mortally wounded on Wednesday, and died the next day. Also that General Dales, commanding a division of Ewell's Corps, was killed on Thursday, opposite Bartlett's Brigade, Fifth Corps.

The Second Rhode Island started home last night. In leaving the front line, where it had been posted the last twenty-four hours, it lost two men wounded. It had lost a dozen men during the day.

QUESTIONS ANSWERED.

HEADQUARTERS ARMY OF THE POTOMAC,
Monday, June 6, 1864.

SEVERAL private letters lately received ask me a hundred questions, the gist of which may be reduced to three, viz.: Has the campaign thus far been successful — reasonably successful? Have not our losses greatly exceeded the enemy's? When *will* we get to Richmond?

It should be understood that Grant's object is not primarily the occupation of Richmond, but the utter destruction of Lee's army. Let people fix this fact in their minds, and they will have a correct point of departure from which to measure the bearing and importance of daily events.

To the first question I answer, "Yes, reasonably successful, highly successful."

To the second I answer, "Not greatly; I doubt if our losses exceed theirs by a single man."

To the third I answer, "Don't, I beg of you, imagine me so presumptuous as to fix a date on which, or by which, we shall occupy the Rebel capital; but take it for Grant-ed that there will be no respite in this campaign till Richmond falls."

The army with which Grant crossed the Rapidan, unre-enforced by a single man, had Lee not been re-enforced by a single man, fighting as it has been fighting, before this date would have broken, dispersed, destroyed, the Rebel army that moved from Madison Court-House. Reduce each army to-day to those men who formed a part of it at the beginning of the campaign, and we should dispose of the Rebel portion before night. I believe this — I know it.

I reason, then, that the heavy re-enforcements each commander has brought to his help will simply have the result of prolonging the campaign, that the end were the same in either case. Breckinridge and Buckner and Beauregard have joined Lee, and they bring with them more men than the latter had originally. Overbearing all these and taking Richmond, the victory will mean fifty times as much, will have fifty times the value, that it would had it been wrested from Lee alone.

Within a very short time the Rebels will be compelled to choose between two things: they may march with their main army westward or southward, leaving an ordinary garrison or no garrison at all in Richmond, and in either case expecting the city to fall into our hands without long delay; or they may make it the "last ditch," concentrate there all they have, and stake the Confederacy upon the issue.

I don't think Grant cares which course they may adopt. If the former, he wins a great victory, moral and material, say by the Fourth of July, and he will have all the fall to push them to the Gulf. If the latter, it may require several months longer to "take Richmond." But at length taking it, and all that is in it, as he surely would, the whole Rebel concern tumbles in one big crash.

As to the comparative losses. The rule is that the general prosecuting an offensive campaign suffers more than his enemy, unless by winning victories he compensates his excess of killed and wounded by an excess of prisoners taken. But while this campaign has been boldly, even daringly, offensive, it has been so conducted that in nearly every collision the enemy has been obliged to become the attacking party. So at the Wilderness, where Lee attacked, and where, when he would no longer attack, Grant *left him.* So on the Po. So on the North Anna. So on the Tolopatomy. Grant attacked here on the Chickahominy, but only in one general assault. In fully half of the fighting here — in all of the night fighting — the Rebels have attacked and been repulsed and slaughtered outright.

[General Grant states his losses at Cold Harbor between May 31, and June 12, as 1,769 killed, 6,752 wounded, and 1,537 missing; a total of 10,058. He says in regard to the flank movement that now began, "Lee's position was now so near Richmond, and the intervening swamps of the Chickahominy so great an obstacle to the movement of troops in face of an enemy, that I determined to make my next left-flank move carry the army of the Potomac south of the James River."]

THE MOVEMENT TO THE JAMES.

THE LEFT FLANK AGAIN. — THE MANNER OF THE MARCH. — SHERIDAN
AND HIS CAVALRY. — THE DUST OF THE PENINSULA.

WITH THE ARMY OF THE POTOMAC,
Sunday, June 12, 1864, 6 P. M.

THE whole army is again in motion. After six days of comparative rest the men march briskly, almost eagerly. They have replenished their stock of fighting endurance, at no time exhausted, but a week ago a good deal tasked, and a rich new wine of battle again courses in their veins and exalts their hope and courage.

It is another flank movement — perhaps the most stupendous of the series. "Enamoured of his left flank," said a Richmond paper lately, in discussing Grant's strategy. And a very good and fruitful thing to be enamoured of, the paper might have added. No mistress fickle and false has the left flank been, but a handmaiden faithful and true to her lord and master.

The Fifth Corps marched yesterday, and was last night at Jones Bridge, on the Chickahominy. It is to make the best possible time to the James River and across it. The Eighteenth Corps (Smith's) is to take transports at White House for Bermuda Hundred.

I have been this week all the way to Washington that I might achieve the novel sensation of cleanliness, and now this march makes my last days worse than my first. I suspect the army has picked itself up and journeyed to the James River at the dictation of no strictly military necessity. It will doubtless further the purpose of taking Richmond, but I believe this to be a subordinate consideration. The paramount reason is to have a grand army Washing-Day! and no stream of less ablutionary capacity than the James will suffice. Dust! thou scourge of the great modern Virginia Desert — ugh! u-g-h! u-g-h! I loathe thee, and I draw thee as though thou wert sweet with the perfumes of Araby the Blest, and Cathay and Oriental spices, into my nostrils, and thou art laden with the seventy distinct stinks of Cologne. I detest thee, and I swallow thee. I abominate thee, and take thee to my bosom. That which I would eschew I chew. I am wretched and I retch.

There are more than 100,000 men marching by, and they are all like unto me, only more abundant is their dust and misery. Calculate the aggregate, and credit it to the Army of the Potomac.

THE MOVEMENT BEYOND THE JAMES.

The Co-operating Column coming from West Virginia. — Progress of the Campaign. — Grant, Meade, and Other Celebrities. — A Headquarters Camp Scene. — "Ole Virginny." — An African Patriarch.

Charles City Court-House,
Headquarters Army of the Potomac,
Monday, June 13, 10 p. m.

THE movement to the James River and beyond it now being made is precisely what was intended when the campaign was first mapped out, in the event that the battles which it was known must be fought on the way should not destroy Lee's army. That they did not so result is due simply and solely to the incomplete success of the various co-operating columns. The check sustained by Sigel in the Shenandoah Valley, and by Crook farther west, enabled the Rebel general to bring to his assistance Breckinridge and Buckner from that quarter. The checks sustained by Butler permitted a large detachment to leave Beauregard, which met us at Cold Harbor. Such heavy re-enforcements added to the shattered army which we had fought all the way from the Rapidan, thwarted us from the complete victory we should have won on the Chickahominy, or yet nearer Richmond, and has compelled us to cross that stream lower down than was intended. But the plan has been only delayed in its execution.

At last affairs in Western Virginia have brightened and permit a resumption of the campaign "on this line." The withdrawal to Richmond of Breckinridge and Buckner gave Hunter a victory at Staunton, and Crook and Averill have joined him at that place, finding nothing in their way on the march.

If you remember, it was during Butler's twenty-one days' possession of the Petersburg and Richmond Railroad that the newspapers of the latter city could not refrain from discussing the exorbitantly high prices of food, and the general destitution that prevailed there. They had a pinched, starvation tone, that ceased only with the resumption of trains on the road that fed them. It is the conviction of those best informed that had we been able to retain that road, the city ere this would have become untenable.

Now, after forty days and forty nights in and out of the Wilderness, the at first apparently detached and isolated operations which marked the initiation of the campaign are seen to bear directly upon a single focus. The first acts of the drama will have contributed to and heightened the effect of the last. Look to see Richmond approached from the interior, much as Vicksburg was, and that right speedily. And if the movement, even so much of it as is already developed, does not raise public confidence and drop the price of gold, then its meaning will not be apprehended.

You should see the brilliant cavalcade and hear the tramp and clangor of hoof and sabre when Grant and Meade and their staffs and the whole mounted retinue of headquarters go sweeping by. Of course the small man on the small black horse leading the troop is Grant. If you did not know it before, the soldiers who rush out to the road, or half halt on the march, and point him out to each other, have told you. The small black pacing-horse, half a queen's pony, half a king's Bucephalus, with arched neck and champing bit, and small, alert, flexile ears, and short, mouse-like hair, and great tail carried royally like a banner, whose form is symmetry, spite of the sloping hips that belong to all pacers, whose muscles are watch-springs, whose impatient air seems to resent his small size, — this little black imp of a horse, a horse that is "all horse," is "Jeff Davis," and Grant is on his back.

The rider sits him with uncommon grace, controls him with one small gauntleted hand, never once regards the torrent of horsemen that follow, looks nor right nor left, but never fails to acknowledge with a quick gesture the salutes of the soldiers. All-absorbed, all-observant, silent, inscrutable, he controls and moves armies as he does his horse.

The rider at his side is not less worth marking well. His horse is the ideal war-horse, tall and powerful, and horse and rider look like a picture of helmeted knight of old, gaunt, tall, grizzled, with the large Roman nose of will and power, and wearing a slouched hat, the wide brim bent down all round, but not concealing the lightning glance of eyes that are terrible in anger, — such is Geo. G. Meade, noblest Roman of them all, relentless fighter and good general, to whose hearty and wise seconding Grant does not, and the country should not, hesitate to acknowledge the greatest indebtedness.

The ride has been from Cold Harbor to Providence Church, a distance of ten miles, and is made in the last two hours of daylight.

The location of the camp has been fixed, fires built, and inquiries are heard about the headquarters train, which must arrive before tents can be pitched and supper had. The evening is chilly, and great coats are taken from the pommels of saddles and put on. Boxes and boards are made into seats, or rubber blankets are thrown upon the ground to lie on, and all gather close to the crackling rail-fire, and wait for the wagons. Grant and Meade are engaged in conversation, upon indifferent topics apparently. Generals Hunt and Barnard discuss guns. General Ingalls sends a man every few minutes to find and hurry up the wagons. Mr. Washburne, here on a flying visit, has gone to sleep, his feet to the fire. Mr. Dana strides up and down as though the day had not afforded sufficient exercise. About ten o'clock it is reported that the train will be up in an hour or two. In crossing a stream on a narrow dam one or two wagons had been capsized, hence the delay. Mr. Dana remarks that it was "evidently a piece of dam(n) folly." Grant rises, steps toward the fire, and says, "If we have nothing worse than this — " The sentence was never finished.

The correlative to the "if" may, however, be imagined. That it was not expressed was because at that instant the general took a brand from the fire and lighted his pipe, an action incompatible with speech. The messenger who brings the report as to the wagons has brought a supply of bread and butter and gingerbread, and a pail of water has been fetched. Everybody lunches. (Mem: A phenomenon — dust is no respecter of persons. General Grant is as dusty as I am.) After lunch all light pipes, and smoke as vigorously and silently as Indians in council — waiting for the wagons. The writer, rolled in a single blanket, falls to sleep; at midnight is wakened to find tents pitched, everybody turning in, and the fire flickering low. The officer whose tent he shares informs him that breakfast is ordered at four o'clock. It seems just no time till the shrill-bugled reveille rouses the camp. Breakfast is despatched, tents struck, horses mounted, all with astonishing celerity, and again gallops headquarters cavalcade. To-day Grant rides his war-horse "Cincinnati," a tall bay, the handsomest horse in the army, and the best.

It is difficult for one familiar with the thriving villages and well-cultivated farms that cover the North to imagine Virginia a populous State. He steams a hundred and fifty miles up the Rappahannock and sees but one village (Port Royal), and but one indifferent city (Fredericksburg), — up the York and Pamunkey a hundred miles, and comes to one or two " Landings " of two or three houses, now deserted. Riding over the country he is struck with the sparseness of the population, even as it must have been before the war. Pretentious names that at the North would mean a community of thousands cover here an insignificant hamlet of a dozen houses. He rides miles and miles between farms, or plantations. The houses are mainly small, unpainted, dilapidated structures, the outbuildings a few negro huts. Riding up to these, he finds them deserted, except, maybe, by a "native" too old for war, or old African cronies, too old to run away. He sees no school-houses — a few churches, but no school-houses. I have ridden over nearly all the roads in the region we have traversed, between the Rappahannock and the James, and I have seen barely one school-house. Curiosity led me to enter. Every seat was furnished with a spittoon! I found one book, a Smith's Grammar, "adapted," as the preface states, "for use in the Confederate States." So far as I can see, the adaptation consists in substituting "C. S." for "U. S.," and the elimination of sentiments in praise of liberty. It was published at Richmond, in the "second year of the Independence of the Confederate States," whenever that may have been.

The better class of houses are usually deserted altogether, but if one is found still inhabited by a "first family" or the remnant of one — I have not yet seen a single able-bodied man, always only women and old men or very young boys — they are always rank, out-spoken Rebels. With the "plain people" it is otherwise. They either pretend to be for the Union, or disclaim having had anything to do with Secession, or having any care which party succeeds, so they may be speedily let alone. They say the Rebel soldiers are as harsh and unsparing as ours; they have had everything taken from them, and can see nothing before them but starvation. They have no crops in the fields. Go into their gardens, and you will find nothing edible growing excepting a little corn and sweet potatoes. But those gardens are one bower of gorgeous June roses, and the peach-trees are laden with green fruit. In New England, when the rose-bushes are in blossom, their foliage is falling; here, it is at its deepest, darkest green, and the effect is surprisingly beautiful.

This morning I rode a half-mile at right angles with the line of march, to a straggling combination of cabins that looked humble, but homelike. Before the door, smoking a veritable corn-cob pipe and mending fishing-tackle, was a grizzled old African patriarch. Seven bright-eyed, kinky-haired youngsters, as I counted them, who crowded the doorways and lounged on the grass, proclaimed him a patriarch. He had a patriarchal name — Eli; had bought his freedom "more den forty years dun gone;" was the father of fifteen living children, nine of whom are boys; has two wives, both living with him, and is the owner of seventy-five acres of soil on which he lives. I wish I could report his conversation literally. Three of his boys "is fightin,' sah, wid you somewhar. *I* sent 'em *Norf*. Dey made 'em work fixin' for de batteries at Richmond, and I was n't gwyne to hab 'em helpin' on *dat* side. 'Spect dey is down in Careliny wid de colud soldiers dat left Washington." The old man intends to go North with all his family; says he shall have nothing to take with him except the deed of his land, which he "worked for and paid for, sah," but "reckins" he can get along "up dah durin' o' de wah, somehow." And I devoutly hope he may.

I remember this colloquy between the two Roman generals: "If thou art a great general, come down and fight me!" "If *thou* art a great general, *make* me come down and fight *thee!*" And I have seen that four times out of five, for we have fought on five distinct lines, Grant, by a single march has made them "come down and fight" him.

Is not the inference from the nature of the fighting clear, that their losses equal or exceed ours? But there is direct proof of it. We have often held the field, or portions of it, and always the dead in Rebel gray have been more than the dead in Union blue.

Now, and probably always hereafter, the nature of the ground will admit of the effective use of artillery. By our immense superiority in that arm, even though we shall be compelled to assault every day, I am greatly mistaken if we shall not still keep the score even, or to our advantage.

It is my rule to religiously refrain from speculation when I do not know, and statement when I do know, as to future movements of the army. But it may alleviate the anxiety which fears terrible losses in the event of an attempt to carry by assault the works now in our immediate front, for me to state that it is not proposed to assault them. We shall go around them. The list of possible flank movements is not yet exhausted.

Anchor your souls to one fact — a fact of which the army is as firmly convinced as it is that the sun shines to-day, or that it will not shine to-night. *This army cannot be beaten back from its purpose.* Its *morale* is held high by continual re-enforcements. It numbers to-day far larger than it did on the Rappahannock. The slightly wounded of the first battles are resuming their places by thousands. The conviction is universal, shared alike by Generals Grant and Meade and the humblest soldier, that this is the last grand campaign, — the last, because it will accomplish the practical destruction of the Confederacy.

I close with the statement that I believe it to be Grant's purpose to compel as many open field engagements as possible, he hopes a decisive one, before he comes to the investment proper and actual siege of the Doomed City.

THE LAST GRAND MOVEMENT.

I.

How the Army Marched. — The Enemy entirely in the Dark. — Crossing Long Bridge. — Passing the Swamps. — Crossing the James River.

Charles City Court-House, Va.
Headquarters Army of the Potomac,
Wednesday, June 15, 6 a. m.

THE works on the Cold Harbor line were not relinquished fully until two o'clock yesterday morning, yet the entire army had reached the James by sunset last night, the average distance marched being twenty-five miles.

When a great army moves, it fills all the roads, it seeks every country cross-road, every farm by-road, and uses it, no matter how circuitous the road, no matter what direction it pursues; so that it intersects some road that does make toward the right point, it must be used. Troops often march ten or fifteen miles, and the point reached shall not be five from that of starting.

The army moved down the Chickahominy in this order: Wilson's cavalry in the advance, followed by the Fifth Army Corps, then the Second Corps, next to the river the Sixth Corps, parallel and to the left of the Second, and the Ninth on the extreme left, each of the last three taking care of its own rear. A second line, perhaps a mile in rear of that fought on, had been thrown up at Cold Harbor. The reserve divisions marched out in the afternoon; those holding the works, as soon as it was fully dark; but not a picket fell back until two o'clock in the morning. The new line was held by a strong picket until daylight.

The withdrawal seems to have been undiscovered. Only at one point had the enemy's skirmishers appeared when the last line was relinquished. In the scores of times we have left the presence of the enemy during the war I do not recall another instance where this device of a second line far in the rear was used. In this case it proved to be unnecessary, but it was a wise precaution, that would have been of vast service had our purpose been divined and the enemy followed too eagerly.

Ten miles down the stream from Cold Harbor is the remains of the Long Bridge, that figures in the narratives of the Peninsula campaign. The causeways leading to it on either side are there still, and in good condition. The bridge proper has disappeared. A few pontoons now fill the breach. The cavalry crossed unmolested, save by the vedettes of a North Carolina regiment, on the evening of the 12th. The Fifth Corps followed early the succeeding morning, and marched two or three miles directly toward Richmond, and formed line of battle nearly up to White Oak Swamp.

If it were the purpose of the enemy to attack, he must come from that quarter. The Second Corps marched to the bridge in the hours between midnight and daylight, and there halted four hours for coffee and a snatch of sleep. Then marching at nine o'clock, it halted only on arriving here, faced up the roads leading toward Richmond, and finally lay down to rest in admirable works of its own construction. At dark the Fifth Corps left its position, looking toward White Oak Swamp, and falling in after the Second, reached here during the night and early yesterday morning.

Meanwhile the Sixth and Ninth Army Corps, moving further down the Chickahominy, crossed on pontoons at Jones Bridge. The former struck the James three miles below here at noon yesterday, the rear coming up by night. This corps marched thirty miles in as many consecutive hours. The Ninth came in at the heels of the Sixth, getting comfortably into camp last evening.

The weather yesterday and the day before was peculiarly favorable for rapid marching, being exceptionally cool and cloudy, and on this side of the Chickahominy the trains moved on different roads from the troops, so that the dust did not trouble us.

The march to the James River, then, has been successfully, rapidly, and smoothly accomplished. I cannot help contrasting it with that other time when the Army of the Potomac marched from the Chickahominy to the James. I need not elaborate the contrast; the bare suggestion is enough to point all the difference between an advance and a retreat, an undisturbed march and a badgered but stubborn flight — stubborn because Sumner and Sedgwick were of the rear-guard. But that was 1862, and this is 1864; and the two years have not been without their lessons, one of which has discovered for us a man.

The Eighteenth Corps, Baldy Smith, as I have stated before, marched to White House to take transports for Bermuda Hundred. Last night it passed up the river, and by this time has disembarked at its destination. It had been away from there but a fortnight; had been to the other side of Richmond by a journey of 250 miles via James River, Fortress Monroe, York River, White House, and a march of twenty miles, and now back again over the same route; had been in two battles at Cold Harbor, and severe skirmishing during a full week; had lost 3,000 men killed and wounded. A good fortnight's work, and an instance of consummate generalship.

Speaking of generalship, it is worth noting that the Richmond papers denounce that which called Breckinridge from the valley, and enabled Hunter to rout their remaining forces in that quarter.

On the principle which led the Roman armies to intrench every night in the regulation manner of the time, even when marching through their own provinces, the army on reaching here faced about toward Richmond, the presumed direction of the enemy, the right became the left, and all could have gone into battle with ten minutes' notice.

Three weeks ago the Engineer Brigade at Washington, under General Benham, was ordered to be ready to take ship, prepared with its pontoon train to lay a bridge across the James. In the exact fulness of time it reached here yesterday noon, and had completed a bridge at dark.

The bridge consists of over one hundred pontoons, about the

same number as that across the mouth of the Chickahominy on McClellan's retreat down the Peninsula two years ago, said to have been the longest floating bridge ever laid. That was placed by the Fiftieth New York Engineers; this by the Fifteenth New York Engineers. The locality is White Oaks Point, half a mile below Windmill Point, and some six miles below Harrison's Landing.

Meanwhile Gibbon's Division of the Second Corps had crossed by steamboat ferry. The remainder of the corps crossed during the night, partly by ferry and partly by bridge. The order was that the Sixth Corps should follow, that to be succeeded by the Ninth, while the Fifth should remain in position, and finally cross last. To-morrow morning will see everything on the other side. And once on the other side, your imagination is as good as mine.

II.

OUR CAVALRY OPERATIONS DURING THE WEEK.

CROSSING THE CHICKAHOMINY. — A SMART FIGHT AT THE RIVER. — ANOTHER AFTER CROSSING. — AN EXTENSIVE SCOUTING PARTY. — THE REBELS DISCOVER OUR FLANK MOVEMENT TOO LATE. — EWELL'S, LONGSTREET'S, AND HILL'S CORPS OFF TO RICHMOND. — OUR CAVALRY OVER THE JAMES. — INVALUABLE SERVICES OF WILSON'S DIVISION.

CHARLES CITY COURT-HOUSE, VA., HEADQUARTERS
THIRD DIVISION CAVALRY (WILSON'S), June 16, 1864.

THE operations of the cavalry during the last four days deserve a separate letter. At the risk of repetition, but for the sake of a connected narrative, I begin with the crossing of the Chickahominy on the night of Sunday, the 12th. To Wilson's Division, consisting of two brigades, commanded by Colonel J. B. McIntosh, and Colonel George H. Chapman (Third Indiana) respectively, was assigned the duty of leading the advance. I was misinformed when I stated, in a late letter, that the crossing was effected without decided opposition and without loss. The fact is to the exact contrary. The Rebel account, in a paper of the 14th, is not far out of the way in the idea which it conveyed of the fighting. It is that "the enemy advanced to the stream at night in masses of cavalry, infantry and artillery, and by virtue of overwhelming numbers, after a severe and well-contested action, compelled us to withdraw."

As to the "overwhelming numbers," etc., Colonel Chapman's brigade did it all, and the Third Indiana, dismounted, did nearly all. The Hoosiers crossed under a fire described by one of their number as "like shaking a pepper-box," in any and every way, wading, swimming, and a number on a fallen tree. Then they discovered, not fifty yards in front, the rifle-pit whence came the shots. Now a bayonet charge, all save the bayonets, for bayonets do not belong to cavalry carbines. The rifle-pit is carried, at a loss of twenty men out of the fifty who charge it. Others come up, and a line is formed, and there is constant firing during the three hours required to construct the bridge. Among the wounded are five pontoniers. It is then daylight. The covering of the building of a bridge under heavy fire had been done by cavalry against infantry,— a thing novel in war. At daylight the whole division came over, and advanced toward White Oak Swamp, on the direct road to Richmond. Warren's Corps followed in feint, as though that was the intended line of advance upon Richmond.

Five miles out, at White Oak Bridge, Chapman got into it again, and fought all day. At night his loss proved to be scarcely less than a hundred. Crawford's Division of the Fifth Corps supported, and threw up works. It withdrew, however, a little before sunset, and a little prematurely, and continued its march toward Charles City Court-House. But the cavalry held on till midnight, though all the while hard up to the Rebel infantry. Being joined at this hour by McIntosh's Brigade, the whole division marched toward the James on the right flank of the line of march of the army, and sent detachments up every road. It was ordered next morning, 14th inst., to push as far as possible up these roads, to keep watch and ward of the whole scope of the country between Long Bridge and Malvern, and to give particular attention to obtaining information of the enemy's movements.

There was absolutely no means of learning anything whatever of the enemy's whereabouts and intentions excepting through the cavalry, and the cavalry could learn nothing except by riding out, finding the Rebels, and coming to such blows as should develop their strength and give us prisoners to question. It did this with such spirit and success that it was ascertained that the Rebels discovered early on the 13th that we had left Cold Harbor, and they began crossing the Chickahominy at various points above Bottom's Bridge during that forenoon. By the morning of the 14th they had established an intrenched line in a strong position extending from the upper part of the

White Oak Swamp, to or toward the James, at a point just above Malvern. This would indicate that they had not penetrated Grant's design of flinging his whole force beyond the James, but expected him to creep up the left bank under shadow of the gunboats!

Yesterday, 15th inst., Colonel Chapman reconnoitred to Malvern-Hill battle-ground, when the enemy formed in line of battle, sent trains to their rear, and moved down as though to meet an army. After a brush with their advance, Chapman rode back a couple of miles; they did not follow. Meanwhile McIntosh, five miles to the right, at White Oak Bridge, had pushed into a warm action. Deliberately and carefully, as a chess-player might withdraw knights and bishops from the presence of queens and castles, he manœuvred back, fighting, bringing prisoners, and losing none captured. The loss in the two brigades during the day was about 100. They had maintained a wide front, as boldly as though they were the advance instead of the rear of a large army. Prisoners taken in the afternoon stated that their army — at least, Ewell's, Longstreet's, and Hill's Corps — began to move before noon toward Richmond and some point on the James above Drury's Bluff, known to us as Fort Darling.

To-day everything has been quiet, but the enemy has kept a force close to both brigades, which hold their positions of last night. To-night they will march down the river ten miles to the pontoon bridge at Fort Powhatan, and the morning will see their five thousand horses unsaddled, and grazing in the rich clover fields on the right bank.

Such is the bare recital. You will have a more just conception of these operations when you are told that the horses have not been unsaddled since the afternoon of the 12th. During four days and nights there has been no hour when it was safe to do so. Neither Wilson, nor Chapman, nor McIntosh has probably slept two consecutive hours, nor hardly a man of their commands. Sleepless vigilance, constant fighting, celerity in movement, and skilful handling of men, have been required and tasked to their limit. Many of the most important movements of the army have been predicated upon, or modified by, or timed in accordance with, Wilson's reports of those of the enemy. His cavalry has been the fingers to feel for, the eyes to see, the enemy. He must watch a front of ten miles. To his headquarters orderlies and officers report — riding up on foaming horses — every few minutes, and then speed away on paths diverging like the ribs of a fan. This squadron on that road is to fall back; that battalion to advance on that other road. This officer must vigilantly patrol between his command and another's. Ascertain if the Rebels are in such a quarter! Drive them at all hazards from such a locality! You must send in some prisoners! I must have information! Are you secure on your right flank? Am afraid the enemy may penetrate what you report to be a swamp. Communicate, if possible, with Colonel so and so on your left! Rations are on the way. Have you sufficient ammunition? I imagine such to resemble the despatches from division headquarters. For those coming, *you* must imagine them.

General Wilson is perhaps the youngest brigadier in the service, certainly not over twenty-five. Educated at West Point, to which he was appointed from Illinois, he is a captain of Topographical Engineers, and has been a colonel on Grant's staff. That general saw in him the qualities of a cavalry leader, nominated him to a brigadiership, during the winter placed him in charge of the Cavalry Bureau of the War Department, and then assigned him to the division which he has handled through the forty-five days of this campaign. In personal appearance he is not remarkable, but he is the best horseman in the army — old cavalrymen tell me so — and rides a little bay devil of a horse to the admiration of his command and the astonishment of all pedestrians. To see some of these cavalrymen "back a horse" must amaze all the gods of the Pantheon, excepting only the Centaurs — if they were deified, as to which I shall not commit myself.

It is hardly credible that the cavalry should be in better condition now than at the beginning of the campaign, but such is the fact. Moreover, it numbers some thousands more. Not less than 5,000 then dismounted have been given horses, and several full regiments have been brought from other quarters.

The cheerfulness and confidence among cavalrymen is more striking than with the infantry, perhaps because with them success is an every-day matter. They expect to yet water their horses in the Gulf.

Some of them have already ridden in scores of charges every whit as glorious as that of the "Light Brigade." Then, on the authority of the Laureate, "all the world wondered" because of the one "wild charge they made." Why, these troopers of ours haven't fingers enough upon which to count a tithe of the wilder charges they have made.

The Rebel soldier, whose letter to his "fair coz" was lately intercepted and published, in disgust of their riders, adjured the young lady "never to marry a cavalryman." As touching our own cavalrymen, the injunction should be reversed.

III.

AROUND PETERSBURG.

OPERATIONS ON SATURDAY.— A CLEAR VIEW OF THE MOVEMENTS OF BOTH ARMIES.— HOW A BATTLE LOOKS TO A SPECTATOR.— SOMETHING ABOUT ARTILLERY DUELLING.

HEADQUARTERS ARMY OF THE POTOMAC,
Saturday, June 18, 1864, 9 P. M.

THE battle of day before yesterday — yes, and of the day before that — of yesterday and of to-day, is not yet ended, unless it has now become a siege. Call it the Battle of Petersburg. I take up the narrative with the operations of to-day, first stating that though not conclusive they have advanced our position fully one mile, and augur great things for to-morrow or the day following. An advance was ordered at four o'clock. The order of the commands was as follows: the right next to the river; Martindale's Division of the Eighteenth Corps, connecting with it Neill's Division of the Sixth Corps; the remaining divisions of these corps were on Butler's line. Closing up to Neill was the Second Corps, at its left the Ninth, with the Fifth on the extreme left. No point on the line, which was four to five miles in length, was nearer than two miles to the city. Beginning at the right on the Appomattox, the general course extended in an ellipse,— a line of semi-circumvallation, but of constant departure. To-night it is a semicircle, for the left has been able to advance most, the right nearly as much, the centre but a little way.

The four o'clock advance was really half an hour later. The fighting was comparatively bloodless. Whether the enemy fell back after severe skirmishing, and *with* severe skirmishing, predeterminately or because he was forced back generally, it was but the ordinary work of a thick skirmish line, covered by such pounding of artillery as gave the echoes no rest,— nothing like the close-range line-of-battle musketry of the Wilderness or of Spottsylvania, unless it was such a few minutes with Hancock and that part of Burnside which extended from his left. Warren, half charging, half marching, half fighting, half picket and skirmish firing, had gained nearly a mile. Neill and Martindale swept up the river some distance, and could have gone further, apparently, but for danger of exposing a flank by breaking alignment with the troops on their left. The works gained by this advance, though nothing like so stupendous as those taken the day before, were quite formidable, such as, if they had been held in force, could scarcely have been carried by assault. The artillery did not halt, but played away until twelve, the hour fixed for another advance.

Not far from the river, and perhaps two miles from the city, on a bold eminence, is the "Friend House." It was one of the fortified positions taken yesterday, and we had advanced from it less than half a mile in the morning. Between it and the city lies a stretch of level river-bottom land, planted with corn and dappled green with scattering trees. From this house I saw the second attack. In the foreground, lying upon their arms in several lines, were our men — Neill's and Martindale's Divisions — and, beyond were those of the enemy, not quite so plainly to be seen. Horsemen are seen riding rapidly along the opposing fronts, preparing, connecting regiments with regiments, brigades with brigades, and dressing the lines. By "left oblique" this body of troops is made to extend the line of the brigades of Gibbon, whose regiments project a little way out of the woods upon the plain, while, by the same movement, Martindale shuts up the space between him and Neill, and the right is advanced somewhat. Here, right by us, is the old Vermont Brigade, General L. A. Grant, in reserve. An officer near me remarks that it is the first time he ever knew that brigade to be the reserve.

There is some anxiety lest the Rebels may have batteries across the river ready to deliver an intolerable cross-fire the moment the attack shall be launched, and General Hunt, Chief of Artillery for the Army, and Colonel Tompkins, Chief of big guns for the corps, are here planting guns to smash any such demonstration. A fort over there has been shelling this hill all the morning, and has been replied to by Harn's and Cowan's (First and Third N. Y. Independent) batteries. It is worth while to watch the duel. Focus your glass upon the Rebel fort, listen for the report close to your elbow of one of Cowan's guns, see the smoke of the shell bursting in or over the yellow earth upon which your eyes rest, even while the shriek of its passage through the air yet rings in your ears, and while the voice of its explosion is yet on the way back.

Wait an instant, and you will see another volume of white smoke rising over there, and hear 20-pound Parrotts coming this way,— the sound of a shell coming toward one is easily distinguished from that of a shell going from one. The former grows in geometrical ratio louder, more discordant and fierce; moreover, one's sensations are different, and the five to ten seconds between the explosion which sped it and that with which it stops are of a prolonged and intense nature. I am half disposed to believe in very truth that these things go from here over there in one-tenth the time required to send one from there here!

But a few musket-shots down on the plain recall our attention to the troops. They are advancing and driving the Rebel skirmishers with a dropping fusillade, and you see the white puff of every shot.

At our feet a smiling valley, rich with springing corn and ripening wheat, orchards already bending with fruit, and in the distance beyond church-spires pierce "the war clouds rising dun," and outlined against the sky, indicate the city you cannot see for suburban trees and shrouding haze and dust and smoke. And these are men, killing each other, and we look on and hope our side will kill the most; and the long line goes glittering on, banging on. This is only a fragment of the battle that is raging. Heavier rolls of musketry than ours, louder pounding of artillery than ours, off in the wood at the left, remind us of this. Of that work we can see nothing. It is in woodland, else belts of woodland intervene, and the ground is cut in every direction by wooded ravines and traversed by several sloughs perpendicular to the river.

There is, however, one point four miles away, on Warren's extreme left, where contending battle lines may be seen, and the same church-spires that we see, but outlined against a different quarter of the horizon. Still, the view is not so good as this; the city is farther away, and the enemy's batteries considerably nearer. We will remain here — and the long line goes glittering on. The Rebels retreat with Parthian shots, holding each orchard and house with some tenacity. This is only a skirmish, remarkable because it can be seen. In the woods, Gibbon and Barlow have all their lines firing; there are "death shots falling thick and fast as lightnings from a mountain cloud." Thus for half an hour. Our line has halted, for it must not go too far unless the left keeps pace with it — otherwise a flank is endangered. And the Second Corps has halted, not "for lack of argument," but from stress of it. Some ground has been taken evidently, and we will mount and ride along the lines, and learn the situation. We find that the Rebels have concentrated in front of our centre, in a good position, covered by ravine and marsh, for that is the key to Petersburg.

Advancing over broken ground the line lost their alignment, which must be dressed up, and heavier masses must be sent in before another advance. Warren's operations had been very like those we saw, with the addition of more artillery from the enemy. At a corps headquarters we learned that yet another general advance is to be made at four o'clock.

I have not been able to ascertain the details of this last attack; I only know that the Fifth, Ninth, and Second Corps, particularly the Second, encountered a determined resistance, and sustained the severest losses of the day, resulting in considerable progress. Everything is now taken excepting the enemy's last position. Taking that, we take Petersburg. But before we shall be able to occupy the city the enemy must be dislodged from certain commanding positions on the other bank of the river, where he has numerous batteries, some of them said to be of siege guns planted.

Official bulletins, based on telegrams from headquarters, will have advised you of any successes obtained within the next day or two, before any speculations of mine can be transmitted by mail.

I believe it is not certain that we have met in these Petersburg battles any of Lee's original army. If we have not, that must be opposed to Butler, and this is probable enough since by breaking through Butler Lee would spoil Grant's combination. It must be on the suspicion that he may attack there that all of Butler's original force has been restored to him, together with two divisions of the Sixth Corps.

Escaped contrabands report the greatest fright in Petersburg, and a hasty hegira therefrom.

Lieutenant-Colonel Locke, Chief of Staff to General Warren, who was shot through the face at Spottsylvania, returned to his post just in season to participate in the movement from Cold Harbor, wearing a deep scar that is still as much wound as scar. There must be thousands at the North wounded at the same time with him, or before, and more slightly, who should be in their places at the front. Send back the "Benschars."

The wounded are rapidly transported over smooth roads to City Point, and instantly placed on ship-board for Washington.

The Sanitary Commission was never so well organized, so prompt, never had such means at its disposal as now, at City Point, and radiating to the field.

General Meade's headquarters are within two and a half miles of Petersburg. General Butler's as near his front. General Grant's at City Point, the best possible locality for instant information from, and wise handling of, the two armies.

HEADQUARTERS OF THE ARMY OF THE POTOMAC,
Sunday Morning, June 19, 1862.

The fourth day of the battle of Petersburg ended last night. If it should open again to-day it will be the siege of Petersburg, briefer perhaps than the battle.

We attacked three times yesterday at four o'clock A. M., noon, and at four o'clock P. M.

Warren joined on the left, and swung around with a skirmishing front half a mile at each advance, taking one line of works, and pressing up to another and the last.

Hancock and Burnside in the centre found more opposition. The former has gained half a mile; the latter more.

The loss in the last assault was particularly severe in Barlow's and Gibbon's Divisions, and the second division of Burnside.

Mill's Division of the Sixth Corps and Martindale's Division of the Eighteenth Corps swept up the river to within half a mile of the town.

One more line and we have the town, which we now semi-circumvallate to its last defences. Colonel Chamberlain, commanding a brigade in the Fifth Corps, is badly wounded in the hip. Captain Byrd of Barlow's staff received a hit in the thigh; Colonel Beaver, One Hundred and Forty-eighth Pennsylvania, in the side.

IV.

WHERE LEE'S TROOPS ARE.

THE DEFENCES ON GENERAL BUTLER'S LINE. — SOMETHING ABOUT GENERAL WEITZEL. — GENERAL HINKS SUFFERING FROM WOUNDS, AND TO BE RELIEVED. — HEALTH OF THE ARMY. — ONIONS. — ITEMS, PERSONAL AND OTHERWISE.

HEADQUARTERS ARMY OF THE POTOMAC,
NEAR PETERSBURG, June 22, 1864.

THE problem of the last few days, other than how to occupy Petersburg, has been to locate Lee's army. It is now pretty well ascertained that after garrisoning Richmond and Petersburg, and holding with slender force the line between, he has not only detached nine brigades to operate against Hunter, but has guarded his still unbroken railroads with large numbers. Meanwhile he provisions Richmond, and looks to wearing us out should he be driven to stand a siege. We have to take Petersburg, when the breaking of all his roads will follow. After the first city falls, the awful wastage of the war, the effusion of so much precious blood, will cease. Then it becomes a work of time and vigilance.

I have to-day ridden along General Butler's lines from the Appomattox to the James. They are immensely strong. The defences of Washington are not more carefully constructed; certainly are not more impregnable. Intended to enable a small force to hold at bay a much larger one, — for during a full month it was within Lee's power to fall upon Butler with all his own army added to Beauregard's, — skill and labor have done their utmost to that end. I am not enough learned in engineering technology to describe them with the professional name for each defensive device, but will endeavor to convey some notion of them to the general reader. It is but two and three-fourths miles from one river to the other, but the continuous line of ditch and parapet and abatis cannot be less than five. Conforming to ridges and ravines, eminences and depressions, according to the rules of military engineering, so as to meet the necessities of cross fire, direct fire, and concentrated fire, that one point shall strengthen another, it is bewilderingly sinuous and zigzag, now semicircling, now turning abruptly right or left at an acute angle, and now at an obtuse one, until, with its isthmuses and peninsulas and tortuous way, only an engineer can pursue it and retain any knowledge of the four cardinal points. The whole length is piled with sand-bags, six or eight deep, and crosswise, forming port-holes for musketeers.

Then there are outworks, complete inclosures, — I think I heard one that looked very formidable called a redoubt, — and inner works, whose cannon bristling through embrasures looked toward us as we followed the line; possibly there are redans, and there are re-entrant spaces with stockades running from point to point, making enclosures; and there are great bomb-proofs, excavations covered with logs and deep-banked with earth, designed by engineers, and smaller ones built by the men of their own accord for safety "when shake the hills with" Rebel "thunder riven;" and there are sally-ports so constructed that from no Rebel standpoint can they be detected; and there are guns, guns, everywhere, trained upon every approach — some oblique adown the line, some straight out into the woods; and be sure there is no road or open ground that is not swept by a score of them. These lines were originally laid out by Captain Farquahr, then chief engineer of this department, but have since been altered, improved, and vastly strengthened by General Weitzel, who seems to have expended upon them all the devices of modern engineering, and then superadded those of his own exhaustless contrivances, resources, and energy. They are pronounced by General Barnard, and other competent authorities who have lately inspected them, marvels of skill and labor, impregnable against assault, no matter by what numbers, and tenable against a protracted siege in force and by regular approaches.

General Weitzel, chief engineer upon Butler's staff, is a curious man. Endowed with wonderful *nous*, located in a big head, set on a long neck, atop of a long body, swung along by pendulum legs, he is — Godfrey Weitzel, and there is none other. Would there were, for the sake of the country, and every one a brigadier-general. After the glorious exhibition of the fighting qualities of the negro last week before Petersburg, he was heard to say triumphantly, "This war is as good as settled — the negroes will fight, *and Baldy Smith says so.*" It must be understood that up to that time General Smith was supposed to distrust negro soldiers, though now unequivocal in their praise. During one of the engagements on this front a soldier cried out to General Weitzel, who was with the skirmishers, "General, a Johnny has got me prisoner! Come out here and save me." The general sprang out, presented his pistols, released the man, and brought in the Rebel, who begged him not to shoot, and was astonished beyond measure when he learned the rank of his captor.

Brigadier-General Carr will probably be assigned to the colored division now commanded by General Hinks. The latter, if he would but take advice, is unfitted for active service by any one of three or four of his worst wounds, particularly by one received as long ago as Malvern Hill; but he insisted upon being permitted to lead the negroes until they had an opportunity of showing their worth. Having done so, he will now accept other and less active duty. That he lives in spite of wounds that would kill another man reminds one of the remark of Rufus Choate, when told that if he persisted in his habit of exhausting labor he would injure his constitution: "Why, I have n't had a constitution for ten years — I 'm living under the by-laws."

That the health of the army continues so good, that there are so few in hospital from disease, is remarkable. And yet these fifty days of campaigning begin to tell upon the men. They need, quite as much as rest, a change of diet, a vegetable diet. With the season, and after so long a course of hard bread and salt meats, they crave vegetables. At a house where I halted on the march from Cold Harbor, the woman, lamenting the robbing of her garden, said, "You Yanks don't seem ter keer fur nuthin but inyuns." The remark is suggestive, and since it is a fact that there is nothing which, as a concentrated antiscorbutic, equals onions, and since they can be as easily provided as potatoes, it seems to me that two or three schooner-loads ought to be immediately despatched to City Point from Weathersfield, Ct., — the world's biggest onion garden. If the children of Israel, while journeying their forty years in the wilderness, had lived on salt pork and hard 'tack, it would not be strange that they longed for the leeks and onions of Egypt. However, their lot was more tolerable than that of our soldiers, for many of them, all of them at the last, were to the manna born. But it may be urged that the objection holds against the introduction into the army of onions, which Dogberry, in "Much Ado About Nothing," makes against comparisons, that they are "odorous." Conceded; so they are. Mrs. Malaprop, in "The Rivals," says "Comparisons don't become a young woman." Nor do onions. But with the soldier it is otherwise. He is not confined to parlors. He ranges all out-doors. He sees only his fellows. Ladies are to him only a memory and a hope. And when this cruel war is over the kiss-welcomes home will not be less sweet that the tabooed vegetable has contributed to his health. Seriously, let the Commissary Department or the Sanitary Commission take this matter in hand, and send the soldiers cargoes of onions and health.

A few bare statements, taken haphazard from my note-book, will eke out this letter.

It is a matter of universal regret — of grief — that General Hancock's Gettysburg wound, breaking out afresh, should have compelled him to relinquish — it is hoped only temporarily — command of his corps. At present General Birney is in command of the old Second.

General Ingalls has established his office, for the sake of having more immediate direction of the immense quartermaster business, at City Point. In his absence from headquarters, Lieutenant-Colonel Batchelder, chief quartermaster of the Second Corps, is acting in that capacity for the whole army.

The Tenth Massachusetts, Second Vermont, and Sixty-seventh New York, their terms of enlistment having expired, have started home. The latter has been known as the First Long Island.

In the cavalry fight near White Oak Swamp last week, Fitzhugh's battery, C, Third U. S. Artillery, occupied the same position and fired in the same direction it did precisely two years before at the battle of Fair Oaks.

A late Richmond paper deprecates in strong terms the habit of questioning Yankee prisoners as to the duration of the war, etc., alleging that no answer is ever given, and no other could be expected, than that the war will not end except with the restoration of the Union, — an unintentional tribute to our poor fellows, which should be held to their credit against the day of their release; pray Heaven that may not be distant.

V.

OPERATIONS ON WEDNESDAY AND THURSDAY OF LAST WEEK.

DEVELOPING THE LEFT AGAIN. — SURPRISE BY THE REBELS ON WEDNESDAY. — THE LOSS OF MCKNIGHT'S BATTERY. — TWO THOUSAND PRISONERS CAPTURED. — WHOLE REGIMENTS TAKEN PRISONERS. — THE LINE REFORMED. — ADVANCE ON THURSDAY, AND THE WELDON RAILROAD REACHED. — WRIGHT IS AGAIN ATTACKED AND DRIVEN BACK. — OUR TROOPS REOCCUPY THEIR INTRENCHMENTS. — BATTLE EXPECTED.

HEADQUARTERS ARMY OF THE POTOMAC,
Thursday, June 23, 10 P. M.

THE operations of the last three days have had for their object possession of the railroads south of Petersburg, — the Weldon and Raleigh road and the Lynchburg. To accomplish this required a hazardous extension of the line far to the left. It was thought possible a surprise might be effected. In that case, planting ourselves on those roads, all would be attained which the occupation of Petersburg would give us. To carry the latter directly, we must expect to sustain large loss. To reach the same end by a sliding movement toward the south was worth the trial. Besides, if successful, it would still further envelop the city, and be another step toward its fall, — a step toward that remoter objective, Richmond. Well, it has been tried, and the result — if we may accept as the result the situation at this hour — is not the most cheerful in the world; not satisfactory, nor yet disheartening, but marred by a disastrous episode, — the loss of prisoners by the Second Corps yesterday. There is this comfort, that the losses in killed and wounded, compared with those of last week, are inconsiderable.

The Second and Sixth Corps were designated for the movement, while the Eighteenth was brought from Butler and with the Fifth and Ninth holds the old works. Thus three corps were stretched over the ground until then occupied by four. The distance from the left of that line, being Warren's left, to the point on the Weldon road which it was thought might be struck, is five miles or thereabout. The Second Corps under Birney had gained position on Warren's left on Tuesday, — so withdrawn, however, as not to attract the attention of the enemy. By yesterday morning the Sixth had assumed a similar relation toward the Second and now the two corps advanced toward the railroad still three miles distant.

Whether the enemy penetrated the design or happened to be making a reconnoissance in force on his own account, he seems to have been moving towards us simultaneously, and the collision was but an hour or two later. The country was utterly unknown to us, or if anything was known as to the direction and termini of roads, and the distances between given points, it was so vague and faulty that it only served to mislead. We found the woods more dense and continuous than any encountered since the Wilderness, — as dense as those, and different only in that there are more cleared spaces. Notwithstanding the brief time the troops had been in the position from which they started, they moved from very tolerable works, — the Second Corps from a continuous line, and the Sixth from a line thrown up by Ricketts' Division, which reached here in advance of the rest of the corps. The enemy must have discovered our advance before we did his, and made dispositions accordingly — to attack us in flank when marching. He confronted the Second Corps and Barlow's Division; the left of that corps was moving still further to the left of Ricketts' Division. Sixth Corps was also moving, and was within a mile and a half of the railroad. Mott's (late Birney's) and Gibbon's Second Corps were in aligned position on the right of Barlow. Gibbon had planted one battery of four guns, McKnight's Twelfth New York Independent. I have been unable to sift a vast contrariety of statements, so as to arrive at even a theory of the precise way it all happened. But the enemy came down with little or no previous indication of his presence in force, struck Barlow, and glanced by him, bearing away prisoners, and then falling upon Mott and Gibbon. Officers in the divisions of the latter insist that the first knowledge they had of the enemy was his presence directly in the rear. Whether he came down between Barlow and the Sixth Corps or behind him and Mott or Gibbon, it is impossible for me to say. It is perhaps certain that Barlow was first struck, that at some points the line was struck from the rear, at others from the front — at all, unexpectedly and disastrously. It was the work of an instant; scarcely any resistance was made, — there was no time for it. Gibbon's staff was eating dinner a fourth of a mile in rear of their advance, and heard no fighting; were confounded at sight of men running. These they rallied into line, but the enemy came no farther. Those that did not run, some of the best troops in the army, were captured by regiments. The First Brigade (Pierce's) suffered most, and without firing a shot, yet this brigade has been the pride of the corps. Somebody blundered, else such soldiers as the Fifteenth, Nineteenth, and Twentieth Massachusetts, Seventh Michigan, Nineteenth Maine, Forty-second and Eighty-second New York, and Thirty-sixth Wisconsin, would have made for themselves an opportunity for fighting. It was the Seventh Michigan and Nineteenth Massachusetts that volunteered to cross to Fredericksburg in boats under a severe fire a year and a half ago, which they did so perilously and so bravely. Some of those regiments were captured bodily, viz., the Nineteenth and Fifteenth Massachusetts and the Forty-second and Eighty-second New York. The brigade has lost five commanders and other officers, and rank and file in proportion, during the campaign. Commanding it have been General Alexander Webb, wounded at Spottsylvania, and Colonels Haskell and McKean, killed at Cold Harbor. The division probably lost a thousand prisoners yesterday, and Mott's and Barlow's together as many. Besides these is the loss of four guns. McKnight stood by them and his colors till a Rebel flag flaunted beside his own, and there was but one man with him. To-day, while talking of the disaster, his voice broke and his eyes filled; the presence of an enemy had never caused the one to falter nor abashed the other.

Dispositions were instantly made to retrieve the fortunes of the day. The Sixth was halted, Ricketts even marching back a mile, and two brigades were sent for from Warren, and reserved batteries prepared for action. Miles' Brigade with certain others retired in — to the line of the morning, and I think it was hoped the enemy would attempt to pursue his advantage. But he knew better, and contented himself with the trophies, already won, 2,000 prisoners and four guns.

Where the blame would rest, if there was fault anywhere, — and it would seem there must have been, — I may not undertake to determine. He must be very astute who is able at this hour to discriminate justly and award righteously.

At seven o'clock in the evening Wright advanced the Sixth Corps. The Rebels had retired leaving a thick skirmish line, which raised a yell and fired a volley, and they fled, like so many pedestrian "Tam O'Shanters." And then such cheers as the Sixth sent after them! The whole corps charged a mile and a half, halting occasionally to preserve alignment, and then bivouacked. The direction pursued had formed it, when halted, at an obtuse angle with the Second. Later in the evening Burnside was attacked strenuously without avail.

To-day at half-past three A. M. the Sixth and Second advanced simultaneously, having during the night perfected connections of brigades, divisions, and corps. Birney barely regained the position lost yesterday. Wright found nothing before him but pickets. He advanced some distance, swinging around Birney. His two left divisions, Wheaton's (late Neill's) and Ricketts' were now hardly more than a mile from the railroad. Captain Beatty with 100 pioneers and sharp-shooters was sent out to reconnoitre. He reached the railroad unopposed and found it without the pretence of a guard, and with his report sent a couple of feet of telegraph wire he had cut from the Raleigh line. The Third, Fourth, and Eleventh Vermont were instantly despatched to take possession, and preparations were made to extend the corps to that point. But by this time the Rebels were fully awake to the situation. It was as vital to them to regain the railroad as it was to us to retain it. Their interior, therefore shorter, lines gave them every advantage.

It is not less than ten miles from our right on the river to the point in question on the railroad. The Rebel communication between the two is not over four, and so they pushed down in overwhelming numbers all of Hill's Corps, and attacked. We had not completed a line, had had no time to intrench, and there was nothing but to fall back. Even that was a matter of some difficulty. The Fourth Vermont lost prisoners, and it was fortunate that the order " As you were !" was issued so promptly. The Rebels followed closely, attacking at the right of the corps and then to the left, and farther to the left, till they found cavalry, and knew they had determined our limit in that direction. It appeared to be his purpose to make a general assault, and it were better to sustain that covered by some sort of works. Hence, in the edge of the evening all the divisions of the corps retired, and now occupy the positions of the morning.

Several brigades have marched over from the Fifth Corps, and it looks as if to-morrow would see a general engagement, though I do not prophesy.

Friday, June 24, 6 A. M.

Sharp spirts of musketry and then booming cannon have disturbed the night. Since daylight, judging by the steady pour of musketry, an engagement has been progressing on the right. No reports yet, and it is not even known what corps are engaged.

The sun is hardly above the horizon and yet the day has become heated and sultry, and the dust of yesterday has not settled.

Colonel Blaisdell, Eleventh Massachusetts, was killed yesterday.

VI.

OPERATIONS ON FRIDAY.

SUDDEN ATTACKS BY THE REBELS ON SMITH'S CORPS. — A LIVELY CAN-
NONADING WITH ALMOST NO DAMAGE TO US. — ONE HUNDRED AND
SIXTY-FIVE REBELS CAPTURED. — NEW STYLE OF RIFLE PITS.

WITH THE ARMY OF THE POTOMAC,
Saturday, June 25, 8 A. M.

DURING two hours yesterday morning, from six to eight, the earth trembled to the thunder of more than 100 cannon. It seemed an artillery carnival raging with a sort of Satanic joy. Baldy Smith was attacked. It will be remembered that he holds next to the Appomattox, within less than a mile of the city. His line stretches across the plain at right angles with the river, while the Rebels have undisturbed possession of the left bank opposite, and a long distance in his rear. On that bank they suddenly uncovered 60 guns, subjecting the Eighteenth Corps to an enfilading fire and reverse fire. With the exception of Gettysburg, the war has not afforded another instance of so many guns concentrated upon one point and firing so rapidly for such length of time. The plain seemed alive with bursting shells, the discharges were as continuous and rapid as the ticking of a watch. It did not seem possible that men could remain there and live, but they did both; so effectually were they covered that two hours of such pounding, though it strewed the ground with fragments of shells like broken crockery around an old tavern, caused a loss of only 30.

Meanwhile our guns replied, and the cannonading ran along the line until the mortars of the Second Corps, miles away, rang the chorus.

At length the enemy attacked, with men as well as cannon. They very foolishly moved a thin line upon our works, since ascertained to be Haygood's South Carolina Brigade of Hoke's Division.

The repulse was the work of a few minutes and was complete; 165 prisoners fell into our hands, among them five commissioned officers, viz.: Captain Henry Buist, Twenty-seventh South Carolina, commanding regiment; J. N. Mulvaney, Twenty-seventh South Carolina; Lieutenant A. B. White, Twenty-seventh South Carolina; Captain J. E. Rayson, Eleventh South Carolina; Lieutenant Clements, Twenty-first South Carolina. Nearly all of these fell into the hands of Colonel Henry's Brigade of Stannard's (late Brooks') Division. By a stratagem on the part of Colonel Henry (observing that the force advancing was so slender that he need not fear it), he at once withdrew his pickets and ordered his men not to fire. The Rebels ran up and took the rifle-pits. Their pickets were then ordered to surrender and compelled to do so.'

These pits were so constructed as to afford no protection to the Rebels when they got into them. They are called French rifle-pits, and are simple excavations shaped like an old-fashioned kitchen dusting-pan, like the half of a square box sawn through diagonally from corner to corner, with the deep end towards the enemy. The deep end is protection to our pickets, and then, if driven out, the next line has a direct fire through the shallow end upon any who may seek shelter in it.

If the Rebels expected with their 60 guns to make the place too hot for us, and thinking they had done so, advanced their line to occupy our works, they were stupendously mistaken.

The affair has done the army a power of good, in the effect it has had upon the morale of the men.

All day yesterday the sharp-shooting was unusually merciless, both sides indulging in the pastime.

During the afternoon, beyond significant movements of troops, nothing of importance occurred, or if there did no word of it has reached me.

Your correspondent is sick with fatigue. The sun broiled his brains, and he was last night placed in hospital, where this has been written. I enclose a "Richmond Enquirer" of the 23d.

AN INVALID'S WHIMS. — HOTTENTOT HEAT. — THE MISERIES OF
CORRESPONDENTS.

WITH THE ARMY OF THE POTOMAC,
Saturday, June 25, 1864.

INVALIDS are proverbially querulous and unreasonable, and because they are invalids it is forgiven them. Their whims and vagaries are humored. They may fret and scold, abuse their toast and their friends, scatter their maledictions and the furniture, and who shall cry them "Nay"? The reader of this, if any there be, is informed respectfully but firmly that the writer, being an invalid, proposes to avail himself of all the privileges which attach to the character. Released from the bonds of the proprieties, for him there are no improprieties. Careless of consequences, careless in rhetoric, altogether careless of everything, this letter that is to be shall write itself. I am an invalid. If any thin stratum of sense or news should happen to crop out between underlying and overlying strata of nonsense, such formation will be accidental, abnormal, unaccountable.

Imprimis: It is hot. It is hotter than yesterday. Yesterday was hotter than the day before. The day before hotter than its immediate predecessor, and *it* than *its*, and so on indeterminately. Purgatory is at least a week back, and hell itself not far ahead. How hot it is now, no thermometer of words will begin to indicate. The boy who extended the comparison of the adjective from hot to hottest, then began again with Hottentot and ended with Hottentotest, made a creditable effort, but failed. In other climates he may be thought to have succeeded. But in the light and heat of this locality I denounce the ambitious youth as unequal to his attempt. It is hot. Has the lower world invaded the confines of this, or is Virginia a part of that world?

This indescribable hotness is a part of the misery of correspondents.

It is dusty. I wrote the de-apotheosis of dust the other day (did you see it in the "Daily —— "?), but failed in the deep damnation commensurate with the subject. Did you ever smile and smile, and feel like a villain? We down here do, whenever we come in dusty from a long ride. Did you ever grit your teeth in rage? We do, whenever we shut our mouths — else we should n't shut 'em. Water, I adore thee; soap, thou art my benefactor; towels, ye are blessed!

Tertiary deposit, good for growing potatoes, but contempt is bred of familiarity with thee — behind me, Satan!

Dust is a part of the misery of correspondents.

A Scene: Three "specials" of metropolitan journals, smoking meerschaums, and conning letters yet to be. Mail arrives with New-York papers. Each reads one of his own letters.

Reading their own letters is a part of the misery of correspondents.

"Herald" special swears oaths both loud and deep: "They have rewritten my despatch!" "Times" special finds something he spoke of as "impudent" pronounced "important." "Tribune" special is amused. He had said certain troops were "handled skilfully;" he is made to say that they "were travelled skilfully." In another place, where he had described foliage as of the "densest, deepest green," it appears that it was of the *direst* green! "Magnificent" is transformed into "magnified" and destroys the point of a quarter of a column of elaborate rhetoric.

Verily, reading their own letters is a part of the misery of correspondents.

Mr. Winser of "The Times" had his horse shot under him at Cold Harbor. Mr. Anderson of "The Herald" was hit in the arm at Wilderness. Richardson and Browne of "The Tribune" have been sixteen months in Rebel prisons. All have had their hairbreadth 'scapes.

Constant danger, without the soldier's glory, is a part of the misery of correspondents.

Abstractly considered, horseback exercise is a good thing. I have known it to be recommended by physicians. Taken in moderate quantities not too long after sunrise, or not too long before sunset, I have myself found it not unpleasant. In imagination I see myself, September next, indulging in flowing rein on smooth beach roads to the murmur of ocean waves, or in the back country, where the foliage is crimson and there are cider-presses in the orchards, following where there are

"Old roads winding, as old roads will,
Here to a ferry, and there to a mill."

That is one picture. Now look on this: Virginia wastes, where only desolation dwells, arid with summer heats, and now four weeks without sprinkle of rain. The sky is brass, heated to a white fervor; the air you breathe heated like the blast of a furnace, and laden with dust that chokes you. A fierce, pitiless sun sheds rays like heated daggers; these impalpable daggers stab you. You broil; you pant; you thirst; your temples throb with thrills of mighty pain; you are threatened with *coup de soleil;* you wish yourself anywhere — anywhere out of such torment.

Pooh, man! You forget that you are a "special," and therefore not supposed to be subject to the laws which govern other mortals. You are a Salamander. You are Briareus. You are Argus. You are Hercules. You are Mark Tapley. Be jolly. Ride your ten, fifteen hours; your twenty, thirty, forty, fifty miles. Fatigue is your normal condition. Sleeplessness ditto. "Tired nature" is yours; the "sweet restorer" somebody else's. "Balmy sleep" is for babies. You are a "special," I tell you.

Incessant riding in the sun is a part of the misery of correspondents.

Composition is pleasant, sometimes. I don't mean the mighty joy of creation of the great author, but the simple pleasure of ordinary mortals writing ordinary things. With dressing-gown elegance, and beslippered ease, a fair prospect out of the window, fragrance stealing through from the garden beneath, tempered by the fragrance of a rich Havana between your lips, a well-ordered desk before you, quill pens, and clear, white paper, a snug bookcase in the corner, a basket of fruit and a bouquet at your elbow, a good dinner in prospect, and a drive at sunset with somebody, your friends to see in the evening, and only a column to write — under such circumstances, "by St. Paul, the work goes bravely on!"

But you are a "special." It is far into the night when you begin. You rode all day and a part of the night, and have only now had your ablution and your supper. You begin, — "squat like a toad" before a camp-fire; a stumpy lead-pencil, and smoke in your eyes, dingy paper, and ashes puffed in your face; no part of you that has not its own special pain and torment. Your brain is in a state of "confusion worse confounded." Your eyes will shut, your pencil will drop from nerveless fingers, but I say unto you, Write! Do you forget that you are a "special," and must write? Force yourself to the rack, tug away, bear on hard, and when you are done, do not read it over, or you will throw it into the fire. Now arrange with the guard to have yourself awakened at daybreak, an hour or two hence, and then lie down, wondering who would n't be a "special."

The necessity of writing just so much every day is a part of the misery of correspondents.

You will inevitably write things that will offend somebody. Somebody will say harsh things of you, and perhaps seek you out to destroy you. Never mind. Such is a part of the misery of correspondents.

Was your horse stolen last night? Are your saddle-bags and all that they contain missing this morning? No matter. It is a thing of course. It is a part of the misery of correspondents.

You are a "special," and who would n't be?

There is news at the front, for I hear great guns; but I am too sick to ride till the sun is lower down the sky. Now, "sweet restorer," now is your time!

HEADQUARTERS ARMY OF THE POTOMAC,
Wednesday, June 29, 10 P. M.

At length, Wilson's cavalry expedition, which marched nine days ago with the purpose of destroying the Danville railroad, has been heard from through other than Rebel sources.

OPERATIONS ON FRIDAY. 147

Captain Whittaker of Wilson's staff, with an escort of 40 men, left the head of the returning column at Ream's Station on the Weldon road, fifteen miles below Petersburg, early this morning, and reached Meade's headquarters at eleven A. M.

He slashed his way through a column of Rebel infantry, which was moving down to intercept our cavalry, losing in the dash 25 of his 40, but he got through.

Wilson's command consists of his own and Kautz's Divisions. Not halting on the way out to more than temporarily break the Weldon road, which he did at Ream's Station, he moved rapidly to Burkesville, the intersection of the Danville and Richmond and the Petersburg and Lynchburg roads, 30 miles from Richmond. Then to the work of destruction with all the might of thousands of active men.

Up to this time he met but little opposition. With headquarters at Burkesville, he despatched commands in each of the four directions where lay a railroad. In this way, on the Danville road he burned bridges forty miles apart, and thoroughly destroyed, to the burning of every tie and the twisting of every rail, some twenty miles between.

On the Petersburg and Lynchburg road he utterly destroyed thirty miles, and fired bridges outside of that distance.

Having effected the object of his raid, he now looked out for his lines of retreat, already threatened by gathering Rebels.

He turned to come back. He met skirmishing, right, left, front, rear, but nothing not easily ridden through until last night at Stony Creek, on the Weldon road, 18 miles below here. There the enemy had concentrated in his front, and themselves attacked late in the afternoon, and a severe engagement ensued, lasting into the night.

He met the same force that had been dealing with Sheridan north of Richmond. The result does not seem to have been decisive, although the losses sustained and inflicted were large. During last night he turned the enemy's flank, coming in between him and Petersburg, preferring that to the other flank and a longer march.

So far as the force he had been fighting is concerned, the

move seems to have been successful. He eluded it, and would have reached our lines by noon, but for the Rebel infantry column which Captain Whittaker discovered and rode through.

What new plan he adopted on meeting this new element in the problem of his return — whether he decided to halt and withstand an attack, or march back on the path he had come — is not known.

Whittaker had scarcely reported when General Meade ordered the Sixth Corps, the nearest, to march to Wilson's support, as an offset to the Rebel infantry, and such of Sheridan's cavalry as had come up from Windmill Point, where it crossed the James, was also ordered to hasten in the same direction.

The Sixth Corps marched early in the afternoon, divested of all impediments, stripped for marching and fighting. Such is the situation as far as heard from, but the collision has doubtless already been precipitated.

We shall hear from it to-morrow. General Wilson was intrusted with an exceedingly important mission. He has accomplished it, and he can afford large loss on his return, and still the raid will be a glorious thing.

When the Danville road was completed two months ago the Richmond papers pronounced it worth more than a victory. By a parity of reasoning the loss of it is worse than a defeat.

General Hancock, on resuming command of his corps to-day, issued a long special order, reviewing the achievements of the old Second, referring to the disaster of last week in terms of rebuke which might be construed as a reflection upon the way the men were handled, rather than upon the men, and finally stirring them with breathing thoughts and burning words to still grander deeds.

By request, I refrain from sending it for publication.

"The Petersburg Register" of yesterday is lugubriously facetious over conchology; states that everybody in the city is learning the art of dodging.

Staid and respectable citizens dodge into the houses of utter strangers, and penetrate even to the cellars, without even saying, "By your leave."

The Eighteenth Corps has adopted a badge, a double triangle inclosed in a quatre-foil. Generals Grant and Butler during the day have visited several corps headquarters, whether for counsel does not appear.

Baldy Smith has dropped a shell into Petersburg every fifteen minutes the last three days. A deserter reports that several struck the Market-House yesterday, that the Rebel pontoon bridge was destroyed by them, and that numbers are killed every day.

Smith silenced two Rebel batteries across the Appomattox yesterday, but this morning they disclose two others in position, which he cannot reach.

Major Merriman, Ninety-second New York, had his arm shattered by a shell to-day. The casualties from sharp-shooting are twenty-five a day in the Eighteenth Corps, and as many in the Ninth.

The other corps maintain informal truce. Lee has but 35,000 men in our front. The Rebels are now conscripting between the ages of 17 and 50; hitherto only between 18 and 45.

If I were operating, I should write privately — *à la* Bull-Run Russell — " Act as though you had heard good news."

THE GREAT CAVALRY EXPEDITION. — RETURN OF GENERAL KAUTZ. — WILSON NOT HEARD FROM. — HIS CAISSONS COME THROUGH. — POWERFUL REBEL CONCENTRATION IN HIS FRONT. — IMMENSE RESULTS OF HIS RAID. — VAST STORES AND MANUFACTORIES DESTROYED.

HEADQUARTERS ARMY OF THE POTOMAC,
Thursday, June 30, 1864.

ALL interest centres in the cavalry, — the return of the Wilson and Kautz expedition from the mission of destruction which it wrought upon the Danville and Richmond Railroad. Kautz got in to-day. His loss does not exceed 350. Wilson has not been heard from since his staff officer cut through yesterday, nor is aught known of the operations of the Sixth Corps, save that it started on a forced march to his relief.

Kautz broke through dense woods, abandoning four guns and his short train. The bridle paths which, through perfect familiarity with the country, he was able to follow, would not permit the passage of these. His men return utterly fagged out.

The excessive heat of the last week contributed largely to their present pitiable condition. Day before yesterday men on the skirmish line, while fighting, fell asleep in their saddles.

I just learn that the caissons of Fitzhugh's battery, the only guns Wilson had with him, have come on through. This implies that the guns are lost.

Wilson will disentangle himself, unless the exhaustion of the men shall prevent marching. Even in that case it is hoped that he will be able to sustain himself until the arrival of Wright's Sixth Corps, since at last accounts he was near Ream's Station, but nine miles from Wright's point of starting at two P. M., yesterday.

The damage inflicted upon the enemy appears to be even greater than I supposed when writing last night. It includes the destruction of immense supplies, sawmills, etc. The guns in the fight at Stony Creek night before last were plainly heard in this army, and it was known it could be nothing else than Wilson fighting his way back.

No means was taken to ascertain whether succor was needed. Hundreds of negroes who had fallen in with the command have probably been retaken. General Smith made a demonstration from his front to-day, but withdrew within his works on discovering that, by the mistake of a brigade commander in marching his men by an observed road, the enemy had seen the movement in time to oppose it with concentration. The loss sustained was 22, although the demonstration wakened all the enemy's artillery, scores in number, at that point.

The Sanitary Commission is beginning to distribute large quantities of vegetables, — sauer-kraut, onions, and dried apples. The soldiers in the trenches are out of tobacco and the time hangs more heavily than ever. I commend the want to the Commission's notice. No rain yet.

Mr. Kent of "The Tribune," was crowded off a pontoon bridge by a passing train and a stupid driver, a day or two ago, himself considerably bruised, and his horse killed, notwithstanding the latter fell uppermost.

GENERAL BUTLER'S HEADQUARTERS,
Monday, July 4, 1864, 7 A. M.

Everything indicates a lively Fourth of July. General Butler has ordered a salute of 34 guns, one for each State, shotted and trained upon the enemy, to be fired at noon, and all the bands to be stationed at the front and play national airs the livelong day.

I presume similar programmes are to be enacted on the line of the Army of the Potomac. The Rebels evidently anticipate some extraordinary demonstration by us in honor of the day, maybe will themselves take the initiative, with the hope of turning its pristine meaning against us. If they do not divine the place and the hour of the thing I know to have been contemplated, I look to see the anniversary yet have for us a present glory added to its traditional significance.

The men in the trenches are much worn. The eternal vigilance which is the price of their lives is more than ordinarily exhausting, owing to the unrelenting heat. Still no rain, albeit one of your contemporaries has a letter dated "Headquarters of the Potomac" which mentions two showers in one day. A letter with such heading, written in New York, should not be so circumstantial. No grand movement may be expected until there is a change in the weather. Grant has now reached a point in his Herculean task where he can afford to require less of his army. He may now take for his motto "*Festina lente*," for he has passed the beginning of the end, and sees the end itself in a straight path before him.

With the destruction of all the roads leading into Richmond begins the practical circumvallation siege of that city. And better to take it months hence, and then and there destroy the

Confederacy, than to celebrate to-day within it, and have Lee's army, unbroken and defiant, posted only a little south of it. The fortunate few in the army who obtain glimpses of Northern papers are astonished at the nervousness of people — at the fluctuations in the price of that said-to-be-barometer of public confidence — gold. Either there was no adequate comprehension of the magnitude of Grant's undertaking, or there is misconception as to the means he is pursuing and the amount he has already accomplished. This much is at all events certain: if he has not kept pace with their great expectations, he has with his own more moderate ones, and while they may despond he only now suffers himself to be fully, altogether, assuredly confident, and he may be supposed to be in possession of the more correct data upon which to predicate an opinion.

Deserters come into General Butler's lines at the rate of ten to fifteen per day, and the rate is steadily increasing. One whole company, led by its captain, recruited in Portsmouth, Va., three years ago and conscripted at the expiration of its term of enlistment, deserted in a body three days ago. Several Tennesseeans arrived yesterday, and these threw up their hats when they learned that Andy Johnson is to be the next Vice President, and one from Georgia, "who did n't keer ter fight fur them aristockers," and who was astonished to hear that General Sherman had occupied Marietta, Georgia, his home. He had never been out of the county where he was born until conscripted, was a poor man, had only one thought — to get back to his wife and children, and said all the soldiers from his locality, every one from "down yender," was of his mind. Several whose homes are in Richmond and Petersburg complained that while they had plenty of food, their families were permitted to starve. It is clear that the greatest distress prevails in those cities. At last starvation is becoming a thing we may count upon, however delusive it may have been heretofore. The cry of "Wolf! Wolf!" was the herald of a fact — a live wolf.

GENERAL BUTLER'S HEADQUARTERS,
Tuesday, July 5, noon, 1864.

Independence day passed even more quietly than other days. Very little cannonading on General Meade's front, though the quarter-hourly shell dropped regularly into Petersburg. No firing on Butler's front save his salute of 34 shotted guns, in honor of the day. Besides being an anniversary salvo, it had the character of a bombardment of the enemy's works. He, however, did not deign to reply, and the afternoon was of Sunday quietude. In the evening a number of rockets were sent up from these headquarters, disclosing high in the sky the national red, white, and blue. The noontide salute and those pyrotechnics constituted the celebration. There was no musketry anywhere during the day except the pitiless sharp-shooting.

On General Burnside's front a mortar shell was seen to throw a Rebel 25 or 30 feet into the air. His body fell outside their works and remains there, for certain death from our riflemen awaits any who should attempt to recover it.

The enemy, in anticipation of attack on our great day, doubled his pickets along his whole line. But we were wiser than to humor his expectation, preferring to let him remain on the *qui-vive*, and to fight him another day. We ate onions — thanks to anti-scorbutic friends — and slept from their soporific influence. True, we had hoped to celebrate the day in Richmond, but satisfied with the progress made, we philosophically bide our time. The offering of vegetables for the Fourth arrived and was distributed just in the nick of time. Doesticks exclaims, "What's a bottle of whiskey among one?" which illustrates the fact that the vegetables sent up this time, evenly distributed, have lasted only one day. The moral is, send more.

General Getty has returned and resumed command of the Second Division, Sixth Corps, which lost the largest percentage in the Wilderness.

General Smith, whom the "London Times" calls "General Baldy," has not availed himself of his twenty days' leave, but remains with his corps.

There are hundreds of officers whose health demands rest, whose bare application would obtain them furloughs, but who remain, and will remain, unless completely prostrated, while the campaign lasts. To use the expression of a division commander, they hang on by their eyelids. It is Elisha Kent Kane pluck that sustains them.

The cavalry, after its late arduous but successful achievements, needs and is being given rest. Having raided all round Richmond, having destroyed all the railroads that centre in that city, until it may almost take up for itself in its specialty the Alexandrine lament of no more worlds to conquer, the cavalry may well rest. Meanwhile clothing is being issued and paymasters have been ordered down. Still no rain. How long, O Lord, how long?

VII.

GOING TO THE FRONT.

HEADQUARTERS GEN. BUTLER, July 15, 11 P. M.

I CHEERFULLY commend and consign this letter to solid nonpareil in an obscure corner of an inside page, for I do not expect to invest with any particular degree of interest a narrative of personal experiences in making the transit from city to camp. Yet such narrative I propose to write. The intention presupposes a vast use of the monolettered pronoun, which must be pardoned along with the culpability of the original purpose. The journey was from Washington to City Point via the Potomac, Chesapeake Bay, and the James. It was not in the least noteworthy. It was not in the least exceptional. It was not in the least eventful. But whoso would come to the army must encounter the same experience, and it is on this account that I tell the tale.

General Ingalls has detailed four steamboats for the route. One leaves City Point each day at ten A. M., and reaches Washington the next day at the same hour. From Washington the hour is two P. M., and the arrival at the other terminus twenty-seven hours later, — an instance, by the way, where the *descensus Averni* requires more time than the getting back again.

On the trip up a week before, I was one of 300 who participated in a free fight on board the "Charlotte Vanderbilt" for 20 staterooms, and was one of 20 who did not lose their temper. It was remarkable that the 20 who retained their temper were identical with the 20 who obtained staterooms. Now I dislike a scene almost as much as the nervous individual in the "Woman in White" and I particularly dislike to part with my temper. Accordingly day before yesterday I was at the foot of Sixth Street an hour before the boat started, with a haversack, a pair of saddle-bags, and the intention of securing a stateroom. The boat was the "John Brooks." As I approach, an officer on the gangway looks at me without seeing me — looks as though "looking at a thought," but extends his hand like an automaton and says one word, "Pass." He does not thereby tender permission to go on board, but demands my authority to do so. I hand him a sesame, "By order of Lieutenant-General Grant." The reticent officer nods. I nod, and the pass is made. I now seek the captain; I respectfully inquire if I can obtain a stateroom. My gracious! how that man did open upon me! Poor man; his boat had no staterooms in her, and his method of telling me so was not agreeable. I pity him, for he suffers terribly from his monomania — his stateroom-phobia. As I started to go on deck I heard another passenger make the same inquiry I had made, and I stopped a moment in pity for the horrid agony which it cost that captain to convey the single idea of a want of staterooms.

The passengers are miscellaneous — of all descriptions and nondescripts. Officers on their way to the front, agents of the Sanitary Commission on their way to the front, agents of the Christian Commission on their way to the front, purveyors and sutlers on their way to the front. Two or three old men, whose sons have been wounded and are now in hospital, on the way to the front. One lady, with pale and mournful face (once I saw her weeping), on her way to the front. A mail agent stretched at full length on a heap of leather bags on the way to the front. And then a half-dozen inscrutables, who may be brigadier-generals or sutlers' clerks, on the way to the front. Down below are a dozen horses, brave war-steeds, restless, pawing, maybe snuffing the battle from afar, on the way to the front. And there are long ranges of hogsheads filled with cabbages, and barrels filled with onions, beets, turnips, etc., on the way to the front.

On the way to the front, and the boat swings into the stream, and the captain is scolding at somebody on the shore. The motley company disperse themselves over the boat. On deck there are fifty of us smoking, twenty-five of us reading, twelve of us have secured resting-places for our feet of equal altitude with our heads, six of us are rapt in the perusal of "Our Mutual Friend" in the August "Harper," and one of us on cutting another leaf is indignant that we must wait a month for another taste of it (note bad grammar, Dickens' use of "mutual").

We pass Alexandria, eight miles down, pass numerous frowning forts (earthworks) on either side, pass Fort Washington, an elaborate stone fortification, ten miles below Alexandria, built years and years ago, pass Mount Vernon, five miles still lower down. We meet numerous craft coming up, and pass numerous ones going down, for the "John Brooks" is the fastest steamer in government employ. The banks of the yellow Potomac are green to the water's edge with a dense fringe of trees and vines. Our rapid motion makes for us a grateful breeze. I smoke Petersburg tobacco, "Zephyr Puff" the label calls it, and time drifts pleasantly away, and the Potomac widens, and I detect in the air reminiscences of the sea it was blowing over but a few hours before, and the sun goes down in a lurid blaze, while a crimson glory transfigures the clouds in the sky; and now the moon is directly overhead, and stars are, timidly at first, but now bravely and brightly shining out, — and supper is announced, and my dreams harshly broken.

Down into a dimly lighted hold, we urge our way by dubious staircases and encumbered passages, encountering at every turn filth and intolerable odors. The table is not inviting.

I am again on deck inhaling air stiff with oxygen and sea-salts, and then exhaling with the addition of the elements of "Zephyr Puff." Four delicious hours, with moonlight so bright that I read over old letters and gaze at certain photographs, and later, when the moon has gone, starlight that reveals all the constellations that I learned to name when I studied mythology and mathematical astronomy, and it is midnight, and the scene is as weird as —

> "In Xanadu did Kubla Khan
> A stately pleasure-dome decree:
> Where Alph, the sacred river, ran
> Through caverns measureless to man
> Down to a sunless sea."

In the stern hold a score of air-discarding individuals were bunked, and are sleeping where only two portholes, the size of cannon-balls, which open just above the rudder, furnish oxygen, and they snooze in the torpor of a Bruin-like hibernation,—a sweaty torpor. Others are sleeping heavily, or restlessly, in the cabins, but little better off. I prefer the open deck, without mattress, or even blanket, with but saddle-bags for pillow, and I remember that my last consciousness was devoted to trying to recall the name of a certain violet-colored star that looked down upon me from the zenith, and was very beautiful. I waken to find the sun shining upon me, and the boat alongside of the wharf at Fortress Monroe. It is still three or four hours to ten o'clock, the hour we start up the James. I breakfast quite tolerably at the Hygeia Hotel, patronize a small boy who sells pears and green apples, and on the arrival of the Baltimore boat at nine o'clock, obtain New York papers, which I read on the deck of the "John Brooks," as we get under way again. There are large additions of passengers from the Baltimore boat, and large additions of Sanitary-Commission vegetables. The former are unable to obtain seats, and the latter fill with barrels and boxes all the passages and lumber-room. Heretofore every effort has been directed to the hospitals, but that was only the ounce of cure. These anti-scorbutics are prevention, and worth a pound of the other. A brigadier-general and his staff have come on board. I am told it is General Shepley, so ably and successfully Military Governor of Louisiana, and now of Norfolk and vicinity,—evidently an able, scholarly, yet executive man, judging by his dignified, manly bearing.

I deliberately go to sleep, and am glad when I waken to find that I have escaped the temptation of going to dinner. I had kept awake until I could get one more look at the spars of the "Cumberland" that more than two years ago went down so gloriously off Newport News; those spars have now been nearly all clipped away for mementos. And I woke when we were opposite Harrison's Landing, where, during the six weeks after Malvern, a mighty and victorious army fortified itself when no man pursued. Less than an hour, and we are at City Point, where the stream is covered with vessels. A new and extensive wharf has just been completed. Alongside of it stands a long train of cars, which to-night will be unloaded within two miles of Petersburg. I am fortunate in obtaining passage, in a special boat provided for General Shepley, from City Point to Bermuda Hundred, a mile across the mouth of the Appomattox. At Bermuda Hundred I met General Graham, in command of the gunboats, who tenders me passage on his flag-ship up the Appomattox four miles to Point of Rocks. General Graham was educated for the sea at the Naval Academy, and has been educated in the army by many battles and by many wounds, and is, therefore, peculiarly fitted for a command half naval, half military. A message transmitted by signals, first to Weitzel's Tower (which is 150 feet high), and from there to headquarters, brings to me my horse, and a ride of a mile or two carries me "home." The transit from city to camp has required only thirty hours, and exceedingly pleasant hours, despite of all drawbacks.

So much by way of personal narrative. I trust events of some importance may claim every line of succeeding letters.

GENERAL BUTLER'S COMMAND. — SHARP WORK BY REBEL ARTILLERY. — ABOUT PRISONERS. — RESIGNATION OF GENERAL BROOKS. — A SMALL RAID.

GENERAL BUTLER'S HEADQUARTERS, July 16, 1864.

THE order of the War Department consolidating the Eighteenth and Tenth Corps, and remitting General Butler to Fortress Monroe, has been suspended, on the request of General Grant, and General Butler's command is likely to be increased rather than diminished.

About seven o'clock this morning the Rebels opened on the pontoon bridge across the James, at Deep Bottom, and upon General R. S. Foster's headquarters on the left bank, with a new battery of Whitworth guns, located a mile below the bridge, at a point but a short distance above Malvern Hill. The gunboat "Mendota," Commander Nichols, which was lying just below the bridge, replied, and soon attracted the Rebel fire. Within the hour she had one man killed and seven wounded, and was compelled to fall down the stream. The Rebels then resumed their fire upon the bridge and Foster's position, but without inflicting damage or loss. One shell knocked to pieces the stove on which had been cooked the breakfast. General Foster and staff were eating not twenty feet distant. Another killed the horse of his adjutant-general, Captain Davis, the same distance on another side, and others still ploughed into the ground, and broke down trees around and among the tents, but somehow managed to strike and burst without hurting any one.

By a coincidence, Generals Grant and Butler had appointed to visit General Foster's lines to-day. The Rebel demonstration did not deter them from the purpose. An hour or two after the firing ceased, General Graham steamed up the river with his flag-boat the "Chamberlain," having Grant and Butler on board. The Rebels opened on them with six guns. The first shot passed between the walking-beam and the smoke-stack and close to the deck, and several subsequent ones came about as near. The "Chamberlain" replied, but kept on her way, and the two generals landed safely, and inspected General Foster's position, even to the extent of going out to the picket line. And they went back the way they came, under the same fire, but this time stopping long enough to silence the enemy, at least temporarily. It is not possible that he knew how distinguished a target he was aiming at, — the lieutenant-general, an outlawed and particularly obnoxious major-general, and a brigadier-general who commands gunboats and has been the special terror of their waters.

There is some prospect that the exchange of prisoners may be resumed. At least some sort of negotiations in relation to it are pending, conducted on our part by General Butler, who is still Commissioner of Exchange with full powers.

Several flags of truce have passed between the lines — one to-day; and while too fond hopes should not be entertained, it may be that the Rebels have seen the folly and untenableness of their position, and will at last consent to a fair cartel. It is supremely absurd for them to refuse to exchange negroes, for it is the same as maintaining that our black soldiers are more valuable than their white ones. On the other hand, if they insist that the negro is property, General Butler has a sufficient number of captured horses to redeem all the colored soldiers in their possession, value for value.

It is understood that General Brooks, for some time in command of the Tenth Corps, has resigned from the army, and that his resignation has been accepted by the War Department. The feeling here seems to be that by some malignant complication of circumstances a deserving officer of long and honorable service is thus lost to the army, and at a time when such men can least be spared.

I believe Major-General A. A. Humphries, so long the admirable chief of staff to General Meade, has already been assigned to the Tenth Corps, *vice* General Brooks, resigned.

Lieutenant-Colonel Patton and 300 men of the New York Mounted Rifles, accompanied by Captains Shaffer and Manning of General Butler's staff, returned a day or two since from a ride across the country to Suffolk. They were absent six days, went and came by different routes, and gathered a great deal of information, captured two signal officers and a number of privates, brought off 200 horses and mules, a score or two of able-bodied negroes, and searched for prowling squads of Rebel cavalry, but which were too wary to risk an encounter, and too fleet to be compelled to one.

The unparalleled drouth has destroyed the crops and dried up the streams of all the region they traversed, considered one of the most fertile in the State. Corn especially seems to be beyond recovery, even should there be early and copious rains. It is quite possible that the remorseless drouth, which not only prevails throughout Virginia, but reaches down into North Carolina, may yet prove a valuable ally to our armies in the destitution — particularly of forage — which it must entail upon the enemy. Beyond temporary inconvenience, it does not affect us, and will not, for the James River, being tide-water, is not likely to fall below navigable capacity, and while it continues to float our keels the army will continue to be supplied.

THE SITUATION. — THE RAID IN MARYLAND.

HEADQUARTERS ARMY OF THE POTOMAC,
July 17, 1864, 8 A. M.

THE Rebel desperation which found manifestation and sought extrication from the ills they had in flight to those they knew not of beyond the Potomac, has not been permitted in the slightest degree to disturb this army in its purpose, or to relax its hold. It may be that it will tend to precipitate rather than to delay further operations.

I find the situation apparently identical with that of ten days ago when I went North. Perhaps there is less sharp-shooting in the trenches, and the weather is certainly much cooler, but still no rain. I pray for the day when I may cease the "damnable iteration" of "still no rain." However, the men are more comfortable than a fortnight ago, have become rested, are stronger, and now begin to speculate as to the next movement, which they universally imagine cannot be far distant. Very few are in hospital, whether from wounds or from disease. At no time since the outset of the campaign have the men been in better condition physically or in morale. Let no one, then, question the propriety of the half a month's respite that they have enjoyed. It has been of immense use; and were not sixty days of constant marching and fighting enough for one spell? Meanwhile the occasion has been seized to thoroughly reorganize the army — consolidation of commands, transfers of officers from commands where the casualties had left a surplus to other commands where the number had become too few for actual necessity; and other changes and reforms for which there had been no opportunity in this grand encounter, where camps have been but bivouacs, and battle-days have been sandwiched between nights of marching, and night marches between days of battles.

I don't know whether I ought to allude to the mingled humiliation and derision felt and expressed by the army on account of the ecstasies of fright which jostled and shivered and upset all Maryland and all Pennsylvania, when some 12,000

Rebels crossed the Potomac ten days ago. At least four weeks ago one of my letters contained the statement that nine decimated brigades of Ewell's old corps, averaging 1,000 each, had marched to meet Hunter. Now, General Grant has kept track of this force, knew that it did not follow Hunter, knew that it did turn down the Shenandoah Valley, and suspected it meant to rob stables and hen-roosts in Maryland, and so apprised the authorities at Washington. This force of 10,000 men, with the addition of such roving bands as Mosby's and Imboden's, has been all of that mighty invading host that raised the teapot tempest. I cannot help suspecting that the Government encouraged, fostered, nursed the fright, and for two reasons, viz. : to induce the Rebels to remain until arrangements looking to their capture could be made, and to induce the Northern States to forward men to hold the border this summer and fall while all the veterans should be sent to the front.

I judge that so far as any advantages the Rebels may reap from their raid are concerned, or so far as we are likely to inflict any loss upon them because of their temerity, the old couplet applies with equal force to either party: —

> "The King of France, with twenty thousand men,
> Marched up a hill and then marched down again."

A REBEL PLOT FRUSTRATED. — GENERAL BUTLER'S KITES. — EXAMINATION OF PRISONERS AND DESERTERS. — A SUNDAY IN CAMP.

GENERAL BUTLER'S HEADQUARTERS,
Sunday, July 16, 1864, 10 P. M.

THE army gunboat "Parke," Captain Fitch, lying off Herring Creek, a little above Charles City Court-House, noticed an unusual stir on shore yesterday afternoon. Men were seen to come down to the river, creep along the bank in the skirt of the woods, stop to peer about, — one of them was seen to gaze through a field glass, — then disappear. Now, Captain Fitch is a man of almost feminine curiosity, though all his other qualities are of the manly type. To see a human being in that quarter astonished him, much as Robinson, surnamed Crusoe, was astonished when he discovered tracks of human feet on the island Juan, surnamed Fernandez; only, his astonishment had no element of terror. With the view of determining the meaning of the phenomenon, he went on shore with twenty-five armed men. There were fifty Rebels there, and they shot at his party and wounded one man. They shot at the Rebels, and the Rebels went away at once, standing on no particular order of going.

Captain Fitch bivouacked on shore, and in the early morning — this morning — sent out scouts. His curiosity was not yet satisfied. One of them made a discovery. Drawn up among the bushes on the bank of Herring Creek were two light boats which had been carted from Richmond and launched in the creek, there concealed. In the boats were twelve torpedoes of the same class which have once or twice exploded beneath our vessels, and shattered them. Each contained 150 or more pounds of powder with anchors and grapples and percussion apparatus which would cause their explosion whenever a boat should pass over. It was evidently the purpose of the Rebel party to plant them in the river last night, and had they succeeded in doing so they could scarcely have failed to cause disaster, — all of which has been frustrated by the vigilance and promptness of the army gunboat "Parke," Captain Fitch commanding, who has since been commended by General Graham, the commander of all the army gunboats. These should be distinguished from the vessels of the navy, which are commanded by Acting Rear-Admiral Lee.

Benjamin Franklin sent a kite skyward, and brought down lightning. Benjamin Franklin Butler sends kites skyward and drops down among the Rebels fluttering hundreds of copies of the President's Amnesty Proclamation. The ingenuity of the device is great in either case, but the latter day Benjamin has a more praiseworthy purpose to serve. He achieves a patriotic end as successfully as the original Benjamin did a philosophical

one. The first fruits were reaped to-day, viz.: a number of deserters, who, on examination, declared that they were induced to come over by "o' lot o' han' bills thet kim down from o' big kite thet scaoted over whar we war."

I was permitted to listen to General Butler's examination to-day of a large number of prisoners, deserters, and refugees. The general, I believe, is noted among the legal fraternity for his skill in the cross-examination of witnesses. His skill and training were apparent in that specialty to-day. Such relentless and successful questioning for truth I never beheld before a jury. It was "as good as a play," and gave me a new idea of the acuteness and godlike divination of the human intellect. The first man to undergo this terribly searching scrutiny was a refugee from Richmond. "Sit down, sir," said the general, pleasantly. "Your name?" "Wm. Jeffers." Then followed a hundred questions in rapid succession and logical order — logical, though it required all my powers to always see their drift and aim. Mr. Jeffers was finally cornered. At first he was a "gentleman." Then he modified his statement; he was a "speculator." A re-modification and he was a "sporting man." And then, "Well — yes — general — I — suppose — they called me a — gambler." And finally, when, in explaining his antecedents, it became clear that he was but lately out of the Penitentiary, he said: "You've got it down pretty fine — I may as well cave." Then he told the whole truth, and I think nothing but the truth. Two other individuals of the same sort, who had come through with him, were examined in turn, and each was beautifully astonished at the self-revelations he was made to make. All had been living upon their wits, had been conscripted a dozen times, had bribed themselves off, until some weeks ago, when even a thousand dollars Confederate money failed to secure immunity, and then concealed themselves, and at last had paid $500 to be piloted through their lines, having first taken an oath not to reveal the name of their pilot. However, General Butler has the name of the pilot, who it appeared, works for gain, not for love of the Union, — traitor to fellow-traitors.

Next in order were the deserters and prisoners.

Before their examination was over, I had learned to distinguish one class from the other before they stated whether they came over voluntarily or had been nabbed. The deserters were intelligent, the prisoners far otherwise, for it is only your fools that are taken on picket, as a rule. The latter knew nothing, and General Butler soon dismissed them, as I do now. But the former were worth more. They each confirmed the statement I have before made, that the Rebel soldiers are told that those who desert are at once forced into our armies. Nevertheless, they do not quite believe it, and it is a subject of constant and earnest discussion among them, for they represent that nearly all would eagerly improve any chance of escaping from further fighting. They were examined separately, and were intelligent, if illiterate, and gave clear, straightforward answers, and all had been decided to come over by the Amnesty Proclamation, which, like the quality of mercy which is not strained, droppeth to the Rebels like the gentle rain, — droppeth not from clouds, but from kites.

To-day has been a real Sunday. Now, army Sundays are usually not distinguishable from other days, but to-day has been serene and almost solemn, like the Sabbath of a rural village. Not a shot has disturbed its supreme peacefulness. The inspections and dress parades which troops in garrison are subjected to of a Sunday, in the field, in face of the enemy, are wisely omitted. Religious services have been held in most of the hospitals, though I am aware of none in the camps. The day has been given to sleep, — literally a day of rest. But in other respects, most of the concomitants of a civilized Sunday have been wanting. No trudging of primly attired children to Sunday School in the morning; no gathering and gossiping before church doors; no flirting of young folks in church galleries; no good old ladies, very fair, very fat, and very forty, "sleepin' in meetin.'"

No conscientious deacons on either side of the pulpit alert for the places where Amens should be inserted, no quiet strolls of lovers in the woods just before sunset. And I am not aware of any courting in any "best room" in this vicinity this evening. But many a soldier has steadfastly gazed on the pictures of his loved ones, or the picture of his loved one, — has written brave words of fondness and longing, and brave words of hope and fortitude, and has communed with them, despite long absence and long distances, till his frame of mind was almost that of religion. Absence strengthens and purifies love. With these soldiers absence strengthens and purifies love, as ye shall all know "when the boys come home."

A BLESSED RAIN. — CAMP LIFE.

GENERAL BUTLER'S HEADQUARTERS, July 18, 1864.

OH, the rain! Not a fitful shower, blowing over from the south, with escort of angry lightnings and boisterous thunderings, as if commanded by Jupiter Tonans in person, then rolling away with rainbow pennant, and the sun shall mock its heels with fierce heats that scorch up from the earth in one short hour all its gratefulness, — but a steady flood, that lay all day yesterday banked up against the horizon between the north and the east and made no sign; only, we saw it was marching this way, and gradually it overcast the sky, and at dark it gave earnest of its approach by occasional drops, like shots of vedettes far ahead on the roads of its march, and then a smarter fusillade of drops like the advance of a skirmish line; and then at midnight it came down in a beating torrent like the resistless sweep of a line of battle, and till morning, and now all day the flood which yesterday we saw in the east has been descending in great riches where there was great poverty. It has been ten weeks of skyey brass and earthy ashes. One hundred thousand men had come to think rain synonymous with comfort and happiness, since the want of it they felt to be discomfort and misery. But the rain, the rain, the God-sent rain, it has come at last, and the more gratefully for its long-wished-for, long-delayed coming.

David of old said, "Let all the floods clap their hands," and Isaiah, "All the trees of the field shall clap their hands." They do so while I write — for the rain still falls, but now, in the waning storm, "as the small rain upon the tender herb, and as the showers upon the grass."

In Broadway, and even in a well-behaved country community, a gun, large or small, fired "on purpose" in the direction of human beings, at effective range, fired with malice aforethought, startles people; otherwise here; we have learned not to mind that sort of thing a bit. It does n't disturb the nap one turns over to take, when he first wakens of a morning, in the least. At the breakfast-table, of which Horace, who four weeks ago was the valet of Colonel Tobb, Fifty-seventh Virginia, is the ministering angel, cut in ebony as he is, the black wizard forever hovering around the sooted and fire-scorched vessels of our out-of-door *cuisine* (a wood fire on the ground, two kettles, two frying-pans, one tea-pot and one coffee-pot), making a weird scene, something like that of the witches' caldron in Macbeth, though the dishes he concocts, while almost as mysterious and composed of nearly as many ingredients as was that hell-broth, are exceedingly palatable, and that other is not supposed to have been especially so, — at the breakfast-table the dull, echo-like sounds which tell of death-shells falling over there into Petersburg do not provoke a remark.

It is so every morning and all the day — why say anything about it this morning? "Horace, did you wash yourself in the Appomattox yesterday?" "Yes, sah, ebery day dis eber so long, when 'cused me dat dis boy was n't 'spectable." "Don't forget to wash your shirt as well as yourself to-night, Horace." "Hab some anty-scobs, Mr. —— ?" says Horace, passing the onions and cucumbers sliced into vinegar in proportions of one to three. Mr. —— is one of "The Times" specials, and one of my messmates. "Anty-scobs" is Horace's contraction of "antiscorbs," the soldiers' contraction of "anti-scorbutics" applied to all vegetables, but particularly to onions. "Times" special helps himself liberally, on the principle that "This Rebellion must be crushed if it takes all the vegetables in the country." Waud, artist of "Harper's Weekly" ("Waud, initialed W.," the brother of his brother, the other artist), emulates his example. "The Tribune" special dextrously separates the milder vegetable from its odorous companion, and partakes largely of the former, and no one at the table scorns both.

In fact, it is remarkable how beefsteaks have ceased to charm, and what a fancy there is for vegetables. Discussion is had at the table of all sorts of things, from the taking of Richmond to the novels which are being read by one or more of the mess, from Grant's campaign to the programme for the day which each has marked out for himself. He of the "Harper" and he of "The Times" contribute the wit, and he of "The Tribune" adds a dash of cynicism, — for the breakfast hour is too early for his habits, and he is in a bad humor, — while the staff-officer at my right is our "Autocrat of the Breakfast-table."

And all the time these guns have been booming away as a matter of course, attracting no attention, suggesting no remark. You think us heartless, unfeeling, extra-stoical. Not so; the very men who fire guns do so in a kind of emotionless routine, and all the other thousands have become so accustomed to the noise they make that they regard it not. Only the sharp-shooter on the line of the trenches is all alive to his work, for with him it is life and death. With him it is constantly the fierce joy of battle, which comes to others only on battle-days, and these are not battle-days.

There is only the friction of armies in close contact, not the awful shock and crush of armies impelled upon each other. The outer particles suffer from the attrition, the main body scarcely vibrates; but soon perhaps it shall be shaken to the core with the quake of conflict, for who knoweth what a day may bring forth?

Having written the above, I swung a rubber coat over my shoulders, and stepped out. Bump, pound, boom! — why, there was heavy cannonading in the distance, and I learned the noise of it had been booming loudly in the humid air for hours. Yet I had not noticed it more than I used to the practice thrumming on a piano in a room beneath my college dormitory. A telegram to these headquarters says it is on the Fifth and Ninth Corps, front, and is doing us no harm, however it may be with the enemy.

COLORED TROOPS.

ARMY OF THE POTOMAC, July 20, 1864.

As bearing with much pertinence and force upon the questions touching negro troops, and for the sake of the information concerning the management in the Department of the Gulf, I make the following extracts from a letter received here which has fallen under my eyes. The writer has a colored command in Louisiana, and writes to his brother, an officer in this army. I extract only those paragraphs that have relation to black soldiers. The letter is under date of July 3, 1864.

". . . Then, too, I believe in General Butler's proper will and understanding upon the colored question. General Smith, too, I am gratified to see, is converted at last, and that by the handsome conduct of the black troops under his command. By George! it was glorious, — just the thing.

"It was most fit and proper that just that thing should happen, that good conduct and very useful service of the colored men. We actually envy you and the men of your corps; we feel as if you had done rather more than your fair share of the hard fighting, and were monopolizing too much of that sense of satisfaction to which men are entitled who have nobly done their whole duty in a trying time — and all this to *our* exclusion, for we *are* excluded. We have done literally nothing but stand agape, or rest upon our spades and wait for news of your exploits. That is our feeling — it is that we have been deprived of a share in just these services which your colored troops have lately rendered to the country, and made the country resound with the fame of it too. . . . *Why don't they order us to go up and help you?* The only thing they give colored troops here to do in the way of duty is fatigue duty, working on the forts, etc., while not a white man of all the thousands of enlisted soldiers here, until yesterday, has been required to lift a spade. No military or other necessity can justify this. There is a whole brigade of 'us' here, but we are not drilled in tactics, are not being prepared for fighting, not being qualified to meet the murdering wretches of Fort Pillow on equal terms. Who can guarantee that some day we may not be *compelled* to meet them? You know me well enough to understand that I am not likely to shrink under *any* circumstances, favorable or unfavorable, but I *demand* the *right* for my people to be disciplined as fighting soldiers. I demand their right to be prepared for every exigency, and then to be put forward in line of battle side by side with the heroes of Petersburg, and not left like rats in a hole, like sheep in a pen, to be butchered with impunity at future Fort Pillows. It was not much better at Port Hudson nor anywise different at Baton Rouge. In this department colored troops have everywhere been treated as though their business was to be exclusively digging, and not fighting. I'll tell you what I think. I think under such circumstances it was a cowardly act to give them arms at all. It seems that they are armed, and some fighting is expected of them in some possible contingencies, say in a tight squeeze, when their help or *any*body's help is gladly accepted. But under ordinary circumstances, when the sky is clear and there is no thick smoke of battle around, it is thought they are only fit to dig, or at least doubted whether they can be safely trusted to fight as soldiers, and therefore never sufficiently drilled to fight as soldiers. Look at the palpable absurdity of the thing — the English of which is a mixture of two mean things. One I have named above when I called it *cowardly*, and I shall name the other when I call it *treachery*. . . . We have been ordered up here to relieve another colored brigade and to dig this fort. One plausible reason assigned for sending us was that we might get recruits and fill the regiments — all skeletons now. We have been here a fortnight and not a solitary recruit has been gained, and we shall not get ninety here in the next ninety days. It was so at Port Hudson, so at Baton Rouge, so at Alexandria, and up Red River.

The colored regiments are not recruited as they should and might be. . . .

"Of what use are we here? Cannot we be got away?

"General Banks will never do anything for us, rely upon that; General Emory don't care anything about us; General Franklin is away on leave; General Roberts would help us to get North if he stays, but I think he will soon leave; General Ullman would like to see us filled up and drilled, but he is powerless.

"You see my reasons for wishing to get out of this department. They are: (1) satisfied by six months' trial that we shall never be recruited; and (2) satisfied by six months' trial (and six months more before I joined) that they will never drill us for fighting, but use us mainly for fatigue and guard duty, even if we should be recruited. Do not doubt this, whatever pretence you may see made to the contrary. Now you are tired of this, and so am I. It is now the 'glorious Fourth' before I have done. Send me a letter soon, and tell me about all your battles. God bless you, my dear brother, and keep you safe. Your affectionate brother."

Now the above statements and revelations by all who know the writer are accepted as unvarnished facts — facts which are all wrong and need righting.

Such outrageous violations of the teachings of the barest, baldest, commonest justice toward these black men, who have now proved themselves to be made of the sterner stuff of which soldiers are made, is simply despicable, — as the writer declares, is "cowardly," is "treacherous." Moreover, "it is worse than a crime, it is a blunder." Let the responsibility be traced, and this wickedness and foolishness be instantly put away. An easy and proper solution of the case would be to forward those troops from that department to this.

There are abundant proofs of wide-spread disaffection in the Rebel ranks! — that whole regiments are tired of the war, are convinced that they can never conquer, and are almost openly canvassing the propriety of desertion *en masse*.

It would "convey information to the enemy" for me to state all that is known as to the prevalence and definitiveness of this feeling in the Rebel army. It can be referred to only as a known fact, the evidence in support of which may not be given. Sufficient to say that it is circumstantial, concordant, cumulative, and will some day have its demonstration in accomplished facts.

By order of General Grant, subject to the approval of the President, Major-General Ord has been assigned to the command of the Eighteenth Army Corps, and Major-General Birney to the command of the Tenth Corps.

The publication of a late order makes it unnecessary to longer withhold the statement that the Nineteenth Corps has arrived from New Orleans. It is an important addition to the army and means business. Scarcely a heavy gun to-day, and but few small ones.

VIII.

AN ARTILLERY DUEL.

CITY POINT, VA., July 20, 8 A. M.

THERE was constant and rapid artillery firing all day yesterday on the front of the Fifth and Ninth Corps, joined in at length by the Second and Eighteenth Corps. The enemy began it. Why he should have desired the myriad shotted duel is inconceivable, for he accomplished nothing, and may have suffered something by it. He should have known that in artillery we are strongest here as well as off Cherbourg, though the demonstration of the fact is not quite yet so palpable. During the day there was no musketry beyond skirmishing, but from this point it was heard in more volume at intervals throughout the night, while the cannonading went down with the sun.

The following order has been made: —

HEADQUARTERS OF THE UNITED STATES,
CITY POINT, VA., July 19, 1864.

SPECIAL ORDERS No. 62 (Extract). III. All troops of the Nineteenth Corps arriving at this point will report to Major-General B. F. Butler, commanding Department of Virginia and North Carolina, at Bermuda Hundred, for orders.

By command of

Lieutenant-General GRANT.

E. S. PARKER, assistant Adjutant-General.
To Major-General B. F. BUTLER, commanding
Department of Virginia and North Carolina.

If anything besides the revocation of the order assigning General Butler to Fortress Monroe were needed to attest a complete vindication and approval of the part he has borne in this campaign, the above would seem to be abundantly sufficient.

AN ARTILLERY DUEL. 175

THE MEN IN HOSPITALS. — RETURNING MASSACHUSETTS REGIMENTS.

GENERAL BUTLER'S HEADQUARTERS,
Wednesday, July 20, 1864.

ALL know how a phrase, a couplet, perhaps only a word, or it may be a few notes of music, with or without as many words of a familiar song, will sometimes haunt one's thoughts till he catches himself incessantly repeating to himself the one little thing, as a refrain to all else he may think, or say, or do. And so something has recalled to me the first two lines of a poem which as a boy I used to declaim of a Saturday in chapel. I can recollect only the one couplet of "Bingen on the Rhine." Strive as I may, all the rest will not come back, but remains like the sense of a dream, the shape of which cannot be defined, while these lines have grown vivid and almost terrible in their haunting power: —

"A soldier of the Legion lay dying in Algiers,
There was lack of woman's nursing, there was dearth of woman's tears."

I think it first came to me one day when walking through a hospital where "soldiers of the Legion lay dying," and there was naught of "woman's nursing," naught of "woman's tears," for there was naught of woman's presence — and it has haunted me ever since.

There were assiduous and kindly disposed men, themselves hardly convalescent, nursing their comrades. These were stricken with fevers and "looking like very old pictures of very young men," and others torn and mutilated by wounds, all suffering, some dying, and only men for nurses. There *was* one woman, and she was ministering to a man who would die before sunset. I doubt not her devotion shrined his departing soul with an efficacy that does not always belong to priestly oil. And that woman, I now know, has the right to come even into a field-hospital, if by that she can relieve a broken heart, for within one year her three sons have fallen in battle.

It is one of the peculiar hardships of the war that these things must be. There is feeling and self-sacrifice and heroism enough among the women of this country, but they may not come to the field. A few may. One in ten thousand is fitted with the extraordinary training and qualification demanded by the nature of the case. And there is proper work for one in ten thousand who would gladly come if they were permitted. But as many ten-thousandth ones as there is work for are here now. I speak of those field-hospitals at the front. In the great hospitals further north it is otherwise. Let noble women go into every ward of them and do their work with all their deft hands and all their tender sympathies.

Yet how our boys here, falling like leaves in this greatest of hero wars, stretched awhile, before they go, on narrow couches, and shutting their weary eyes to think of their homes and the dear ones there — homes dear to them as "Fair Bingen on the Rhine" to the "soldier of the Legion" — would have joy, some of them, maybe, would have life itself, come to them could woman's hovering presence, her gentle hands, and gentler voice be with them in their weary, weary hours of waiting. It is pitiful.

It is comfort to know that there are other fields where the good and brave women of the country may labor, and I know there are thousands of whom it may be said, "Drums do not throb like these hearts; bullets do not patter like these tears!" There must be women the power of whose souls has been vitalized and expanded by this war, who are even now contriving and toiling for "our boys." God speed them!

Regiments are continually going home on the expiration of their terms of service. Among the last which have gone are the Eighteenth and Twentieth Massachusetts, historical regiments. Would that I could catalogue the names of the heroes, Bay-State born and nurtured and taught, who have fallen from these.

Practically, the most important consideration is that so many trained and valuable officers are thus lost to the service. Of the Twentieth, Oliver Wendell Holmes, Jr., the "Captain" of "My Hunt" in an Atlantic of two years ago, was an officer. Captain Holmes served more than two years sturdily and chivalrously as a line officer, was three times severely wounded, and in this campaign has been zealous and indefatigable as a member of the Sixth Corps staff, has always been conspicuously daring, and capably efficient, and he goes out of the service because his regiment does, not because he would taste the sweets of home and Boston.

Another instance. First Lieutenant Fisher A. Baker has been adjutant of the Eighteenth Massachusetts during its three years of service, than which no regiment has a better reputation, and next to the colonel an adjutant helps to make a regiment. All through the Peninsula campaign, at the Second Bull Run, at Antietam, Fredericksburg, Chancellorsville, Gettysburg, Rappahannock Station, and now from the Wilderness to Petersburg, the Eighteenth has been one of those trustworthy regiments that commanders learn to depend upon, and through it all Lieutenant Baker has been the adjutant, escaping promotion because he was so good an adjutant that the colonels would not let him go to higher rank in other regiments. I said this regiment had gone home. Nevertheless 150 of its veterans have re-enlisted and remain. It would be a good thing if with these for a nucleus the organization could be preserved by additions of new men. Raw troops would so speedily crystallize about the veterans, would so soon learn to take pride in the fame and traditions of the regiment, would so soon gather *esprit de corps*, that it were a great pity not to retain for the war the Eighteenth Massachusetts. The regiment has graduated two brigadier-generals, General James Barnes, and General Joseph Hayes. The former brought it into the field, and the latter was its colonel during some of its hardest fights, and was promoted soon after being severely wounded in the Wilderness.

REBEL NEWS. — JOE JOHNSTON SUPERSEDED BY GENERAL HOOD. — ALLEGED DEATH OF LIEUTENANT-GENERAL GRANT.

GENERAL BUTLER'S HEADQUARTERS,
Thursday, July 21, 1864, 8 A. M.

RICHMOND papers of yesterday announce that General Joe Johnston has been superseded by Major-General J. B. Hood, who, it will be recollected, lost a leg at Gettysburg, and was immoderately praised by the correspondent of "The London Times."

The same papers announce and comment on the death of General Grant. (I saw the general yesterday, apparently very much alive.) They state that his death — he being a general who led his men to slaughter, but never to victory — is a great loss to their armies, unless, since we were so stupid as to consider him a very Napoleon, his loss shall cast despondency upon the whole North, armies and people.

THE SANITARY COMMISSION.

CITY POINT, VA., Saturday, July 23, 1864.

IN my note-book are several pages of memoranda touching the Sanitary Commission, its organization, its methods of operation, and the work it is doing in this army; and the arrangement into something like order of these memoranda must constitute to-day's letter.

Simultaneously with the marching of the army from the Chickahominy for the James, and with the clearing out of the hospitals at White House, the Sanitary Commission, men and effects, shipped for City Point, and reached here in advance of the troops.

At White House stores had been distributed through its agency at the average rate of $5,000 per day; $50,000 during the ten days of service there.

AN ARTILLERY DUEL.

It must not be supposed that the Commission had hitherto neglected this department. On the contrary, during the early summer, when this department had a campaign of its own, a fair proportion of its goods — goods material and goods otherwise — had been diverted in this direction, where Dr. McDonald, the same who was captured at Gettysburg and held several months in Richmond, was in charge, and had his organization "well in hand."

The main work is always at its water base, which is always the same as that of the army. Dr. J. H. Douglas, associate secretary of the commission, is its "lieutenant-general commanding" its operation before Richmond, and here are his headquarters. Next in authority is Dr. A. McDonald, with the rank of inspector. Two other inspectors are on the ground, viz.: Dr. W. F. Swalm and Dr. W. C. Stevens, each with his appropriate and distinct duties. Mr. John A. Anderson has charge of the transportation and issuing of supplies, controls the boats, and makes the requisitions on the home depots, is in short quartermaster of the commission. These are all located here. On the immediate front, the superintendent of "Field Relief" is Mr. J. Warner Johnson; and with the hospitals and ambulance trains, as superintendent of the "Auxiliary Relief Corps," is Honorable F. B. Fay, late mayor of Chelsea, Mass.

All told, the persons attached to the commission number some 200, but the force is always largely increased by volunteers from Washington and elsewhere, who are set to work with the special relief corps under Mr. Fay. About fifty of these are regular employees, and have been working as now through all this campaign, and many of them much longer.

The first thing is to get the stores here from the grand depots at Washington, Baltimore, and Philadelphia. For this the Commission has two steam propellers regularly chartered and in constant service, and then in emergencies steamers are chartered for the trip, as in the case of the "Commander," from New York, with vegetables, lately, and another of the same class from Philadelphia.

Then here at City Point are a number of commodious barges:

the receiving barge, from which goods are issued in the original packages, and the issuing barge, on board of which are the offices, and where packages are broken for distribution in certain channels, as will be explained anon. Besides, there is a little tug necessary in the harbor for the timely towing about of these barges and the transportation for short distances of small cargoes.

The land transportation consists of 23 four-horse wagons, 128 wagon horses, and 18 saddle horses, all in constant use.

The manner of distribution is through the "Field Relief" and the "Auxiliary Relief," the former at the front with the troops, the latter at the hospitals. In an emergency, like that the day before the Fourth of July, when there is a large quantity of perishable articles to be issued at once, wagons are asked and obtained from the army authorities. On that occasion, by order of General Grant, his chief commissary, Colonel Morgan, took charge of the matter and afforded means and facilities; but usually the Commission's own means are sufficient.

The Field Relief has an organization in each corps, ramifying to divisions and brigades, and also has a branch with the navy. These make requisitions from day to day upon the depot at the water base for such things as are needed at once; wagons immediately start out with them, and they are distributed prudently, evenly, and systematically. To each division there is a "Sanitary" wagon and a "Sanitary" tent. The organization with the hospitals is not less perfect. To each of these also there is a wagon and a tent and a body of men, to which is added a kitchen, where articles of light diet are prepared for the patients.

No article is ever issued except on the requisition of a responsible party, usually either an agent of the Commission or a surgeon, who, as occasionally happens, is unable to obtain from the Government supplies the things he requires.

But the active benevolence of the Commission does not end in judicious and systematic distribution of supplies. It is "zealous in good works," instant in season and out of season, and does with all its might whatever its hands find to do. Many of its agents are young men preparing for the ministry, theological students from Andover and elsewhere, who, administering and ministering, are passing their novitiate in the best possible school of training and of usefulness, to which pulpit and parish will be largely indebted years and years hence. These are ubiquitous, in the trenches as well as in the hospitals. They write letters for those too feeble to otherwise send a word to their friends.

After battles, when the wounded pour into the hospitals in overwhelming numbers, they aid the surgeons by dressing the more trifling wounds, and as their assistants in the more serious cases. At those times feeding stations are established at different points, and food is given to all who are hungry, for it always happens that men, besides the wounded, during and just after an engagement, become separated from their commands and channels of supply. On such occasions, not only crackers and coffee are found to be needed, but arm-slings and crutches. Even now, when there has been no late battle here at City Point, no returning regiment stops an hour on its way home without being given a substantial meal at the hands of the Sanitary Commission, and many a man of them gets a shirt or a pair of pantaloons, that he may be presentable when his friends meet him.

All the burials from hospitals the last forty days, from Belle Plain to City Point, have been made by the Commission, always with a decent interment, and generally with religious services by a clergyman. In every instance a head-board, properly and indelibly marked, is placed at the grave, and a record is kept and forwarded to the Hospital Directory of the Commission at Washington, in the following form: —

```
Name . . . . . . . . . . . . . . . . . . . .
Rank . . . . . . .  Company . . . . . . . . .
Regiment and State  . . . . . . . . . . . . .
In  . . . . A. C. . .  Div. Hospital, at  . . . .
Date and place of death. . . . . . . . . . . . . .
Cause of death  . . . . . . . . . . . . . . .
Where buried . . . . . . . . . . . . . . . .
The above statement was taken by . . . . . . . . 186
```

The effects of the deceased are then collected and sent to Washington, and if his friends are known are despatched from there by express, accompanied by a letter of particulars and of sympathy.

Such, then, in brief, is the work of the Sanitary Commission in this army, and it is fully appreciated by officers and soldiers. Dr. Douglas has received grateful letters from Smith, Burnside, Warren, and other generals, from division and regimental surgeons, and even more grateful ones from rank and file. When a Sanitary wagon appears in the camps, the jolly glee with which it is welcomed, the shouts of "Good for you, Sanitary!" "Here's your bully San. Com.!" "How are you, Sanitary Onions?" and all that sort of good-humor testify what "the boys" think of it. One of them lays by for it $2 out of his monthly $13, because the Sanitary took care of him at Gettysburg.

Some interesting — almost romantic — incidents might be woven into this letter if the writer were not sleepy. One must be told — how a soldier in hospital was given a towel and told to keep it for his own; how the next day he shouted to the agent till he got his attention, and then said : " You know that towel you gave me ? I know where it came from. Look here, that's my mother's name in the corner ! She gave it to the Sanitary and — is n't it funny ? — it came straight to me. That's what I call jolly." And so it was, for there was only one chance in a hundred thousand that the old lady's offering would reach her own boy.

Were I to make a suggestion to the Commission, and to the benevolent who sustain it, I would say, give the boys a supply of tobacco !

IX.

IN FRONT OF PETERSBURG.

THE REGULARS.

HEADQUARTERS OF GENERAL BUTLER, July 26, 1864.

ON the breaking out of the war, and with the first call for volunteers, two lieutenants of the regular army sought and obtained permission to take service in volunteer regiments. Their applications were the first of that nature made, and were the first granted. By a coincidence, their requests bore even date, as did their order of detail. These two officers have since become pretty widely known as Major-General Warren and Brigadier-General Kilpatrick. The former took the field as lieutenant-colonel of the Fifth N. Y. (Duryee Zouaves), and the latter with the same position in the Harris Light Guard (cavalry). They saw that the war must be mainly fought by volunteers, and hastened to identify themselves with the arm most likely to afford the largest opportunities for service; and the course of the war has shown the correctness of their forecast. The regular army as a distinct organization has been overshadowed by the volunteer host, and the officers named have borne a more prominent and honorable part than they could have made for themselves serving strictly in their own corps, — though such a soldier as G. K. Warren must have been a marked man, and have risen to high command in any war the world ever saw.

But as the armies swelled, others of the regulars took rank as volunteers, the more prominent as general officers, those less so with regiments, usually of the States from which they originally went to West Point, while a still larger number were distributed on staff duty. Then, with the reorganization by Congressional enactment of the old army, the creation of new regiments, and the consequent transfers and vacancies, a great many captains and lieutenants in nowise superior to those of the same grade in volunteer regiments were appointed to the regulars from civil life. Recruiting at that stage of the contest was easy, and the ranks were filled with the same material that swelled the ranks of the volunteers, with only a bare nucleus of veterans in each regiment. So that from all these causes the distinction between the one and the other, even so long ago as the Peninsular campaign, was more nominal than real. It will be conceded, however, that the regular regiments earliest became well drilled in tactics, but owing to a sprinkling of old sergeants and the like quite as much as to any superior discipline enforced by officers of higher grade.

Five regular infantry regiments — the Tenth, Eleventh, Twelfth, Fourteenth, and Seventeenth — have formed a part of the Army of the Potomac from the outset. These, with the Fifth New York Volunteers, and a number of other New York regiments, whose numbers I have forgotten, constituted on the Peninsula and until after Antietam the First Division, Fifth Corps, commanded by General Sykes, when that officer succeeded to the corps, and General R. D. Ayres assumed the division. Finally, in the reorganization of commands just prior to the opening of this campaign, the regiments named, with the One hundred and fortieth and One hundred and forty-sixth New York, still under General Ayres, became a brigade of Griffin's Division. It is of the services of this brigade, now the First Brigade, General Joseph Hayes, Second Division, General Ayres, Fifth Corps, Warren's, since the army crossed the Rapidan, of which I propose to now speak particularly.

I remember that Griffin's Division led the advance on that first day of the campaign, and on that first night took position on a ridge in the Wilderness, facing the quarter whence the enemy might come — whence he did come. The order of march for the next day contemplated that Griffin should continue marching, leaving his position on the right to a division of the Sixth Corps, for there was no intention of fighting in the Wilderness, and there was to have been another day's march before the enemy was expected. But Lee was too swift to permit it, and early that Thursday morning Griffin reported Rebel columns moving toward him down the roads from Mine Run, and on the ground of his first night's bivouac he fought them two days. It was the centre of our line, and Grant and Meade established their headquarters directly in its rear. Griffin advanced two brigades, Ayres' and Bartlett's, and brought on the battle of the Wilderness, which, and not Antietam and not Gettysburg, was the culminating battle of this war. These two brigades, then, first grappled with the Rebels on the highest historic ground of the country.

Both suffered severe loss, but Ayres' regulars lost in one-half an hour one-fourth their number — a stern initiation to a campaign which 80 days have not ended. Two days on that dark and bloody ground, and then the Fifth Corps, again in the advance, is the first to meet the enemy at Spottsylvania, and then again the regulars and their companion regiments are put into the thickest, and again acquit themselves as of the bravest, and are again more than decimated. Their next severe engagement was on the right of the line at Cold Harbor. There the two brigades of Bartlett and Ayres interposed, and first stayed, and then repulsed an entire corps of the Rebels that rushed down like a torrent upon the Ninth Corps, which from fancied security was in no position to breast the storm when it suddenly burst. But so great and instant service could not be rendered without proportionate loss, which again fell most heavily upon Ayres' Brigade — indeed the losses in this brigade have been exceptionally severe in nearly every engagement. Since Cold Harbor the brigade has borne its share of the marching and fighting. Its losses since the 5th of May now amount to something over 2,000, including over 70 officers — 2,000 from one brigade in one campaign! Had all the army suffered as severely, the entire loss would be fully double what it is.

Some weeks ago, General Ayres, having disciplined and fought the brigade till it had come to be pointed out as a model, was raised to the command of the division, and General Joseph

Hayes, just returned to the army recovered from a wound received at the Wilderness, and with the eagle he then wore exchanged for a star, was assigned to the brigade, which is still the largest in the corps. General Hayes was by profession a civil engineer, but with such military instincts as made him captain of an independent company in Davenport, Iowa, just before the war. Offered the colonelcy of a regiment from that State, he declined it for a majority in a Massachusetts regiment — the Eighteenth. His intimate friend and associate in railroad engineering accepted an Iowa regiment, and is now Major-General G. M. Dodge, commanding a corps in front of Atlanta. General Hayes' present command is the first instance where the regulars have been commanded by a volunteer officer, an evidence of the confidence reposed in him, a young brigadier, and that there are now no jealousies between regulars and volunteers.

Such, then, is an inadequate sketch of the services, the battles and losses of one brigade. I do not hold it up as unparalleled; on the contrary, it is but one of many, between whom no distinctions may be made. But I have thought it worth while to note the deeds of these regulars, not for the sake of the officers, but that of the rank and file, who, not accredited to any particular State, have lost, perhaps, something of the recognition due them. Nor should the volunteer regiments serving in the same brigade be lost sight of; one of them, the Fifth New York, was trained by a lieutenant-colonel, who now, as major-general, commands the corps of which it is a part. In no soldierly quality has there been a shade of difference, fighting side by side as they have been, between regular and volunteer. After three years of such war, who shall claim better training, more veteran skill, than those who responded to its first blast and have not once faltered until this day?

At present, the brigade, — remember its style, First Brigade, Second Division, Fifth Corps, when you come to read accounts of succeeding battles, — like most of the army, is in that admirable condition best described by one word, *effective*.

GENERAL BUTLER'S HEADQUARTERS,
Thursday, July 28, Sunrise.

Hancock and Sheridan marched night before last all night, and yesterday at one P. M. began crossing the James, on a pontoon newly laid, a little below the one connected with Foster's lodgment at Deep Bottom, on the left bank. Barlow's Division, the first over, pushed rapidly ahead, swinging up the river, and flanking the Rebel position opposed to Foster. 230 men of the Eighty-third Pennsylvania, Colonel Lynch, Miles' Brigade, charged and captured a battery of four 20-pound Parrotts, with a loss of only 20. The guns proved to be those of Ashley's battery, lost by General Smith in the early part of the campaign. While this attack was making in flank, Foster demonstrated in front, which, doubtless, helped toward the result. Hancock then, as his divisions came over, advanced a mile up the river, and Sheridan, Torbert's and Gregg's Divisions, crossing immediately afterward, turned off on his right, and with Merritt's Brigade, struck the New-Market and Long-Bridge road at its intersection with the Malvern-Hill road, some four miles above the latter place. One regiment charged and stampeded 300 Rebel cavalry, taking a dozen prisoners. The position now was, Foster with troops from the Tenth Corps, with his left resting on the James, the Second Corps on his right, then Sheridan's cavalry feeling out all the roads, and swinging round upon the enemy's left flank, the general direction of the line being from southwest to northeast. But the Rebel position was a range of hills, very strong, and he was known to have two full divisions,— Kershaw's, of Longstreet's Corps, and Wilcox's of Hill's. It was almost night, and no further advance was attempted. The casualties number perhaps 50. In simply holding his line the day before, Foster had lost as many. Fully 100 prisoners were taken; 200 was the number reported, but I could not count so many. If the day's operations did not effect all that was expected, and if nothing more should come of it, the movement may be considered successful, and rather useful in the cheering effect of guns and prisoners taken without loss, and in the treat it affords in the breaking of the monotony, that had begun to look like a siege. Generals Grant and Ingalls were on the field.

THE OPERATIONS OF THURSDAY.

HEADQUARTERS OF GENERAL BUTLER,
Thursday, July 28, 1864.

THE operations on the left bank of the James to-day have been more stirring than important. About ten o'clock an infantry brigade with a body of dismounted cavalry attacked Gregg's cavalry on our extreme right.

Gregg fought his men dismounted, was driven at first with a loss of one gun, but finally stayed their advance. At one o'clock Merritt's Brigade of Torbert's Division, posted some distance to the left of Gregg, and next to the infantry, sustained, dismounted, a regular line-of-battle attack, and the fight was sharp and well sustained.

The First United States, Sixth Pennsylvania, and Sixth and Ninth New York, sustained the shock of double their own numbers of veteran Rebel infantry. The First United States particularly distinguished itself. At the end of half an hour we still held the ground, and the enemy sullenly withdrew.

Our loss during the day is 157 killed, wounded, and missing; only 19 missing.

We captured two battle flags and lost one gun, buried 158 Rebel dead, and have 106 prisoners.

The enemy was all day moving troops from Petersburg toward Richmond. It is probable that the demonstration beyond the James is to induce him to do that particular thing.

THE OPERATIONS OF WEDNESDAY.

HEADQUARTERS OF GENERAL BUTLER,
July 28, 1864.

A DESPATCH transmitted to you this morning gave the manner and the results of the operations of yesterday, but it has occurred to me that there was material for a letter in a personal narrative of the day which should include more details of its events, — hence the present writing.

All the night before, infantry and cavalry and artillery and wagon trains were marching by these headquarters. The night was very dark and fires had been built along the roads to direct the line of march. The Second Corps had been in reserve on Meade's line, and was chosen for the demonstration on the left bank of the James, 15 miles distant. The marching must be at night, else the enemy would make a parallel column and defeat the movement. At four o'clock P. M. the rank and file struck and packed their shelter tents, and the different headquarters located in the edge of woods and beneath sheltering bowers a little reluctantly and disconsolately saw their camp gods (classic for camp-comforts) stowed in close compass, and piled into mule-drawn wagons, and these wagons formed into the "Headquarters train," which they should see again, — doubtful when. Orderlies brought horses, all groomed and saddled, to the spot, and as the soldiers form, with slung knapsacks and shouldered arms, headquarters gallops to the head and the order is "Column, — *for-w-a-r-d!*"

The first half of this march is to the pontoon, near Point of Rocks on the Appomattox. It is two miles over a plain, stumpy, brambled, and cumbered with fallen timber, and then through pine woods, by crooked army roads, and then by the "river road," an old country road, which is one long vista, straight and arched by rows of cedars four miles further ; and when beyond that, winding to the left, down a steep hill to the bridge. And the long column files over the muffled way, muffled with strewn hay, that no sound of its myriad tramplings shall be borne to the enemy, and the long bridge, resting literally on the element "unstable as water," is as true as if based on ledges of granite, though it rises and falls with dreamy undulations, like those which fleck with light and shadow prairie wheatfields, when summer winds are blowing.

Over the Appomattox and now up a sinuous gorge, the bed of which great labor has made into a road. Emerging from the gorge, by the light of a great fire at its head, the column wheels square to the right, and then, following a chain of guide-fires, passes a little in front of my tent, and disappears in the deep gloom of woods that extend nearly to the James River, five miles away. Say that it is midnight, and a very dark midnight. Just opposite us is one of the fires that blaze the way, affording light, as they pass on this side of it, to show us a little of the stream at a time, — a dozen soldiers moving in rapid order, coming out of the night and going into the night, and others take their places, and disappear like the first, and so continually, except anon it may be a few horsemen at the head of a brigade or regiment, and then we hear a clatter of sabre-scabbards; or perhaps a battery is going by, and we catch in our eyes a sheen of light, glancing from the brightness of the guns, — but these only briefly, for close after either and all is that flow of armed men, like a river, passing, still passing, but never passed. It was still passing two hours later, when I crept beneath the mosquito bars, whose folds hang in elegant drapery over a bed of two blankets, spread upon elastic pine saplings, raised a foot from the ground.

The head of the column reached James River at sunrise and began crossing at seven o'clock; meanwhile Sheridan's cavalry had also been marching all night, crossing the Appomattox on the lower pontoon and falling in behind Hancock.

In the early morning (yesterday), after breakfasting more rapidly than is recommended by "Hall's Journal of Health," "George" brings around my horse and straps a rubber coat to the pommel of the saddle, while "Horace" crowds a luncheon of beef sandwiches and jelly, a flask not filled with water, and a dozen cigars into the saddle pouches, and then a jolly gallop to Jones' Neck, the tongue of land from the extremity of which are laid the pontoons over which the troops are still tramping when I arrive. Pressing over the bridge and up the bank, I meet four big black 20-pound Parrotts (guns, not birds, though they have a way of talking loudly and well sometimes), which have already been taken by the One hundred and Eighty-third Pennsylvania, Barlow's advance. It is a rough ride across a deep-furrowed field. (I never yet crossed a Virginia field parallel with its ditches and I think they must have a trick of swinging around broadsides on the approach of a horseman, compelling him to take them transversely.) To the point in the skirt of the woods where the guns were taken, Barlow had advanced over this field on the enemy's flank, turning his works. At the same time Foster with his brigade of the Tenth Corps from his position higher up the river was threatening in his front. The pressure was too great and those Rebels did not stay to make much of a fight, — they gave us the four guns which I saw going to the rear. Each was inscribed "Before Richmond, May 29, 1864," and we recognized them as the guns lost near Fort Darling on that date. Two or three dead men in Rebel gray lying in the trench close by indicate the precise place where they were planted. They had been brought out only that morning and had not yet opened their grim mouths.

We have now struck the river road from Malvern Hill to Richmond. A twitch of my right heel (I wear spurs) encourages my horse. Does "The Tribune" know what an efficient servant it has in "White Frank"?— enduring as iron, ambitious as Cæsar, tireless and powerful as watch-spring muscle can make a horse, endowed with his full share of horse-sense, proud of the races he has won, as he has been the pride of two colonels shot from his back at Gettysburg and Wilderness. There are woods on either side of this road, and on its left are the Rebel works, relinquished only two hours ago. A mile and we (not you, reader, but Frank and I) emerge on open ground to find we are on the front, to see General Hancock sitting in his shirt-sleeves close by, the picket line a little way in the field beyond, occasionally firing, Gibbon's Division in line of battle following the contour of the woods where we are, and on the range of hills, across the fields, the position to which the Rebels fell back and where they can be seen as plainly as though only across Broadway. Barlow is pushing through the woods off on the right. With Hancock are Sheridan and staff. General Sheridan physically is the smallest major-general I ever saw, but mentally one of the largest.

I ride with general and staff (I have a friend on that staff), by a wide detour through wood-roads that nothing but cavalry could ever have found, till we strike the head of the cavalry column, which is to operate miles away on our right, and if possible on the enemy's left flank. Debouching on the New-Market road the enemy's cavalry is seen on the hills beyond; not waiting to ascertain his numbers, a regiment is rapidly deployed and scampers over the ravine, and up the rising ground. We have dismounted in order to get nearer and see all within carbine range. Now an actual cavalry charge is not the ideal cavalry charge. The riders do not go all abreast, in a serried phalanx. They go all in a scamper according to the speed of the horses and the daring of their riders; two variable quantities that scatter the cavalrymen like so many stampeded wild horses. But the sight is none the less exciting, and some of us do not repress a cheer or two. The enemy, though 300 strong, do not stand, and we have a dozen prisoners.

A dismounted horse or two passes, then Sheridan and staff mount and ride headlong back to Hancock, this time by nearer roads cleared of Rebels by Barlow in the meantime. It is now sunset, and judging that there will be little more done to-day I ride back to the river and back to my quarters. Three miles of the way is by a narrow but straight bridle-path cut through a dense growth of pines. Frank must have the rein to himself, and must pick his way through the stumps and the night. It is thick dark. All alone, seeing nothing but the darkness, a little tired and a good deal hungry, three longer miles were never ridden. Miles away there are guns firing, miles away there are drums beating — these only for companionship, and it is *so* dark. Another cigar for me, Frank, and a cheery word for you, and a supper by and by for us both. And we at last break out of the woods and see the lights of the camp not far away. Frank with an impatient whinny and a great leap breaks into a mighty gallop, and makes for them straight as an arrow. A few more miles of that, and it would be the "Ride to Aix" and Roland and I over again, barring any great good news.

Excuse me: the mail is in, bringing a package of letters to —

X.

THE MINE EXPLOSION.

GOING TO WORK. — A REBEL FORT BLOWN UP.

BEFORE PETERSBURG, Saturday, July 30, 9 A. M.

AFTER three days of manœuvring, with marching and some fighting, the grand assault upon Petersburg was made at half-past four o'clock this morning, and is still progressing, it is thought favorably. The movement of Hancock and Sheridan to the left bank of the James was a feint to draw the enemy in that direction, and was successful.

Yesterday, to confirm him in his impression that Grant proposed to make the fight, three trains were sent over from here in his plain sight, — the long transportation wagons of the Sixth Corps being used for that purpose. Then at dark last night Hancock began marching this way, and before daylight had his corps in close reserve. General Hunt, chief of artillery, had 94 guns and 15 mortars in position.

The explosion of an immense mine on Burnside's front was the signal for them to open. The main attack was to be from the centre by the Ninth Corps, while the Eighteenth and Turner's Division of the Tenth should be massed on the right rear of the Ninth, and the Fifth on the left of the Ninth; part of the Second to take a portion of the line near the river, but nearly all to support the Ninth.

The mine had been pushed out 400 feet, radiating into three branches beneath a Rebel four-gun battery. The powder, exploding five to fifteen feet underground, was equal to a chamber train fifteen inches in diameter and 250 feet long. The world shook when it was fired. A column of yellow earth spouted into the air broad and high as Bunker Hill Monument.

THE MINE EXPLOSION.

The echo of the awful blast had not come back from the woods behind when the hundred guns open from the rising ground in Warren's front. I could see the line of belching fire, the great volume of white smoke, and hear the noise of it all. And the enemy angrily replied; heavy musketry volleyed in the centre, only heard in the momentary intervals between the guns, heaviest just when the sun's blood-red disk whirled into sight. Was it the sun of another Austerlitz? Great masses of white powder-smoke, hugging close to the earth or reluctantly rising and resting on the treetops, obscured the view. The flashes of the guns in the haze, projecting many feet from the muzzles, could be seen — nothing else. The church spires of Petersburg were lost from the picture. And the smoke lodged behind and banked up against the sun till his great disk was dim and bleared.

At last, just before six a fresh breeze cleared all the prospect as by magic. Each man now to his field-glass, and we strain our eyes and sweep the glass from point to point. In the groups are Generals Warren, Hunt, Cutler and Ayers, and their staffs.

Still no word from the front as to how it is with ours. There we can only look and exchange thoughts and hopes and knowledge of what each sees. At just six the Rebels are running. One and then another is certain he sees them flying. The naked eye soon confirms that which was "seen through a glass darkly," and the rascals are running in great flocks.

One more glance from this point and then to another. At our elbows a battery is throwing four-and-a-half-inch shells, and the enemy occasionally reply with those of equal metal and with good aim. The Regular brigade is engaged at our left. A column of black smoke rises from Petersburg, and clouds in the sky indicate that the city is burning.

A signal station by a battery hard to the front is waving merrily its little flag, — flag that talks; I do not comprehend it. Generals Grant and Meade are at Burnside's headquarters. There I learn that the mine accomplished its purpose. The explosion carried three of the four guns above it and many men. While the earth still trembled the Fourteenth New York Heavy Artillery, Second Brigade of Ludlie's Division, rushed upon the spot and broke the enemy's line; over 800 prisoners were taken. Prisoners are coming in, — 200 already. There is no straggling.

We have certainly carried some of the enemy's works. Here at headquarters the impression is that we shall before the sun goes down unfurl THE flag in Petersburg. There are still fresh troops enough at hand to pour a new column upon the Rebel centre every hour till night if that shall be necessary.

Of course nothing is known yet in detail, nothing as to the losses and where they have fallen heaviest. Sheridan's cavalry is moving round to our left on the enemy's right. The battle has raged four hours without cessation. How much longer of this depends upon the Rebels giving way, not on our giving up.

XI.

A LETTER FROM THE HONORABLE BEN WOOD.

GENERAL BUTLER'S HEADQUARTERS, July 31, 1864.

THE following letter, although franked "B. Wood, M.C.," and addressed to "Captain E. G. Dejarnette, Prisoner of War, Fortress Monroe, Virginia," will probably be read in "The Tribune" a long time before it falls into the hands of the man in whose case his friends — B. Wood and others — "apprehend no difficulty."

OFFICE NEW YORK DAILY NEWS, No 19 CITY HALL SQUARE, NEW YORK, JULY 25, 1864.

DEAR: Inclosed find "personal" from late Southern papers.
Yours, &c.,
B. WOOD, per G. W. S.

CAPTAIN E. J. DEJARNETTE, PRISONER AT FORTRESS MONROE: Your communication has been received; your friends apprehend no difficulty in your case. You will hear from us more particularly in a few days. I. H. DEJARNETTE.

New York News please copy.

Addressed — Captain E. J. DEJARNETTE,
Prisoner of War.
FORTRESS MONROE, VIRGINIA.

If gone, please forward to next destination.

It seems this "personal" first appeared in a Richmond paper, was then, according to request, copied into the "New York News," from which it was clipped by "B. Wood, M.C." and mailed under his frank to Rebel Captain Dejarnette.

In a late number of "The New Régime," a paper published at Norfolk, was published, among other proceedings of a military commission, the findings and sentence in the case of two men,

Lewyllan and Mull by name, accused of harboring Rebel spies. They were found guilty and sentenced to one and two years in the penitentiary. One of the spies harbored was Captain E. J. Dejarnette, who, when captured some weeks after by a nicely laid trap, represented himself as a signal officer in the service of the Confederates. It is a question of some interest how intimately the Honorable Ben Wood is connected with this Rebel spy. What is the nature of the connection?

The weather has lapsed back to its old condition of intense heat. Five men of Turner's Division, Tenth Corps, died to-day from sun-stroke or from immoderate drinking of water while on the march. Poor fellows, they could not resist the temptation of a wayside spring, and in the quaffing of refreshing waters, they quaffed their death.

The following is an accurate statement of the issues of the Sanitary Commission of vegetables to the troops in the trenches from June 18 to August 1, 1864:—

3,842	bbls.	potatoes.	1,480 bbls.	pickled cucumbers.
443	"	pickled onions.	2,600 "	fresh onions.
355	"	sauer-kraut.	453 "	dried apples.
64	"	beans.	383 "	beets.
133	"	turnips.	54 "	curried cabbage.
152	"	assorted vegetables.	3,930 head of cabbages.	

1,367 boxes and 45 bbls. of canned tomatoes.

If a single soldier has been omitted or slighted in these distributions, it is the fault of their officers, whose reports of the number of men in each command to the agents of the commission are the basis of distribution. However, the system is so perfect that there are few, if any, who have not had their full share.

XII.

THE NORFOLK AND PORTSMOUTH ELECTION.

BUTLER'S HEADQUARTERS, August 1, 1864.

IN the custody of the provost marshal at these headquarters there is to-day one Edmund K. Snead. This Snead was living on the eastern shore of Virginia before and during the Rebel possession of that part of the State. By his own confession, when interrogated by General Butler last night, he practised as a lawyer before the Rebel courts up to the time the Union forces put an end to them. However, in November last he took the oath of allegiance, it being about the time that Governor Pierpont ordered an election for Judge of the Circuit Court, for the district of six or seven counties which include the cities of Portsmouth and Norfolk. Votes were polled in only those two places, less than 700 in the former, and 70 in the latter, whereupon Pierpont declared Snead elected Judge and so commissioned him.

On the 30th of June last the Major-General commanding the Department made the following order, the necessity of which is fully and forcibly set forth therein.

HEADQUARTERS DEPARTMENT OF VIRGINIA AND NORTH CAROLINA.
IN THE FIELD, VIRGINIA. June 30, 1864.

GENERAL ORDERS No. —. The City of Norfolk having once been in rebellion against the lawful Government of the United States, and occupied by the enemies thereof in the summer of 1862, was captured by the armed forces of the United States under command of Major-General Wool, and has since been occupied by a military garrison and with its environs have become subject to the law martial.

At the request of a portion of its citizens and by permission of the Major-General then commanding the Department of Virginia, the inhabitants were permitted to endeavor to establish for themselves a municipal civil government under such restrictions as were consistent with the safety of the city and its occupation as a military post.

Such city government was attempted to be established by a vote of about one hundred of its citizens, all that would vote therefor, and civil officers were elected. But upon a full and fair trial of the experiment, such government has been found wholly to have failed, and to be inadequate to perform the duties of preserving the public peace, protecting the city from fire, cleaning and repairing the streets, wharves, and bridges, establishing schools, and feeding and maintaining the poor, and to do those acts to accomplish which civil government is established and maintained in well-regulated and peaceful communities. Whether this incapacity arose from the necessities of the case, because of military operations, or because of the want of confidence among the citizens, in the persons administering the Government, or because of their incapacity, or from the inherent weakness of such a government in a disturbed and disorganized society, resulting from a state of war, it is not now necessary to determine. Certain it is that the experiment has wholly failed.

By that municipality, persons have not been protected, property has not been safe, the streets have not been cleaned, the fire department has not been kept up, schools have not been established, and the poor have not been fed or cared for. Therefore it was that Brigadier-General Shepley, commanding the District of Virginia by direction of the Major General commanding the Department, called upon all the qualified loyal voters, by their ballots, to pass upon the following questions.

HEADQUARTERS DISTRICT OF EASTERN VIRGINIA,
NORFOLK, VIRGINIA, June 22, 1864.

SPECIAL ORDERS No. 50. Many loyal citizens of Norfolk having represented to the military authorities in this Department that they do not desire a continuance of the Municipal Government that has heretofore been recognized by the commanding-general, it is determined, before any final action is taken upon those petitions, to take an expression of the preference of the citizens themselves at the polls.

On the day of the ensuing municipal election in the city of Norfolk, a poll will be opened at the several places of voting, and separate ballot-boxes will be kept open during the hours of voting, in which voters will deposit their ballots, "Yes" or "No," upon the following questions: —

Those in favor of continuing the present form of municipal government during the existence of military occupation will vote "Yes." Those opposed to it will vote "No."

Persons otherwise entitled to vote, and who have taken the oath required by the Amnesty Proclamation of the President will not be considered as disqualified from voting on this question by reason of their not having taken any other oaths, but will be allowed to vote upon this question if qualified in other respects.

The Provost Marshal will appoint persons to receive and count and declare these votes in case the Commissioners of Election or other officers presiding at the polls shall fail to do so.

By command of
         Brigadier-General G. F. SHEPLEY.

GEO. H. JOHNSTON, Captain and Assistant Adjutant-General.

Upon the day of the recurrence of the annual election for city officers, and at the same time that a vote was taken for the choice of those officers the fullest discussion of the questions was had.

Meetings were held in which they were canvassed. Interested men falsely charged corruption, oppression, and wrong upon the military administration of affairs.

A pamphlet was published by a person who called himself Governor, and whose means of living largely depended upon the votes cast in favor of civil government, upon the "abuses of military power."

A proclamation was issued to intimidate the citizens from voting, by the same person, pretending to be the head of the restored Government of Virginia, which Government is unrecognized by the Congress, laws, and Constitution of the United States.

The loyal citizens of Norfolk determined with an unanimity almost unexampled — by a vote of THREE HUNDRED AND THIRTY TO SIXTEEN — against a further trial of the experiment of a municipal government which gave as results to them only taxes and salaried officers, without any corresponding benefit. It will be observed that this vote was more than three times as large as that by which the experiment of civil government was set on foot. Some doubts upon the legal formality of this vote were attempted to be cast by interested parties, and proclamation was made that the adherents and salaried officers of the restored government should not vote upon the question submitted; yet that it was an overwhelming expression of the opinion of the citizens, is seen from the fact that 350 votes were cast upon the questions, while only 109 were cast by all parties for their respective candidates to fill the several offices.

Now, as there were at least two sets of candidates voted for, containing a list of some forty-five officers who would have place in the civil government in each set, it would seem that but twenty votes were cast for city officers except by those who were interested in being elected, assuming always that the men running for office in a city vote for each other.

It is the duty and province of the Government of the United States to afford protection to all its citizens in the manner most effectual and beneficial to them, and, so far as consistent with the Constitution and laws, in such manner as they desire; and all experience has shown that in a disorganized state of society incident upon a state of war, and especially civil war, a military government properly administered affords the best protection to property, liberty, and life.

Whether the military government has been properly administered in the City of Norfolk during the two years that it has been under military rule, and especially whether that military government has been administered during the past eight months, and has secured the substantial benefits of good government to the City of Norfolk, it is not proper for this order to state.

The citizens of Norfolk have spoken upon that subject with sufficient distinctness to inform the judgment of the commanding general.

Therefore it is ordered, That all attempts to exercise civil office and power, under any supposed city election, within the City of Norfolk and its environs must cease, and the persons pretending to be elected to civil offices at the late election, and those heretofore elected to municipal offices since the Rebellion, must no longer attempt to exercise such functions, and upon any pretence or attempt so to do, the Military Commandant at Norfolk will see to it that the persons so acting are stayed and quieted.

The commission for the care of the poor of Norfolk will see to the relief of the needy inhabitants as heretofore. The Superintendent of Prison Labor will take charge, as heretofore, of the streets. The Fire Department organized under the military government will be charged with the protection of the city against burning.

The Provost Marshal will see to the police of the city as heretofore. Provost Court will try all minor offences against the public peace and the Military Commandant will organize a competent commission to re-establish the schools for the white and colored children of Norfolk — separate schools for each.

The Military Superintendent of the Gas Works will see that the city is properly lighted as heretofore.

The wharves and docks will be placed under the superintendence of the Harbor Masters.

In fine, such orders will be given and dispositions made as will insure tranquil quiet, within the City of Norfolk and its environs, with safety to the property, persons, and lives of those that behave themselves well, and prompt punishment to those doing ill.

All taxes, licenses, and imposts of whatever description heretofore accustomed to be paid to the civil government will be paid into the hands of a financial agent to be appointed by the Military Commandant, and disbursed by him, upon requisitions to be approved by the Military Commandant, with fidelity and economy, accurate accounts being kept of all receipts and expenditures.

No salaries will be paid to any salaried officers of the United States for any service beyond that fixed by law, and no other or greater salaries than were paid heretofore for like services will be paid to any civilian whom it may be necessary to employ to aid in the administration of the government. To the end that the citizens of Norfolk and of Virginia may find, when in happier times, soon to come, they may resume that government which from the necessities of the case and at their own request has been assumed by the military authorities, that efficiency, economy, fidelity, and probity had characterized the military government as an example to those who may come after it.

By command of

Major-General B. F. BUTLER.

R. S. DAVIS, Major, and Assistant Adjutant-General.

In compliance with this order the city of Norfolk has since been governed under the direct supervision of General Shepley. All the departments of the city government have been admirably conducted, — with the advantages to the city of order and economy, and to the country of a searching and watchful loyalty careful that the "Republic shall receive no detriment" through disloyal inhabitants. Such, then, was the state of the case a few days ago, when this man Snead advertised in the city papers that he should hold a term of the Norfolk Circuit Court on Tuesday, August 2. Thereupon General Butler sent for the would-be judge to these headquarters, where he arrived last night and was immediately given audience.

General Butler asked him if he was aware of the order of the 30th of June, prohibiting the exercise of civil office under any supposed civil elections. Snead was aware of it. Did he propose to go ahead and hold a court in contravention of that order? He did. He considered the order illegal, a flagrant usurpation. Was there any occasion, necessity, or exigency demanding a term of his court at this time? He did not know that there was. Indeed he would confess that his object was to test the question of jurisdiction. He had consulted with Attorney-General Bates, and that functionary had advised him by all means to hold the court to make the issue. He was not only acting with the knowledge and sanction of Mr. Bates, but under his direction.

The examination finally ended by Snead's refusing to take his parole that he would in no way oppose the military orders of the commanding-general, whereupon he was put in custody, and the following order was made.

HEADQUARTERS DEPARTMENT OF VIRGINIA AND NORTH CAROLINA.
IN THE FIELD, VIRGINIA, July 31, 1864.

Edward K. Snead, Esq., of the City of Norfolk, having taken measures to oppose and hinder the execution of the military orders of the Commanding General of this Department, especially General Order No. — of 30th June last, and upon being sent for by the Commanding General and asked if he intended to oppose the execution of the military order of this Department, replied that he did. Upon being further asked if the supposed Court of the City of Norfolk which he had advertised to be held was to be held in subordination or opposition to the military of this Department, replied "it would be held in opposition to such military orders."

The Commanding General therefore orders and directs that Edward K. Snead, Esq., be stayed and quieted until he gives his parole that he will in no way oppose the military orders of the Commanding General of this Department. This, the said Edward K. Snead declines to do, and therefore he will be kept in custody until he shall give such parole with full intentions to keep the same.

In the meantime, to be treated with tenderness and care, so that he may take no detriment in sharing with the soldiers of the United States the fatigues necessarily incident to camp life.

All communications by said Snead will be passed through these headquarters.

By command of

Major-General BUTLER.

R. C. DAVIS, Assistant Adjutant-General.

Mr. Pierrepont, ex-Governor of the State of West Virginia, now claims authority as Governor of the State of Virginia, while it is notorious that he has neither power nor people nor territory. His "restored Government" has never contributed a man or a dollar to the Union cause. If a conscription were to be had to-morrow in such portions of the State as our armies control, seven eighths of the men it would carry into the war would desert and fight on the other side, where their hearts are. Only their treasure is on this side, and that alone has induced them to remain. The city of Norfolk is a nest of viperous Rebels. Too cowardly to fight on the side they love, they would treacherously serve their master Jeff Davis quite as effectually in a thousand other ways if not subjected to firm military control.

A seaport city in a military department where our largest army is operating, a majority of whose inhabitants are rank Rebels, eager to embarrass us and aid them, and yet these men, Pierrepont and Snead *et al.* — semi-disloyalists themselves — talk glibly about the "interference of the military with the civil government," and are counselled to a course of factiousness and anarchy by the Attorney-General of the United States. General Butler saw no other way that would be just or beneficent or safe towards both the inhabitants and the United States than the one he adopted; and since it has secured all the order and justice and safety and beneficence — the latter being abundantly proven by the votes of all those who were so far loyal as to take oath of allegiance — it is not likely he will swerve a hair's breadth from his course or tolerate any ill-advised and disloyal opposition to it. Mr. Snead will hold no courts, and Mr. Pierrepont will exercise none of the functions of a State Governor, unless indeed they shall be supported and General Butler stopped by a higher authority than Mr. Bates. But it is probable that the President's great good sense will prevent him from interfering to subordinate a military department under military law, where the loyal are numbered by hundreds and the disloyal by thousands, where the interests of a great army are concerned, — interfering to subordinate those to trumped-up provisional authorities calling themselves governors and judges.

XIII.

THE FEELING OVER THE MINE DISASTER.

THE EXPLOSION BEFORE PETERSBURG. — ITS EFFECT PASSING AWAY. — PLUCK OF THE ARMY. — CHEERING GOOD NEWS.

GENERAL BUTLER'S HEADQUARTERS, August 11, 1864.

THE affair of Saturday, July 3d, in front of Petersburg, has already come to seem almost as old a thing as either Bull Run. That there was extreme disappointment, and, for a time, great depression throughout the army, may not be denied, — better face the fact. And better face, too, the one alarming element of that fact: that the disheartenment was altogether disproportionate to the calamity which induced it. Men asked each other if a simple repulse, with a loss small compared with that of any one of half a dozen other days of this campaign, could now produce such dispiritment, would not a greater disaster utterly break the power of the army for immediate offence? Some reasoned thus, who, from their rank, should at least never have expressed such a fear. These must by this time, have "stayed and quieted" all such misgivings, else they have not noted the present feeling in the ranks and over the ranks.

It required but a few days for reflecting men — and none others affect at all, or help to constitute the *morale* of an army — to begin to suspect that they had been a little infected with panic. Looking at it coolly they saw that the Rebels were no stronger and we scarcely weaker for the one unlucky day's work, that we had lost nothing of position, that despite the rebel raiding north coming right on the heels of a repulse here, there seemed no faltering in the purpose to fight it out on this line — that here the army was planted and here its great leader was determined it should hold on. They knew also, and better than the people of New York, the desperate strait of the rebels, the strait they can escape only by causing this army to let go this hold, yield this vantage ground, whether by direct battle or by the ruse of a grand invasion of Pennsylvania. And looking around the horizon they saw what Sherman had done, and dwelt on the fact that he had inflicted losses three times as great as those he suffered. And now comes the good news from Mobile, and the later good news from Averill, till *there is spontaneous cheering in the camps.* When these men cheer of their own will, and with a will, for victories far away, know that they crave one more for themselves, and will fight for it. Letters come here from all over the country asking if the army is n't going back to Washington — is n't going here, there, or elsewhere. Now there is not a soldier in all this army that has any such notion. Not one intelligent man, even at his heart-sickest moment, on account of hope deferred has dreamed that thing — that the campaign is to be backed out of. *Vestigia nulla retrorsum* — few of them know the dead language but they all have the live idea.

It is somewhat the habit to represent a body of troops, known to be brave and effective, as "eager for the fray," "burning to be led against the foe," or, less elegantly, "spoiling for a fight." Writers who indulge in the use of such phrases, know nothing of armies, or do not state what they know, or rather state what they do not know, unless indeed they know it to be false. The soldiers themselves laugh at these expressions when they see them, and none laugh heartier than those a score of times conspicuous for the cheerfulness with which they have gone into battle and their steadiness and pluck under withering fire. They are not conscious of any particular "eagerness for the fray," any amorous inclination toward bullets, any penchant for meeting shells half-way, any longing for a short sleep, and a shortened limb under the surgeon's hands, any especial haste to be mustered out in this, and to be mustered in in another world. The man who affects any of this fine frenzy is a coward. Let it be understood that troops never "rush frantically to the front" for the love of the thing — at least not after they have been in one fight. After that, they are sure to know better. Hence it is that the first battle does not distinguish the brave from the cowardly. It is the second one, with the recollection of the carnage and narrow escapes of the first before him, which tries a soldier and tests his metal — and his mettle. One who was recklessly, unthinkingly brave on his first field, has learned to realize the peril on the second, and may run away; while another who ran the first time, now plucks up courage, having seen that it is quite as safe to go ahead, or having, through pride, mastered his fears.

But if there is no beautiful, sentimental itching "to be led against the foe," on the other hand, men do not go in sullenly, doggedly, or with any sort of apparent reluctance. They go to an encounter with something like solemnity now, with elastic step and cheerfully, but with set teeth and earnest faces. Set it down to the credit of pluck — sheer pluck, clear, clean, square, stern, quiet, solid, honest pluck. It was this which fought Antietam, notwithstanding the Seven Days, Gettysburg, notwithstanding Chancellorsville, and it is this which would yet give to this army the clarions of victory, notwithstanding twenty 30ths of July like the last. That day has ceased from troubling the army and is become like any other of the defeats of three campaigns — to be offset, when thought of, against some one of the successes of these three years, and, depend upon it, the successes are oftenest recalled.

There is no reason why we should "bate one jot of heart or hope," but there is every inducement and warrant why we should "still bear up and steer right onward."

XIV.

TOBACCO FOR SOLDIERS.

HEADQUARTERS OF GENERAL BUTLER, August 12, 1864.

PROPOSITION: Even unto this day the children of Darkness are sometimes wiser in their generation than the children of Light. Illustration: The Confederate Government issues to its soldiers a tobacco ration. Our Government does not.

That Senator Wilson's proposition of last winter, to add tobacco to the soldiers' regular ration, did not meet the approval of Congress, is not simply a matter of regret, but an open shame, which the next session must be induced to remedy.

It is not understood to be in accordance with the theory of our institutions to compel one set of men to follow the notions of another set on questions of diet and medicine. And yet here are a few scores of Congressmen with hypercritical, super-refined, extra-punctilious notions and theories on the great Tobacco question forcing some half a million of soldiers, *citizen*-soldiers, to adopt in practice their side of the issue. It is pure unadulterated tyranny, and of the meanest sort, — that which would make your conscience the rule of another man's actions. History does not accord to the Stuarts any great regard for the rights of their subjects when their own ideas or convenience ran counter to them; but King James contented himself with writing his "Counterblast" against tobacco. He neither procured an act of Parliament nor promulgated an edict prohibiting its use. It remained for the Congress of the United States to dictate thus unrighteously, for under the circumstances the refusal to issue tobacco amounted to a deprivation of it. This on two insuperable accounts: first, that the soldier not being paid regularly often has no money to purchase; second, that during active operations sutlers are excluded, and there is no tobacco to buy. Congress was told this, knew this, but, with quids in their mouths, voted down the amendment and then went complacently home to enjoy the post-prandial cigar, with all the sweets of digesting dinner and tobacco-reverie. Were none of them disturbed by visions of haggard soldiers in heated trenches, eating a junk of meat and three hard crackers, and then restless and discontented for want of the pipe which was their solace in all the old home-days they remember and would now make more tolerable these long, long days? Deprive these men of tobacco — it is more than unjust, more than unmerciful, it is worse than folly or blunder, *it is mean!*

Look at it as it is in this army now. The men cannot obtain tobacco. They have not money to buy, and there is little tobacco to be bought. Men who had used it every day for ten and twenty years have not smoked nor chewed since they exhausted what little stock they may have had when they left the Rappahannock. If any have been able to procure a supply since, they have paid twenty prices for it — say half a month's pay for a common plug, enough for a week, which Government could issue at a cost of twenty-five cents. There are teamsters whose occasional trips to some water base have enabled them to traffic in a small way, who have made thousands of dollars, for they sell at an advance of five hundred to one thousand per cent. And this is wrenched from a stipend of sixteen dollars a month — and Congress is responsible.

The question whether the use of tobacco works in the world more harm than good does not enter into the case, for the case is anomalous, exceptional, and transitory. Concede that the nicotian plant is as hurtful as its enemies insist, to deprive the armies of it on compulsion during this war would not push the "Progress of the Age" very considerably, nor, on the contrary, will its free use by the same block the wheels materially. One of the arguments urged by grave senators against tobacco for the soldiers was that it would be injustice to those who do not use it. Well, quite as many do not eat beans, quite as many do not drink coffee, quite as many discard any one of the articles of the regulation ration, while this is the only one the want of which to those who do want it is a real hardship.

So far I have treated the question mainly as a matter of justice and kindness. But there is another line of argument even more telling. Tobacco saves soldiers' lives — and in two ways, the one direct, the other indirect. The best medical authorities, in this army, some of them men who do not themselves use it, declare that it is a natural antidote to the malaria that lurks in this climate, and slowly poisons our soldiers. The hospital records show that in the case of officers — the test cannot be applied to the men, for, poor fellows, they have none of them used it, bitter thanks to Congress — those who have been sick with camp-fever and diarrhœa come in a much larger proportion from the non-smokers and non-chewers than from the opposite class.

If such is the case with men who have simply continued in their former habits, how much worse would be the showing among those who have been compelled to cease, just when most required, a habit of years' standing? The indirect effect upon their health and spirits is, however, perhaps the more injurious of the two. Night-marches have seemed as long again for want of tobacco. Picket duty has been more wearing and wearisome for want of tobacco. Time has hung heavily and cheerlessly in the trenches for want of tobacco. In camp the hours have passed restlessly, discontentedly for want of tobacco. The first result is that your confirmed nicotian loses in spirit and then he loses in health. Why, there are thousands here who long for the "piping times of peace," not because they are times of peace but because they are pipe-ing times.

I remember these lines, written by my college chum, years agone —

>To happiness there are two ways,
>   For every youth beneath the stars,
>The girls must make his holidays,
>   Or else Havana's prime cigars.

I do not quite subscribe to the philosophy, but verily believe if anything can at all compensate for absence from home and friends, it is tobacco — the digestive pipe and the sedative quid. The idea may not be romantic, the fact may not be creditable to human nature, but they are truth, nevertheless.

Well, the remedy. Not Congress till next winter. The Sanitary Commission must take it up, else the boys must continue to suffer. The Commission has seen the need all these months, but has not felt authorized to divert means contributed for other purposes to this. The only way left would seem to be to raise a special fund, to be put into the hands of the Commission for expenditure. Tobacco for the soldiers, — and every man who enjoys cigar, pipe or quid, to contribute that the boys may have that

"Plant divine, of rarest virtue."

whose

"Clouds all other clouds dispel."

New York raised an "Onion Fund." That was hailed by the soldiers with all thanks and joy. But let there be a Tobacco Fund, and the boys will — take Richmond!

In relevant conclusion, and from memory this, which I have never seen in print.

"I look upon this round green ball
 Where poets sing and warriors fight,
Where statesmen on their parties call,
 And true men struggle for the right,
Where 'mid the sin and woe and strife,
 True hearts still bear this heavy life, —

And see that all the mighty men,
 Whose names like beacons shine from far,
Who wield the sword, and wield the pen,
 Each loves and smokes his good cigar.
In spite of all that has been spoke,
 The wreath of fame's a wreath of smoke!

And, leaving earth, my eyes I bend
 To heaven, and see that every star
Is but the burning, flaming end
 Of some tall angel's lit cigar!
And where the baldric's white stream dashes,
 Is but the place they knock the ashes."

XV.

THE WOOING AND WEDDING OF JOHN KICK.

GENERAL BUTLER'S HEADQUARTERS, Aug. 13, 1864.

LAWRENCE, in his last novel, "The Quadrilateral," indulges in some reflections on the often-happening fact that a man falls sick among strangers, falls into kind hands, falls under the nursing, particularly during his convalescence, of a lovely young woman, and finally falls in love with the fair nurse, and while he is still pallid from illness — there is a wedding.

I am about to present an illustration of these truths.

John Kick, of Buffalo, New York, is a private in the Second New York Mounted Rifles, which regiment, notwithstanding its name, is not mounted, but serves as infantry — "mounted," if it refers to human legs and feet, being a palpable superfluity. Pushing along, sunned on, and dusted on during the march from Cold Harbor to James River, John, surnamed Kick, was stricken with deadly sickness. John could go no further. John was not simply tired out, exhausted, knocked up, played out and done for, but he was sick. He fell out of the ranks. His comrades thought him sun-struck. A learned surgeon hazarded the expression of an opinion that the man was suffering from aggravated *coup de soleil*, induced by exhaustion and the climate. His comrades bore John to the nearest house. The nearest house was the late residence of the late John Tyler, accidental President, defunct ex-President, whose picture, of large nose and brow of swift backward aslant, contradicts all rules of physiognomy and phrenology. There John was left and his fellows went marching on. There was a young lady in the house, Anna Maria Tyler, niece of the once President. A month, nearly two months, passed, and John, surnamed Kick, was not heard from. Was John still sick? Was John lingering in pain and helplessness? Had John gone over to the Johnnies after recovering? Or had Kick kicked the inevitable bucket that awaits all mortals? Would John ever be heard of again? Would Kick ever again pedestrinate with his fellow Mounted Rifles? Nobody could answer. Kick was supposed to have kicked out of the service. His enemies hinted that he had gone over to the enemy, in fact been Tylerized. They were mistaken. Kick had not been Tylerized, but Tyler had been Kicked. Anna Maria took tender care of John. She did pity him like another Desdemona. True, he was a Yankee, but Othello was a Moor. Perhaps Anna loved John for the dangers he had seen. At any rate she loved John in spite of the fact that he had done the State some service. And John loved Anna Maria (tiler). As the flush of returning health came to John's cheek, Maria grew pale, — pale, but interesting. John saw, and then John began to feel. Here I ought to write five chapters, and quote Tennyson, by way of describing the fusing of their two hearts, but I won't. I have related the "Veni" and the "Vidi." Only the "Vici" remains. Now John was n't agoin' to let concealment feed on his cheek. John spoke. Anna Maria spoke back. She was a rebel, but she did not rebel. Both Barkises were willin'. A local preacher lived in a "hard town small by." This announcement did not appear in any newspaper the following day, but ought to have done so:

MARRIED: — On the —— inst., at the residence of the late ex-President John Tyler, by Rev. Close Atthande, John Kick, private 2d N. Y. R., U. S. V. and Anna Maria Tyler, niece of the ex-President. "No cards."

Kick (prenomen John) and Kick (née Tyler) were happy. "Whoso findeth a wife findeth a good thing and obtaineth favor of the Lord," is Scripture. Doubtless the converse should be understood. They were happy, but — (The reader will begin with this "but" and moralize as much as he pleases.) A cloud shadowed the honeymoon. John must go to his regiment and Kick away his other half. But still he lingered. Duty called, but Anna pleaded. It was kicking against the pricks to think of parting. Four weeks passed, at last John wrenched himself away. Kick, afoot and alone, cross lots and crying, left his brided ex-President's niece, and wended his sorrowful but proud way "on this line" till he reached our pickets. And so a few days ago John Kick, private husband of Anna Maria Tyler Kick, presented himself at these headquarters. He told his tale. He was no deserter. On the contrary he was the wedded husband of — his wife, and he told who his wife was and how he came to have her for wife. He produced a letter to the commanding general, signed "Anna Tyler Kick," begging that her spouse might be granted furlough for 30 days, and pass north for self and wife "to arrange domestic affairs." The letter was evidently that of a cultivated lady — in an exquisite hand, on exquisite paper, couched in well-considered, well-phrased, and touching terms, giving lucid and cogent statement of the case, and pleading for furlough for Kick, and pass for Kicks, as only woman ("in our hours of ease, coy, etc., but etc.") can plead. The 2d N. Y. M. R. happen now to be in General Burnside's corps. It was not in General Butler's power to grant the request. However, he gave Kick a letter to General Burnside, recommending that the request of the other half of Kick, late Tyler (niece of ex.-P. J. T.) be granted, and commending John Kick (Private N. Y. M. R. U. S. V., late of Buffalo, N. Y.) for successful union strategy. I understand that furlough and pass have been granted, and that Kick (John) and (Anna) Tyler have gone north. So let it be.

Meanwhile widow ex-President John Tyler writes the "Herald" from her present house on Staten Island, that a daughter of the late ex-P. has *not* married a private in the Union Army. Mrs. T. is right. It is a niece and not a daughter.

Two old friends meet after long separation; one says to the other, "George, are you married?" "No, but I have been *exposed* several times," was the reply. And so there are doubtless others of the She-chivalry who would succumb to even privates in the Union armies, if they were only exposed as this one was.

GENERAL BUTLER'S HEADQUARTERS,
Monday, Aug. 15, 7 A. M.

Turner's and Ferry's Divisions of the Tenth Corps (Birney's) crossed to Deep Bottom during the night before last.

Hancock's Corps came by boat from City Point, and did not disembark till nearly noon yesterday. Meanwhile Foster's Brigade, which had so long held Deep Bottom, was advanced by Birney a little after sunrise, pushing the Rebel skirmish line some distance. The Twenty-fourth Mass., Colonel Osborne, charged, carried the line, capturing seventy prisoners. Gregg's Cavalry was already clearing the roads for Hancock, who during the afternoon got into position on Birney's right along the Newmarket Road. Just before dark Birney assaulted the works in his front and captured six guns and two mortars.

The particulars of this assault have not reached me, but our loss was small. The loss of the whole day will not exceed three hundred and fifty. Generals Grant and Butler were on the ground from morning to night.

XVI.

OPERATIONS NORTH OF THE JAMES.

BIRNEY WITHIN SIX MILES OF RICHMOND. — COURAGE OF THE COLORED TROOPS. — A FRESH WATER FRESHET AND SALT WATER JOKE.

GENERAL BUTLER'S HEADQUARTERS,
Aug. 16, 1864, 7 P. M.

THE operations of to-day on the north bank of the James require but few paragraphs. During the night Birney with the Tenth Corps left his line of the day before and assumed Hancock's, from which he advanced a line early in the morning without opposition, Hancock taking the reserves and left flank. Foster's old position at Deep Bottom was left with a few negro troops. Nearly all day was occupied in skirmishing and learning the ground. Gregg's Cavalry on the extreme right, rested its right on the Charles City Road, seven miles from Richmond. One brigade of the Second Corps connected it with General William Birney's provisional division of the Tenth Corps, consisting of the colored brigade lately from Florida, and two brigades of Turner's Division of the Tenth Corps.

General Turner was left in command of Butler's line from the Appomattox to the James. Terry's Division was next to the left, and Barlow's Second Corps on the refused flank. This line extended from the Charles City Road to the New Market Road, the Central Road being midway, at which point we were but six miles from Richmond. The line more nearly faces the river than it does Richmond, extending at an obtuse angle from the right of the line the day before.

The country is very thickly wooded, — all woods save narrow cleared patches. The day was by the thermometer the warmest known this summer, and no air was stirring, hence little could be done in the middle of the day.

OPERATIONS NORTH OF THE JAMES. 219

About noon the Rebels attacked Gregg's Cavalry and bore it back, whereupon Birney sent a brigade square out to his right in charge of Captain Briscoe of his staff, which struck the Rebel force on its right flank and forced it to slide out from between this brigade and Gregg. This, however, measured by the losses, was little more than skirmishing.

At five o'clock General William Birney's and a part of General Terry's Divisions advanced the line, in order to prepare itself for the final charge, pushed through the dense growth but slowly, and it was after six before it became actively engaged. The negro troops, Seventh, Eighth, and Ninth United States, and Twenty-ninth Conn., heroes of Olustee, went in magnificently with the heartiest cheer I have heard since the earlier battles of the campaign. By dark considerable distance had been gained, and work for the day ceased.

The losses are very small, between one and two hundred, and perhaps as many more sick from the excessive heat.

At one time in the day General Birney's headquarters were under a very bitter fire of case shot and musketry. The chair upon which the General was sitting was struck.

There was just a little sprinkle of rain near night and there was the same at these headquarters and at City Point, while in the trenches in front of Petersburg a tremendous freshet fell in but half an hour from one great cloud. The ravine in front of the Eighteenth Corps rose so rapidly outside its banks as to wash away hundreds of tents. Fourteen soldiers who were asleep are known to have been drowned. The water in the valley was ten feet deep and more, and raged like an ocean surf. One man, noted as a wit, was rescued, when nearly drowned. At last, heaving a groan, he opened his eyes and gasped out, a word at a time, "I — am — Captain Semmes — where — is — the — 'Greyhound'?"

DETAILS OF THE BATTLE OF DEEP RIVER.— HARD FIGHTING.— REBELS DRIVEN.— TWO OF THEIR GENERALS KILLED. — A MILE OF GROUND GAINED. — NEGRO VALOR.

GENERAL BUTLER'S HEADQUARTERS,
August 16, 1864, 10 P. M.

IT has been a good day's work — the battle of Deep River. We have four Rebel battle flags, over four hundred prisoners; the bodies of two Rebel generals, and nearly or quite a mile of advance ground.

Without a reader has a map before him he will hardly obtain any clear notion of the topography of the field of operations from any written description.

At nine in the morning General Terry's Division attacked from the right of the line held by the Tenth Corps the night before. A part of Brigadier-General Wm. Birney's troops were also in this attack, the remainder of his division being in close support and under fire. Of the Second Corps, only the brigades commanded by Colonel Craig (Second and Third Divisions), Birney's old Peninsula Brigade, participated in the fight. At about the same time, Gregg's Cavalry, supported by Miles's Brigade, Second Corps, was engaged, far to the right on the Charles City Road.

The first Rebel line was carried with little difficulty. At ten o'clock a push was made for the second line by the same troops. It required an hour's close fighting to carry it, but it was done. The whole affair was in the woods and the opposing lines fought at very short range — so short that a man seen was a man shot. The principal loss of the day was here. Colonel Craig was mortally wounded, and Colonel Osborne Twenty-fourth Massachusetts, an excellent officer, also commanding a brigade (Second of Second Division, Tenth Corps) was hit in the face, severely but not dangerously.

The second and main line being finally carried, the men were instantly set to work to turn it against the enemy. But little had been done, however, when the Rebels ebbed back to retake it. Four distinct desperate attempts were repulsed, and the fifth would have been if our men had not got short of ammunition. Owing to this alone on the fifth trial the enemy repossessed a portion of the line. In one of these assaults General Gerardy, lately promoted from a major and staff-officer for services the day Burnside's mine was sprung, fell, and his body remained in our hands.

In his fight on the Charles City Road, Gregg had killed the Rebel cavalry general, John R. Chambliss, and brought off his body, and forced the enemy to retire with loss. Just at night, assisted by two brigades from the Second Corps, Birney renewed the engagement with the purpose of getting back the ground he relinquished earlier in the day for want of ammunition. Your correspondent left the field before there was any result.

Meanwhile General Butler and staff had ridden to Dutch Gap, the scene of Major Ludlow's canal-cutting operations, to direct a diversion by the force there, and by the force under Colonel Wooster at Deep Bottom. It must be remembered that General Birney's line faced the river, and that the enemy were between him and the positions of Dutch Gap and Deep Bottom, which are four miles apart as the river runs. Butler had Major Ludlow's transport, half his command and eight hundred men, in boats, two miles down, to land at Aikin's Wharf — five hundred of them were colored. Major Ludlow then moved three miles square across the isthmus to Cox's Mills or Cox's Ferry, skirmishing on the way, and cutting off and capturing a portion of the pickets the enemy had left to make a show opposite his position at Dutch Gap.

He found the enemy pressed by Birney had abandoned very strong works at Cox's Ferry, into which he threw his men, and where he will be by the morning too strong to be easily dislodged. This position is considered very important, and has been much coveted. The force at Deep Bottom also advanced the enemy's rear some distance, but met little resistance.

At Deep Run, General D. B. Birney commanded on the field, all troops of both corps likely to become engaged reporting to him, while General Hancock had general direction of all the forces. The Tenth Corps stood the brunt of the work, while the Brigadier from the Second went in where required. Barlow's Division Second Corps lay on the left, and near Gibbon's Division, same corps, now under General Smythe, connected Barlow with Foster's Brigade, the left of the Tenth.

The loss in the Tenth is estimated to-night at one thousand, the loss in the Second at four hundred, in the cavalry one hundred. Colonel McGilvery, Birney's Chief of Artillery, lost a finger and Captain Briscoe, senior A. D. C., suffered a painful contusion from a ball grazing his abdomen. Colonel Gregg, commanding Cavalry Brigade, brother of the general, is quite severely wounded. Major Patton, Twentieth Massachusetts, leg broken. The lieutenant-colonel and major of the Thirty-sixth Wisconsin are both wounded; Captain Nolan, Twenty-eighth Massachusetts, killed; Captains Lewis and Woodruff, Sixth Connecticut, killed. The lieutenant-colonel of Eighth Maine, arm amputated. Lieutenant-Colonel Plimpton, Third New Hampshire, and Major Wabath, One-Hundred-and-fifteenth New York, killed. Captain Hooker, Eighty-fifth Pennsylvania, badly wounded. The Third New Hampshire lost very heavily, — it had but five days to serve. Batteries D, First United States Artillery, Lieutenant Sanger commanding, and Fourth New Jersey, Lieutenant Doane commanding, both of Tenth Corps, planted on the front line, did excellent service. Colonel Macy, Twentieth Massachusetts, who had two horses killed under him Sunday, the second of which fell upon and badly injured him, will scarcely recover.

I saw not less than fifty colored wounded and was told by General Birney that the negroes behaved admirably, equal to any.

General Hill commands the Rebels. Their force consists of parts of nearly all their corps.

It is understood that General Warren was to engage the enemy on the Petersburg line, and heavy cannonading in that quarter gives color to the supposition that he did so this afternoon.

The heat on the battle-field to-day was greatly relieved by a smart shower in the afternoon.

On the person of General Chambliss was found an elaborate topographical map of the country and fortifications around Richmond.

The wounded are instantly placed on shipboard to be taken to the sea-shore hospitals.

GENERAL WARREN'S MARCH. — THE WELDON RAILROAD HELD. — HANCOCK'S AND BIRNEY'S WORK, SO FAR. — WHERE THE REBEL FORCES ARE. — OUR LINE TWENTY-FIVE MILES LONG.

WASHINGTON, August 20, 1864.
GENERAL BUTLER'S HEADQUARTERS, August 18, 1864, 10 P. M.

GENERAL WARREN marched with the Fifth Corps at daylight this morning towards the Weldon Railroad, below Petersburg. At 8 A. M. he was driving in the Rebel pickets. At noon he had possession of the road, and set to work intrenching his command for several good days' work of destruction. The intention is to destroy that road thoroughly this time.

The operations of Hancock and Birney have accomplished these things : —

First — A successful action, giving us guns, battle-flags, prisoners, and inflicting greater loss than has been suffered :

Second — They have deterred the enemy from sending more troops to the valley, and have brought back at double-quick troops already started.

Lastly — And this was the main object — they have drawn troops from the Petersburg front and enabled Warren to get a fair start on his mission.

These operations had no relation whatever to the Dutch Gap project ; and the papers which vaulted to the conclusion that Hancock meant Drury's Bluff, are informed that that position is on the left bank of the river, and something further from Richmond than Hancock is to-night.

When the enemy found, late to-day, that we were demonstrating below Petersburg, he attacked Hancock to ascertain whether he had withdrawn, was satisfied on that point, and soon desisted.

The canal is progressing satisfactorily and will be completed within the time originally estimated. Lieutenant Michie, assistant engineer of the department, is the engineer in charge, and Major B. C. Ludlow commands the forces.

Major Mulford goes up with a flag of truce boat to-morrow; will probably return with a number of sick and wounded prisoners.

Exactly one half of the Rebel forces in Virginia are in the Shenandoah Valley, awaiting Sheridan. The other half hold the line from Richmond to Petersburg.

From General Birney's headquarters, the right of the line of operations, to General Warren's extreme left is a distance of over twenty-five miles by the shortest roads. The whole distance is intrenched and two large rivers straddled. Grant, having much the larger army, can afford to stretch the line of operations and thus attenuate Lee's forces. I transmit a list of casualties.

XVII.

REPLY TO EDMUND K. SNEAD.

HEADQUARTERS OF GENERAL BUTLER,
August 20th, 1864.

"THE TRIBUNE" of yesterday surrenders more than three columns to an article headed "The Norfolk Difficulty," and signed " Edmund K. Snead," which seems to demand from me a brief counter statement. I must needs address myself to Mr. Snead, the ostensible author of the article, although the probability is that Mr. F. H. Pierpont has used him to cover a studied attack upon General Butler, and an elaborate statement of his own side of the "Norfolk Difficulties," for I have grounds for the suspicion that my letter to "The Tribune" was but made the pretence through which to obtain the use of the columns of so widely-read a journal in behalf of Mr. Pierpont and his "restored government."

Mr. Snead classes me among "anonymous and stipendiary scribblers," and terms me one who ventilates his rhetoric under the euphonious *nom de plume* of "C. A. P." Upon which I remark that when he calls a correspondent writing under his own initials "anonymous," and when he terms a writer's own initials, no matter how "euphonious" they may be, a "*nom de plume*," he ventilates *his* "rhetoric" after a manner most writers would prefer should be buried under a fictitious, rather than acknowledged under a real name. If by the epithet "stipendiary" he means anything beyond the fact that I receive a proper "stipend" for services rendered to the newspaper of which I am a regular correspondent, I oppose to the insinuation a square denial, with the remark that "The Tribune" would not retain in its service an instant a correspondent who should become anybody's "stipendiary," anybody's paid claqueur. No hightoned paper would suffer such prostitution of its columns.

It is the business of a correspondent to report events, facts, and news. In the strict line of that duty, certain facts which I conceived to be of interest having come to my knowledge — that Mr. Snead was here under arrest, and the reasons why he was so held — I reported them. Lo! three columns by way of indignant protest! Mr. S. says: "He (I) displays his ignorance of the subject upon which he (I) presumes to write." I concede it. Had I not been partially ignorant of the subject upon which I wrote, the letter to which he takes exception would have been made, in its statement of facts, even more damaging to him, — as, since he provokes it, this shall be.

He says, "I (he) am willing to be judged by my (his) record." By the record, then let it be; although were he as honest as the Irish culprit who, when assured by the judge that he should have justice, replied, "Bedad, yer honor, it's jist joostis that I'm afraid of; it's to be claired that I'm after," — if he were as honest as Pat he would ask to be relieved from the "deep damnation" of that same record.

He admits, as a part of his record, that he practised his profession during the time the Eastern shore was in Rebel occupancy, but attempts to parry any inference of disloyalty by exclaiming, "With the same propriety might this potent logician affirm that every farmer, storekeeper, physician, shoemaker, and blacksmith who followed his regular avocation while living under Rebel rule was a traitor." Not quite, Mr. Snead! By practising before a Rebel court you acknowledged the jurisdiction of that court, while farmers might plough and physicians might heal without in any way acknowledging Rebel authority. Most "potent logician" thou?

The following is an extract from a pamphlet written and published in January last by Hon. Joseph Segar. It throws some further light upon Mr. Snead's record:

"And now as to Mr. Snead. Some time after the secession of Virginia a Federal invasion was reported in the neighborhood of Pungoteague. The Second Regiment of Virginia militia was called out by Colonel Finney, and assembled at Pungoteague. The alarm proved a false one, and in the evening several persons were called upon for speeches. Among the speakers was Mr. E. K. Snead. The substance of that speech, as furnished me by those who heard it, was, that *it was the time for action and not speaking — that he (Snead) had come at the call of his country to repel the invasion of her soil and would be the last man to falter — that if any man should run, he (Snead) would shoot him, and if he (Snead) should run, he hoped some one would shoot him (Snead) down.* The vote for Jeff. Davis is acknowledged by Mr. Snead, and I give him the full benefit of his explanation of that vote. He was appointed a Commissioner of elections, and, being so appointed, he could not vote but the Rebel Presidential ticket. Bought off from loyalty by the very cheap honor of an appointment as an officer of the Polls! His loyalty could not have lain very deep. Why did he not decline the appointment and thus save himself from this connection with treason and rebellion? I would have seen the earth reel and totter before I would have consented, as Mr. Snead did, to keep the polls of treason and then cast a vote for the arch-traitor. Nor was this the only disloyal vote cast by the gentleman. He voted for a member of the Rebel Congress, and for a secession member of the House of Delegates."

Mr. Segar also states, in a letter which I have seen, that he knows "from personal inspection of the Roll-books of Accomac county, that Snead voted for Jeff. Davis." So much for the record by which he is willing to be judged. A plea of repentance might be in order, but, on the record simply, I was wrong in prefixing "semi" to the word "disloyalist." In his communication to "The Tribune," Mr. Snead says:

"On the 28th of September last . . . I was elected Judge of the First Judicial Circuit, without opposition. I was called to the position by the spontaneous action of the loyal people of those cities (Norfolk and Portsmouth) without any solicitation or effort on my part."

In my letter which called forth his communication, the types made me say that he received 700 votes in Portsmouth and less than 70 in Norfolk. Instead of the former number I wrote 100, having been informed that his entire vote was about 170. Now this was one of the statements wherein I was open to his charge of ignorance of the subject upon which I wrote. I am therefore happy to make the *amende honorable*. Mr. Snead *received at that election* 25 *votes only*, and not 170 as I stated, nor yet 770 as I was made to state. But he says he "was called to the position by the spontaneous action of the loyal people of those cities." Then there are only 25 loyal people in those cities? And this is the constituency back of his Judgeship? And this the loyal community now ground beneath the heel of military despotism?

In his "concise history" of three columns he introduces "C. H. Porter, Esq.," his co-laboring "Commonwealth's Attorney," who accompanied him to Washington to see the President and Mr. Attorney-General Bates. This Mr. Porter is now in charge of the Provost Marshal at these headquarters, having been sentenced by military commission to six months' confinement at such military post as the commanding general should designate. Four charges were preferred against him, with one or more specifications under each charge. Charge First: "Using seditious and treasonable language against the United States." Charge Second: "Conduct prejudicial to good order and military discipline." Charge Third: "Using contemptuous and disrespectful language of the President of the United States and against the Congress of the United States." Of these three charges he was found guilty. The following is the language he was proven to have used in a public drinking saloon in Norfolk, viz.:

"This Government is all a G—d d—d humbug from beginning to end, and if you could have seen what I did in Washington you would say so, — I mean what I say, I have been there and seen it all, Abraham Lincoln is doing anything he can for his election. If Abraham Lincoln allows the military authority to go on as it is here I would rather live under Jeff. Davis's Government than this."

And upon being reprimanded and cautioned by some one present, and upon being asked if he really meant that he would rather live under Jeff. Davis's Government than under this, he answered:

"Yes, by G—d. I stand here now in the City of Norfolk and proclaim it boldly and above board that the United States Government is a bogus, rotten, and corrupt government, from beginning to end."

It should be stated, if it is thought to be any palliation, that Porter was intoxicated at the time and smarting under an unsuccessful mission, undertaken in company, as before stated, with Mr. E. K. Snead to the President.

It is submitted whether it was very far out of the way to class these men as semi-disloyalists.

The vote in Norfolk on the 24th of June, the day of the election for city officers, upon the question of military or civil government, when there were 330 votes for the former and but 16 for the latter, is an ugly fact for Mr. Snead to explain. The only plausible point he makes is that "112 voted (109 he should have said) for municipal officers, thus indirectly voting for civil government." But it does not follow that these 112 voted indirectly for civil government. It is quite as likely that many voted against civil government and yet voted for municipal candidates — reasoning that should civil government prevail they were entitled to their voice as between candidates. Again, in the words of General Butler's order:

"As there were at least two sets of candidates voted for, containing a list of some forty-five officers who would have place in the civil government, in each set, it would seem that but twenty votes were cast for city officers except by those who were interested in being elected; assuming always that the men running for office in a city vote for each other."

As to Snead's charges of military intimidation at the polls, of threats of discharge from employment, etc., and to his "analysis of the vote against civil government," they scarcely deserve serious attention. They are of a piece with the loyalty of his record, *Falsus in uno, falsus in omni.* The man who, having practised in Rebel courts, harangued a Rebel mob, and voted for Jeff. Davis, can brazenly say, speaking of the oath of allegiance, that "no one ever supposed there was any reason for requiring *me* to take it," would naturally not be very scrupulous in statements put forth for a purpose. The fact remains that Norfolk is now well governed, economically, justly, and in the interest of the Union, being in every particular in direct contrast to the former rule. General Butler has and deserves the gratitude of the loyal citizens of that city, for securing to them, through martial law, all the blessings of good government.

It does not devolve upon me to enter into a discussion of all the questions touched upon by Snead in his three columns. If General Butler needed any defence — and he does not — I do not know that it would be my place to take up the cudgels in his behalf. And as to all the questions of jurisdiction, etc., involved in that of the "restored government," they will have to be subordinated to "military necessity" as may seem good in the eyes of commanding generals. However, it is notorious that licenses to sell liquor levied by the "restored" legislature, are the only sources of revenue known to the "restored government," that the only money it has ever disbursed has been for the salaries of the officials, and that these officials (pseudo) appear to be so indignant and factious because military rule, cutting off the only source of revenue, cuts off their salaries.

CHAS. A. PAGE.

XVIII.

THE COLORED TROOPS.

GENERAL BIRNEY'S CONGRATULATORY ORDER. — SPLENDID BEHAVIOR OF
OUR COLORED TROOPS. — LATEST MOVEMENTS.

HEADQUARTERS OF GENERAL BUTLER,
August 21, 1864, 10 P. M.

GENERAL BIRNEY has published the following to his corps : —

HEADQUARTERS TENTH ARMY CORPS,
FUZZLES' MILLS, VIRGINIA,
August 19, 1864.

GENERAL ORDERS. — The major-general commanding congratulates the Tenth Army Corps upon its success. It has, on each occasion when ordered, broken the enemy's strong lines. It has captured during this short campaign four siege guns protected by formidable works, six colors, and many prisoners. It has proved itself worthy of its old Wagner and Sumter renown.

Much fatigue, patience, heroism may be still demanded of it, but the major-general commanding is confident of the response. To the colored troops, recently added to us, and fighting with us, the major-general tenders his thanks, for their uniform good conduct and soldierly bearing. They have set a good example to our veterans by the entire absence of straggling from their ranks on the march.

By order of Major-General D. B. BIRNEY.

E. W. SMITH, Lieutenant-Colonel and Assistant Adjutant-General.

General Butler, in a despatch to the Tenth Corps, on receiving official report of its work, said : " All honor to the brave Tenth Corps ; you have done more than was expected of you by the Lieutenant-General."

The loss in the four colored regiments is about three hundred. The Seventh United States Colored on the first day carried, with fixed bayonets, a line of rifle-pits, and carried it without a shot, but with a loss of 51. It was one of the most stirring and gallant affairs I have ever known.

Perhaps the star regiment in the fight of the last week is the Thirty-ninth Illinois, the only regiment from that state in this army. Its colonel, lieutenant-colonel, major, and two senior captains have lost either life or limb within two months, and men in proportion, and yet its spirit remains unbroken. On the sixteenth there were individual instances of gallantry in this regiment which would, could they be recorded, vie with the wildest tales of romance.

The Second and Tenth Corps recrossed the river last night. The Second marched to the support of the Fifth, which is known to have been heavily engaged on the Weldon road. The main Rebel force north of the James, after being repulsed in its assault of Thursday night, and being apprised of Warren's operations south of Petersburg, marched that night in that direction, and was a part of the force which engaged Warren on Saturday.

I send extracts from Rebel papers of yesterday. General Joseph Hayes, whom they claim to have captured, was in command of the regular brigade of the Fifth Corps, and was one of the most promising and trusted of the younger brigadiers — not a man to surrender except in extremity. No particulars of the engagement have been received here.

XIX.

ON THE WELDON ROAD.

GENERALSHIP. — THE COLORED TROOPS. — THE FIGHTING ON THE WELDON
R. R. — LEE'S TASK.

HEADQUARTERS DEPARTMENT VIRGINIA AND NORTH CAROLINA.
IN THE FIELD, August 25, 1864.

THE eight or ten days of active operations seem to have ceased, though not for "lack of argument." It has been a pure, keen matching of generalship. Grant's object was to extend his cordon of impregnable works to the Weldon road south of Petersburg. Lee could not know his purpose, but must watch and strike counter and parrying blows. The Tenth and Second Corps were thrown across the James, and it looked like a rush for Richmond. It was not, though it had all the opportunities of an optional movement which could be made more or less of, according as the enemy might manœuvre. Hancock and Birney demonstrated and fought more or less on each of four days. Their loss all told was scarcely less than two thousand. The enemy's is judged to have been greater, for he made successive efforts to dislodge us, charged in deep masses on good works, and was repulsed with such loss that, on one occasion, one regiment, the Seventh United States Colored, buried eighty-two that had fallen on less than two acres in its front, while the loss of that regiment was two! North of the river, then, we inflicted excessive losses, and by the movement distracted the enemy's attention from the real thing intended. Besides, it was again proved that the colored soldiers are good soldiers — incontrovertibly proved — and thus the base stigma sought to be stamped upon them for the affair of the mine explosion, has been cleared away beyond all plausible cavil.

Meanwhile Warren has marched to the Weldon road: it was a detached movement. He made no attempt to retain communications, but left them to be established, when he should have become firmly fixed, and there should be troops enough, by the return of the Second Corps, to fill out a continuous line. He deliberately subjected himself to all the chances of a detachment, severed from any support. He must take care of front, right and left, with the knowledge that the enemy might mass upon either, and that he could not know which a moment before the event; he must, in consequence, hold in reserve the main body of his corps, ready on the instant to support either flank, or the front, if the Rebels, contrary to habit, strike there. They chose to strike the right flank held by Ayres's Division, and they came down through the woods, much as Stonewall Jackson burst upon the Eleventh Corps at Chancellorsville; but, unlike that affair, this was no surprise. True, by force of numbers and impetuous attack, they bore back our men, and took in a half an hour 1,800 prisoners, but then, so soon as they could be opposed by equal numbers, they in turn were routed. That our loss in prisoners was not made good by an equivalent number taken from them, is explained only by the precipitation of their retreat. In killed and wounded they suffered most; this is known since those of both sides fell into our hands. I repeat, this affair was no surprise; our loss in prisoners was not the result of want of watchfulness, or want of gallantry, but an untoward chance that had to be risked, and which the wily enemy saw and improved. The Regular brigades suffered most severely, General Joseph Hayes commanding; after having his horse shot under him, General Hayes had reformed his brigade in comparative order, and was withdrawing it himself on foot and closest to the enemy, when a sudden dash cut him off; his fate was not known until the Richmond papers reported him a prisoner.

Our revenge came on Sunday morning, two days later. By that time portions of the Ninth and Second Corps had filled in the gap. We held a well defended line from the Appomattox due north of Petersburg to the Weldon Railroad, due south a distance of ten miles. The enemy massed upon the extreme left, and assaulted with all his might. He surged around the salient point on the railroad and came on us as though he thought he had turned the flank, but he was trapped. Warren had a refused flank at almost a right angle down the railroad, and the crowded Rebel masses fell a prey to the dispositions made to welcome him. Our men had it all their own way, — theirs the slaughtering, theirs very few of the slaughtered; and yet the enemy madly poured into that slaughter-pen more and still more men, and they were each a mass still swept down. They were in full sight in a broad field — our men behind earthworks. The range was short to the woods out of which they broke, and our men stood thickly and fired rapidly, many of them with aim. For every prisoner lost, the revenge was a man killed or wounded, before they went back — "all that was left of them."

Summing up, then, the brightest, welcomest thing, because it must be confessed that it is a little novel, is this, leaving prisoners out of the account (of which roughly stated we have lost 200 and taken 1,000), the Rebels have lost in killed and wounded, on the estimate of the least sanguine of those who have had the most and best data for judging, twice the number we have. The Richmond papers are particularly lugubrious over the losses in the repulse they suffered at the hands of Warren, Sunday morning. In general officers they concede the following killed during the week of fighting, viz.: General Sanders, General Lamar, General Gerrardey, General Chambliss, and General W. H. F. Lee, and these wounded, viz.: General Barton, General Finnegan, General Anderson, General Clingman, and General Conner, in all ten generals. And they mention other field-officers, colonels, etc., in the same proportion. Since it is precisely men, and precisely good officers which they can least afford to lose, the fact that in these they have lost so heavily, should be made of large account in arriving at a just estimate of the week's fighting.

But we hold, and will continue to hold the Weldon Railroad. They used to run ten to fifteen trains per day over it. Only the Danville Road is now left to them. Of how much advantage the loss to them of this road will be, time alone can determine. But the persistence with which they have defended it and the desperate efforts they have made to regain possession of it, serve to show what value they placed upon it, and how great a blow its loss is to them. More than six weeks ago Grant attempted to possess it. Foiled then, he has succeeded now,— and his persistence in manœuvring for it may be taken as evidence of the value he attaches to it. It has already been thoroughly destroyed, to the burning of every tie, and the twisting of every rail — for a distance of ten or more miles, being from within two miles of Petersburg, to a point several miles below Reams's Station. The destruction has been mainly performed by Barlow's Division of the Second Corps, with Gregg's Cavalry for guard to men at work.

The extent of the line now held by Meade's and Butler's armies, reckoning by the shortest roads, is not less than thirty miles. And Lee has to meet Grant on every point of this tremendous line. It will task even his powers, with his far inferior force. Nevertheless, it must be remembered that it is one of the maxims of war that the offensive army must be twice the numbers of the defensive army, in order that it shall have equal chances of success. We shall see.

XX.

THE NEW POSITION.

IMPORTANCE OF THE NEW POSITION. — EXTENT OF OUR LINES. — GRANT'S ADVANTAGE. — PRECARIOUS CONDITION OF LEE. — RETROSPECTIVE. — SHORTCOMINGS OF THE CAMPAIGN. — LOST OPPORTUNITIES. — WHAT MIGHT HAVE BEEN.

HEADQUARTERS OF GENERAL BUTLER,
Sunday, August 28, 1864.

THE line now held by these armies is so long that it is beyond one man's capacity to be an eye-witness of all of even the most important events which occur. Everybody in the army depends upon the New York papers for knowledge of what the army does. Even corps commanders have no other means of learning details of movements wherein their own corps do not participate.

Of the heavy battle of Thursday on the Weldon road nothing is yet known here definitely. It was twenty miles south of here — left of here — beyond the province of your correspondent at these headquarters, and beyond the path of duty of any one on the hither side of the Appomattox. Perhaps one third of the soldiers of Grant's army are not yet aware that their comrades have again been in battle. It follows, therefore, that if I would write at all I must speculate on the general situation, else make up a letter of unimportant matter — in fact, create a letter.

One fact which may, I think, be stated, is pregnant with a world of meaning. The railroad now and for some time in operation from City Point to the very confines of Petersburg, is to be extended eight miles to Warren's position on the Weldon road, south of the city. The preliminary survey has been completed, and it is calculated that it can be built — the bed graded, track laid, and cars running — in ten to fifteen days!

Enough of rails have been reserved from the destruction of the Weldon road to lay the entire distance. The purpose which this indicates is apparent, — need not be enlarged upon. That the occupation of Petersburg would make Richmond untenable is conceded by the Rebels. Let Grant reach and hold all the railroads south of Petersburg, and it amounts to the same as the reduction of that city.

He now semi-circumvallates the city with a chain of strong works which may be held with slender force. He holds from a point due north to a point due south — let him reach around until he shall be due west, cutting the Lynchburg road, and the end will not be far distant. And while doing this the Rebel leaders must look out that he does not pierce their line at some point which they may happen at some time to hold but weakly. Grant has a choice of thirty miles, where to strike ; and let him attack at any point, the Rebels must concentrate there ; and still Grant may reserve his decision whether to make the movement more than a feint. If he sees success within his grasp, then push on there.

If he finds the enemy massed upon his point of attack — finds that he has none of the advantage of a surprise, then and there, while that movement shall still seem to be pressed with all his might, he may strike elsewhere on the line, or project that line another reach of the clasp about Petersburg. The result is not the less certain, is all the more certain, that in the nature of the case it cannot be compassed save by slow steps. It will be the sure end which always follows when great ability, wielding great means, uses the *festina lente*. Much, of course, depends on how promptly the strategy which Grant must from time to time bring into play shall be seconded by those intrusted with its execution. In the handling of a great army everything hinges on time.

This is no new truth, but one that has had a score of almost startling illustrations in this campaign. Time and again a movement has been utterly foiled, or only partially successful, which should have been a grand triumph, and would have been, but for the slowness of some body of troops. The nick of time passed and they did not reach the nick of place. A certain corps was to have occupied Spottsylvania at a certain hour. Had it done so, it would have interposed between the wings of Lee's army, and that day must have destroyed the enemy. Wilson's Cavalry got on the ground, cleared it of Rebel cavalry, skirmished with Longstreet coming from one direction, and with Hill coming from another, — and at the same time Warren was attacking Hill's rear. McIntosh's one brigade of cavalry held the gap for hours and vainly waited for that corps which should have been there, — held it as a forlorn hope, willing to hold it at any price, if that corps would only come.

But it did not come. It was four hours, only four hours behind time, but those four hours have cost us many thousands of lives, and will yet cost us more thousands. A delay of ten hours in the arrival of the pontoons, when the head of the army reached the James, lost us Petersburg, — which, taken then, would have given us Richmond long ago. These are two instances. There have been many others like unto them.

This slowness is a "monster of such hideous mien" that it would be supposed to be the one thing each general shuns, avoids, hates. On the contrary, it is "seen too oft, until, familiar with its face," too many have learned to endure it with the most complacent and philosophical composure.

To these often failures on the part of subordinates to come to time must be attributed the fact, that this campaign has, like a wounded snake, or an Alexandrine rhyme, dragged its slow length along with only measurable success. That there has been any degree of success must be attributed to the persistence and fertility of resource of the lieutenant-general, and to the peerless fighting of the rank and file.

Sedgewick, marching forty miles in one day, to be in at the battle of Gettysburg; Hancock, crowding his corps by forced march to a junction with the rest of the army on the morning of that Friday in the Wilderness; Warren, but the other day, projecting his corps through that other Wilderness, detached from all connection and support of other corps, and fixing an unrelaxing clench upon the Weldon road, — these are conspicuous instances of promptness.

But there should be *no* failures in point of time, without the responsibility being stamped where it belongs, and the officer upon whom it falls should never have another opportunity of doing harm, of frustrating the best-laid plans. And on this philosophy, which I have from the lips of a major-general who does come to time. Said he: "When I order an officer to do such a thing by such a time, and he fails in point of time, there is at once a question between him and me. The onus is upon him. He must leave my department unless he can show that it was impossible to execute my orders by the time specified. If he can show that *I* am the party to blame, I am convicted of issuing orders which it was impossible to obey, I am shown to be incompetent to my position. In that case, I will go. *But as the Lord liveth, if a man is ten minutes behind time, he must go, unless he shows cause — in that case, I will go, for I ought to.*"

If these reasonings and this conclusion obtained in higher quarters, there would be fewer failures.

FIVE DAYS OF QUIET. — THE FALL SEASON AND THE SOLDIERS. — TOBACCO FOR THE ARMY. — HOW OUR BOYS CRAVE IT. — GENERAL BUTLER AND THE NEGRO SOLDIERS. — PICKET HUMOR. — ARMY HOSPITALS. — THE PAYMASTER.

HEADQUARTERS GENERAL BUTLER,
September 2, 1864.

TO-DAY has been the fifth consecutive day of absolute quiet — of entire cessation from firing of guns large and small, of weather comparatively cool by day and exceedingly chilly by night. Last night especially was very cold — toward morning unbearably so, unless one had an extra blanket within reach. In this latitude as the fall comes on, mid-days may be of scorching heat, while mid-nights shall be shivering cold. It may be owing to this fact that September is considered the most unhealthy month of the year — more so than the excessive heats of July and August. Still, I doubt if it will be much worse for these soldiers. It will be no worse for them, and perhaps much better, if the fall clothing can be given out — say everything but great-coats, which will not be needed for some time yet — immediately. One fortunate circumstance is, that this is a wooded country, and a few such nights as the last will set a fire to blazing for every corporal's guard in the army; and these densely-grown pine-lands will be rapidly cleared when a hundred thousand men set to chopping fuel for twenty thousand fires in the open air.

In the July dust we longed for rain. With August came rain — rain every day. Some of us thought that a little too much fell, but anything was preferable to the dust. Some one apostrophized a late storm, after the manner of the forbearing lover to his mistress, thus : —

"With all thy *falls* I love thee still."

Yet the waters scarcely diminished the heat, and some of the most trying marches the army has known, have been over earth, slippery wet, and between fitful showers, but in air stifling as the blast of a furnace, and enervating and emasculating as sniffs of chloroform.

But now with the first days of fall, that, too, is past, and there are hours after each sunrise and hours before each sunset so deliciously bracing, hours when the air is brave with strength and life, that one would almost risk the fever bred of sultry noon and chilly daybreak, for the sake of wantoning in lusty life the rest of the time. Why, the very horses feel the difference, and manifest it with a pawing delight, an eager spirit of *go*, an airiness of carriage, a snuffing of the air of inhalation and a snorting of the air of exhalation, which tempts to the saddle, while it dissuades from the spur.

Two days ago, while threading my way through a camp, a good-looking, cleanly dressed, full-bearded soldier attracted my attention by a gesture which was half salute and half beckon. Reining up, for I thought I detected a desire to speak with me, the man advanced, and, folding his arms and standing at his full length, began: "Sir, do I look like a beggar? Look at me and say if I appear as if I were in the habit of begging?" I answered in the negative, and desired to know whether he had anything to beg for then — and I got his story. Said he, "Do you chew or smoke? Now I don't know whether you are an officer or a chaplain, or a sutler, or a quartermaster's clerk, but if you have any tobacco with you, for God's sake divide with me. You see I have not been paid for five months, so I can't buy any, and I *must* have a smoke — can't stand it any longer, am home-sick as a school-girl; be hanged if I have n't come confounded near deserting. (Here he stopped to light a cigar I had handed him, along with a more-or-less of Killikinnick.) When (puff) I get back (puff, puff) to Connecticut, I mean to raise (puff, puff, puff) — raise tobacco by the acre, and hang me (puff, puff) — hang me if I don't give it all away to poor devils that have n't money to — (puff, puff, puff) — poor devils that have n't money to buy any." Conversing with him further, he declared that he would re-enlist if he could be sure of obtaining tobacco regularly, and he would not re-enlist unless he could be sure of it.

The moral to this incident is easily enough deduced — tobacco for the soldiers.

The negro soldiers believe in General Butler with all their might. Some weeks ago a squad of them presented themselves at the office of Lieutenant Brown, then mustering officer here, and demanded to be mustered out. They had heard that General Butler's "time was out," they had enlisted to fight under him and they "was n't goin' t' hab any udder man generalizin' fer dem," and they were quieted only by the assurance that General Butler's time was not out.

The humor that crops out between pickets furnishes a good many funny incidents. Major Ludlow was lately showing his lines to a party of civilians, one of whom was conspicuous for his hat, a tall, silk tile hat, new from an establishment beneath the Astor House. The individual of the hat had just said to the Major: "Is that man in drab clothing, just out there under the tree, one of your pickets?" when the "man in drab clothing" brought his gun to his shoulder and shouted: "Say, you feller with the stove-pipe hat! ef you don't take that hat off d—d suddent, I'll shoot ye!" And he of the hat *did* take it off "suddent," and for the rest of the way carried it something nervously in his hand.

Not long since Surgeon R. K. Smith reported for duty to General Butler in person. The general told him he should order him to Norfolk to report to General Shepley, who would direct him to inspect all the hospitals in that vicinity, with a view to clearing them of all convalescents fit for duty.

The doctor asked if in every case he should use his own discretion as to whether a man was fit for the field. "Yes, sir," said the general, "and you are not to credit any yarns they may tell you. I'll give you a good rule to work by, I'll take it from Hoyle. Whenever you are in doubt *take the trick*." Dr. Smith proceeded to the different hospitals about Norfolk, and has already sent nearly or quite a battalion to their regiments.

It is not to be doubted, that were the hospitals throughout the North subjected to a thorough overhauling, the army would be the gainer by some thousands. The difficulty is, that the men once in hospital, even those slightly wounded, who when a few weeks have healed their wounds are hardy and able, do not come back. They are absorbed in a dozen different ways. Some become nurses, some wardmasters, some cooks, others are taken up as hospital guards, as orderlies for the surgeons, as musicians for the hospital band, which has been organized to swell the importance of the surgeon in charge, until, in many hospitals, there are as many well soldiers as sick ones.

And so it is that stalwart men, trained veterans who should be in the field, toot serenades, simmer broths, bend over washtubs, polish surgeon's boots, carry *billets doux* for young Mr. Doctor, even scrape their chins and mend their stockings, if the soldier should once have been barber or tailor. I repeat, a thorough overhauling of all the northern hospitals would send to the field some thousands of good soldiers.

At last, we have a paymaster among us. Several millions of

dollars have been paid to this army within a fortnight, and how the sutlers do thrive! Communication with the North is so easy, and the army being quite permanently located, sutlers and their goods are allowed to come to the front, that all the luxuries of the season abound. One may see any morning at City Point and Bermuda Hundred, heaps of mellow apples, peaches, and vegetables that would not discredit Washington and Fulton markets. Fresh fish, not twenty-four hours from the sea, fresh figs, not twenty-four hours from the tree ("In the name of the prophet, *Figs!*") and "Syllabubs and jellies and wines, pies, and other such lady-like things," all brought from the vicinity of Norfolk, may be had of your enterprising sutler, if one will bear the swindle. Mr. Sutler often deals in literature. He will sell you the "Atlantic" or "Harper's" for half a dollar, the latest novel for twice the sale price printed on the cover, or he will sell you a half-dozen rolls of cough candy, or quinine by the dose, or a pair of spurs, or a shirt, or perfumed note-paper, fit for letters to your sweetheart. He keeps postage stamps. He deals in Bibles. He has several cords of canned fruits and half a dozen barrels of eggs, nature's own device in the way of canned fruit. In the way of cutlery, pocket knives and cork-screws he is sure to have, scissors usually, and surgical instruments occasionally. Great is the sutler. Like Shakespeare, he is "a many-sided man." Like Sam Slick's wife, one cannot live without him nor scarcely with him. Like the Miller's Daughter, he has "grown so dear, so dear." Like Robinson Crusoe, "his right there is none to dispute."

GENERAL ORD ON SICK LEAVE. — A SALUTE FOR SHERMAN. — THE SOLDIERS ON MCCLELLAN. — THE DUTCH GAP CANAL.

HEADQUARTERS OF GENERAL BUTLER,
September 5, 1864.

GENERAL ORD, who has been in command of this Department during General Butler's absence, goes North to-day on sick leave. Major-General Gibbon of the Second Division of the Second Corps throughout the campaign is temporarily assigned to the Eighteenth Corps in place of General Ord.

Beginning at midnight last night, a salute of 100 guns was fired in celebration of Sherman's great victory and the fall of Atlanta. The guns were shotted and trained upon Petersburg, and provoked a reply from the enemy's artillery. In consequence the cannonading did not cease with the salute, but vexed the whole night with great noises. Nobody on our side was hurt by it.

Our army comment on the taking of Atlanta is "bad for McClellan. He can't stand any victories." His nomination produces no excitement, much less any enthusiasm. The army, if it could be polled to-day, would show a decided majority against him. I have heard many a man say he would vote for him if it were not that he won't be seen in such bad company. — For Vallandigham and the Woods are cordially hated by every soldier in the army.

Besides, the whole army knows that the army it is fighting desires nothing else so much as that Mr. Lincoln shall be defeated, and that knowledge tends to make our soldiers anxious that he shall be elected.

The Dutch Gap canal — as a canal — is so far completed that its success is beyond question. The river will be taught a new and better channel, and commerce will be forever facilitated. But of how much use as a military expedient the canal may be, remains to be seen. It will by no means open the river to Richmond. The Rebel gun-boats are now a mile or two above it. Fort Drury is above it, and there may be obstructions in the channel above it. However, by means of it we shall flank Howlett House battery, which is almost as formidable as Drury's Bluff, and shall cut off six miles of river.

The work is nearly all being done by colored troops. They work steadily and quietly under heavy artillery fire, which the enemy is able to rain upon the position.

The work goes on constantly, day and night, excepting only five hours in the heat of the day.

General Butler is expected back to-morrow.

XXI.

FROM THE ARMY OF THE JAMES.

THE NEW ARMY TITLE. — PROVOST MARSHAL'S OFFICE, WHAT IT IS AND WHAT IT DOES. — STARVATION PRICES IN RICHMOND. — WHAT THE PROVOST MARSHAL KNOWS. — FACTS ABOUT THE REBEL ARMY.

HEADQUARTERS OF THE ARMY OF THE JAMES.

BY recognition as such by the War Department, the army commanded by General Butler has become officially, as it was first in fact, "The army of the James."

Hence your correspondent at these headquarters assumes the new style in the caption of his letters.

My tent adjoins the office of the Provost Marshal, and the scenes enacted there are so directly beneath my eyes, that I cannot but note them to myself as I now do for you. A Provost Marshal's office is a safety-valve, an escape-pipe, a clearing house, a court of justice, a bureau of information, a headquarters of detectives, — a place where, besides its own regular business, all the fag ends of business that belong nowhere in particular come, and are attended to. Here all prisoners, deserters, and refugees are examined, and information obtained from these and other sources. Here soldiers, teamsters, sutlers, negroes, and rebel residents report their grievances, obtain a hearing, solicit privileges, or are brought, examined, and disposed of when guilty of any sort of misdemeanor.

The Provost Marshal must be an officer of peculiar qualifications: of courteous manners, that every person coming before him may be perfectly at ease, else the culprit, deserter, or what not, will not be able to tell his story clearly or consistently.

He must be an officer of keen and accurate perception and discernment, else he will be imposed upon by got-up tales and information.

He must have aptness for affairs and promptness in decision, else he would never dispatch the immense business that comes into his hands. In short, he must have *faculty* — which is a word used in the "Minister's Wooing" to characterize Mrs. Kate Scudder, she "was a woman of faculty." These qualifications are indispensable. Better yet, if to these he adds a cunning pen, which shall in brief time draft an order or a letter or a dispatch without circumlocution, perspicuously, and forcibly. And still better if he be a short-hand writer, able to take a *verbatim* record of an examination, the accuracy of which shall be unquestionable.

Deserters now come over at the rate of a dozen or more a day. Each of these is examined separately and a record taken. Unless there are suspicious circumstances, these are permitted to take the oath of allegiance and are furnished subsistence and transportation to any point within our lines which they may choose. They belong to all the Rebel States, though a larger proportion are from regions which have been possessed by our forces, Tennessee, and Western Virginia. They manifest great pleasure at the reception they meet, and invariably declare that large numbers of their late comrades are deterred from desertion only by the fear of being pressed into our service.

Besides, they have been led to believe that the North is on the point of yielding; that therefore there will be little more fighting; that peace will be declared and their independence acknowledged soon after the election of McClellan in November; and this induces them to hold out the two intervening months.

But to the Provost Marshal's office again. The Provost Marshal, Lieutenant John I. Davenport, as I write, is examining a number of refugees, eight or ten who left Richmond last night. They are nearly all Irishmen, have been employed in the Confederate Arsenals at eight dollars per day, and have left rebeldom because they could not live on their wages. They avoided the Rebel pickets, were taken up by ours, and have finally brought up before the Provost Marshal.

A more ragged, poverty-stricken, out-at-the-elbows, and down-at-the-heels set of beggars you never saw, — they actually looked pinched and famished. Yet they had eight dollars a day, Rebel currency. But flour was five hundred dollars a barrel, and green corn ten dollars a dozen ears, and they were starved out of Richmond. They were able to subsist themselves until we grasped the Weldon Road, when prices of food rose at a jump beyond eight dollars a day for enough to feed a laborer. Like the deserters, they will be permitted to take the oath of allegiance, and be sent wherever within our lines they please, all but one. His first story was, that he had been living in Richmond five years, had not worked for the Government, had not been drafted, had eluded the authorities.

His mother kept a small grocery and had fed him the last year. This tale the Provost Marshal did not believe, and simply telling him that it was not possible that he had so long kept out of the Rebel army by secreting himself, remanded him to the guard-house. In less than an hour he asked to be taken to the Provost's office again, where he amended his tale; now it took this shape. He was a private to the Nineteenth Virginia, had been detailed as a blacksmith at the arsenal, had deserted on his detail being revoked, and had destroyed his order of detail, thinking he would be better treated as a refugee than as a deserter; and this last story is probably the correct one.

So perfect is the information in the Provost Office that the deserter or refugee who attempts to palm off a false story is pretty sure to come to grief. Once in a while a straggler from our own army reports himself as a deserter from the enemy, but only to be unmasked. The Lieutenant knows the organization of the Rebel army — could give an almost perfect roster of its officers. He knows, too, the locality of every Rebel Brigade now and at any time the last three months. Let a straggler pretend to belong to any one of them, and he must give answers corresponding with the record or he is shown to be an impostor, and who and what he is, is soon ascertained.

You should see the blank stare of surprise when a deserter sees how much is known about the Rebel army. A man is asked his company and regiment, and perhaps is then told the names of the officers commanding his company, regiment, brigade, division, and corps, and from what locality he deserted. From that instant he tells the truth, for he does not know how much more may be known; the strength of his company is obtained from him with other valuable information — as that which astonished him had been from some comrade deserter or prisoner previously here.

In the course of each few weeks, men from nearly every Rebel regiment pass through this office, and the information obtained, collected, and tabularized, ready for instant reference, is of vast service to the commanding General. It is in this way more than from what may be learned in all others, that the rapid decrease in the Rebel Army is proven. It may be known that in a given engagement the enemy lost severely, but when a company which was forty or fifty strong before, is now found to have dwindled to ten or twelve, fit for duty, the fact assumes a more definite form. It is a fact that the Rebel regiments are smaller to-day than ours, yet they were fully as large in the spring. And they have the habit of consolidating depleted commands to a greater extent than we have yet done.

The record of the Rebel organization, as I have just examined it, shows very many references to the margin, where it is explained that this or that regiment was, on or about such a date, consolidated with this or that other regiment; that this or that battalion has been broken up, and the remnant of men added to this or that other organization. And it is the same with brigades and divisions. For instance, the old "Stonewall Brigade" no longer exists, — all fought away, so many times smashed, that but a few splinters remained to be incorporated with any other body.

It would be tiresome to speak of all the suspicious characters with whom the Provost Marshal has to deal. Their name is legion. Nor will I more than advert to residents within the lines, begging a guard, begging rations, begging all sorts of privileges; to the negro who has not been paid his last month's wages, and seeks justice at the hands of the Provost; to the contraband fresh from a Rebel master, whose eyes roll in jolly whiteness when told that he can go to work for wages; to the women captured while trying to carry through to the enemy a pound of quinine, a hundred letters, a new bonnet, and the one thousand and one other feminine necessities; to the Rebel spy, with the plan of a fort in his foot; to the soldier guilty of assaulting his officer; to the officer guilty of maltreating a soldier, — all these individuals have been before the Provost Marshal, and have been passed on to their fate.

GENERALS WEITZEL AND TERRY. — GENERAL BUTLER AT WORK. — GENERAL TURNER'S RECOVERY. — REBEL HOPES FOR MCCLELLAN'S ELECTION. — DESERTIONS.

HEADQUARTERS OF GENERAL BUTLER,
Sunday, Sept. 11, 1864.

MY chief motive in writing is to say that the days pass here eventless. Generals Weitzel and Terry have been made Major-Generals by brevet. No one conversant with the record of each of these officers will question the propriety of this recognition of their services. Sheer merit, attested by three years of conspicuously able service, have made Lieutenant Godfrey Weitzel of the Engineers, and Colonel Alfred Howe Terry of the Seventh Connecticut, Major-Generals. The double stars seldom adorn such worthy shoulders.

Immediately on his return, General Butler set to work upon the business which had accumulated during his absence with his own unequalled capacity and tireless indefatigability. Besides commanding a large army in the field, he is Major-General commanding a large Department and Commissioner of Exchange. His great aptness and inexhaustible industry enable him to give personal attention to all the details of these three distinct orders of affairs and duties. He is like Frederick the Great in his personal attention to subordinate as well as to the ruling affairs within his control. For instance, his rule is to condemn no man — no officer who has been tried before court-martial, no citizen or other person who has been tried before Military Commission — without first giving him a personal audience, with perfect opportunity to state his case. Besides, he examines deserters, prisoners, and refugees himself when there appears to be anything special in their cases, or in their stories. Considered irrespective of everything else, there is something as unusual as it is wonderful and praiseworthy in the "workful" energy and omnipresent personality with which this man labors, and with which he commands.

General John W. Turner, who has been so sick for a fortnight that during many days his life was despaired of, is now thought to be beyond danger. General Turner is a young man — not thirty — the eldest son of John B. Turner, Esq., of Chicago, President of the Galena and Chicago Union Railroad Company, a graduate of West Point, and an officer much beloved and respected. His dangerous illness cast a shadow over his division — Second, Tenth Corps — which only his return to command can disperse. The part borne by him and his division on the day of the mine explosion is the only white spot in the affair — he was the only division commander who led his men that day.

A deserter came over yesterday who says the understanding prevails throughout the Rebel ranks that hostilities will cease with the election of McClellan, which they believe will be a certain thing. Articles from "The New-York World" and kindred papers are eagerly reproduced in all the Rebel sheets, until their armies look to the success of McClellan and the independence of the South as certain and simultaneous events. This deserter, James Haggerty, Seventeenth Virginia, also says that they believe there will be little or no fighting before Richmond in the meantime, and that for this reason they will not desert or throw down their arms until we have had our election. That such ideas are talked in the Rebel ranks cannot be doubted. Every deserter and prisoner confirms it. They are talked across to our pickets every day, and by the time one of our men has bandied words once or twice with a Rebel soldier, and finds him anxious for the success of the Chicago nominee as the assurance and prelude of peace on *their* terms, the Union soldier, no matter what his predilections, has determined to assist in spoiling their hopes by voting for Lincoln.

This same deserter reports that twenty-one men of his regiment, whose original enlistment had expired, provided themselves with sixty rounds of cartridges each, and taking their muskets started away in a body a few nights ago, avowing their intention of making their way home, and of defending themselves, if molested. Their homes being in a part of the State held alternately by each army, it is possible that they may make good their escape and safety.

The suggestive feature of this man's story is, of course, the statement that large numbers are deterred from desertion only by the conviction that their trouble will all be over in two months, at which time they expect the election of a peace President, and peace itself, and Southern independence as a natural consequence. This statement has daily confirmation in conversations between pickets, and from other deserters.

The army has not yet felt the brisk volunteering which is said to be going on at the North. Its strength has, however, been more than kept good by the return of convalescents; so that, despite the fact that so many are going out of the service, this volunteering will be so much clear gain.

The voice of the army is, enforce the draft without delay in every locality where the quota is not made up by the stipulated time.

PRACTICABILITY OF TAKING RICHMOND. — WHY THE MOVEMENT IS NOT MADE. — REBEL RELIANCE ON MCCLELLAN'S ELECTION. — HOPELESS WEAKNESS OF THE REBELS.

HEADQUARTERS OF THE ARMY OF THE JAMES,
Wednesday, Sept. 14, 1864.

THERE is authority for the statement that the Lieutenant-General is convinced that the forces now here — the Army of the Potomac and the Army of the James — are competent, without the addition of a man, to the reduction of Richmond, whether by defeat of the Rebel army and a consequent evacuation of the city, or by a defeat of that army which shall carry the city with it. Then why is the army quiet; why is it not put to work and the task accomplished?—it is asked. If there is force enough here now, why not use that force at once, and gain the end so ardently desired? For this reason — a reason, too, that is conclusive that General Grant is not the cold, calculating, flinty-hearted commander, the man utterly regardless of human lives and human suffering, which Rebels and Copperheads would have us believe; and a reason, moreover, which appeals to all who have friends in the army, and who have not friends in the army.

General Grant believes that it would be unjust to these men who have gone through so much, who are the heroes of so many battles, and the chosen ones miraculously preserved while so many of their comrades have fallen. General Grant believes that it would be an unnecessary and unjustifiable sacrifice to subject these to the losses of another series of battles, when it is within his power to so soon and so largely re-enforce them and thus distribute the loss, if further loss there must be, among a larger number, or, perhaps, enable him, by means of a larger army, to achieve the same end with far less sacrifice of life. These men, by virtue of heroism and baptism of fire and blood, have become the Old Guard of the Republic, and it were a grievous wastage of tried and precious things to sacrifice these in other than the Republic's extremity — and, thank God! that extremity is past. And you remember that Napoleon's Old Guard was never called upon except in the last extremity, unless it was to ride the crest of a victory and make it a triumph. No, these veterans will be subjected to no uncalled-for sacrifice, and when they are again called upon there will be other thousands to stand by their sides.

Do I seem to be writing very hopefully? I hope I am. Otherwise, I should not be true to my convictions. I have been with the army since the first day of May. I have participated in its feelings of depression and of exultation, and I but participate in its present hope and spirit when I write hopefully — for I believe that

> "The gods, who live forever,
> Are on our side to-day."

There is warrant for the belief. General Butler, who, perhaps, by natural parts and the training of a lifetime is best fitted of all the generals of the army to comprehend the situation, as he certainly is in point of opportunities for pertinent and relevant and conclusive information,— General Butler, I am warranted in stating, believes that the Rebels have only one ground of hope, only one bond of coherence; and that is, that the pending election may result in their favor; in other words — may result in favor of the Copperheads, and their Chicago nominee. And as all in the army believe that McClellan will not be elected — cannot carry three States — they feel that for the Rebels to lean on that hope is to lean on a broken reed, and accordingly, they expect to see the whole Rebel concern fall apart and go down soon after November — as well from all loss of hope on the part of the Rebels as from the potency of the Union armies, whose puissant blows will fall again and again before that time.

By reference to "The Richmond Whig" which I mailed to you last night, you will see that on their own calculation, there remains in the whole South but 132,000 men between the ages of sixteen and fifty. These they style *exempts*. By enactment of their Congress all residents between those ages are in their military service. From these exempts only can they recruit their armies. But these 132,000 are all men who have been detailed for duty considered, up to this time, as virtually important as service in the army, and not all of them, nor any large proportion of them, can be spared from their present avocations — as overseers of plantations, as workmen in the Confederate arsenals, as manufacturers of articles which must be obtained. Hence there is no basis of addition to their armies. They have already "robbed the cradle and the grave," and to-day there is not left to them even the resource of the Imperial city, when

> "Sempronius Atratius
> Was left in charge at home
> With boys and with gray-headed men,
> To keep the gates of Rome."

REBEL PICKET-FIRING AND ITS CONSEQUENCES. — PETERSBURG BOM-
BARDED. — OFFICIAL CHANGES. — HEALTH OF GENERAL BUTLER. —
THE SITUATION.

HEADQUARTERS, ARMY OF THE JAMES,
Thursday, Sept. 15, 1864.

THE incessant picket firing, when no advance is attempted by either side, has been so murderous and yet so useless, that our officers have determined that the wanton bloodshed shall cease. That portion of the line next to the Appomattox, and nearest to the city, formerly held by the Eighteenth and Ninth Corps, has been particularly noted for this kind of warfare. The Tenth Corps, General Birney, took this line some weeks ago. He at once caused the Rebels to be informally notified by our pickets that there would be no sharp-shooting except when they should begin it, and in that case we would not only return their fire, but open upon Petersburg with fifty guns, more or less. In consequence for ten days the sharp-shooters were idle. But day before yesterday the Rebels began again. As good as his word, about midnight before last General Birney began to bombard the city, and he continued the bombardment until noon yesterday — twelve hours. The firing was exceedingly rapid — that devoted city has never been subjected to a more terrific shelling. Should the Rebels again try their skill upon ours, their musket balls will again be repaid with cannon balls.

The position at Deep Bottom is now garrisoned entirely by negro soldiers under General Paine. The operations at Dutch Gap are being prosecuted by a force of negro soldiers, and a fair proportion of the trenches are held by the dusky patriots.

Major George C. Dodge, two days ago, relieved Colonel Howard as Chief Quartermaster of the Department. Major Dodge has long been known as one of the most capable and efficient officers in his branch of the service.

Captain Isaac C. Seeley is announced as Assistant Adjutant General on the staff of General Butler.

General Hickman, lately exchanged at Charleston, on his return from a short leave, will report to General Butler instead of to General Banks, which was the terms of his first order. He will be assigned to a Division either of the Tenth or of the Eighteenth Corps.

Captain John Cassels has not been relieved from his position of Provost Marshal of the Department, as might be inferred from a paragraph in the " Herald " correspondence.

Captain Conrad, of the Provost Marshal department of the Army of the Potomac, has been ordered to duty at Fortress Monroe. The rumor that Captain Cassels had been relieved probably grew out of this, and the assumed necessity to find a reason for the change doubtless caused the statement that Captain Cassels was deposed for uncourteous demeanor in the discharge of his duties.

General Butler, with Dr. McCormick, Captain Puffer, and Lieutenants Davenport and De Kay of his staff, went to Fortress Monroe yesterday afternoon on the special steamer " Greyhound." The General is not in good health — in fact is threatened with a fever, and his physicians insisted that he should give himself the benefit of the greater quiet and the better air of Old Point Comfort.

As regards the military situation, it may be summed up briefly thus: —

There is no occasion for General Grant to initiate active operations immediately, and the enemy will not dare to do so until he shall have re-enforced himself either from Early or from Hood. It is known that not a man has yet come back from the Valley, and it is not known that any have been detached from Sherman.

RESIGNATION OF COLONEL SHAFFER. — REBEL DESERTERS. — RETURN OF GENERAL BUTLER.

HEADQUARTERS OF THE ARMY OF THE JAMES.
Sept. 18, 1864.

COLONEL J. W. SHAFFER, Chief of Staff to General Butler, has resigned his commission, his resignation has been accepted, and he goes in a few days to his home in Illinois.

Commissioned at the beginning of the war, Captain and Assistant Quartermaster he served in that capacity some time at the West, was then made Colonel and Chief Quartermaster of the Department of the South, stationed at Port Royal. Thence he was ordered to Washington to be sent as Chief Quartermaster of the armies on the Mississippi; but New Orleans having been taken about that time, he was despatched forthwith in the same capacity to that place, where during eight months his labors were so arduous that in January, 1863, he was obliged to come North in very poor health.

His originally fine constitution seeming to be so shattered as to preclude the hope of returning to active duty, he tendered his resignation. Secretary Stanton, however, positively refused to permit him to resign, saying he might have time to recover his health, but should not leave the service.

General Butler, on being assigned to the Department of Virginia and North Carolina, tendered Colonel Shaffer the position of Chief of Staff, which he accepted, although still in delicate health. Since then, he has performed the duties of that position, to the entire satisfaction of even so exacting an officer as General Butler. And if his efficiency has met the approval of the General, not less has he by force of character and social qualities won the respect and love of his brother staff officers, and all others who have come in contact with him.

Sometime ago, when it became apparent to his friends and to himself that he must quit the service or become hopelessly broken in health General Butler finally consented to part with him, and with ample testimony to the great services he had rendered, forwarded his resignation and procured its acceptance.

Colonel Shaffer will shortly go West, where so far as his strength will permit he will aid in the political campaign, since he believes that on the defeat of the Chicago nominees at the polls depends the defeat of the Rebel armies in the field.

General Weitzel will succeed him, at least temporarily, as Chief of Staff.

Among the desertions from the enemy yesterday were a Major and two Captains. No wonder the men desert when the commissioned officers set the example. It is known that several plans have been concerted to come over in large bodies, but have been frustrated at the last moment by treachery. The only men who can get away are those placed on picket, and these have no chance except in a very few localities. Probably not one in fifty of the Rebel army has had an opportunity the last month which did not involve too much risk — for to try it, and to fail is to be remorselessly shot.

The devices they adopt to get away are often ingenious. One man goes for water between the lines, another for forage for his horse, another for roasting ears, or he crosses to our lines to exchange papers or traffic tobacco for other luxuries. But no suspected man is permitted any of these privileges; hence those who escape successfully are those against whom suspicion has never been excited.

Two lately came over whose home was Atlanta. In their own words — " When we heer'd you'd gut thar we kincluded Jeff. Davis was a dead coon."

General Butler has returned from Fortress Monroe much better in health. In General Grant's absence he commands all the armies operating against Richmond.

EVENTS OF THE AUTUMN.

THERE is an hiatus in the correspondence of Mr. Page from the last quoted letter to the close of the "grand campaign," early in December, 1864; it therefore seems necessary, in order to give a connected view of the intervening events, to draw some accounts from other eye-witnesses, and also to take a brief glance at the general situation.

On July 18th, 1864, President Lincoln ordered an additional draft for 500,000 men. This order was issued at a time when the North was thoroughly tired of the war, and an almost universal opinion prevailed that an honorable peace might be made with the Confederacy that would not involve a dissolution of the Union. A large party in Congress were of this opinion, and opposed to a vigorous prosecution of the war, as involving a useless waste of life and property. Hence the draft order would, doubtless, not have been issued but for the personal influence of President Lincoln. The circumstances attending its issue are strikingly illustrative of the character of Mr. Lincoln; and they are not irrelevant here as, without the issue and enforcement of this draft, General Grant could not have suppressed the Confederacy. The circumstances as related at the time to the writer by General Garfield — who was then a member of the Congressional Committee on Military Affairs — were as follows.

"The army at this time numbered about seven hundred and fifty thousand, but one day Mr. Lincoln came to the room of the Military Committee, and told them what he did not dare to say in public, or disclose to the House of Representatives — that at a certain time, not long ensuing — say, one hundred days — the term of three hundred and eighty thousand of those men would expire, and the army be reduced to below four hundred thousand. 'Unless I can replace those three hundred and eighty thousand,' he said, 'we not only cannot push the Rebellion, but we cannot stand where we are. Sherman will have to come back from Atlanta, Grant from the Peninsula. I ask you to give me the power to draft men to fill the ranks.'

"Some of his Republican friends on the Committee remonstrated with him; represented that we were just on the eve of his re-election; that the North was tired of the war, and would not tolerate another draft; that men who had already paid large sums for substitutes to meet the quotas, would not submit to be drafted, and would raise a tempest that would carry the country for the Democracy.

"Mr. Lincoln raised his tall and manly figure up to its full height as he answered, 'Gentlemen, it is not necessary that I should be re-elected; but it *is* necessary that I should put down this Rebellion. If you will give me this law, I will put it down before my successor takes his seat.'"

Thereupon the Committee drew a draft bill, and reported it to the House. It was voted down by a two-thirds majority. The Democrats were not very numerous at that time in Congress, but they were joined by a large number of Republicans, who were on the eve of a re-election and feared to face an angry constituency. When the voting was over, General Garfield moved a reconsideration, and made a speech full of fire, and bristling like a regiment of bayonets. It carried the House by storm, and Mr. Lincoln made the draft for five hundred thousand men.[1]

The draft met with much public disfavor, but its enforcement was greatly aided by the explicit declaration of Jefferson Davis to the writer of these notes that the Confederacy would make no peace except on the basis of Southern independence. This declaration, scattered very widely over the North, satisfied all but those willing to acquiesce in a dissolution of the Union that there could be no saving of the country without a vigorous prosecution of the war; still the States fell behind in the filling of their quotas, and, nearly sixty days after the issue of the draft

---

[1] See "Personal Recollections of Abraham Lincoln and the Civil War," by James R. Gilmore (Edmund Kirke). L. C. Page & Company.

Eng'd by A H Ritchie

Edwin M. Stanton

order, General Grant sent the following despatch to the War Department:—

"CITY POINT, 10.30 A. M., September 13.

"HON. EDWIN M. STANTON, *Secretary of War:*

"We ought to have the whole number of men called for by the President in the shortest possible time. Prompt action in filling our armies will have more effect upon the enemy than a victory over them. They profess to believe, and make their men believe, there is such a party North in favor of recognizing Southern independence that the draft cannot be enforced. Let them be undeceived. Deserters come into our lines daily who tell us that the men are nearly universally tired of the war, and that desertions would be much more frequent, but they believe peace will be negotiated after the fall election. The enforcement of the draft and prompt filling up of our armies will save the shedding of blood to an immense degree."

This, and a similar despatch from General Sherman had a marked effect on the filling up of the Union armies.

The general situation at about this time was succinctly described by General Grant to the Hon. E. B. Washburne.

"DEAR SIR: I state to all citizens who visit me that all we want now to insure an early restoration of the Union is a determined unity of sentiment North. The Rebels have now in their ranks their last man. The little boys and old men are guarding prisoners, guarding railroad bridges, and forming a good part of their garrisons for intrenched positions. A man lost by them cannot be replaced. They have robbed the cradle and the grave equally to get their present force. Besides what they lose in frequent skirmishes and battles, they are now losing from desertions and other causes at least one regiment per day.

"With this drain upon them the end is not far distant, if we will only be true to ourselves. Their only hope now is in a divided North. This might give them re-enforcements from Tennessee, Kentucky, Maryland and Missouri, while it would weaken us. With the draft quickly enforced the enemy would become despondent, and would make but little resistance. There is no doubt but the enemy are exceedingly anxious to hold out until after the Presidential election. They have many hopes from its effects.

"They hope a counter revolution; they hope the election of the Peace Candidate. In fact, like Micawber, they hope for something to turn up. Our peace friends, if they expect peace from separation are much mistaken. It would be but the beginning of war with thousands of Northern men joining the South because of our disgrace in allowing separation. To have 'peace on any terms' the South would demand the restoration of their slaves already freed; they would demand indemnity for losses sustained and they would demand a treaty which would make the North slave-hunters for the South. They would demand pay for the restoration of every slave escaping to the North."

One of the prime objects of the movements of General Grant's army was the cutting off of supplies from the Confederate forces, and the principal storehouse for feeding their armies near Richmond was the Valley of the Shenandoah. Through this outlet into Maryland and Pennsylvania the Confederates were able to secure for themselves about all the horses, live-stock and provisions they could carry away; and all the efforts to cut off this source of Confederate supply had been fruitless, owing — as General Grant thought — partly to the incompetence of some of our commanders, but mainly to the interference of General Halleck and Secretary Stanton, who hampered our forces with instructions which aimed to keep Washington constantly covered from the enemy. Grant's orders sent through the War Department were either modified or pigeonholed altogether, and the consequence was that the evil continued. He had repeatedly asked to have General Sheridan placed in command of that department, but the Secretary of War had objected, on the ground that he was too young for so important a command. General Hunter occupied that position on August 1st, when Grant decided to exercise his right as Commander-in-Chief of all the armies. On that day he wrote General Halleck at Washington: "I am sending General Sheridan for temporary duty whilst the enemy is expelled from the border. Unless General Hunter is in the field in person, I want Sheridan put in command of all the troops in the field, with instructions to put himself south of the enemy, and follow him to the death. Wherever the enemy goes let our troops go also. Once started up the Valley they ought to be followed until we get possession of the Virginia Central Railroad. If General Hunter is in the field give Sheridan direct command of the Sixth Corps and Cavalry Division."

Two days later President Lincoln wrote General Grant, strongly commending this movement, and adding: "I repeat to you it will neither be done nor attempted unless you watch it every day, and hour, and force it." Grant, in answer, telegraphed to the President: "I will start in two hours for Washington."

This he did, but, without stopping there, he went directly to the Monocacy, where he found General Hunter and his army encamped, and "scattered over the fields" in a state of masterly inactivity. He inquired of the general where the enemy was. Hunter answered that he did not know, that he had been so embarrassed by orders from Washington, moving him first to the right, and then to the left, that he had lost all trace of the enemy. Grant, to whom the enemy was always the first objective, replied that he would soon find out where the enemy was; and at once he ordered up a railway engine, and proceeded up the road to a point a few miles above Harper's Ferry. Returning soon to Monocacy, he wrote out instructions for the movement of the troops, but before handing them to Hunter, suggested to him that he should establish his department headquarters at Baltimore, or at any other point that he might choose, and relinquish to Sheridan the command of the army in the field. To this Hunter replied that he thought he had better be relieved entirely; that General Halleck seemed to distrust his fitness for the position, and he did not wish in any way to embarrass the cause of the country, — "thus," remarked General Grant, "showing a patriotism that was none too common in the army. There were not many major-generals who would voluntarily have asked to have the command of a department taken from them on the supposition that from some particular reason, or for any reason, the service would be better performed." Grant merely said "Very well, then," and telegraphed to Sheridan to meet him on the Monocacy.

Sheridan came by a special train, and Grant met him at the railway. There he invested Sheridan with the command of the Department, gave him the written instructions he had prepared for Hunter, and a few hurried oral directions for the movement of his army of thirty thousand men, and then started back to his own headquarters near Richmond. The appearance of Grant and Sheridan on the Monocacy was, as Grant had anticipated, at once followed by a concentration of the forces under General Jabal Early, and the relief of Pennsylvania and Western Maryland from the raids of the Confederates.

The forces under Early were at this time about equal in number to those under Sheridan, and the relative strength of the two armies is to be measured by the military skill of its respective generals; it was therefore fortunate for the country that the Union forces had such a leader as Sheridan.

To prevent Lee's sending such overwhelming re-enforcements to Early, as would be likely to crush Sheridan, Grant set in motion a portion of his own army as if for an attack upon Richmond. Hancock's Corps, a part of the Tenth Corps under Birney, and Gregg's Division of Cavalry were transferred to the north side of the James and kept in a threatening attitude; and General Meade, at Petersburg, was directed to keep a close watch upon the enemy in that quarter. The result was that few, if any, re-enforcements were sent to Early.

At the same time, General Grant despatched the Fifth Corps, under General Warren, to capture the Weldon Railroad, another important source of supplies for the Confederate forces. This was accomplished with great loss of life, and much severe fighting; but the road was taken, and held continuously up to the close of the war. This reduced General Lee's sources of supply to the Danville Railroad and the Valley of the Shenandoah. The latter cleared of Early's forces, a heavy blow would be struck at the Confederacy.

Sheridan had delayed a forward movement to get his men well in hand, but on the 10th of August he advanced up the Valley, Early falling back to Strasburg. Two days later Grant learned that Lee had sent to Early twenty cannon, two divisions of infantry, and a considerable force of cavalry. This information he sent to Sheridan by a special messenger, who found him just preparing to attack Early in his intrenchments, but these tidings threw him back on the defensive, and obliged him to wait for re-enforcements.

By the 15th of September Sheridan was ready to advance with an army numbering, of all arms, 45,000, with twenty batteries of artillery, of six guns each; and on that day Grant set out from City Point to visit him and direct the opening of the campaign. He says, "I knew it was impossible for me to get orders through Washington to Sheridan to make a move, because they would be stopped there and such orders as Halleck's caution suggested (and that of the Secretary of War) would be given instead, and would, no doubt, be contradictory to mine. I therefore, without stopping at Washington, went directly through to Charlestown, some ten miles above Harper's Ferry."

There Grant awaited the coming of Sheridan, and on his arrival asked if he had a map showing his own position and that of the enemy. Sheridan drew one from his side-pocket, which showed the various roads and streams, and the camps of the two armies, and proceeded to explain how he would handle his force to defeat the enemy. Grant had brought with him a plan of the campaign; but, seeing that Sheridan's was so admirable and he was so confident of success, he made no reference to it, but simply said, "Go in." The advance being decided on for the ensuing Monday morning, Grant returned at once to City Point, arriving there on the morning of Sheridan's first great victory.

It was a great victory: "It," said General Grant, "electrified the country." Measured by the forces engaged it does not equal that of Gettysburg, Nashville, Stone River or Vicksburg; but in its political consequences it is not surpassed by any other. Said Horace Greeley in the "Tribune," "Sherman's capture of Atlanta, and Sheridan's victories in the Valley, coupled with the emphatic declaration of Jeff. Davis to Jaquess and Gilmore, carried New York State for the Union; and thus secured the re-election of Mr. Lincoln." Also, as a mere military achievement it will doubtless rank in history among the most remarkable and decisive contests of our Civil War. In some respects it stands by itself. The completeness of the victory, the utter demoralization of the enemy, and the vigor and pertinacity of the pursuit for more than one hundred miles through the almost impregnable positions of the upper valley of the Shenandoah, are scarcely equalled by anything in the history of campaigning. Space will not permit a detailed account of these battles, and in lieu thereof we append Sheridan's brief and modest reports to General Grant.

At this time the main body of General Early's army was in the vicinity of Bunker Hill, northwest of the position held by General Sheridan. By a rapid advance along the Winchester road, General Sheridan could gain the rear of the enemy, and he quickly embraced the opportunity. The Sixth and Nineteenth Corps began to move at three o'clock on the morning of the nineteenth. General Crook followed three hours later, and joined the main column at the crossing of the Opequan. This advance was stubbornly resisted, and the first and second lines were temporarily thrown into confusion.

But the artillery being brought into position, the ranks were re-formed and a severe contest ensued. At some points the opposing lines were not more than two hundred yards apart. By a successful cavalry charge the enemy were thrown into confusion and driven from the field. The enemy retreated toward Fisher's Hill, a short distance south of Strasburg, closely followed by General Sheridan. That evening he sent the following despatch to General Grant:

WINCHESTER, VIRGINIA, September 19, 7.30 P. M.

LIEUTENANT-GENERAL U. S. GRANT:

I have the honor to report that I attacked the forces of General Early over the Berryville pike, at the crossing of Opequan Creek, and, after a most stubborn and sanguinary engagement, which lasted from early in the morning until five o'clock in the evening, completely defeated him, driving him through Winchester, capturing 2500 prisoners, five pieces of artillery, nine army flags, and most of their wounded.

The Rebel generals Rhodes and Gordon were killed, and three other general officers wounded.

Most of the enemy's wounded and all of their dead fell into our hands.

Our losses were severe, — among them General D. A. Russel, commanding a division in the Sixth Corps, who was killed by a cannon ball. Generals Upton, McIntosh, and Chapman were wounded.

I cannot tell our losses. The conduct of the officers and men was most superb. They charged, and carried every position taken up by the Rebels from Opequan Creek to Winchester. The Rebels were strong in numbers and very obstinate in their fighting.

I desire to mention to the Lieutenant-General commanding the army, the gallant conduct of Generals Wright, Crook, Emory, Torbert, and the officers and men under their command. To them the country is indebted for this handsome victory.

P. H. SHERIDAN,
Major-General commanding.

On September 22 General Sheridan attacked the enemy's position at Fisher's Hill, and by forcing back the left of his line and throwing a force in his rear he compelled him to abandon it. He thus described and reported his success: —

HEADQUARTERS MIDDLE MILITARY DIVISION, SIX MILES FROM WOODSTOCK, 11.30 P. M. September 22.

LIEUTENANT-GENERAL GRANT:

I have the honor to report that I achieved a most signal victory over the army of General Early at Fisher's Hill to-day. I found the Rebel army posted with its right resting on the north fork of the Shenandoah and extending across the Strasburg Valley, westward to North Mountain, occupying a position which appeared almost impregnable.

After a great deal of manœuvring during the day, General Crook's command was transferred to the extreme right of the line on North Mountain, and he furiously attacked the left of the enemy's line, carrying everything before him. While General Crook was driving the enemy in the greatest confusion, and sweeping down behind their breastworks, the Sixth and Nineteenth Army Corps attacked the works in the front, and the whole Rebel army appeared to be broken up.

They fled in the utmost confusion. Sixteen pieces of artillery were captured, and also a great many caissons, artillery horses, etc., etc.

I am to-night pushing down the Valley. I cannot say how many prisoners I have captured, nor do I know either my own or the enemy's casualties. Only darkness has saved the whole of Early's army from total destruction. My attack could not be made until four o'clock in the evening, which left but little daylight to operate in.

The First and Third Cavalry Divisions went down the Luray Valley to-day, and if they push on vigorously to the main Valley the result of this day's engagement will be still more signal. The victory was very complete.

P. H. SHERIDAN,
Major-General commanding.

The number of prisoners taken was 1100. The pursuit was continued to Staunton, which place General Sheridan occupied with his cavalry and inflicted much damage upon the enemy. He then leisurely and destructively fell back toward Strasburg. The losses of the enemy in these battles in killed, wounded and missing was estimated at nearly ten thousand men. The losses of General Sheridan were also severe.

While General Sheridan was at Staunton all public property was destroyed, including the railroad and factories. His cavalry then proceeded to Waynesborough for the purpose of destroying the iron railroad bridge, and all the barns and mills in that section of country. The force of General Early, in the meantime, had retreated through Brown's Gap with their wagon trains, but on learning of the operations of the Federal cavalry, Kershaw's Division of infantry and Fitzhugh Lee's cavalry were ordered to march in their rear and cut off the command of General Torbert at Waynesborough. The latter, however, marched all night by way of Staunton and escaped.

General Sheridan thus reported his march back to Woodstock:—

WOODSTOCK, VIRGINIA, October 7, P. M.

To GENERAL U. S. GRANT:

I have the honor to report my command at this point to-night. I commenced moving back from Port Republic, Mount Crawford,

Bridgewater and Harrisonburg yesterday morning. The grain and forage in advance of these points had previously been destroyed in coming back to this point.

The whole country from the Blue Ridge to the North Mountain has been made untenable for a Rebel army. I have destroyed over 2,000 barns filled with wheat, hay, and farming implements; over 70 mills filled with wheat and flour; four herds of cattle have been driven before the army, and not less than 3,000 sheep have been killed and issued to the troops.

This destruction embraces the Luray and Little Fork Valleys as well as the main valley. A large number of horses have been obtained, a proper estimate of which I cannot now make.

Lieutenant John R. Meigs, my engineer officer, was murdered beyond Harrisonburg near Dayton. For this atrocious act all houses within an area of five miles were burned. Since I came into this valley from Harper's Ferry, up to Harrisonburg, every train, small party, and every straggler has been bushwhacked by people, many of whom have protection papers from commanders who have been hitherto in that valley.

The people here are getting sick of the war; heretofore they have had no reason to complain, because they have been living in great abundance.

I have not been followed by the enemy up to this point, with the exception of a small force of Rebel cavalry that showed themselves some distance behind my rear-guard. To-day a party of 100 of the Eighth Virginia Cavalry, which I had stationed at the bridge over the North Shenandoah near Mount Jackson, was attacked by McNeil with seventeen men, while they were asleep, and the whole party dispersed or captured. I think they will turn up. I learn that 56 of them had reached Winchester. McNeil was mortally wounded, and fell into our hands. This was most fortunate, as he was the most daring and dangerous of bushwhackers in this section of the country.

P. H. SHERIDAN, Major-General.

A correspondent who was present with Sheridan's army describes the scenes of this march as follows: —

"The atmosphere, from horizon to horizon, has been black with the smoke of a hundred conflagrations, and at night a gleam brighter and more lurid than sunset has shot from every verge.

"The orders have been to destroy all forage in stacks and barns, and to drive the stock before us for the subsistence of the army. The execution of these orders has been thorough, and in some instances, when barns near dwelling-houses have been fired, has resulted in the destruction of the latter. In no instance, except in that of the burning dwellings within five miles, in retaliation for the murder of Lieutenant Meigs, have orders been issued for the burning of houses, or have such orders been sanctioned by General Sheridan. Such wholesale incendiarism could not have been pursued, however, without undue license being taken by the worst class of soldiers, and there have been frequent instances of rascality and pillage. Indiscriminating (for with such swift work discrimination is impracticable), relentless, merciless, the torch has done its terrible business in the centre and either side of the valley. Few barns and stables have escaped. The gardens and cornfields have been desolated. The cattle, hogs, sheep, cows, oxen, nearly five thousand in all, have been driven from every farm. The poor, alike with the rich, have suffered. Some have lost their all.

"The wailing of women and children mingling with the crackling of flames has sounded from scores of dwellings. I have seen mothers weeping over the loss of that which was necessary to their children's lives, setting aside their own, their last cow, their last bit of flour pilfered by stragglers, the last morsel they had to eat or drink. Young girls with flushed cheeks, and pale with tearful or tearless eyes, have pleaded with and cursed the men whom the necessities of war have forced to burn the buildings reared by their fathers, and turn them into paupers in a day.

"The completeness of the desolation is awful. Hundreds of nearly starving people are going North. Our trains are crowded with them. They line the wayside. Hundreds more are coming; not half the inhabitants of the Valley can subsist on it in its present condition. Absolute want is in mansions used in other days to extravagant luxury.

"The entire loss of property was estimated by a committee of thirty-six citizens and magistrates, appointed by the county court of Rockingham, at twenty-five millions of dollars. It was rendered necessary by Grant's plan of the campaign for the reduction of Richmond; nevertheless, it fearfully illustrates the horrible barbarity of war."

Sheridan, having practically driven the enemy out of the Shenandoah Valley, suggested to Grant the reduction of his force, and the sending of his surplus troops where they would be more useful. This reduction was about to be put in execution, when Sheridan, on his way to Washington,—whither he had been summoned in consequence of some orders he had received from the Department, contradictory to those from General Grant,—when he heard from General Wright, whom he had left in command, that a despatch had been intercepted from Longstreet to Early, directing the latter to be in readiness to move and crush Sheridan as soon as Longstreet should arrive. Sheridan at once ordered a concentration of his forces, and continued on to Washington. This was on the 15th of October. On the 18th Early was ready to move, and during that night succeeded in getting his force in the rear of the Union left flank, which broke, and fled precipitately down the Valley, losing eighteen pieces of artillery and about a thousand prisoners. The Union right, under General Getty, kept a firm and steady front, falling back to Middletown, where it took a favorable position, and made a stand.

Sheridan, having left Washington on the 18th, arrived at Winchester that night, and on the following morning set out to join his command. He had scarcely ridden out of the town before he met some of his panic-stricken troops fleeing from the front, and heard heavy firing from the direction of Cedar Creek. He at once ordered such cavalry as he had at Winchester to be deployed across the Valley to arrest the stragglers, and set out in hot haste, with a small escort, in the direction of the heavy firing. As he rode on he ordered the fugitives to turn back, saying, "You are going the wrong way, boys." His presence at once restored confidence, and many who had fled ten miles from the enemy returned to do execution on them before nightfall. This was that famous "Sheridan's Ride" which has been celebrated by Thomas Buchanan Read, in lines that will, no doubt, live as long as the memory of the Civil War.

The following are Sheridan's reports of this battle of Cedar Creek.

CEDAR CREEK, VIRGINIA,
October 19, 10 P. M.

LIEUTENANT-GENERAL GRANT, City Point :

I have the honor to report that my army at Cedar Creek was attacked at Alacken this morning before daylight, and my left was turned and driven in, in confusion. In fact, most of the line was driven in confusion, with the loss of 20 pieces of artillery. I hastened from Winchester, where I was on my return from Washington, and found my army between Middletown and Newton, having been driven back about four miles. I here took the affair in hand, and quickly marched the corps forward, formed a compact line of battle to repulse an attack of the enemy, which was done handsomely at about one o'clock P. M. At three P. M. after some changes of the cavalry from the left to the right flank, I attacked with great vigor, driving and routing the enemy, capturing, according to the last report, 43 pieces of artillery and very many prisoners.

I have to regret the loss of General Bidwell, killed ; and Generals Wright, Grover, and Ricketts, wounded. Wright is slightly wounded. Affairs at times looked badly; but by the gallantry of our brave officers and men disaster has been converted into a splendid victory. Darkness again intervened to shut off greater results. I now occupy Strasburg. As soon as practicable I will send you further particulars.

P. H. SHERIDAN, Major-General.

On the next day he further reported as follows : —

CEDAR CREEK, VIRGINIA,
October 20, 11.30 A. M.

To LIEUTENANT-GENERAL GRANT, City Point :

We have again been favored by a great victory, won from disaster by the gallantry of our officers and men. The attack on the enemy was made at three P. M. by a left wheel of the whole line, with a division of cavalry turning each flank of the enemy. The whole line advanced.

The enemy, after a stubborn resistance, broke and fled, and were pushed with vigor. The artillery captured will, probably, be over fifty pieces. This, of course, includes what were captured from our troops early in the morning. At least 1,600 prisoners have been brought in, also wagons and ambulances in large numbers. This morning the cavalry made a dash at Fisher's Hill, and carried it, the enemy having fled during the night, leaving only a small rear-guard.

I have to regret the loss of many valuable officers killed and wounded. Among them is Colonel James Thorburn, commanding a division of Crook's command; Colonel Sherwood, commanding a brigade, but would not leave the field. I cannot yet give a full account, as many of our men who were captured in the morning have since made their escape, and are coming in. Ramseur, commanding a division in Early's army, died this morning.

[Signed]   P. H. SHERIDAN.

With the exception of a few collisions of small consequence this battle closed the military operations in that region for the remainder of the year. Early's force took a position farther up the Valley, while Sheridan's forces were scattered in small detachments, capable of speedy concentration, and Wright's Corps and two other divisions were ordered back to the Army of the Potomac. The Valley of the Shenandoah was of no further use to the Confederates, and General Grant states that "Early had lost more men in killed, wounded, and captured than Sheridan had commanded from first to last," which would make his losses mount up to the enormous number of 45,000.

On the ensuing 14th of November the War Department issued the following order: —

"That for personal gallantry, military skill, and just confidence in the courage and patriotism of his troops displayed by Philip H. Sheridan on the 19th of October at Cedar Run, whereby, under the blessing of Providence, his routed force was reorganized, a great national disaster averted, and a brilliant victory achieved over the Rebels for the third time in pitched battle within thirty days, Philip H. Sheridan is appointed Major-General in the United States army, to rank as such from the 8th day of November, 1864.

"By order of the President of the United States."

Sheridan, in his pursuit of Early up the Shenandoah Valley, got beyond where communication could be had with Washington, and President Lincoln became alarmed for his safety. He feared that Sheridan in his hot pursuit had got in advance of Early, and that the latter, re-enforced from Richmond, might come upon him in overpowering numbers. Grant replied that to prevent this he had on the 28th September sent Ord with the Eighteenth Corps, and Birney with the Tenth Corps, to threaten Richmond, and thus prevent the sending of re-enforcements by Lee to the Shenandoah. The movement was intended primarily to protect Sheridan; at the same time it was assumed that if the advance was successfully resisted, it could only be done by the withdrawal of such a force from the south side of the James as would materially aid the Army of the Potomac in a contemplated movement on the enemy in the vicinity of Petersburg.

General Ord was to cross the James eight miles above Deep Bottom; General Birney at Deep Bottom to capture the enemy's works there, gaining possession of the New Market road, which leads directly to Richmond; and the two forces were to form a junction near Chapin's Bluff. This was successfully done, but the enemy's works at this point were very strong and very intricate. A division of the Eighteenth Corps captured Fort Harrison, sixteen guns, and a considerable number of prisoners; but as the works were evidently very formidable, it became necessary to organize a regular assaulting column. This delayed the assault till early in the afternoon, which gave Lee time to send up re-enforcements. As the Union troops advanced they could see these re-enforcements entering the works. From this cause, and the strength of the works, the attack was unsuccessful, though the troops behaved with great gallantry. Two regiments of colored men reached one of the Confederate forts, and found there a ditch ten feet wide and eight feet deep, between them and the parapet. More than a hundred of these brave fellows plunged into the ditch, and helped some of their comrades to mount the parapet by letting them climb upon their shoulders. About a dozen did so, but the force that had thus bravely pushed on was far too small for successful assault, and the attack was abandoned with a loss of about eight hundred in killed, wounded, and prisoners.

On the 30th the Confederates attempted to recapture the works which had been taken, but were repulsed. The Union troops fortified their new position, bringing Fort Harrison into the new line, and extending it down to the James. This brought the opposing lines within a few miles of each other, and they retained these relative positions until the capture of Richmond.

The subsequent movements of both armies were comparatively unimportant during the remainder of the year.

The condition of the 'country around Richmond, at this time occupied by the two armies, is graphically described by a correspondent of the "Tribune" in the following letter, dated:—

"HEADQUARTERS ARMY OF THE JAMES, NEAR RICHMOND, VIRGINIA, October 21, 1864.

" A ride over the fields where our besieging army lies intrenched before the gates of the Rebel capital does not afford much information that is proper to communicate to a public anxious only to know how we are progressing in the great work of ending this Rebellion; and yet there is a painful interest in a gallop over these desolated plains, ribbed with long lines of intrenchments, and dotted with bristling forts, or skirting the edges of forests flushed with the hectic of the waning year, when the white tents and blue uniforms of our soldiery form poetic contrasts of color with the deep, cold green of the pines, and the yellow and crimson of the oak, the dogwood, and the maple leaves.

"The weather is magnificent. The sunshine of the Indian Summer lies mellow and golden along the landscape at our feet, and fades away to the distant heights yonder overlooking the beleaguered city. Peaceful corn-fields slope to the river's edge on the west, and behind the fresh-plowed ground has been hastily abandoned by the affrighted farmer, who has fled, leaving the harrow standing in the half-sown field. Nature is beautiful, poetic, peaceful, and one could almost believe that this war, which is all about us with its fearful destruction and desolation, is only a fevered dream. Nay, one can hardly believe as he gazes northward, where the silver waters of the James stretch flashing in the sunshine toward the Rebel capital, that two hundred thousand armed men confront each other here; that bristling cannon are ready to belch forth quick destruction at a moment's warning; that the faint martial music which swells gently on the October breeze shall perhaps in a day, or possibly even in an hour, wail the requiem for thousands mangled, dying, dead, hurried to swift destruction.

"This at the front, while in our rear the sunshine shimmers with so warm a glow, the autumn wind breathes gently on our cheek; but desolated fields are seen, where the unharvested grain is trampled down, and dismantled and demolished houses bespeak the blighting trail of marching armies. Deep gashes furrow the face of the country, where the red earth has been piled in long lines of traversing intrenchments, edged with slashing and abatis, or heaped in fortifications bristling with threatening cannon. White tents dot the open fields and fade into the edges of the circumjacent forests, while long lines of army wagons wind like serpents away as far as the eye can reach. From time to time the dull boom of distant cannon falls upon the ear and mingles with the hum of assembled thousands in the busy camp, the clatter of galloping orderlies, and the shout and boisterous merriment of light-hearted, careless soldiers.

"Fences disappear as if by magic, and each night feed the fires of the merry bivouac, the one feature in the experiences of the field which is always cheerful, always beautiful, always welcome to the weary soldier.

"All is haste, bustle, confusion, preparation; loads of forage, ammunition, subsistence, tents, camp-fixtures, and officers' baggage are wagoned by. Great guns on merry wheels are dragged with tedious labor to the front; cavalry dashes past; long columns of infantry move with glistening bayonets and measured tread, their blankets twisted over their shoulders and their dirty knapsacks on their backs. In the fields, here and there plowed and scarified with shot and shell, dead horses and mules lie festering in the sun; and yonder, saddest sight of all, the graves of noble-hearted soldiers, cut down in their prime, vigor, and manhood, like the grass, are sprinkled thicker than the harvest sheaves.

"Down in the valley great herds of beeves graze continually, and flocks of horses and mules are gathered in corrals.

"It is a noisy, busy scene, and to a contemplative mind furnishes food for thought, anxiety, and sadness, as well as hope. Who shall tell what may be the issue of to-day, to-morrow, or the next? Who can say when the battle shall begin, or, if begun, who its victims or its heroes of all this busy throng? Yonder marching line of soldiers, in their uniforms of bonny blue, tread proudly, firmly on. Perhaps to-morrow they may be scattered like the leaves when the autumn winds have blown. Adown yon road, where the wagons go and the wagoners merrily ride, perhaps ere the sun goes down shall file a slow, sad line of ambulances freighted with the maimed and torn and bleeding from the battle-field, and wounded men toil feebly along with great rents and gashes, whence the life-blood oozes as they pass.

"All behind is desolate as a grave. Houses and out-buildings are torn down and carried away to construct temporary shelters for the men of the adjacent camps; everything which can be made of use to hungry, wearied soldiers is laid hold of and made to yield a momentary enjoyment. Refugees come in with their starving, half-clad families asking for protection and for food. Destitute wives, widows, and children, and helpless parents of Rebel husbands and fathers who are fighting against us in the Confederate armies, with hate in their hearts but words of humility upon their tongues, ask also to be protected and fed. The former are sent to places of security, and the latter to their friends beyond the lines, for where their treasure is there will their heart be also.

"Deserters come in in squads to claim, and are sent away to receive, the pardon for past sins which the Government has proffered to all who will lay down their arms and fight no more in the Rebel cause. Scowling prisoners in filth and tattered raiment march by, guarded by negro soldiers, for the enslavement of whom the war was first begun, and which will probably cease forever when the war shall stop.

"Destruction goes before and desolation is left behind! Oh! who is there that would not, does not, pray that this war may cease? And who is there that, seeing the misery, the want, the wretchedness, the destruction of life and property and law, the wives made widows, the children fatherless, the parents bereaved and desolate, would not rather, ten thousand times, continue this contest till the cause which brought the struggle on is effectually removed, than to stop it now and leave the viper of Secession and Rebellion to sting our children and our children's children in the years to come, and to desolate again this empire which we leave them for a heritage?"

We have come now to the close of this six months' campaign, — a campaign as bloody and destructive as any recorded in history, — and it seems appropriate to here reckon up its gains and losses. Its gains were that it saved the city of Washington; that it got Grant's forces a few miles nearer to Richmond, but with Lee — his army still intact, and able to promptly send a formidable force to the defence of any menaced point — standing an impenetrable wall between Grant and the Confederate capital. Also, Grant had closely imprisoned Lee within his own lines, and forced him to draw his entire subsistence from a single line of railway. These are the gains. The losses in killed, wounded, and missing in the three armies operating against Richmond — that of the Potomac, the James, and of the Shenandoah Valley — cannot be stated with equal exactitude. They probably reached a total of 120,000 men, not counting those who died of disease, or were sent home to die of their wounds, or to linger in life for a few years, a burden to themselves and to others, and then to drop into their graves, unknown and unwept by all save their immediate connections. The following table, compiled by an officer of General Grant's staff and published in the book entitled "Grant and his Generals," and republished in the

"American Conflict" by Horace Greeley—who was skilled in statistics—gives the losses of the Army of the Potomac. It does not include the Army of the James, or the forces operating in the Shenandoah Valley. Grant states in his "Personal Memoirs" that the Confederates under Early lost in the Valley more men than Sheridan had from first to last—and at the battle of the Opequan, Sheridan had 45,000. He says his losses were severe. They could not well have been less than one third of the Confederate loss. Set at this figure—15,000—and estimating the losses of the Army of the James at an equal number, we have a total loss of about 120,000.

CASUALTIES IN THE ARMY OF THE POTOMAC FROM MAY 5, 1864, TO NOVEMBER 1, 1864.

Battles.	Dates.	Killed.		Wounded.		Missing.		Aggregate.
		Officers.	Enlisted Men.	Officers.	Enlisted Men.	Officers.	Enlisted Men.	
Wilderness	May 5 to 12	269	3,019	1,017	18,261	177	6,667	29,410
Spottsylvania . . .	May 12 to 21	114	2,032	259	7,097	31	248	10,381
North Anna . . .	May 21 to 31	12	138	67	1,063	3	324	1,607
Cold Harbor . . .	June 1 to 10	144	1,561	421	8,621	51	2,355	13,153
Petersburg	June 10 to 20	85	1,113	361	6,492	45	1,568	9,665
"	June 20 to July 30	29	576	120	2,374	108	2,109	5,316
"	July 30	47	372	124	1,555	91	1,819	4,008
Trenches	August 1 to 18	10	128	58	626	1	45	868
Weldon Road . . .	August 18 to 21	21	191	100	1,055	104	3,072	4,543
Reams's Station . .	August 25	24	93	62	484	95	1,674	2,432
Peebles's Farm . .	Sept. 30 to Oct. 1	12	129	50	738	56	1,700	2,685
Trenches	Aug. 18 to Oct. 30	13	284	91	1,214	4	800	2,417
Boydton Plank Road	Oct. 27 to 28	16	140	66	981	8	619	1,902
Totals . . .		796	9,776	2,796	51,161	775	23,083	88,387

NOTE.—The first line of the above table includes several days' desperate fighting at Spottsylvania in which our losses were fully 10,000. Our actual losses in the Wilderness were rather under than over 20,000, and at Spottsylvania just about as many. These corrections, however, make no difference in the aggregate given above. The losses of the Army of the James and of the Union forces in the Shenandoah Valley are not included.

Part Third.

THE FINAL CAMPAIGN.

MARCH TO MAY, 1865.

At the opening of this final campaign the forces under the immediate command of General Grant occupied a line extending a distance of fully thirty miles. The extreme right was at Fort Harrison (Chapin's Farm), on the north side of James River, a few miles below Richmond. Then the line crossed the river at Bermuda Hundred, and extended around Petersburg, and as far southwest as Hatcher's Run, a few miles from that city. The line was strongly intrenched everywhere, and from the Appomattox to Hatcher's Run was a series of formidable connected works, between which were mortar batteries.

The Confederates were the first to begin offensive operations in this campaign. About daylight on the 25th of March they made a strong attack on Fort Steadman — one of these connected works — capturing the garrison, and inflicting a total loss on the Union force of about one thousand; but they were speedily repulsed, driven from the fort, and from their own intrenched picket line, with a heavy loss in killed and wounded, eight battle-flags, and over 1,900 prisoners.

Indications were soon apparent of the weakness of the Confederates, and the impending fall of Richmond and Petersburg. Grant construed this attack on Fort Steadman as intended to mask Lee's design to abandon Richmond and Petersburg, and retreat to Lynchburg, and accordingly he made such disposition of his own forces as would tend to balk this design and lead to a final surrender. Various collisions occurred during the following week, with considerable losses on both sides, and on Saturday, April 1st, came the struggle which virtually decided the fall of Richmond. And this is a fitting point to resume Mr. Page's correspondence.

A GLANCE AT THE SITUATION.

DROP an old swimmer into the water and he — swims. So I, ex-war-correspondent, having dropped into the army for two days, write. If the necessity be not so palpable in the one case as in the other, it is — my word for it — quite as imperative. Having been in both situations, I know.

The man who never before saw a city is not more astounded by Broadway, not more bewildered in threading the modern Labyrinth known as Boston — more intricate than the Cretan of old — than are most civilians who, "unused to war's alarms," come into the midst of this army to face its bustle and thread its intricacies. An appreciation of this fact led my friend, the Honorable ——, to ask me to go with him to the front; not exactly in the capacity of "guide, philosopher, and friend," for the philosophy of the *duumviri* is rather more his than mine. The friendship we divide. The guidance I at first assumed, but soon relinquished. His acquaintance with major-generals showered upon him all courtesies and facilities, until the advantages of my own long apprenticeship shrank into Toots' "no consequence."

The weather deserves a complimentary paragraph. Out of deference to Northern latitudes and Northern prejudices, this letter bears date December 2. Nevertheless, the almanac to the contrary notwithstanding, the season is spring and the actual date is May 2. I never was strong in chronology, and would not commit myself, without first referring to the Book of Genesis, to more than a mild insinuation of an opinion that Adam and Eve were cotemporaries — a direct statement to that effect would be too hazardous. But this *is* spring. I feel it, therefore I know it. The evidences of one's senses may not be disputed. Predispositions imbibed from books must vanish in the light of every-day experience. This is spring. Nor is it so wonderful that it should be. Did n't the sun sit up all night, that Joshua might have time to send the Canaanitish squatters whirling through some oriental Winchester ? Was n't there some atmospheric phenomenon compensating for the sun while Moses should make available that great prototype of the Dutch Gap Canal through the Red Sea ? — which, by the way, differed from the modern mainly as to the relations, one to the other, of the land and the water. Is it not, then, reasonable, that the seasons should conspire for General Grant, and that he will, "before the going down thereof" (for antecedent see " sun," four sentences back, and then take it figuratively as meaning season), achieve his purposes ?

This discussion has involved three things. First: The premises assumed, viz.: That the present season is spring; rightfully assumed because an apparent, therefore a conceded truth. Second: An inquiry as to why spring should appear out of the usual order, eliciting historic parallels in transposition of natural phenomena. These always to subserve one of two belligerents, and always crowning that one with victory. Third: The inevitable deduction, which is, since our side is the party aided by this spring-in-autumn, that our side is to accomplish what it proposes.

If it should snow to-morrow it will not be the fault of the argument! Words aside, the campaign depends on a continuance of the present warm and dry weather. Two weeks more of it may remove these headquarters to the Spottswood House, or perhaps the Ballard, in case General Grant should select the former for his own. To make the exchange, or to gain any decided success, involves heavy fighting notwithstanding the Rebel force in Virginia is less than one-half the number they had last spring.

The remaining half is all concentrated about Richmond. Early's forces have been recalled from the Valley, and very few are guarding the Lynchburg and Danville roads. A cavalry expedition, under General Gregg, down the Weldon road yesterday and day before, found only a few hundred in that quarter.

A GLANCE AT THE SITUATION. 285

Nor have they despatched any large force to Georgia — none but Heth's Division, and that a small one, from the Petersburg front. Confronting us on the north bank of the James they have more than at any time since Butler effected the lodgment here, having been lately re-enforced by Kershaw's Division of Early's Corps. And they have constructed a magnificent line of works hard up to our own, and interior line after interior line is plainly visible. These facts, together with the every-day clamor of the Richmond papers for the last inhabitant to be ready to help to man the trenches, are proof that the enemy expects a terrific assault on *this* side of the river. These same papers assert that Butler and Porter are preparing a tremendous naval armament to attack in conjunction with the first flow of water through the Dutch Gap Canal.

Well, the truth is, it behooves them to be in readiness to withstand all these — and more too. I may say particularly the "more too."

The Eighteenth and Tenth Corps, which have hitherto constituted the Army of the James, have been abolished, the white troops of both going to form a new corps, to be numbered as the Twenty-fourth, and to be commanded by General Ord, while the colored troops of both, with those of the Army of the Potomac, are to form the Twenty-fifth Corps, under General Weitzel. The change was demanded by several considerations, of such weight that at last the separation has been decreed. Prominent among the reasons requiring it, is that due credit may be awarded wherever it may be earned. In the army the division is the unit, and let a division do well, or let it do ill, the fact is soon known in every other division. But before the country the corps is the unit, and each has its own fame, while few have suggested to them the record of a division or a brigade, by simply seeing its number. Therefore the colored troops have been given a corps of their own, and will have to make a name for it.

And it is no unwarranted stretch of the imagination to say that the Twenty-fifth will hew for itself a niche in history alongside of the already household words, the Sixth, the Fifth, the Second, the Eighteenth, and others not less glorious. The ability and earnestness of the new corps commander is of itself a pledge for this. General Godfrey Weitzel, although a young man, being in his 29th year, and, with the exception of General Custer, the youngest major-general in the service, is an old soldier. A lieutenant of engineers, he commanded one-half of the company of regulars which with loaded pieces, capped and at half-cock, guarded the presidential carriage at the inauguration in '61. That same night he lay, with 64 men, in a barn adjacent to the building in which was held the inauguration ball, General Scott having received word that a set of Baltimore roughs were likely to make a disturbance. Having prior to the war served four years under one Major Beauregard in the construction of the defences of New Orleans, when General Butler sailed against that city Lieutenant Weitzel accompanied him as engineer officer, and assisted in reducing the works he had helped to construct. Some months a staff officer, he was at length made a brigadier-general, and given an independent field command in the up-country, where he fought several battles, and each battle a victory. His later record is familiar to the country.

General Grant lately remarked that "the boys must finish up this war." He meant such men as Sheridan, Warren, Custer, Merritt, and Weitzel, — all young men; and he meant such striplings as were first to lay hands on the rebel flags in the Shenandoah fights.

Generals Terry, Stannard, and Devens will have divisions in the Twenty-fourth Corps. This will be the largest corps in the service by some thousands, since it comprises all the original troops of the Tenth and the Eighteenth. It has but to prolong the reputation of these last, and the same men are there to do it.

I know how hackneyed are the expressions, "the army is in good spirits," "the army is in splendid condition," "the army is eager for the fray," and similar sayings — "with the variations," which are ever and anon Heralded to the country, and I hesitate and quibble with myself as to how I shall convey the thought I wish to without repeating some old and by-everybody-distrusted assertion. Let me say that the army is *effective*. As to numbers, Grant menaces Richmond with about the same force as that with which he fought the battle of the Wilderness — with which he started from the Rapidan. He needs good weather, that only.

The struggle which finally decided the fate of the Confederacy occurred before Petersburg, and is vividly described in the following despatches.

FIVE FORKS.

GENERAL SHERIDAN. — HIS PART IN THE FIGHTING.

GENERAL SHERIDAN'S HEADQUARTERS, IN THE FIELD,
Wednesday Night, March 29, 1865.

THE cavalry command, consisting of General Crook's Division and Sheridan's Cavalry, moved out on the Jerusalem Plank-road this morning about three and a half miles from Hancock Station, where they took the country road leading across the Weldon railroad at Reams's Station, and into the Vaughn road one mile from the Dinwiddie Court-House, General Crook's Division going in advance. They reached Dinwiddle Court-House about four P. M., after some slight skirmishing on the way with Rebel cavalry, resulting in the capture of some 15 prisoners by our side. General Devens camped on the Crump plantation, one mile from the Court-House, General Custer being ten miles back on the road, in charge of the wagon-trains, which were greatly delayed on account of the wretched condition of the roads.

In the meantime the Fifth and Second Corps of infantry had been moving in a parallel line on the Vaughn road. General Grant's headquarters to-night are on the Boydtown Plank-road, in the neighborhood of Gravelly Run. General Sheridan's headquarters are at Dinwiddie Court-House. Reports are current this evening that Griffin's Division of the Fifth Corps had a fight with Bushrod Johnson's Division, driving them back and capturing about 100 prisoners, and inflicting a large loss in killed and wounded.

Thursday Evening, March 30.

Rained very hard nearly all day, having commenced during the night. Roads in a terrible condition, and wagon-trains still ten miles in the rear, the whole of General Custer's command being employed in corduroying the roads to get them along.

At eight A. M. Merritt moved out on the road crossing White Oak road, leading to the Southside railroad — moved out three miles, skirmishing with the enemy's cavalry, until he reached Brooks's Corners with Devens's Division. There the division was massed, and strong reconnoitring parties sent out on all roads leading to the Southside railroad. From Brooks's Corners, three miles from Dinwiddie Court-House, the Fifth and Sixth regular cavalry, under Major Morris of the Sixth, were sent out on the road leading to the Five Forks, five miles distant. He moved out, skirmishing with the enemy, until he crossed Chamberlain Bed Creek, where the enemy made considerable resistance, but were driven back within half a mile of the Five Forks, where the enemy's infantry were found posted behind breastworks. Major Morris, in pursuance of orders, made strong efforts to drive the enemy and gain possession of the Five Forks, but after an hour's hard fighting, was obliged to send for reenforcements, as he had only about 140 men in his command and was nearly out of ammunition.

In this fight he lost two officers wounded, — Captain Leib of the Fifth, slightly, and Lieutenant Denny of the Fifth, severely; Lieutenant Nolan of the Sixth, captured; enlisted men killed, 3; wounded, 15; and missing, 14. At one period during the fight Major Morris was driven back, and these 14 men were dismounted before they could reach their horses. At this time Lieutenant-Colonel Lepper of the Sixth Pennsylvania, commanding a detachment from his regiment and the First United States Cavalry and First Massachusetts Cavalry (General Gibbs's Brigade), had been sent on the direct road to the White Oak road, three miles distant. After he had proceeded about one mile a brigade of Rebel cavalry, afterward ascertained to be Roberts's Brigade of William H. Lee's Division of cavalry, was found in his front. Colonel Lepper ordered a charge with the sabre, and drove them in great confusion back to their infantry support on the White Oak road, capturing twenty prisoners, including a lieutenant-colonel and captain, and losing Captain Cooles of the First Massachusetts, captured, and ten men killed and wounded.

Another reconnoitring party went out toward the White Oak road, by the Five Forks, about a mile and a half distant from the route of each of the other parties, and consisting of the First New York Dragoons, under Major Smith of Colonel Fitzhugh's Brigade. They also pushed Barringer's Brigade of Rebel cavalry to the White Oak road, where infantry also was found behind breastworks. These reconnoitring parties had ascertained the position of the enemy, and General Merritt, wishing to develop their strength, sent out a portion of the Michigan Brigade to the support of Colonel Lepper, and Colonel Fitzhugh's Brigade to the support of Major Morris, while Gibbs's Brigade was kept in reserve. Each brigade commander carried out the orders to the letter, made a fierce attack upon the enemy, ascertained their exact position, character, and strength, captured a few prisoners belonging to Johnson's Division of infantry, and then fell back one mile and went into camp, the total loss in Devens's Division being about 100 killed, wounded, and missing. It rained very hard all day, the roads and ground everywhere being very unfavorable for field movements.

General Sheridan is very well pleased with the result of the day's operations. The cavalry pickets communicate on their right with the pickets of the Fifth Corps on the left of our infantry line. General Devens's Division is in camp in the neighborhood of Brooks's Cross Roads; General Davies's Brigade of Crook's Division is camped about two and a half miles from Dinwiddie Court-House, along the north bank of the Chamberlain Bed Creek, and communicating with General Devens on his right. The rest of General Crook's Division is at Dinwiddie Court-House. General Custer is still in the rear, working hard to bring up the wagons.

March 31, 6 A. M.

Wagons still stuck in the mud, six miles back — Custer working like a Trojan to bring them forward. Raining very hard and roads almost impassable. Forage becoming scarce, but everybody in good spirits. Skirmishing between the pickets all along the cavalry line. Enemy evidently closing up, and disposed to fight. Sheridan disposed to gratify them.

One A. M. — Fighting commenced by a portion of General Smith's Brigade, Crook's Division, posted at the crossing of Chamberlain Bed Creek on the Dinwiddle Court-House and Five Forks road, the enemy evidently attempting to cross the creek and flank General Davies. General Smith's Brigade being ordered in attacked them, drove them back in great confusion, capturing twenty prisoners, and killing and wounding a large number, the enemy leaving their dead and badly wounded on the ground. Failing in this attempt, they next attacked General Davies, and succeeded in driving him back a short distance; but Davies, being supported by Colonel Fitzhugh's Brigade, Devens's Division, drove them back and re-established the line. The enemy lost heavily in this attack, as they were very much exposed to the fire of our men, who were protected by the timber.

The enemy were evidently in strong force, and information received from prisoners proved that Bushrod Johnson's and Pickett's Divisions of infantry and General Fitzhugh Lee's and General Wm. H. Lee's Divisions of cavalry were in our front.

The enemy were now quiet for some time. About eleven A. M. they recommenced the attack along the whole line. General Devens's Division was very much exposed to being flanked, a considerable portion of it being in advance of the rest of the command and without any support on the right. Our ammunition wagons having failed to come up, the cartridge-boxes were nearly empty.

General Custer, who was back about six miles from Dinwiddie Court-House, was ordered to leave one brigade in charge of the wagon-trains, and move rapidly to the scene of action. Before he could arrive, however, General Devens began to retire. The whole of his men were fighting on foot (the nature of the country making it impossible to fight mounted). About half-past three P. M., he was ordered by General Merritt to retire on the Brooks's road and cover the Boydtown Plank-road. He retired slowly and in good order before the enemy, closely contesting every foot of the ground. The enemy then swung their left upon General Davies's right and drove him back also, until they reached a point within about two miles of Dinwiddie Court-House. At this juncture, General Custer's well-known flag was seen coming to the rescue. His arrival was greeted with hearty cheers by the men of General Crook's Division and General Gibbs's Brigade, which had been cut off from General Devens's left. Up to this time the enemy had succeeded by overwhelming numbers in driving back our whole cavalry line, but with a terrible loss on their side.

General Merritt ordered General Custer into position, and this checked the enemy's advance, and they began throwing up breastworks.

The enemy did not seem disposed to continue the contest that night, and as darkness was approaching, our troops went into camp in their front. The result of the day's operations was decidedly to the advantage of the Rebels as regards position and ground gained, but they paid dearly for these, their losses being very large — definitely ascertained to be over two thousand killed and wounded, while our loss did not exceed four hundred killed, wounded, and missing.

At this time the wagon-trains were still in the rear, coming up as fast as the roads could be corduroyed by the troops of Colonel Well's Brigade of General Custer's Division, who were guarding them.

GENERAL SHERIDAN'S HEADQUARTERS, IN THE FIELD,
Saturday Evening, April 1, 1865.

"Boot and saddle" sounded at five A. M. Morning clear and beautiful — all quiet along the lines. Everybody in good spirits. The horses had been fed, and ammunition having been served out during the night, the men all seemed anxious to go in again and regain the ground lost yesterday. Generals Sheridan, Merritt, and Custer rode out from their respective headquarters at and near Dinwiddie Court-House, down to the front and examined the enemy's line. They had thrown up breastworks and had a strong position under cover of the woods. About this time it was reported that the Fifth Corps (General Warren) had been ordered to report to General Sheridan, and that it was moving upon our right to attack the enemy.

The report soon spread among the cavalrymen, and they at once began cheering, and General Merritt, finding them in the right humor, ordered an advance.

General Devens took the road to Brooks's Cross Roads, driving the enemy back and regaining the position held yesterday morning. Colonel Stagg's Michigan Brigade marched out on Five Points Road, Colonel Fitzhugh's Brigade being on his left, General Devens's Regular Brigade remaining in reserve. At the Brooks's Cross Road, the advance of the Fifth Corps joined General Devens, and were massed in the field, near Brooks's House. At this time General Sheridan and staff rode down the road. As soon as his presence was known the greatest excitement prevailed, and the Fifth Corps infantry pressed down to the sides of the road to get a sight at the conquering hero of the Shenandoah Valley. As he passed, they swung their caps in the air, and cheered as long as he was in sight.

General Merritt rode with General Sheridan, and these two famous cavalry leaders appeared to be in earnest consultation. General Sheridan looked exceedingly belligerent. He rode his favorite horse — the one made celebrated by Buchanan Read in his verses entitled, " Sheridan's Ride from Winchester." He is an enormous coal-black charger, very fleet and powerful. Sheridan, like Grant, is an inveterate smoker, and, as usual, he was indulging in the weed. The short, quick puffs of smoke, the sharp glance of his eye at the arms and accoutrements of the troops, as he passed by them, and the quick gestures of his right hand showed the native energy of the man.

General Merritt, a handsome young officer, was a captain in the Second United States Cavalry, was formerly Chief of Staff for General Buford, and commanded the First Cavalry Division until the cavalry of the Shenandoah Valley started out on the first of March, when he assumed command of the cavalry belonging to Sheridan's army, which was selected for the late raid on the Virginia Central railroad and James River Canal. He has an army reputation as a cavalry officer second to none, and is admired by his fellow-soldiers for his gallantry under fire, and for the rare good judgment shown in the splendid manner in which he handles his troops on all occasions.

General Custer had gone in with the Second Brigade of his Division, with Pennington's and Capehart's formed on the Dinwiddie Court-House and Five Points road. The Second Brigade found the Rebels about two miles from the Court-House, and pushed them back until it crossed the Chamberlain Bed Creek, where it met with considerable resistance, but, about one P. M. joined Devens's left, he having driven the enemy back to within half a mile of Five Forks. Here the enemy made a stand and the firing became more rapid. All our men were dismounted except the Regular Brigade and First Michigan Cavalry (Lieutenant-Colonel Maxwell). A line was formed and an advance ordered, but very little progress was made at first. About half an hour later a gallant mounted charge was made by the First United States Cavalry, under Captain Floyd, and the First Michigan, under Lieutenant-Colonel Maxwell. They drove the enemy's skirmish line and charged through the woods up to breastworks, where a heavy infantry line of the enemy was developed. They returned, bringing with them 160 prisoners, belonging to Pickett's Division. There was now a cessation of small-arm firing for a while, but the Rebels kept up a heavy fire from their batteries, the shot and shell from three batteries tearing and screaming through the deep pine woods like something infernal — all wondering what our side was waiting for.

At last a few shots were heard on our right and soon a crash of musketry showed where the Fifth Corps were engaging the enemy. The bugle sounded and the cavalry went in, and the contest soon became very severe. For about a half-hour the firing raged furiously and many officers and men were brought to the rear wounded. Among these were Major Smith, First New York Dragoons; Lieutenant-Colonel Maxwell, First Michigan; Major O'Keefe, Second New York; Lieutenant-Colonel Robinson, Third New Jersey; Captain Drummond,

Fifth U. S. Cavalry, mortally; Captain Norton, Second Ohio; Lieutenant Smith, Second Ohio; Captain Houghton, Second Ohio; Lieutenant Bosworth, Second Ohio; Captain Chester, Second Ohio; Lieutenant Hough, Third New Jersey, killed; Lieutenant Jenbourne, Third New Jersey, wounded; Adjutant Stickles, Third New Jersey, wounded; Lieutenant Ackerman, Third New Jersey, wounded; Captain A. N. Parmlee, First Connecticut, wounded; Lieutenant Byrne, First New York, Lincoln Cavalry, killed; Captain Brownson, First New York, Lincoln Cavalry, killed. Some 300 enlisted men were killed and wounded.

At last, General Merritt made the grand charge, the bands striking up Yankee Doodle, and above the howl of shot and shell and the crash of musketry, could be heard the huzzas of the dashing light cavalry. They moved steadily on and soon poured over the Rebel breastworks. At the same time the infantry marched upon the flank of the enemy, and Custer sent in Wells's and Capehart's Brigade, mounted, and the whole force closed in around the confused and bewildered Rebels, who, almost *en masse*, threw down their arms and surrendered. Some 5,000 prisoners and muskets were captured. General Custer, with his mounted command, pursued the remainder of the enemy until long after nightfall, when the recall was sounded, and our tired troops went into camp near and upon the battle-ground. The houses in the rear of the late Rebel lines were found filled with wounded. Our loss is estimated at about 300 infantry and 800 cavalry.

The loss in officers is said to have been more than usually severe, some 20 per cent of the officers in the Cavalry Corps being either killed or wounded. Many of the cavalry are only slightly wounded. Lieutenant Boehn of General Custer's staff was severely wounded.

General Custer had a sharp fight with W. H. Lee's and Fitzhugh Lee's Divisions of cavalry at one time, but they could not stand before his fiery onset, and were soon driven away. At one time General Custer was charging at some distance in advance of his line of battle and narrowly escaped capture, but was rescued by a portion of the First New York (Lincoln) Cavalry after the sharpest sabre fight of the campaign. General Custer exchanged pistol-shots with the Rebel general.

The cavalry captured some 1,000 prisoners and two guns, taken by Colonel Fitzhugh in person. The cavalry claim that a large number of the prisoners gave themselves up where the firing was "least effective in the infantry line."

THE PETERSBURG BATTLE.

A GLORIOUS DAY. — PREPARATIONS FOR THE ASSAULT. — THE ASSAULT. — OPERATIONS OF THE DIFFERENT CORPS. — THE REBEL LINES PIERCED. — GENERAL ORD.

HEADQUARTERS ARMIES OPERATING AGAINST RICHMOND, NEAR PETERSBURG, Sunday Night, April 2.

THIS has been a glorious day for the armies operating against Richmond. For the first time in its annals the noble old Army of the Potomac, ably assisted by a portion of the army of Major-General E. O. C. Ord, has achieved a grand and almost overwhelming victory over the best army of the bogus Confederacy, — a victory which will, in all probability, be crowned to-morrow morning by its triumphant entrée into the city of Petersburg. For the first time in its history this grand old army of battle-scarred veterans, whose breasts have been bared to the storms of a hundred battles, has almost at its mercy the thoroughly beaten, disheartened, and demoralized army of their vaunted Rebel chieftain, and to-night rests on its laurels full of hope for the morrow. At Gettysburg, and on a score of other battle-fields, it rolled back the assaulting foe, awarding him a bloody repulse; and on a hundred other occasions its own assaults have resulted only in its discomfiture and defeat. True, it has at times succeeded, by dint of determined valor, in achieving important advantages, but all these have been eclipsed by the glorious results of to-day's engagement in front of Petersburg.

In accordance with the programme arranged last night, the attack upon the enemy's lines on the east and south of Petersburg was made simultaneously at daybreak this morning by the Sixth and Ninth Corps, Turner's and Foster's Divisions of the Twenty-fourth Army Corps, and Birney's Colored Division of the Twenty-fifth. The Second and Third Divisions of the

Second Corps likewise assaulted the enemy's lines in their front at a later hour, and after a brief but sharp contest with the opposing pickets drove them into their works across the Boydtown Plank-road, and pressing forward were soon in undisputed possession of the Rebel line, having met with comparatively trifling resistance, and having captured several hundred prisoners. Preparations for the assault were begun along the Sixth and Ninth Corps front several hours before daylight. The troops were massed as quietly as possible for the attack at daybreak, but, notwithstanding, their manœuvres were discovered by the enemy, who at once opened a terrific artillery and musketry fire upon them, continuing it until they moved outside of their works for the grand charge which resulted in such signal success. It was yet dark when our forces began their march for the enemy's line in the face of a fierce and incessant fire such as has seldom been exceeded during the war. The firing of the enemy was wild and inaccurate, however, and our troops suffered less while moving to the charge than when massing two hours before.

At the time before mentioned the line of the Ninth Corps was advanced from the Appomattox to its left, near the Weldon railroad, and after a short but desperate contest was in possession of the greater portion of the Rebel line east of Petersburg, including most of the formidable salients. The division of Wilcox, resting its right on the Appomattox, was afterward furiously attacked and forced to retire to its original position, while those of Potter and Hartranft, further to the left, still held tenaciously the greater portion of the enemy's line, notwithstanding the desperate attempts made to dislodge them. Fort Mahone, in front of the notorious Fort Hell, and three other formidable earthworks to the northward, had been carried by storm, and the enemy, maddened at the success of our assault, were in turn assaulting, now driving our men from the works, and again being hurled back leaving them in our hands. The history of the fighting of the Ninth to-day is made up of a series of charges and counter-charges, finally resulting in our retention of the works carried by Potter and Hartranft in the morning, with the exception of Fort Mahone, one portion of which is still in the hands of the enemy. General Potter was severely if not fatally wounded while fighting his Division this morning.

To the gallant old Sixth was reserved the honor of carrying the whole Rebel line of works on their front, of sweeping down to the left to the Appomattox, southwest, and two miles from Petersburg, of cutting the long-coveted Southside railroad, and of capturing some 2,000 prisoners, 20 guns, and a number of battle-flags. Brig.-General L. A. Grant, commanding the Second Brigade of Getty's Division, was severely wounded in the head by the fragment of a shell while preparing his command for the charge an hour before daybreak. The corps was massed for the attack as follows: In the centre deployed in line of battle the division of General Getty, supported on the left and right respectively by the divisions of Generals Seymour and Wheaton, moving in échelon. The division of Getty, leading the advance, was formed from left to right of the Second Brigade, Lieutenant-Colonel Tracy of the Second Vermont temporarily commanding, the First Brigade, General Warner, and the Third, commanded by Colonel Hyde of the First Maine Regiment. Under the fire of four rebel batteries, and in the face of a storm of bullets, the different divisions, in the order mentioned, moved steadily on to the attack, driving back the Rebel skirmishers, piercing two lines of abatis, carrying at the point of the bayonet the whole line in their front, and making the important captures referred to. The first regiment entering the enemy's works was the One Hundred and Thirty-ninth Pennsylvania, of the Second Brigade of Getty's Division, led by Colonel Mundee, on the staff of General Getty. The line wrested so gallantly from the enemy was but a mile from the Southside railroad, toward and across which the troops of the corps were immediately thrown, with the left of our new line resting on the Appomattox, west of Petersburg. All attempts of the enemy to repossess this line having resulted in his repulse, he withdrew between ten and eleven o'clock across Town Creek to his inner line of earthworks, in the immediate vicinity of the city.

The enemy having thus been completely cut in two, dispositions were immediately made to roll up his right wing in the direction of Dinwiddie Court-House, the Second Division of the Second Corps, led by General Humphrey in person, being at once despatched down the Cox road running towards Dinwiddie Court-House, between the Boydtown Plank-road and the Southside road, for the purpose of environing the Rebels on the north, while Sheridan, supported by the Fifth Corps and Miles's Division of the Second, cut off their retreat southward. How far we have succeeded in accomplishing this result has not transpired at the hour of writing. It is generally believed that the portion of the enemy cut off in the direction of Sutherland's Station will make every effort to escape without giving battle, but it may very reasonably be supposed that our cavalry, with the aid of the infantry supporting it, will be able either to capture or annihilate the whole of the Rebel force. News from Sheridan's army may be expected to-morrow, and there is every reason to believe that it will be of the most gratifying character.

The command of General Ord was also hotly engaged this morning. From its position across Hatcher's Run, the troops at daybreak charged the enemy's works, carrying them and driving the enemy in confusion. In obedience to orders, General Ord then moved up from his position on the Run, and formed to the support and on the right of the Sixth Corps. Full details of the operations of this command are not at present available, but his troops are known to have been equally successful with the Sixth in the capture of works, guns, and prisoners.

Every one confidently believes that Petersburg will be abandoned during the night, the enemy retiring to his works north of the town. It is possible that Lee may essay desperate efforts to break Grant's lines, which now half encircle the city; but it is far beyond the range of possibility that he will succeed.

Not content to rest upon the new laurels he has won, General Grant will to-morrow follow up to-day's achievement by another assault upon the enemy. Preparations are now going forward for to-morrow's work. The Appomattox is being pontooned for

THE PETERSBURG BATTLE. 301

the crossing of troops to the west and northwest of Petersburg; and unless Lee retreats to-night, ten hours hence must witness the annihilation of his army. When it is known that we have possession of the Southside railroad, and that we cannot be dislodged by any force the enemy can bring against us, the extremely critical position of Lee will at once be fully comprehended.

Our casualties in to-day's engagement are represented by general officers as comparatively light. It is impossible at this time to form any accurate estimate of our killed and wounded, which will not probably exceed 2,500 or 3,000. Among the killed is General Russell of the Twenty-fifth Corps, and Lieutenant-Colonel Crosby of the Sixty-first Pennsylvania; and among the wounded, Brigadier-General Grant of the Sixth Corps, Lieutenant-Colonel E. D. Holt of the Forty-ninth New York, mortally, and Lieutenant-Colonel D. J. Caw of the Seventy-seventh New York, in the breast, severely.

There is a report, lacking confirmation, however, that the Rebel General Hill was killed in to-day's engagement.

Major-General Ransom of Hill's Corps is wounded, and a prisoner. His wounds are believed to be mortal.

Thus far official reports of 45 guns, a large number of battle-flags, and about 10,000 prisoners, have been received at General Meade's headquarters. Of this number of prisoners Sheridan captured about one-half in his brilliant fight yesterday P. M. at the Five Points, or Forks, northwest of Dinwiddie Court-House.

Major-General Warren, commanding the Fifth Corps, was relieved last night by General Sheridan, and ordered to report to General Grant for orders. The cause generally assigned is the refusal of Warren to obey an order of General Sheridan, to whom, with his corps, he had been directed to report. It is reported that General Sheridan's present force, both of cavalry and infantry, constitute an army of his own, and that he reports directly to the Lieutenant-General for orders.

Everybody is jubilant over to-day's grand victory. Generals Grant and Meade's headquarters to-night are at the Ritchie

House, on the Boydtown Plank-road, and three miles from Petersburg.

April 3, half-past four A. M. — News has reached us of the evacuation of Petersburg.

GLAD NEWS. — THE SIXTH CORPS. — PROGRESS OF THE FIGHT. — APPEARANCE OF GENERAL SHERIDAN. — THE TWENTY-FOURTH CORPS. — FIVE THOUSAND TAKEN PRISONERS.

IN THE FIELD WITH THE ARMY OF THE
POTOMAC, April 2, 1865.

TO-DAY I have glad news to communicate. After a series of hard-fought actions this army forced out of their strong lines the enemy who have so long held it at bay. At half-past four A. M. a general attack was made by all the corps, which resulted in this great success. The left of our long line, with the cavalry on its flank, turned that of the enemy, who threw back their right from point to point as our army gained ground; and at the end of a glorious day they were found clinging to their last line of defences on their left. I will give a brief report of the action of each corps in this great operation, as far as it was possible for one person to see not gifted with the power of ubiquity, and will begin with the Sixth Corps.

At half-past four A. M. the Sixth Corps, under General Wright, left its lines to attack that part of the enemy in its front who formed their left centre. The corps moved in this order: On the right was the First Division, in échelon of brigades, left in front; then came the Second Division, in two lines, and next was the Third, in the same order as the first. This échelon order was used to enable the corps to throw forward its left and flank the works of the enemy one after another. In a very little time the picket line of the enemy was driven away from its pits, and the line swept on in fine order. Soon a battery of four guns opened upon the First Division, but it did not fire many rounds, for in a rapid charge by the First Brigade it was at once taken, and thus the first work was out of the way.

The batteries of the enemy now opened from every point, and shells flew about the lines, but on they went gallantly. The left soon got near some works in its front, and one by one these fell into our hands. At half-past ten a grand picture of war presented itself. The line of the corps, with its left in advance, was to be seen sweeping on toward two heavy forts of the enemy, and in rear of its left was the Twenty-fourth Corps in support. At this time the enemy plied their guns vigorously, and shells flew about and burst thickly over our line. The scene was a fine and thrilling one. In the rear, too, were to be seen crowds of men standing upon our earthworks to get a view of the great tableau.

On pushed the left division until it struck the line of the Southside railroad; and against the two forts swept the Second Division, under General Getty. At the same time the batteries of the latter, posted on rising ground, kept up a sharp fire upon the forts, which did not relax their fire until our men were close up to them. Then a dash was made upon the works, but it was repulsed. Again it was tried, and this time it met with success, but so resolute were some of the enemy inside that they used the bayonet for a short time.

As these two works fell into our hands a loud cheer rent the air, and the enemy were seen hastily retiring to their works next in line, which at once opened sharply in an effort to stay our advance.

About this time General Sheridan came upon the field, and was greeted by a loud cheer from the Sixth Corps, who look up to him with great respect. This must have been a glad moment for him, and the writer never beheld a finer sight as the Sixth and Twenty-fourth Corps swept on to victory. At this time our entire line was changing its long front to the right, and slowly before it the broken line of the enemy was falling back upon rear defences.

From Battery No. 45 the enemy now fired sharply upon the line of the Second Division, which massed under cover of the two captured works, and got ready for the new work before it. At the same time three batteries were posted at easy range from the Rebel works, and plied them with shell, until they had forced the gunners to leave their guns, and lie under cover of the parapet.

In the meantime the Twenty-fourth Corps came into line on the left of the Sixth, and the First Division of the latter was sent round to support the Ninth Corps, which had the heaviest part of the great work to do. Against the line of defences that the enemy had now fallen back upon, a heavy force was now pitted, and formed in this way: On the left was the Twenty-fourth Corps (two divisions), and the Second Division, Sixth Corps; to their right was the Second Division, Twenty-fifth Corps (colored), and lastly, on its right, was the Third Division of the Sixth Corps. All these, except the Second Division of the Sixth Corps, were fresh troops, and the negro division was eager for the fray. As this new line was being formed the enemy shelled it sharply, but the hollows in the ground at that point enabled the dispositions to be made with little loss.

A lull took place when all this force was ready, and it was plain that a distinct action was about to take place. In fact, all the day long the fighting was a series of actions rather than a continuous battle. The enemy had time to gain fresh breath for the coming attack, and looked on quietly at our half-hidden lines reserving their fire for a good mark.

Up to this time the trophies gained by us at this point were some 2,000 prisoners, four flags, and 25 to 30 guns; and with pleasure I write that three of the guns were taken by the Sixty-fifth New York Volunteers, of the First Brigade, First Division, Sixth Corps, who took them by a gallant charge very early in the day. Those were, I think, the first guns taken by the corps, the battery lying first in its way, and not far from the Rebel line of pickets. There were four guns in the battery, and the fourth gun was taken by the Ninty-fifth Pennsylvania Volunteers, in the same brigade.

Dusk stole over the scene before the force set against the Rebel line at this point was ready, and the attack was deferred

THE PETERSBURG BATTLE. 305

for the next day. It was too serious to attack this line of the enemy hastily, for it was their main one. In line the two divisions of the Sixth Corps, the Twenty-fourth Corps, and the negro division lay at a rest until dark, and then stacked arms, to light fires and cook some food. Tired with the day's fight the men soon lay down and fell asleep on the field of their glory.

The Twenty-fourth Corps lay in the morning in the new line that it had won the day before in front of our left centre, and at half-past four A. M. it took its share in the general fight by carrying, with the Second Division, Twenty-fifth Corps, the Rebel works in its front. The corps then moved by its right to extend aid to the Sixth, which had such a heavy task to perform. On coming up, it first lent support to the Sixth, and afterward entered into line on its left. The service it did in that position is stated under the action of the Sixth Corps, so that I need not go again into an account of it, and space will not allow me to write details.

The action of the Second Division of the Twenty-fifth Corps was so connected with that of the Twenty-fourth Corps (with which it acted, as a part of the same corps) that I will not say more of it than what appears in my account of the action of the Sixth.

There is a report that the Twenty-fourth Corps lost its leader, General Gibbons, during the day, and I have not heard the report contradicted so far.

In the day's great work the part played by the Fifth Corps was a very high one. On the left of our line, with the cavalry on its left, the Fifth Corps did the great service of turning and driving back the right of the Rebel army, formed of their First Corps, which was transferred from their left, in order to meet the danger threatening their right.

The success met with by the Fifth Corps was great, though I am unable to give details of it. The results were some 4,000 to 5,000 prisoners, taken mostly from Pickett's Division, and whom the cavalry was most active in capturing, though to both belong the honor. The entire force was under the command of General Sheridan.

Late in the day it was reported that the Rebel First Corps was cut off from the rest of its line by the Fifth Corps, which got upon its left. By this it added another laurel to its wreath.

The Second Corps, which in every fight has played so high a part, did to the full its share in the battle of to-day, under General Humphrey.

The corps lay on the left of our line, connecting with the right of the Fifth, and had some very rough ground to fight upon, as well as a brave foe to fight with, in the Rebel Third Corps (under General Hill). In spite of all, however, it drove the enemy in its front, back, step by step, losing many gallant men in the effort. It may not be too much to say that from half-past four to-day until dark the Second Corps had rather the most to do, the nature of the ground — thick pine woods — enabling the enemy to fight stubbornly. To all the corps, division generals, and to its commander much praise is due for its untiring valor.

The line of Rebel defences in front of the Ninth Corps, was stronger than those at any other point, and consequently the corps had heavy work to do. At the ordered time, half-past four, it made an attack upon the Rebel line of defences stretching to the Appomattox, and carried some of the outer defences. Here the Rebel Second Corps (under General Gordon) fought. It was this body that made the at first successful attack upon the line of the Ninth Corps on the 25th ult., and to-day its line was in turn attacked. In the course of the day the Ninth Corps delivered many assaults upon the Rebel lines and met with some successes, but lost many men. At the end of the day it found itself close up to the main line of the defences, but unable to go any further.

The First Division of the Tenth Corps lent its support to the Ninth Corps, and aided it in the great work.

The Cavalry arm was the first to begin the great work of turning the right of the enemy, and under its dashing leader, General Sheridan, it to-day played a very high part in the battle. The Fifth Corps sent it strong support, and to this body it owes the aid that enabled it to recover from a check and to attack the enemy again under General Fitzhugh Lee, with most of their First Corps in support of him. From the latter was taken in the fight on the 1st the 3,000 men of Pickett's Division.

It was thought to-day that our cavalry had got round upon the enemy's line of retreat upon Lynchburg.

The Rebel line was formed of four corps in this order: On their right, with the cavalry on the flank, was the First Corps. Next to it was the Fourth Corps, then the Third, and lastly, with its left resting upon the Appomattox, the Second Corps.

There were Fitzhugh Lee, Hill, Gordon, and Anderson, and under them were such men as Heth, Wilcox, Evans, and others.

Coolly directing the battle in this crisis was General Lee, who, it must be said, made a hard fight of it, and showed his usual ability. He fought against numbers and made the best of it. His total force did not exceed 60,000 men of all arms.

INCIDENTS OF THE OCCUPATION.

THE SCENES ON THE MORNING OF OUR OCCUPATION. — APPEARANCE OF THE TOWN ON ENTERING. — A BREAKFAST AT THE JARRATT HOUSE. — A SICK REBEL'S SUDDEN CONVALESCENCE. — DAMAGE DONE TO THE CITY BY OUR SHELLS. — A STRANGE RUMOR SATISFACTORILY EXPLAINED.

PETERSBURG, VIRGINIA, Tuesday, April 4, 1865.

IN my letter of Saturday lack of time compelled me to omit several items which may prove interesting to "The Tribune" reader.

As the writer rode through our lines toward the city at daybreak, the troops were all astir; knapsacks were being slung, blankets rolled, and every preparation made for an immediate advance. Portions of our troops had, as has been already stated, occupied the town two hours before, but the majority were denied the enviable pleasure of breakfasting in the Cockade City. A general fusillade was sounding along our whole line, and, as if it were impossible to indulge sufficiently in other noisy demonstrations, muskets were emptied of their charges to add to the universal din. Bands were playing "Hail Columbia," "Yankee Doodle," "Kingdom Comin'," "We'll all Drink Stone Blind," "Lanigan's Ball," polkas, waltzes, in fact almost everything of a patriotic or an enlivening character. It seemed as if Orpheus himself had gone mad, and was trying to render from all his creations of lighter music a grand, triumphant, and heaven-swelling chorus in honor of the occasion. Amid this torrent of mellifluous sounds arose from one of the bands that grand old refrain, —

"Praise God from whom all blessings flow,
Praise him ye people here below : "

indicating that some, at least, believed it but just and proper to blend thanksgiving with the general jubilation. And thus did the noble old Army of the Potomac, and its brethren from above the James celebrate the victory won by their long years of persevering toil.

But few evidences were discovered, on entering the town, of great destruction of life on the Rebel side. They had removed their dead and wounded, to hide from the eye of our victorious army the full extent of their disaster. Along the Boydtown road leading to Petersburg, I noticed but one poor fellow (yes, poor fellow, although a Rebel) sacrificed to the devilish ambition of his implacable masters, Davis and Lee. He was dead; but the dark, swarthy countenance almost led one to believe, until he touched his cold and pulseless hand, that life still lingered in his emaciated, half-clad body. He lay in a ditch or gully along the highway, with the water from a pure, perennial spring above trickling musically beneath him; his blanket was neatly rolled and slung across his shoulder; his head was resting upon his arm as if in repose, but the death-glaze upon his eyes told that he slept the sleep which knows no waking. A hideous orifice in the side of the head, surrounded by clotted gore, showed where a fragment of shell had saved him from living to see the overwhelming shame and disgrace which awaits the deluded followers of his former leaders.

The city presented the appearance usually noticeable in every Rebel town falling into our possession. Doors were closed and window-blinds shut; but, if I mistake not, I saw many a curious eye intently peering into the street. True, the number of contrabands of all ages and sizes congregated on street corners was legion, and of ancient and crippled whites not a few; but the fairer sex kept close within doors, disdaining to exhibit their peerless charms to our men in blue. Well, the Union boys took it philosophically enough, seeming to care but little for Confederate calico or linsey, and went marching along as if only intent on the capture or dispersion of Lee's defeated army.

Stopping at the Jarratt House, on Washington Street, we requested breakfast for our party, and were referred by the guard to a colored native, who seemed to be, from his deportment, both proprietor and chief steward of the establishment. After considerable hesitation, and on being fully assured that we intended to remunerate him liberally for the entertainment, he set to work and soon produced a repast, consisting *only* of bread of a tenacious tendency, and scraps of bacon of a toughness and elasticity which defied the persistent attempts of cuspids and molars to accomplish its necessary mastication.

Having Confederate notes about us, we decided to test the mercenary African's confidence in Rebel currency, and offered him in payment for our breakfast a handful or two of the article. Viewing it for an instant, he placed his hands in his pockets, and looking at us in astonishment ejaculated: "Lord bress ye, massas, I got heaps o' dat ar' stuff, more as a mule can tote; has n't ye got any Yankee money?" "But see here, John," we replied, "here is over five hundred dollars for our breakfast; that surely ought to pay you!" "I know it's a heap o' money, but I don't want it, massas; you alls is welcome to your breakfast, if dat's all de money you's got." We finally astonished his optics with a V of the "Union persuasion," and he was appeased. Thinking a little genuine Confederate apple-jack necessary to our temporal well-being, we requested him to produce the article. With a decided shake of the head he informed us that it would be utterly impossible to comply with our request. "De Rebs took eberyting wid 'em; we's got nuffin." "But," replied we, "we have greenbacks to pay you for it." "Well, now you alls just go in dar," pointing to an anteroom, said he, his face again brightening, "and I'll see what I can do." We did "go in dar," and were soon favored with the genuine Virginia stimulant known as apple-jack or apple whiskey.

Previous to leaving the Jarratt House, a rather ludicrous incident took place, which I will record. Happening in the large stable of the hotel, and naturally inquisitive under the circumstances, we were peering into the different apartments contingent. One door, although not locked, seemed to resist our first efforts to open it, and, redoubling our exertions, it finally swung back, revealing to our gaze a genuine grayback, sitting on the floor, his blanket around him, hatless, and with his hair unkempt projecting in every direction. His blanched face, on seeing several citizens, showed that he was either very ill or excessively frightened; and on asking him why he was there, he faintly replied that he was very ill, — in fact, that he had no confidence in his ability to prolong his existence further than an hour at most.

"But why did n't the Johnnies take you with them in an ambulance or place you in hospital before they evacuated?" one of us inquired. Springing to his feet, his face radiant with joy and relief, he confessed himself a Rebel deserter; stated that he was perfectly well; that he had on the previous night secreted himself there, and that he had been afraid to venture out for fear the Rebel rear-guard had not yet left the town; and that when he saw us he was uncertain whether we were Yankees or Confederates. He stated that he desired to take the oath, and requested us to take him to the house of a friend before delivering him over to the provost marshal, which we did.

The eastern portion of the town exhibits on every side marks of the solid shot and shell thrown by our guns during last summer. The buildings in Bolingbroke Street, which run nearly east and west, are literally perforated in every part. Chimneys have been razed on every building, windows knocked and splintered to pieces, brick walls crumbled and torn, porches carried away — ruin and desolation reign supreme.

Petersburg was undoubtedly before the war one of the very neatest of Virginia towns, and even now is attractive in appearance. Market Street contains, perhaps, the finest residences, while Sycamore can boast of stores and warehouses which would certainly not disgrace a Northern city. It was in the first-named street, in a fine brick dwelling with beautiful grounds in front, that Generals Grant and Meade made their temporary headquarters yesterday before leaving for Sutherland Station.

A singular rumor was in circulation yesterday to the effect

that a party of Johnnies still held a certain fort on the line south of the city; that they refused to surrender, and that our forces there had deemed it most judicious to starve them out without shedding the blood always attending an assault. Reports of cannon were occasionally heard during the afternoon in that direction, which seemed to give an air of trustworthiness to the strange rumor; but, nevertheless, no one attached sufficient importance to the story to investigate it. It was explained this morning, and proved to have originated in the explosion of shells lying around the works by some of our stragglers, who were strolling about outside the city, and who fired them by means of trains for their own amusement. This incident is given only to show the absurd rumors or "chin music" which are constantly set afloat by soldiers of vivid imagination.

The fall of Petersburg involved the fall of Richmond. Hearing of the latter event in Washington, Mr. Page set out at once for the fallen city. He relates the incidents of his journey in the following letter to the "Tribune."

RICHMOND.

TIME, eleven A. M., Monday, April 3, 1865; place, the Treasury Department, Washington, where at his desk sat the writer hereof. An abstruse calculation corrugated his brow, while an undercurrent of thought eddied among the pros and cons of the question — would he win that hat he had wagered that Richmond would fall within forty-eight hours?

Of the two questions, one as to the exchange to be allowed on the drafts of the Honorable Politikalie Exeyell, Minister to the Windward Islands, and the other as to the contingent hat aforesaid, the latter was the first solved.

A wild shout, exultant and prolonged, — a shout that grew into a great storm and whirlwind of voiced joy as hundreds of bellows-like lungs were added to its forces; this thousand-throated voice came surging up the broad stairways and went reverberating adown the long corridors, and called all forth to ask hungry questions; and these were answered with one word : " Richmond ! "

Now, in the Peninsular Campaign I had climbed tall trees to see but the glinting spires of Richmond, — always careful to keep the body of the tree between my own body and those spires, the former being better calculated to stop bullets. Again, last summer, I climbed other trees for the same purpose. What more natural, then, than for me to be seized with the magic of the old slogan (much abused, but always right) : " Onward to Richmond " ? Besides, the instincts of a retired army correspondent asserted themselves and bade me go once more to the front and to once more write to " The Tribune." And so, all-athrob with the thought of seeing Richmond, I set about the requisite preparations, in quite as much haste to get there as was Davis himself to get away from there.

The course of the War Department toward newspapers and their correspondents during the whole war has been marked by petty tyranny, by a caprice that would be funny if it had not been so troublesome, and by the most consummate ignorance, short-sightedness, and folly. Perhaps the conglomerate word "pig-headedness" well sums up my indictment. The procurement of passes for correspondents has always developed on the part of some one or other of its officials with whom one came in contact the above-mentioned quality. I remember when Grant was about to set out from Culpeper an order was issued that correspondents must be registered as such in the army, and the construction placed upon it by the War Department was that passes could not be granted prior to such registration, and that the registration must be done in person. In other words, one must be in the army in order to be registered, at the same time he could not go to the army until he was registered. And telegraphic correspondence with provost-marshals at the front, and a series of interviews with officials at the Department, only befogged the matter. At length the dilemma was submitted to A. Lincoln, the Commander-in-Chief, who granted unconditional passes to half a dozen of us — and he told us an apropos story.

Bearing the past in mind, I was not at all surprised, on calling at the Department at noon on Monday, to find that, from Secretary down, no one had authority to grant passes. "The late successes so changed the circumstances that probably a new policy as to passes would be required," and would I "call to-morrow?" I determined I would not call to-morrow, particularly as I thought I could find an old pass, "By order of Lieutenant-General Grant," bearing the indorsement, dated last May, "extended until further orders," and I had heard of no "further orders" touching it. As I hoped, that pass admitted me on board the "James T. Brady" at three P. M.

Similar considerations to those which started me to Richmond had the same effect upon two other veteran correspondents, — Whitelaw Reid, the "Agate" of "The Cincinnati Gazette," and L. L. Crounse, the Washington editor of "The Times," — gentlemen with whom it is a pleasure to travel, even on board of one of General Ingalls's line of steamers to City Point. Being anxious to forget the unnecessary annoyance and discomforts of my many trips on these boats, I forbear a description of the one in question. I wish I could as easily dismiss it from my dreams, for it has since formed the substance of the only nightmare by which I was ever ridden.

We reached Varina Landing, fifteen miles from Richmond, as runneth the New-Market road, at sunset Tuesday, the most interesting event on the way being the meeting of five or six steamboats crowded with Rebel prisoners, who cheered lustily as they passed. Our party, now consisting of Mr. Reid, R. T. Colburn, of "The World," and myself (Mr. Crounse had stopped at City Point), was anxious for instant transportation to Richmond — our Mecca. A mail ambulance, the only vehicle at the wharf, could not accommodate us, and we were mustering courage to start on foot in company with a score or two bound for the same destination, when General Weitzel's four-horse headquarters wagon drove up. It had come down from the city with a party of ladies, escorted by Major Graves, of Weitzel's staff. Luckily the major was an acquaintance of mine, and our greetings were cut short by my initiating negotiations for seats in the wagon on its return passage. With warm thanks for his ready assent, we three, with all the flourish of an old-time stage-coach, and to the no small envy of a dozen others, rattled off on the corduroy road. But not all the way to Mecca that night. Although plied with the contents of flask and pocket-book, the driver could not be induced to travel after dark, alleging torpedoes, which, should he stray by night from the straight path and the narrow gate which leads through the Rebel fortifications, might be exploded and *kill his horses!* The sublime self-abnegation of that driver, and his great love for his horses, begat our respect. We pardoned him his want of consideration as to our own safety, and assented to his proposition that we should pass the night at the now abandoned headquarters of General Weitzel, ten miles on the hither side of Mecca. These headquarters consisted of a village of deserted huts. The sole inhabitants were a colored sergeant with a guard of six men, left in charge of certain unremoved stores. We at once established ourselves in Weitzel's own hut, and by the potency of greenbacks soon had the entire population of the village working and contriving for our comfort. One proceeded to cook our supper. A second started a cheerful wood-fire. A third foraged for furniture, procuring three cushioned and two rocking chairs, a centre table, and three sofas — originally the spoils of deserted houses in the neighborhood. Awaiting supper we spied out the vicinity. On our return Sergeant Ebony informed us that he had brought us for our toilet water and towels, but "I 'se not got no comb, na' no har-brush, na' no toof-brush;" and his surprise was open-mouthed when each of us in turn produced from his own diminutive travelling-bag these articles. A supper of coffee, bacon, and pones, alias corn-dodgers, was to us as nectar and ambrosia. My own subsequent cigar (knowing that my companions never smoked, I took care to offer each a prime Havana from my own store) had a perfume sweeter than odors of Oriental gardens, and induced a reveried satisfaction more blissful than dreams of hasheesh eaters. Sergeant Ebony piled still higher the crackling fire, and in the cheer of its glow the conversation turned to reminiscences of nights each had passed in camps and on battle-fields, which had not been comfortable, of marches, sieges, battles and campaigns, of adventures ludicrous or dangerous, ending with one accord in expressions of satisfaction that they were all so soon to become things of the past, — that now, at last, the war was most over.

Now Reid is a man six feet and one inch in stature, and neither of our sofas would accommodate so great length of limb when horizontally disposed; so Sergeant Ebony was required to arrange one bed on the floor. Colburn is of less stature, but even he appropriated the longest sofa. Not being myself of such commanding proportions, with some grumbling I accepted their decision that I should occupy a shorter sofa. But I had my revenge the next morning, when I accused Reid of prolonged and stentorian snoring, and Colburn of three times visiting my flask during the night. My indignation having cooled, I now publicly confess that each accusation was false. Nevertheless, by steady persistence in them, backed up with much circumstantial detail, they at the time became firmly convinced of the truthfulness of the charges.

By arrangement of the night before, we were awakened promptly at four in the morning, and our boots, well polished by Sergeant Ebony, brought to us. We drank coffee at half-past four, and at five our coach-and-four whirled to the door, and we were off for Mecca. A jolly ride, that. The sun rose with a glory that crimsoned the whole East, and the balm of the air, and the green of the fields, and the buddings of the trees — and we Mecca-bound. It was intoxicating. On the left, now near, now far, as if timidly coming toward us, anon as if coquetting away from us, was the river. And there were our gunboats above Dutch Gap, above Drury's Bluff, ay, within shot of the farthest house in Richmond. All around, everywhere, were the yellow parapets of the concentric lines, so well defended, so well besieged, the great guns still planted upon them, but the host of the enemy gone. A dozen negro soldiers trudging on to Mecca were the only men we saw in all that ten miles. The smoke of the fire still clouded in gloom over the southern half of the city, but the whole remaining half, all clothed in morning light, showed spires of churches, the dome of the State House, stately mansions, and, sprinkled nearer to us, suburban cottages. It was beautiful. Up Main Street, and up a long hill, — for Richmond, like Rome, sat upon her more than Seven Hills, — and making a wide détour to avoid the burned district, we reached the Spottswood House. A front parlor on the second floor, with adjacent bedrooms, received the three scribes and pilgrims to the Mecca of the war. "Towels, John — and some water." "My name's Ben." "Very well, is there a barber-shop in the house, Ben?" And quickened by the magic of money in fractional postal-green, Ben made us comfortable.

My letter written at the Spottswood three days ago would come mainly under this head.

[The letter referred to is here inserted, this being its appropriate position.]

A DIARY OF EVENTS.

SPOTTSWOOD HOUSE, RICHMOND,
Thursday, April 6, 1865.

ONWARD *into* Richmond, at last, and the representative of "The Tribune" is at the "Spottswood."

At half-past eleven o'clock Sunday morning, while seated in his pew at church listening to the lucubrations of the Rev. Dr. Hoge, Jeff. Davis was handed a despatch from General Lee. Thereupon he instantly arose and walked hurriedly down the aisle, beneath the questionings of all the eyes in the house. The despatch was to the effect that Richmond must be evacuated during the coming night. And so his ex-Excellency, the late President of the late Confederacy, went forth from the sanctuary where prophesied the favorite high-priest of his realm, to pack up his "portable property" in hasty preparation for a journey on the Sabbath day. Like a thief in the night, he stole away with trepidation and fear, and with an agonizing sense of the shortness of time.

As the preacher closed the services the colored sexton handed him a note from his ex-Excellency. The face of the preacher waxed sickly with despair, while that of the sexton glowed with joy too great for concealment. The chagrin of the one was quite as marked as the grin of the other. The former begged his congregation to tarry, and told them in sad utterances that he did not expect to minister to them any more. His farewell over, he too proceeded furiously to the packing of "portable property" — he also intended to journey on the Sabbath. This Dr. Hoge, it will be remembered, visited England two years ago, ostensibly to procure a supply of Bibles, but really as an emissary of the Rebellion. He was largely fêted by the British adherents of the South, and doubtless did much harm. Since his return he has been in the habit of making camp speeches, full of hot unction and perorated with presumptuous appeals to the God of battles. A pro-slavery fanatic of considerable ability, he has been petted and used by Davis, whose own enormous cunning and wickedness have nothing of the

element of fanaticism. The two worthies fled together. *Requiescat!*

The evacuation, though suddenly determined upon, had evidently been some time contemplated and provided for. Correspondence of their Treasury and other Departments shows that as long as a month ago many of the public effects were sent to Danville, Augusta, and Charlotte. But the event, when it came, was under more stress and urgency than could have been expected; still it was conducted very systematically and with much completeness.

The overthrow of their army south of Petersburg on Friday, Saturday, and Sunday, by the magnificent fighting of Sheridan and the storming of the works in front of that city by Wright, — all in pursuance of a combination involving forced marches, timely demonstrations, and successful ruses, though conducted thirty and forty miles away, — these won for us the city. Military considerations overruled moral ones, pushed aside the dictates of pride and state-pretence, compelled the evacuation; and the decision so promptly made was as promptly acted upon. Their government offices were stripped of their effects, the banks and treasury of their coin, the houses of the officials of their valuables; all the available means of transportation, both of cars on the Danville road and of horses and vehicles in the city, gathered together; laborers, white and black, impressed; orders issued for the troops to be withdrawn, for the destruction of the iron-clads, navy-yard, arsenals, and laboratories, for the tobacco warehouses to be fired, for all stores of provisions and a large amount of whiskey to be destroyed, — in short they were a wondrously busy set of men, those officials.

Very few of the citizens, while they conjectured that the city was being abandoned by the Government, dreamed it was to be done that night. They had no means of going themselves, had they been never so much disposed to. They seemed to have looked on in grim and stupid amaze, and to have been wakened to the actual fact in the early morning by the terrific explosions and raging flames, — wakened to find the Rebels gone, the Yankees come.

And now let me narrate how the latter came.

When Grant began the movement General Weitzel was left in command of our line north of the river, with two divisions of his own corps — the Twenty-fifth, colored, and General Devens's Division, the Third of the Twenty-fourth Corps. At half-past three A. M. Monday, Captain Bruce, of Devens's staff, being in charge of the picket line, visited the outposts, and, his suspicions for some reason aroused, he sent three men to reconnoitre. They penetrated the Rebel line and reported no enemy. These three, like the three children of Israel despatched by Moses, spied out the land of Canaan. At once advancing his whole picket line by skirmishers, and opportunely falling in with a deserter by whom he was piloted, he himself first passed through. The deserter pointed out a tortuous path through three lines of *chevaux de frise*, which had been used for egress and ingress of their picket reliefs, and was, unlike the rest of the line, free from thickly planted torpedoes. Ordering his men to deploy widely and continue to advance, Captain Bruce rode rapidly to General Devens, who instantly telegraphed the facts to Weitzel. That energetic officer by daylight was advancing his entire force. By that hour a series of heavy explosions, and the smoke and flames of Richmond burning, put the fact of the evacuation beyond question. Major Stevens of Weitzel's staff, Lieutenant W. J. Ladd of Devens's, and Major Brooks of the Eighth Vermont, were the first in the city — by virtue of the excellence of their horses. Within that hour Weitzel, Devens, Ripley, Shepley, and other generals had come up ; the heads of their columns were pushing up parallel streets, and all the prominent points were in our possession. It is said to have been a jolly sight, the colored troops marching in great rapture, with long strides and ecstatic shouts, their welcome by their brethren in the city, who, men and women and piccaninnies, embraced them, ran by their sides, cried and laughed, and, in their own extravagant way, thanked the Lord and took courage.

But the city was burning down ; had been burning three hours. To prevent large quantities of tobacco and other stores from falling into our hands, on the direct order of Breckinridge, millions of private property was subjected to the flames, and one of the fairest cities on the continent ruined. Indeed, it is said that Breckinridge, in person, superintended the great arson, and left by the last train only twenty minutes before we came in.

That the entire city was not destroyed is due entirely to the Union army. The first order issued was for every exertion to be used to stay the conflagration, while regiment after regiment, without orders other than from their own officers, stacked arms, piled knapsacks, and lent willing and tireless energies to save the property of their enemies. Whole squares were tumbling and smouldering to ruin, and when the flames were extinguished, the *débris* and the smoke, the crumbling walls and the tottering chimneys of a thousand structures, many of them costly, all of them valuable, testified to the relentless cruelty of the Rebel authorities, — unpitying even to their friends and their dupes. Included in the destruction are the large mills and warehouses on the river, and the entire business part of the town.

During the night, stragglers from the retreating army inaugurated a reign of terror and pillage. Jewelry, clothing, and liquor stores, and a few private houses, were sacked. The fire revealed immense amounts of provisions, — whether the accumulations of the Government or of speculators does not appear, although citizens say the latter. Thousands immediately engaged in the scarcely reprehensible work of removing to their houses family supplies. "The niggers got it all," said a leading citizen, with a wrath he made little attempt to conceal. I do not doubt they "toted off" largely. Hunger stimulates thrift, and there was no fear to restrain. Meanwhile the more substantial citizens, the actual sufferers by the wanton destruction, looked on with an apparent unconcern approaching apathy. They have been too sternly disciplined these last four years to exhibit any intense consternation.

I entered the city by the New Market road, the same over which the troops advanced. There are seven distinct lines of fortifications, — very formidable, but no more so than those encountered at Petersburg. Nearly all were overgrown with last summer's vegetation, while some were badly washed by late rains. The enemy removed none of the heavy guns; their black forms dot the parapets, and you look into their black throats as you approach the city. Nor does one turn aside from the road, lest his step explode a villanous torpedo. Several of the first lines are strengthened against assault by a new device, in the nature of *chevaux de frise*. Sharp-hewn stakes, say eight feet long, are driven through a long pole in such a way that four to six rows of them project from a common centre, like spokes from a wheel. Indeed, the device may be described as one long hub extending miles, resting on long sharpened spokes, while the remaining spokes project into the air — radiating so thickly that one cannot creep through, while if he should be able to roll the thing over, he but turns up other spokes to meet him in the face.

Nearly all the houses on the way had been abandoned, yet two miles out of the city a man was plowing in a magnificent field stretching along the river bottom, and I was told he began betimes Monday morning — the day after the evacuation.

Near "Rocketts," a mile below the city on either side of the river, are the smouldering ruins of their Navy-Yard, and several of their rams and gunboats. One of them would have been launched within a fortnight.

Passing up Main Street, at the left were the crumbling walls and tottering chimneys, and the smoke still rising from the *débris* of the great fire. At the right, the sidewalk covered with negroes and poverty-stricken whites, timid women peering from the windows, or bolder ones in untidy garb standing in the doorways, or the doors were closed and the blinds shut — the denizens gone or hiding within. At length, forced by the cumbered street to turn into another, the signs attracted my attention.

There was "The Southern Literary Messenger," published by Thompson (John R.) and Wedderburn; "Dispatch" office, only the walls standing; "Richmond Examiner" likewise burned. The editor, John M. Daniels, died the Thursday before the

Sunday on which his paper and the Rebellion he had served so well went down in one common and irretrievable ruin. E. A. Pollard, the associate editor, the man who violated his parole granted him by General Butler, under the terms of which he was to effect an exchange for Richardson of "The Tribune," is at large in the city, boarding at the Spottswood, unmolested and saucy. "The Inquirer" was also destroyed, leaving of the five Richmond dailies only "The Whig" and "The Sentinel" in existence. One of the sub-editors of the former has been permitted to continue its publication as a Union paper. In his issue of yesterday, a dingy single sheet 10 by 14 inches size, he announces that he expects to secure as editor "one of the most brilliant and vigorous writers in Virginia," understood to be John M. Botts.

The street I was following led me to the Capitol grounds; and as I strolled through them and looked out upon the city — for the State House occupies a commanding site — I thought that before treason and war and sorrow came with their black wings to hover over and settle down upon the place, it might have passed for the "City which is called Beautiful," — it must have been fair and lovely.

In the public buildings were the evidences of hasty leave-taking. Documents and papers littered the floors of the rooms where sat in wordy war — with open doors, anon in secret conclave — the two houses of their Congress, and the two houses of the State Legislature. Copies of "Statutes at Large of the Confederate States," reports of the different cabinet officers, copies of bills, of resolutions, — they covered the tables and you tripped your feet against them strewn upon the floor. Indeed, acres of ground, and all the streets, and the very air were thick with paper — flying with the wind, picked up by the curious, gathered in baskets by negroes; papers and letters, papers and letters everywhere.

A bird's-eye view from "Gamble's Hill," an abrupt bluff just above the city, was worth to me the journey from Washington. Imagine the scene as I try to describe it. Looking south your eye follows down the river; at your feet a torrent tumbling among rocks, a mile down, where it meets the tide, placid as a lake. Where tide and torrent meet is the celebrated Richmond water-power, and there were great flouring-mills there three days ago. You now see only the blackened walls. The smoke on either side of the river still further down rises from where in navy-yards and arsenals were prepared the appointments of Rebel armies, and were built sundry abortive rams for their navy. In the middle of the river below us is "Belle Island." You start, for you remember how our boys, the poor prisoners, were starved and frozen there. Yet it looks now, from this distance, like any other island. Oh, the deep damnation those Rebel fiends deserve! And among the ruins in the burned district, which extends a mile down the left bank of the river, do you see those two large brick buildings, the only ones spared in a dozen blocks? — Libby Prison and Castle Thunder; and to-day they have both come back to plague the inventor, for now they are full of Rebel prisoners. As we look at the wide area over which swept the fire, and note those two buildings, is it not suggested that if the lash has been repaid by the sword, so base cruelty has been repaid by fire? But let us turn our eyes up the river — you catch the gleam of its winding course for miles. Your back is toward man's work, the city, your face toward God's, the country, and you heave a great sigh of relief. A moment and the marble-sprinkled sod of another city fixes your attention. It is a city that has not been evacuated. Ah, but its population has greatly increased during this war, its streets stretched out longer, and its habitations huddled closer. General A. P. Hill was buried there a few days ago, — one of twenty thousand soldiers who rest there, the fitful fever o'er. Saddened we turn to go, and you will carry that picture, vivid in color and distinct in outlines, while you live.

President Lincoln's visit, coming so soon after the occupation, was a matter of intense interest to the entire population. Crowds — thousands — rushed out for a glimpse of his tall figure, as he walked into the city attended by a few friends and an escort of a score or two of soldiers. The enthusiasm was, however, confined to the negroes, the foreigners, and exceptional Virginia-born citizens. But the joy of the negro knew no bounds. It found expression in whoops, in contortions, in tears, and incessantly in prayerful ejaculations of thanks. The President proceeded to General Weitzel's headquarters, the late residence of Jeff. Davis. I do not imagine he went there for the sake of any petty triumph, but simply because it was the headquarters of the general commanding. Many officers and citizens of Richmond came to pay their respects, after which he rode about the city. He slept on board one of the gunboats, and last night returned to City Point.

Among the first to seek an interview with the President was Judge Campbell, one of the three commissioners whom he met at Fortress Monroe. The interview lasted half an hour, and was followed by a second of longer duration yesterday. It is known that Judge Campbell concedes the hopelessness of the Rebellion, and is only striving for terms. To what extent he is authorized to act for Davis and Lee I do not know, nor is it known what was the President's response.

It is wholly unnecessary to say that every colored man is a loyal man, and is overflowing with expressions of his loyalty — triumphant through great tribulation. With the citizens generally it is otherwise. With one exception I saw but one blatant Rebel. Generally there is a disposition to acquiesce in a return to the Union, and I think the majority will, with little hesitation, subscribe to the oath of allegiance; not that there is not a deep sense of humiliation, for that is too apparent to be ignored; they will simply yield to necessity — grimly and sullenly at first, but with the consciousness that such is the only road to quiet and a return of prosperity. The blatant Rebel to whom I referred just now is a lawyer by the name of Crane, who told me that he had been, during several weeks in 1861, "Lincoln's district attorney;" that he shed tears when he saw the old flag taken down from the State House; "but," he added, "I shed more tears, and more bitter ones, when I saw it put back there." He confessed that he was almost alone in his bitterness, and wrathfully deplored the weakness of those "who are thinking of going back to Egypt."

I cannot ascertain that there has been anything approaching actual starvation, and yet everybody was pinched to the last degree. A letter which I append, addressed to Governor Extra Billy Smith, and found in his house, — which, by the way, belongs to the State, and is occupied by the successive governors, — is evidence of what extraordinary exertions were necessary, even in the Governor of Virginia, to supply his family, and how thankfully small favors were received.

[Filed on back, "J. M. Wade, Nov. 19, 1864."]

CHRISTIANSBURG, VA., Nov. 19, 1864.

DEAR SIR: According to your request I have purchased you a cheese from Mrs. E. Phlegar. I could only succeed in procuring one weighing about five pounds, for which I had to pay $10 per pound, which I consider a very high price, although the cheese is of a superior quality. I expect to visit the city in a few days and will bring it down.

Very respectfully, your obedient servant,

J. M. WADE.

To his Excellency WM. SMITH, Richmond, Va.

This is but one out of a score, all relating to the question of the Governor's daily food, and the raiment wherewith to be clothed. As to clothing, notwithstanding yesterday and to-day have been very warm, it is remarkable how universally such ladies as appear on the streets have worn heavy furs. The reason would seem to be that costly furs are very respectable, and, despite the oppressive weather, are worn in default of other garments that are respectable. With both gentlemen and ladies the different articles of clothing comport badly, — an elegant coat and a shocking hat, — boots out at the toes and fine cloth pantaloons, an elegant silk dress and cashmere shawl and a horrid old bonnet. Nor could either the gentlemen or the ladies refrain, in conversation, from hinting that they once were arrayed in purple and fine linen, and fared sumptuously every day.

Day before yesterday Mr. Chester, the colored correspondent of "The Philadelphia Press," was seated in the Speaker's chair of the Rebel House of Representatives, quietly writing to his paper. A scion of a first family discovered him thus and it kindled his ire. He ordered Mr. Chester to "kim out o' thar"—which he did n't, as Pip's Joe the blacksmith would say. Then the scion laid hold of him to take him out. Then Chester planted a black fist and left a black eye and a prostrate Rebel. Then the Rebel rose and asked an officer, who was a witness of the scene, for his sword "to cut the d—d nigger's heart out." The officer declined on the ground that he did not have two swords, that he might also give one to Chester. However, if the scion desired it, he would see fair play for a fair fight, at the same time expressing the opinion that he would "get thrashed worse than Lee did the other day." The scion bottled his wrath and skulked away; meanwhile Chester was coolly writing.

To-day the mail-boat will come up to the city instead of stopping at Varina Landing. The old post-office rooms, beneath the Spottswood, will be occupied by the army post-office.

All trading is done upon a greenback basis; not a man has been found whose faith in the stability and solvency of the Confederacy extended to his pocket.

Major B. B. Hammond, paymaster, paid here in the city yesterday the Fifty-eighth Pennsylvania, and other paymasters are at work paying to-day.

Generals Weitzel and Shepley attended the theatre last night on the occasion of its reopening. It was profusely decorated with Union flags, and the audience, being composed mainly of soldiers, never got tired of cheering them.

Mrs. Lincoln, Secretary Harlan and wife, Senator Sumner, with a large party, arrived at City Point to-day and will reach here to-night.

The best of order prevails in the city.

The first thing that struck me was the number of the colored population, perhaps, because they were all out of doors. In the State-House grounds, where they had never before been allowed to enter, not less than a thousand were congregated, strolling about with curious eyes upon every Yankee, or huddled in groups upon the ground, basking in the sun, there too following with their eyes the Union soldiers, especially those of their own color. It was impossible to mistake the great glee that shone in all their faces. In my hearing one of them said to half a dozen of his friends: "We uns kin go jist any whar — don't keer fur no pass — go any whar yer want 'er. Golly! de Kingdom hab kim *dis* time fur sure — dat ar what am promised in dé Generations to dem dat goes up tru great tribulations."

A citizen told me that a few hours before three of his slaves came and explained to him that they were a committee to inform him that the twenty-seven he owned were free, but would continue to work for him on condition that he would pay them wages *in greenbacks*. I suggested to the irate ex-master that the appointment of committees was a distinctive feature of enlightened communities, and in any case indicated a very high order of civilization and a capacity for self-care. He replied, "Well, I told the whole crew to go to ——, and they all left; it's my opinion they 'll all get there soon enough," and turning upon his heel he went away with the air of an injured man.

One fact is certain, namely: that there is not a negro in the city who does not know that he is free, and that does not count largely upon it. Nor do the majority look forward to a simple heaven of laziness. A dozen with whom I talked were anxious to get to work for wages. " Not for none of dis yer money which ain't *werf* nuffin, but de money dat *you* has. Dis chile 'd like to hab a heap o' *dat*," said one, exhibiting perhaps a thousand dollars of Confederate issues, and also exhibiting white teeth in a broad grin.

I found General Devens and staff quartered in the house lately occupied by Governor Extra Billy Smith. His wife, daughter, and nieces were still there, and anxious for permission to go to friends in Baltimore. The furniture, owned like the house by the State, remained. The ladies said nothing belonging to the State was removed, except a valuable table, service and other plate, marked with the State arms, which had been taken to the Exchange Bank for safety, and was there burned on Monday morning. It is more probable the ladies were mistaken, and that those valuables were carried off with the coin of the bank.

The State gardener, a Swiss, gave me a choice bouquet from the conservatory, and then tried to enlist my services in procuring for him a pass North. It is remarkable how many desire to get away. The office of the provost-marshal is thronged from morning to night, mainly by people pleading for passes to Baltimore. At present none are granted, principally for want of transportation.

Next I called on General Weitzel, at the house for which the city paid $65,000 in gold and presented to Davis when he removed his Government from Montgomery. In the parlor, on the point of setting out for an interview with Mr. Lincoln on one of the gunboats, was Judge Campbell, an elderly bald man, bowed, pale, and with a look on his face full of all disappointment and sadness, yet of great dignity. I could but note the contrast afforded by Weitzel, who, in full uniform, with sword at his loins, was to go with him to the President. It was the contrast between sorrow and joy, between bitter failure and glorious success, between a thwarted and broken conspirator, whose age precludes any honorable retrieval, and a soldier who, though not yet thirty, has served his country well, won her greenest laurels and the respect and gratitude of good men, — the contrast between Catiline defeated and Cicero in his triumph. The very courtesy of Weitzel's demeanor toward the old man but pointed the difference each must have felt in his consciousness.

Here I met many officers whom I had known in the "armies operating against Richmond." By the way, those armies are operating elsewhere now, and it behooves Grant to choose another designation to replace the one he has caused to become a misnomer. Among them were General Shepley and Colonels Ed. Smith and Fred. Manning, late of Butler's staff. Having had large experience in the governing of captured cities and turbulent communities, I found them very busy, as I know they are very useful men. The former said he had received not less than fifty applications from citizens living in splendid houses to have officers quartered upon them, — of course with a view to protection, and immunity from confiscation. Apropos to the possession of houses, a good story is told of General Shepley, the military governor. A party claimed that he had leased his house to one of the foreign consuls, and that, therefore, it should not be occupied now or at any time confiscated. The general said to him, " Bring me the lease, sir; I will examine it, and if I find upon it the stamp required by the revenue laws, I will consider your request. Of course, if the lease is not stamped I am not bound to respect it." Whether the party appreciated the reasoning did not appear, but he evidently understood the decision, for he went away.

It was mournful to walk about the city. So many houses deserted, so many ladies in mourning, — all I met were in mourning, — so many old men, broken with premature age, their hats made respectable by the dingy crape that told of sons slain, and then that broad black waste where stood the busiest part of the city — it was pitiful.

And so the forenoon was spent, and I returned to the Spottswood. The chivalry used to rate this house as we do the Fifth Avenue and the Brevoort, though I do not see how, if it were in New York, it could ever have been considered more than a fourth-rate hotel. The dinner was not inviting. Among the guests were Honorable Roscoe Conkling, Assistant-Secretary Dana and wife, and C. C. Coffin, of " The Boston Journal," who, since the war began, has always managed to be at the point of interest, whether it were Vicksburg, Chattanooga, the Wilderness, Savannah, Charleston, Wilmington, or Richmond. Near Mr. Dana sat Pollard, late of "The Examiner," though I think neither ex-editor was aware of the other's presence.

During the day, from soldiers and negroes and by my own foraging among the heaps of papers flying about, a large number of autograph letters of distinguished Rebels fell into my hands. H. S. Foote excuses himself from breakfasting with Governor Smith in a long note in his usual verbose style. General McCausland pronounces General Lomax " no cavalry general." Governor Brown of Georgia won't let Governor Smith have a train of Georgia cars to bring up supplies. Senator J. L. Orr has a bile on his neck, so he cannot breakfast with Smith. Indeed, that breakfast must have been a failure, for half a dozen write to decline, and another half-dozen to excuse themselves for not going. Perhaps forty plead their destitution to the Governor as reason why they should be given employment in some office. Secretary of War Seddon and Smith quarrel, in half a score of letters, over details and exemptions. "Anonymous" — so filed on the back in Smith's own hand, though the body of the letter shows that he was simply afraid to sign his name — writes from New York of politics and of torpedoes, but despairs of the Rebel cause. "Anonymous," it appears, voted for McClellan. But these letters will bear publication in full, and I refrain from noting more.

By a lucky chance I discovered late at night that I could obtain passage in a headquarters mail-wagon back to Varina the next morning. It was an opportunity not to be slighted, especially as a little calculation made it appear that by hitting all the connections I might make New York Friday night in time for Saturday's paper. In that view, Richmond became Sodom, and New York Mecca, for be it known that the correspondent who is ahead in point of time is most valued by his paper. Powers of observation, the ability to tell a story in passable English, and a gentlemanly presence are requisites, but they are all secondary to energy that never flags and gets the news back to the home office on time.

Picking up Messrs. Reid and Colburn at daylight, — for I had slept in another part of the city, and they determined to go only when I called for my baggage, — by a second judicious use of the potence of flask and pocket-book upon the driver, we made the boat at Varina by half a minute. Thence, tediously, by boat to Baltimore, via Fortress Monroe; thence, a train to New York; all told, thirty-six hours from Richmond. Then four hours' tough work, resulting in three columns in the next morning's paper, embodying the main facts of the evacuation and occupation of the Rebel capital — and the five days of my trip to Richmond and back were over. The trip probably closes my relation of army correspondent, which fact may excuse so much of personal matter in this article.

With the foregoing letters Mr. Page furnished to the "Tribune" some extracts from the "Richmond Whig," an old and influential journal, and one of the only two that survived the destruction of so large a part of the city. They are of interest as describing the then condition of Richmond by an eye-witness, who was a Virginian. He gives the following incidents of the evacuation.

"Sunday morning, April 2, broke upon Richmond calmly and pleasantly, and without anything portentous in events immediately transpiring. There were rumors of evacuation, but very few supposed the event was upon us and at hand. The church bells rang as usual, with nothing of alarm in their tone, and worshippers were as prompt and devout as was their wont. But by the hour of noon nervous people began to snuff danger in the air, and one's ears were filled with the most terrible rumors. Then there came an unusual increase in the number of wagons on the streets; boxes and trunks were being hastily loaded at the departments and driven to the Danville depot. Those who had determined to evacuate with the fugitive Government looked on with amazement, then, convinced of the fact, rushed to follow the Government's example. Vehicles with two horses, one horse, or even no horse at all, suddenly rose to a premium value that was astounding, and ten, fifteen, and even a hundred dollars in gold or Federal currency were offered for a conveyance.

"Suddenly, as if by magic, the streets became filled with men, walking as though for a wager, and behind them excited negroes toting trunks, bundles, and luggage of every description. All over the city it was the same, — wagons, trunks, band-boxes and their owners, a mass of hurrying fugitives, filling the streets. The banks were all open, and depositors were as busy as bees removing their specie deposits; and the directors were equally active in getting off their bullion. Hundreds of thousands of dollars of paper money were destroyed, both State and Confederate. Night came, and with it came confusion worse confounded. There was no sleep for human eyes in Richmond Sunday night. The rapid tramp of men upon the streets, the rattle and roar of wagons, the shouts of soldiers retreating through the city to the south side, went on the whole long, long, weary night.

"One of the pillaging soldiers engaged in robbing the stores on Main Street, Monday morning, was shot from the inside by the proprietor, while he was knocking in the show-glass. A charge of buckshot entered his stomach, and it was believed he died in a short time, but we could not learn what became of the body.

"At daybreak on Monday morning the scene at the commissary depot, at the head of the dock, beggared description. Hundreds of Government wagons were loaded with bacon, flour, and whiskey, and driven off in hot haste to join the retreating army. Negroes with their peculiar 'heave oh!' sweated and worked like beavers; but the immense piles of stores did not seem to diminish in the least. Thronged about the depot were hundreds of men, women, and children, black and white, provided with capacious bags, baskets, tubs, buckets, tin pans, and aprons, cursing, pushing, and crowding, awaiting the throwing open of the doors, and the order for each to help himself. When the Government wagons had gotten off all the stores possible, it was found that several hundred barrels of whiskey remained in the upper story.

"One after another, in hasty procession, the barrels were rolled to the hatchway, the heads knocked out, and a miniature whiskey Niagara poured continuously down, pouring into the dock in a current almost strong enough to have swept a man off his feet. Between 200 and 300 barrels were thus poured out, — a big drink to the finny inhabitants of the river.

"About sunrise the doors were opened to the populace, and a rush that almost seemed to carry the building off its foundations was made, and hundreds of thousands of pounds of splendid bacon, flour, etc., went into the capacious maw of the public.

"And here we may remark that while the Confederate Government was making such a poor mouth over the reported failure of supplies, while the people were being starved that the army might be fed, this immense storehouse was bursting with fulness and plenty, to come finally to utter wreck and waste.

"While hundreds of families have been rendered homeless and houseless by the conflagration, a great many persons who live in sections spared by the flames have accumulated small fortunes by rescuing large quantities of goods from the burning buildings. Clothing, shoes, dry goods of every description, were saved in large quantities, and are now stored away in the houses of those who saved them. Part restitution would be the proper thing in cases where the owners were known.

"A whirlwind sweeping through dead leaves in autumn scattered them no more wildly than official documents, pamphlets, etc., were scattered on Monday morning. Confederate bonds, Confederate notes, bank checks, bills, flecked and whitened the streets in every direction, — all so worthless that the boys would not pick them up.

"While the city was burning, about nine o'clock on Monday morning, terrific shell-explosions, rapid and continuous, added to the terror of the scene, and led to the impression that the city was being shelled by the retreating Confederate army from the south side; but the explosions were soon ascertained to proceed from the Government Arsenal and Laboratory, then in flames.

"The military authorities, in view of the destruction of the bridges across the James, have thrown across the river below Mayo's bridge one of their firm and very durable pontoon bridges to facilitate travel and transportation to the south side.

"The insurance offices, being mostly located in that portion of the city destroyed, are included among the buildings burned, — with their books and accounts in many instances. Hundreds of the sufferers hold policies of insurance on their property in these offices, but whether they can ever realize a cent under the present circumstances is a grave question.

"Captain Warren M. Kelly, Tenth New Hampshire Volunteers, was in command of the skirmish line of the Second Brigade (commanded by Colonel Donohue, Tenth New Hampshire Volunteers), Third Division, Twenty-fourth Army Corps, which was the first organized body of troops to enter the city, under the direction of Lieutenant-Colonel W. W. Barnberger, Fifth Maryland Volunteers, division officer of the day.

"Captain Kelly advanced his line of skirmishers through several of the streets of the city, and halting in front of Jeff. Davis's mansion, divided his command into squads and patrolled the city until relieved by the arrival of other troops.

"The visit of his Excellency President Lincoln was the event of yesterday afternoon.

"The President, accompanied by Admiral Porter of the United States Navy, with an escort of army and navy officers, was landed at Rocketts about three P. M., from a gunboat, and was enthusiastically cheered by the populace and Federal soldiers all the way up Main Street to the market, and up Franklin Street to Governor Street. The President was on foot and walked rapidly, towering above the crowd, flanked on his right by Admiral Porter, on his left by his son Thaddeus.

"The President was dressed in a long black overcoat, high silk hat, and black pants, giving to his form a very commanding appearance. The President and escort moved up Governor to Twelfth Street, out Twelfth to Marshall Street, and the mansion of Jeff. Davis, late President of the Confederate States, and now the headquarters of Major-General Godfrey Weitzel. The crowd surrounded the mansion, and sent up cheer after cheer as the President entered the doorway and seated himself in the reception room and reception chair of Jefferson Davis. Three cheers for Admiral Porter were then proposed, and given with a hearty good-will.

"A brilliant collection of Union officers assembled in the hall were then presented to the President, and afterward the citizens generally were allowed the opportunity of shaking the President of 'our whole Union' by the hand. Subsequently the President and suite, with a cavalry escort of colored troops, appeared on the square, drawn in a carriage and four, which was driven around the walks, the President inspecting the condition of the troops and exhibiting an unwonted interest in everything.

"Everywhere the reception was the same, the bands playing

and the people besieging the grounds, each anxious for a closer inspection of the distinguished occupants of the carriage.

"While these ceremonies were going on a salute of guns was fired from the steamers at Rocketts.

"The President is still in Richmond, we believe, but we are not informed what are to be his future movements.

"The theatre will be reopened to-night under the management of Mr. R. D'Orsay Ogden, who may now exclaim, 'Richard is himself again.' The play selected for the occasion is 'Don Cæsar de Bazan.' Mr. Ogden will personate Don Cæsar, supported by the company recently performing at the theatre.

"Invitations have been sent to President Lincoln, General Grant, General Weitzel, General Shepley, and other officers of distinction. An efficient guard has been detailed by the provost-marshal to preserve order."

A further description of the state of things in the doomed city is in the following letters from another eye-witness, Charles Carleton Coffin, the widely known war correspondent. The first is dated —

RICHMOND, April 5.

The Richmond "Whig" was issued yesterday afternoon as a loyal paper. The editor and all who have heretofore controlled its columns fled on Sunday night. The proprietor and one *attaché* of the editorial corps remain. They have taken the oath of allegiance. The issue of last night says: "'The Whig' will be issued hereafter as a Union paper. The sentiment of attachment to our whole country, which formerly characterized it as a journal, will again find expression in its columns, and whatever influence it may have for the restoration of the national authority will be exerted."

The "Sentinel" office was not destroyed. I saw the proprietor to-day. He formerly did the government printing. We had a pleasant interview.

"I was sorry," he said, "to see the Stars and Stripes torn down in 1861. It is the prettiest flag in the world, but I shed tears when I saw it raised over the Capitol of Virginia on Sunday morning."

"Why so?" I asked.

"Because it was done without the consent of the State of Virginia."

"Then you still cling to the idea that a State is more than the nation?"

"Yes. State rights above everything."

"Don't you think the war is almost over — that it is useless for Lee to contend further?"

"No. He will fight another battle, and he will win. He can fight for twenty-five years in the mountains."

"Do you think that men can live in the mountains?"

"Yes; on roots and herbs, and fight you till you are weary of it, and whip you out."

I give you the conversation as near as I can recall it, that you may understand the insanity of the secessionists. They have no conception of the great principles which underlie this mighty struggle. They are clinging to the abstractions of the past, — State rights, State sovereignty, — and are impelled by State pride. They talk of the proud Old Dominion, the State which has raised up presidents, of their ancestors and all that, — living in the past, without comprehending the revolution of the present, which has precipitated them from power, and brought liberty to a despised race.

A friend called upon one of the most aristocratic families of the place last night, — a family which has had a great name. He found them exceedingly bitter and defiant. They never would yield; no — never! They would fight through a generation and defeat us at last.

There are many people in Richmond who are glad to see the old flag here once more; they love the Union, they say, but cannot bear to "see a nigger parading about the streets." And this brings me to the subject of negro troops.

I have taken especial pains to ascertain the truth about negro troops in the Rebel service. A great meeting was held in the African church some weeks ago to fire the African heart. The church was crowded with colored people. The newspapers since then have made frequent mention of the volunteering of colored men, and the public have been made to believe that several regiments were being enlisted. I have the testimony of a dozen men, white and colored, that the entire number did not exceed fifty! — and these were boys, who were ready to parade the streets, and live on Confederate rations, but who had no idea of fighting. "Dey was mostly poor Souf Carolina darkies

— poor heathen fellers, who did n't know no better," said one negro, in response to my inquiries.

"Would you have fought against the Yankees?" I asked of a colored man, dressed in butternut-colored clothes, who stood near by.

"No, sir. Dey might have shot me through de body wid ninety thousand balls, before I would have fired a gun at my friends."

"Then you look upon us as your friends?"

"Yes, sir. I've prayed for you to come to get here for a long while, and do you think that I would have prayed one way and fit de other?"

He said it with spirit, as if a little hurt that I should question his sincerity.

"I'll tell you, massa, what I would have done," said another, taking off his hat and bowing; "I would have taken de gun and when I cotched a chance, I'd 'a' shooted it at de Rebs and den run for de Yankees."

This brought a general explosion from the crowd, and arrested the attention of some white men passing.

I look back with pleasure to the scene. It was in the street directly west of the Capitol — the dilapidated building with decaying walls and broken windows. I had but to raise my eyes to see the Stars and Stripes waving in the evening breeze. A few paces distant were the ruins of the Rebel war department, from whence were issued the orders to starve our prisoners at Belle Isle, Salisbury, and Andersonville. Near by were the walls of Dr. Reed's church, where a specious gospel had been preached. A stone's throw in the other direction was Dr. Hoge's church, where Jeff. Davis' heart quailed on Sunday last. The street was full of people. I was a stranger to them all, but I ventured to make this inquiry: —

"Did you ever see an abolitionist?"

"No, massa, I reckon I neber did," was the reply.

"What kind of people do you think they are?"

"Well, massa, I specs dey is a good kind of people."

"Why do you think so?"

"'Case when I hear bad white folks swearing and cussing about 'em, I reckun dar must be something good about 'em."

"Well, my friends, I am an abolitionist; I believe that one man is just as good as another if he behaves as well, and that I have no more right to make a slave of you than you have of me."

Every hat came off in an instant, and a dozen hands were reached out toward me, and I heard from a dozen tongues a hearty "God bless you, sir!"

There is freedom of speech in Richmond now. White men heard me and scowled. Last Sunday, had I uttered those words, I should have dangled upon the nearest lamp-post in five minutes; but to-day, those men who stretched out their hands to me would have given the last drop of their blood before they would have seen a hair of my head injured, after that declaration.

The fire which licked out with forked tongues of flame the heart of Richmond on Monday last, which surged from James River to the Capitol, from Belle Isle to Rocketts, which made the place a scene of indescribable desolation, left the Libby Prison unharmed, though nearly all other buildings around it were burned.

Libby Prison! What horrors have been witnessed within its walls! What sighs and groans! What prayers and tears! What dying out of hope and wasting away of body and mind! What nights of darkness settling on human souls! Its door an entrance to a living charnel-house — its iron-grated windows the loop-holes of hell! Death was the warden. Whoever entered there stood on the verge of the grave and met Death face to face.

This morning, accompanied by friends, I visited the prison, which now contains about five hundred Rebel prisoners. They were peeping out from the grated windows, looking intently and sadly upon the scene of desolation around them, — a city in ruins, still smouldering and smoking. A large number were upon the roof, breathing the fresh air, and gazing upon the fields beyond the James, green now with the verdure of spring. Union prisoners never had such liberty. Whoever approached the window bars, or laid his hand upon them, fell dead the next instant.

There was a crowd of women with pails and buckets at the windows, giving the prisoners provisions and talking freely with their friends, who came not only to the windows but to the door, where the good-natured sentinel allowed conversation without restriction.

The officer in charge conducted our party through the wards. The crowd of filthy wretches gazed upon us with curiosity, wondering what was the purpose of our visit. The air was fetid with vile odors, arising from the unwashed crowd, from old rags and filthy garments, from choked-up urinals and sinks, from puddles of filthy water which oozed from the leaky conductors, dripped through the floor, ran down the walls, sickening to all the senses. From this prison, on Sunday last, fifteen hundred men were hurried to the flag-of-truce boat, that they might be exchanged before falling into our hands. Many thousands of men have lived there month after month, wasting away, starving, dying of fever, of consumption, of all diseases known to medical science, — from insanity, despair, and idiocy; having no communication with the outer world, no food from friends, no sympathy, no compassion, denied everything, starved to death, tortured to death by rigor of imprisonment, — by men whose hearts grew harder from day to day till they became fiends in human form.

"Please give me a bit of bread, aunty, I am starving," was the plea made one day by a young soldier who saw a negro woman passing the window. He thrust his emaciated hand between the bars and clutched the bit which the kind-hearted colored woman cheerfully gave him; but before it had passed between his teeth he saw the brains of his benefactress spattered upon the sidewalk by the sentinel!

Where on the page of history is there such a damning record of crime as that written in Richmond, — at Libby, at Belle Isle, at Castle Thunder, the jail, and the penitentiary? Andersonville, and Salisbury, and Millen are parts of the Richmond record of crime, for all orders were issued from here.

At the jail Major Stevens, the provost-marshal, found a crowd of starving wretches — men, women, and children, blacks and whites — incarcerated for petty crimes.

"What are you in here for?" he asked of a little girl.

"For stealing a piece of bread, sir. I was hungry and my mother was starving," she replied, the tears starting down her cheeks.

Major Stevens ascertained that nearly all were imprisoned for petty offences, — driven to crime by necessity, — and opening the door, told them to go where they pleased.

Barbarity and inhumanity are characteristics of slavery; which have shown themselves on the plantation, in the slave mart, and in the prison, — to slaves and prisoners of war alike.

"I intend to treat the prisoners well. They have murdered our men, but I shall not retaliate except with kindness," said the officer who conducted us.

The prisoners were playing cards, cooking their breakfasts, baking hoe cakes by the fire.

It was gratifying to see the flag of the Union floating over that accursed prison-house, with the soldiers of the Union pacing their beats before the doors, — to see the motley crowd peeping from the iron-barred windows. It was not a feeling of resentment, but of satisfaction that at last there was an end to human torture on that spot; that it should be no longer the prison-house of despair.

How strange the action of the rebel leaders! They burned the tobacco warehouses that the tobacco might not fall into our hands; they destroyed the city wantonly, reducing their best friends from affluence to poverty, and yet suffered Libby Prison to remain a monument of their infamy! They were anxious that it should not be destroyed, as I am informed by Captain Stewart, who has been the United States agent for the distribution of supplies at this place.

Like the Bridge of Sighs, it will be a memorable place — forever an object of interest, waking harrowing feelings and melancholy thoughts in the minds of all visitors to Richmond. The great lock of its largest door has passed into the hands of Senator Sumner, who arrived here to-day, accompanying Mr. Lincoln.

Charles Sumner in Richmond! The hated, despised, maltreated fanatic of other days, whose life was sought, who was received only with haughty, insolent contempt from his compeers in the Senate of the United States, walked the streets of Richmond to-day, entered the Capitol of the Confederacy, while ex-Senators Mason, Hunter, Breckenridge, Benjamin, and Davis are fugitives. It is not Senator Sumner who has triumphed. Men are God's instruments. Justice and righteousness have won the mighty victory.

CONDITION OF THE SOUTH.

RICHMOND, April 6, 1865.

IT is possible that General Lee may be able to fight another battle, for there is strength even in despair; but that the long conflict is over and the rebellion crushed must be evident to any fair-minded person.

A letter from Adjutant-General Cooper to his wife has fallen into my hands, which was written April 1, which presents a vivid picture of the Rebel cause as he looked upon it on the morning after the great Rebel victory of Hatcher's Run, in which Sheridan was repulsed. Being a military man, the Adjutant-General of the Confederacy, he saw the approaching doom. He says: —

"I was pained on reading your letter that your mind is made up on coming to this city; you know not what you would have to encounter here, nor is it possible for you to know (unless you were here) of the privation which you would encounter here if you came. You say there is no place safer than where you are except in Richmond, and that you expect to leave Clifton for this place in three weeks, by which time the roads will be passable.

"Let me beg and urge you *not* to come here, and do not let your fancy picture comfort and safety to you here.

"Think of the distresses in Savannah and Columbia when Sherman's army took possession of those cities, and do not suppose that the same scenes may not be enacted here, under like circumstances.

"I met Mary Lee yesterday and she told me her mother and sisters would *not* remain here, and also said the ladies in Savannah were selling their own clothing to buy themselves food. In all places the enemy have captured, the Confederate money is considered by them as trash, and is not taken for the sale of any commodities. So will it be here. You know I have nothing but Confederate money; and how can you live upon that here under these circumstances? You will be reduced to starvation. That is lingering death, to be sure; but it is not the less certain. You could not live upon your relations and friends here, as you seem to think, for a time, for they could no more live on the same means than yourself, and you would all be reduced to the same necessities and *despair*. Call your mind to these facts and do not let your apprehension as to your present situation sway your judgment; and as you place *faith* in the protection of the Almighty, do not let that faith be shaken by the fear that he will fail you in the hour of need, which would only prove a doubt of his powers or purpose to *save*.

"Mrs. Davis and her children left here yesterday for the South, and other families are preparing to leave. Your sister Nannie, I understand, is much disturbed as to what to do, and inclines to leave the city. Grant is making every effort not to fight battles, but to starve the city and Lee's army by cutting off communications for supplies, and in that way gain an easy victory.

"P. S. Mr. Ambler says your sister Eliza, Mrs. J. M. Mason, is going to Halifax for safety."

I have omitted portions of the letter which are of a private nature. The missive is like a candle in a dark room; we can look in and see the darkness and gloom. General Cooper says he has nothing but Confederate money. The same kind of currency is plenty in Richmond. One-thousand-dollar bonds are trampled in the streets, — of so little value that men will not take the trouble to pick them up. A few days ago the rebel authorities confiscated the coin of the Louisiana banks and of the Richmond banks, — stole it, rather, — and the people are penniless. They talk of maintaining the fight, but the great concern with many soon will be how to live. Pride and power are going down. Old families are decaying, and never so fast as now. The old families will find themselves pushed aside by new families. The old merchants will see new firms carrying on the trade of Richmond. Already the Yankees are here opening stores and carrying on a brisk trade. The Spottswood hotel already is overflowing with visitors, and Northern men are here, talking of going into business.

Yesterday and to-day there have been jubilee meetings in the African churches, conducted by members of the Christian Commission. They are purely religious in their character. The colored people are an excitable, demonstrative race, and at such a time as this cool, calm words are best. I attended the meeting held this afternoon. It was a vast assembly. Every seat, every aisle, every inch of room was appropriated. A black cloud of men hung around the door, peeped into the windows, and even mounted the walls in rear of the church. A half-hour before the time appointed the church was full, and all were singing, giving utterance to their joy.

Professor Barrows, of Andover Theological Seminary, preached a plain, practical sermon. Another meeting will be held to-morrow, and so on through the week. The reception of their liberty, so sudden, so long prayed for, is marked by devout thanksgiving and gratitude to God. Every allusion to their freedom brought spontaneous shouts of "Glory!" They instinctively feel that the Yankees are their friends. They have always been faithful, true, and trustworthy to our prisoners, to our generals and soldiers. Our battle was theirs. What a hard life they have led!

"I paid forty dollars a month for my time before our money

became worthless," said one bright fellow, who has been an assistant in a drug store. He added: "My master thought I was going to run away to the Yankees, and sold me a while ago; and he was my own father, sir!"

AFTER THE EVACUATION.

RICHMOND, April 8, 1865.

THE telegraph has given you intelligence of the breaking up of Lee's army; how Ewell and three other major-generals and prisoners by the thousand and guns without number have been captured near Amelia Court-House. I cannot be there to see it, for just now there are important matters to look after in the city. The Rebellion is about finished. Sheridan has captured a despatch-bearer from Lee to Davis, in which Lee states that the men will not fight. As he nears the Carolina line his army will melt away. Virginians will not leave the State. Even if they were to do so it would make no difference. Grant outnumbers Lee three to one. His men are flushed with victory. They can go where they please. Grant alone is able to cope with all the combined armies in the Confederacy. Deserters are coming in this city hourly. About five hundred have come in voluntarily since the occupation four days ago.

There is a distinction between feeling and opinion. They are not synonymous terms. The people of Richmond feel intensely. It is easy to get at their feelings, but more difficult to find out their opinions.

The suddenness of the evacuation, the action of the authorities in destroying the city, the terribleness of the event were stunning and stupefying. It was like a thunderbolt on a cloudless day. They trusted their leaders. They believed in General Lee. Their newspapers were as defiant and confident as ever. The very peacefulness and calm of Sunday made the blow more appalling; and when it fell, all their hopes, all their trust, all their confidence — all went except their pride. All their property went down in an instant. The foundations were all broken up, and they beheld themselves on Monday morning utterly powerless, helpless, weak as a starving infant abandoned by its unnatural mother, mocked, derided, deceived. Like the rebellious angels hurled from heaven, when overthrown in the great battle once fought on the celestial plains, they found themselves engulfed by a sea of fire. As I entered the city on Monday night and saw the poor, pale, emaciated, heaven-stricken people moving along the streets over the hot pavements — lost at times to sight beneath the murky clouds of smoke, I thought of the rebellious host of heaven, as described by Milton, walking over the burning marl of hell!

The secessionists are just awakening to a sense of their lost condition. Some of them are as bitter as ever they have been. There is another class who are looking toward reconstruction, who talk of an armistice, of coming back into the Union. President Lincoln while here had an interview with Judge Campbell, and made a memorandum, not signing it, as I understand, but simply making a minute on paper that he was desirous of doing what he could to aid Virginia to come back into the Union, and expressed a desire that the Legislature would reassemble for that purpose.

There was a meeting yesterday of those members of the Legislature who did not leave the city. Some citizens were present. Those attending were Messrs. English, Hull, Ambers, Burr, Scott, of the House of Delegates, Messrs. Marshall of Fauquier and Garrison of Accomac, of the Senate, the mayor of the city, Mr. Mayo, Mr. Thomas, city auditor. General Joseph R. Anderson presided. He is proprietor of the Tredegar Iron Works and has been a brigadier in the Rebel service, but resigned his commission about one year ago.

Judge Campbell made a statement concerning his interview with President Lincoln. He said that Mr. Lincoln would give passports to Governor Smith and the members of the Legislature to come within the Union lines to Richmond to decide upon the future destiny of Virginia. The desire was expressed by several gentlemen that four commissioners should be sent to General Lee with the terms of President Lincoln, to see if an armistice could not be obtained.

Senator Marshall proposed that Charlottesville be made neutral ground and that the Legislature assemble there. The meeting was private, but the above information may be relied upon as being in the main correct. What will grow out of it remains to be seen.

General Anderson, as above stated, is proprietor of the Tredegar Works, and has been in the Rebel service. The fortifications around Richmond, around Charleston, around Savannah, contain hundreds of pieces of heavy ordnance which were cast at those works; hundreds of field pieces now in Rebel hands bear on their trunnions the initials J. R. A. He has built up a splendid fortune out of the Rebel government, — estimated to be worth three millions of dollars in greenbacks. By his genius and enterprise he has done quite as much as any other man to help on the Rebellion.

The Rebel authorities sent a man to fire the works when the city was evacuated, but General Anderson saved them. I heard him say: "The works are private property, and the Rebel Government has no right to destroy them, even if they have been run upon government work." Perhaps General Anderson may turn round and say that the United States cannot confiscate private property. General Anderson and Judge Campbell represent one class of Union men, — those who want what was discussed in the Virginia Legislature three weeks ago in secret session: a recognition of State rights, no confiscation of property, but protection to property, which means no interference with slaves. Such questions were discussed. Judge Campbell and General Anderson propose terms: armistice, neutrality, peace commissioners, non-interference with slavery.

But there is another class of Union men whom President Lincoln has not seen, men who are yet to be heard from. They are men of wealth, character, slaveholders, but yet uncompromising Unionists. They held an informal meeting last evening at a private residence to talk over the great question of the hour. They will not ask for a cessation of hostilities, an armistice, a neutrality, a calling together of a runaway legislature, a recognition of State rights, or protection to slave property, but they will ask for a prosecution of the war till every Rebel lays down his arms; they will ask for a convention of the people for the abolition of slavery, although one of the number owns two hundred slaves. It is refreshing to talk with these men. They are emphatic, earnest, and determined. They say that the time has not yet come for action; that they will not recognize William Smith as Governor; that he is a tyrant; that he was elected under secession, and is not Governor of the State. I shall have more to say of these men in another letter.

The time has not yet come when the State should resume its place in the nation. President Lincoln's action in the matter is somewhat criticised. The men of this city, who have stood up for the Union under one of the worst despotisms the world ever saw, who have suffered, some of them, imprisonment in Castle Thunder, where the floors are inches thick with filth and vermin, will have nothing to do with a milk and water policy, which is policy and not principle, which looks only to selfish interests and ends. These men are for a radical work. They mean that the barbaric features of the past, that slavery shall be abolished, and that when Virginia starts again it shall be with a motive power which will lift her to her true position among the sisterhood of States. If the President had talked with these men before his interview with Judge Campbell perhaps he would not have made the memorandum which gave rise to the proposition for an armistice and neutral ground in the meeting to-day.

Andrew Johnson is here, accompanied by ex-Senator Preston King of New York. He rode round the city to-day. He remarked that the white people were exceedingly morose. He did not see them smile, except the poor whites, but the negroes were jubilant. Mr. Johnson has no sympathy with half-way Unionism.

It is impossible to convey an idea of the destitution of the poor whites. The Christian Commission gave supplies to more than two thousand persons to-day — a pint of flour to each. It was a sad spectacle, that crowd of famished women, victims of the rebellion. Many of them had not tasted flour for months together. It was a motley crowd, a rag-pickers' fair; women in faded, tattered garments, reaching out their long bony fingers to receive the pittance, while tears of gratitude and thanksgiving rolled down their sunken cheeks. The Commission is doing a blessed work.

Among the papers left behind by the Secretary of the Treasury is the correspondence had with the British Government in regard to employment of bank-note engravers. They were hired from the British Government! What will the London "Times" say to that neutrality? CARLETON.

SUNDAY IN RICHMOND.

RICHMOND, April 10, 1865.

TIME brings wonderful changes. The second Sunday of April, 1861, was a day of wild excitement in this city, marked by thanksgivings and praises over the fall of Fort Sumter. Then the old flag of the Union was laid away to be seen no more, except in secret by those who loved and cherished it, till Monday morning last, when with tearful eyes they gazed once more upon its folds.

I had a curiosity, laudable I trust, to be an observer of the temper of the people at church yesterday. It was a beautiful day — warm and sunny. The churches were all open, and at the hour of worship the streets were thronged with people. The African churches were crowded. It has been a jubilee week to the colored people. They have given thanks from overflowing hearts. The other churches were well attended, many officers and soldiers availing themselves of the opportunity to be present at public worship.

Two of the clergymen of the city, after preaching to their congregations a week ago, in the forenoon of Sunday, took a journey toward Danville or Lynchburg in the afternoon, — Rev. Dr. Hoge of the Presbyterian, and Dr. Duncan of the Methodist Church. Here let me make a correction. I have stated in a former letter that Jeff. Davis attended Dr. Hoge's church; not so, he was an attendant at St. Paul's, where Rev. Mr. Minnegerade, a German, who speaks broken English, officiates. Jeff. Davis's pew had no occupant yesterday.

The lesson for the day in the Episcopal service was the forty-fourth Psalm, in which are several passages which probably were not very comforting to the worshippers in Richmond.

"Thou hast cast us off and put us to shame, and goest not forth with our armies.

"Thou makest us to turn back from the enemy and they which hate us spoil for themselves.

"Thou makest us a reproach to our neighbors, a scorn and a derision to them that are round about us."

There is not a passage in the Bible more full of humiliating confession of weaknesses and inability. The prayer for the President was omitted, and the minister, after a little haggling, prayed "for those in authority." So in times of emergency the authority of the bishop is set aside, and ministers exercise their own power to omit or alter the church service.

In Dr. Hoge's church, where Dr. Bevins officiated, the minister prayed for "those who are in rightful authority."

There evidently had been a consultation among the pastors of the churches to frame a uniform course, for I have reports from friends who attended other churches that other ministers used similar phraseology. The hymns, the sermon, and the prayer at Dr. Hoge's were as if it was a funeral occasion. Two thirds of the congregation were in mourning for friends killed in battle. Many tears were shed as the thoughts of the great humiliation came upon them. What a humiliation it is! Never has there been a sterner pride than that of Virginia, never a pride more haughty and arrogant. But all power of resistance is gone. They struggle hopelessly with destiny. They might as well attempt to stop Niagara as to stem the mighty current which is sweeping them away. If they but knew the things which belong to their peace, they would cease to struggle with pride, accept the humiliation, acknowledge their errors, their criminality, and adapt themselves to their changed condition.

It is a great change, and it is not yet over. The people are beginning to see that we are not a vandal horde. The Yankees had not been in the city a half-hour before they had an organized force at work with the fire engines, to put out the fire which the retreating army had kindled. They brought law and order. Not a man, woman, or child has been insulted by white or black soldiers of the Union. The retreating army broke open stores, the incoming army protects life and property. The streets are peaceful at night. There has not been a mob, not a disturbance of any kind. The ladies of Richmond have manifested no such venom as the ladies of Fredericksburg were accustomed to exhibit two years ago. Some of them may already be seen walking and riding with Union officers.

It has come to light that the question of firing the city was discussed and resolved upon in secret session in Congress, and that Ewell and Breckenridge were only acting under orders when they applied the match. This fact, this wanton, wicked act, — the disregard for life, for property, the inhumanity of the rebel authorities, civil and military, surpassing all conception, — is making a great change in public opinion. The people begin to see how they have been misled, cheated, robbed, and plundered by a set of miscreants. They contrast their past with the present. The fact that the army of the Union undertook to save the city from destruction; that they did save it; that instead of insult and hatred they are receiving nothing but kindness; that the Christian and Sanitary Commissions, and the Government, are relieving the necessities of the destitute; that there is security to life and property; that money is not worthless paper; that provisions are becoming plenty; when they contrast this with what has been, they feel that they have been woefully deluded. Kindness kills hate and malignity. I can see a change coming over the feelings of the people. Most of them will accept the conquest as an inevitable decree which cannot be reversed.

The author of the "Southern History of the War," E. A. Pollard, and his brother, H. E. Pollard, were arrested last night and committed to Castle Thunder. They were connected with the "Examiner," and have been and are now exceedingly bitter against the United States Government. Mr. E. A. Pollard, as will be remembered, was for a while prisoner in Fort Warren, was paroled and allowed to come to Richmond to be exchanged for Mr. A. D. Richardson, but before his arrival here Mr. Richardson made his escape from Salisbury. General Butler says that he was to be exchanged for Mr. Richardson and no one else. He has been at large through the week and has not bridled his tongue.

He was arrested by Colonel Coughlin, of the Tenth New Hampshire, who is provost-marshal of the District of Virginia, an able and efficient officer. When brought before Colonel Coughlin he said: "Do you take away my parole?" "Oh, no, you may keep your parole. I do not arrest you because you have been connected with the 'Examiner,' or for what you have published, but for what you have said since the occupation of the city."

When informed that he was to be sent to Castle Thunder, his countenance fell. He asked permission to take his clothes, which was granted, and at sunset Saturday night he and his brother entered the door where many better men than they have suffered long imprisonment, — eaten by vermin, suffocated by intolerable stench, and starved till they were walking skeletons. So the wheel turns, grinding the grinders.

CARLETON.

RECONSTRUCTION MOVEMENT IN RICHMOND.

RICHMOND, April 12, 1865.

AN address will be issued in a day or two to the people of Virginia by a few men who have held various official positions in the State, — members of the old Assembly, which dissolved suddenly a week ago; also by members of the new Assembly, elected on the 23d of March,

I believe, — an Assembly which never will have a speaker, which never will meet as a legislative body. Other men will append their names, — Judge Campbell, perhaps, who once had a seat on the Supreme Bench of the United States, but who became a Rebel, who was one of Jeff. Davis's peace commissioners to confer with Secretary Seward. He is not a Virginian, but hails from Alabama, I believe. The address probably will bear the name of J. R. Anderson, who owns the Tredegar Iron Works, whose initials may be found on the trunnions of two thirds of the cannon which the Confederacy ever owned. He has been a general in the Rebel service, and commanded a brigade, I think, at Antietam.

These signers of the address will call upon the members of the old Assembly to return to Richmond and resume their legislative functions. They have procured safe conducts from General Weitzel for the members, and for Governor Smith and the lieutenant-governor. The intention is to get the machinery of civil government going again — to call a convention of the people by delegates to vote the State back into the Union, or, as the words of the address will be, "the restoration of peace to Virginia and an adjustment of the questions involving life, liberty, and property that have arisen in the State as a consequence of war."

It is understood that this is a movement inaugurated by Judge Campbell. It is a movement which demands the attention of the whole country as well as of the people of Virginia. It is based upon the theory that Virginia is out of the Union, — a theory which has not been accepted by the Congress of the United States.

The action of Congress on the admission of West Virginia and the recognition of Governor Pierpont as Governor of Virginia, has settled it that Governor Smith cannot be recognized as Governor of the State. He has not sworn to support the Constitution, neither the laws of the United States. Neither has the Legislature, which has been owing fealty to the Confederacy and which has passed laws repugnant to the Constitution and laws of the Union. The Legislature may meet, but whatever action may be taken will be of no more force than that of a village debating-club. In law, unless there is a legal premise, there can be no constitutional action. In architecture, without some sort of foundation there can be no superstructure. With no legal status to begin with they cannot call the people of Virginia into legal convention.

Regeneration, and not reconstruction, is needed just now, — a change of heart and purpose on the pàrt of those who have been Rebels, rather than scheming how to recover lost political power and influence. Governor Smith made a speech on Sunday afternoon while the evacuation was going on which was very bitter against the Yankees. He fled on Sunday night. He has shown no signs of repentance. He has not manifested by word or sign, so far as is known here, that he desires to return to the Union. Neither has Senator Hunter. The true Union men, who have borne insult and outrage through the terrible years of the war, do not believe in the method of reconstruction proposed by these men. They believe in the work of regeneration before reconstruction, — of a full and hearty recognition of the United States laws and authority before a reinvestment of privilege and position in the exercise of citizenship is granted to men who have done all that they could to overthrow the Government, and who would now be fighting against us were there any hope of success.

Profane swearers and robbers are not admitted to church-membership till they manifest a disposition to turn from their evil ways; why, then, should the so-called Governor Smith, who has forsworn himself, who has shown himself to be an uncompromising, inhuman enemy, be recognized as a friend and restored to his lost position of political power, till he acknowledges the authority of the United States?

To reconstruct the State by such a method as is proposed would be like the attempt of an unlearned country carpenter to erect a stately edifice by the old-fashioned *scribe* rule, instead of by the regular rules of architecture.

The work to be done is too solemn to be trifled with. The Union men feel it. They know what it has cost to demolish the barbarism of the past. Their houses are in ruins — burned by the hands of the enemy, who were false friends. Some of them have been incarcerated for months in Castle Thunder, for no crime but that of loving the Union. They are strenuous in their opposition to this movement.

I have conversed freely with all classes of citizens, Unionists and secessionists, and it is my conviction that the time has not yet arrived for any action toward the re-establishment of civil authority.

The work of regeneration is going on, and if left to itself will work out a glorious redemption for the State. The middling class of men — those who have not been distinguished for political influence — will be heard from by and by.

The action of General Weitzel in granting passes to these Rebels to assemble is not at all relished by some of the officers here. He has shown clemency to the clergymen who don't want to read prayers for the President of the United States, and the colored soldier who has faithfully guarded the premises of General Lee has been displaced by a white soldier, not because he was derelict in duty, not because General Weitzel is not in favor of colored troops, but because Mrs. Lee's friends were sensitive upon the matter.

It is rumored that the friends of General Lee are asking for permission to make him a present of several thousand dollars in consideration of his services in the Rebellion.

Next to Judge Campbell, the men most active in bringing about the reassembling of the Legislature are General J. R. Anderson, before mentioned, and Wm. R. Crenshaw, who is one of the wealthiest men in the South. He has accumulated an immense fortune by blockade running, as Anderson has in casting cannon, shot, and shells. Vice-President Stephens occupied one of Crenshaw's houses, opposite Jeff. Davis's mansion. It is now occupied by Major Stevens, provost-marshal of the Army of the James.

Crenshaw is exceedingly anxious to secure the return of R. M. T. Hunter to Richmond.

Mention is made of these matters that a clear understanding may be had of the character of the men who are engaged in the new reconstruction plan.

The true Union men have no one to speak for them. They never have been in political life. They are business men. Having been invited to their parlors, having heard their tales of horror — of the terrible despotism which they have borne, having heard their frank avowals, their declarations of love for the old flag, I speak in their behalf. They ask for delay. They ask for the administration of military authority till the true Union sentiment of the State can have time to develop itself; then they believe that the people will forever hurl from power the men who by treason have made the State a desolation.

CARLETON.

THE

OBSEQUIES OF ABRAHAM LINCOLN.

WHILE these things were going on in Richmond, Grant and Sheridan had enveloped the army of General Lee, and forced from him a surrender. This event was quickly followed by the assassination of President Lincoln. During this period there is an hiatus in the correspondence of Mr. Page; but it is resumed with the obsequies of Abraham Lincoln.

THE DEPARTURE FROM WASHINGTON.

BALTIMORE, Friday, April 21, 1 P. M., 1865.

THIS morning, at half-past six o'clock, appropriate religious services were held at the Rotunda of the Capitol, over the remains of the late President, which had rested there since the funeral on Wednesday. These services were conducted by the Rev. Dr. Gurley, in the presence of the pall-bearers, the Congressional committees, the entire Cabinet, governors of States, and many distinguished officers of the army and navy, including General Grant and Admiral Farragut. All these followed the honored ashes to the special train at the depot. A vast acreage of people had gathered thus early in the day and looked mournfully on while the cortège passed to the slow music of a dirge between lines of soldiers standing at a present-arms, the usual position of respect.

Without confusion, almost noiselessly, while thousands stood by with uncovered heads, the bier was transferred to the funeral car, and promptly at eight o'clock (the appointed hour) the train moved slowly away, — with no discordant sound of the whistle of the locomotive, but on the slight tinkle of a small bell.

One group on the platform consisted of Secretaries Stanton, McCulloch, Usher, and Welles. Their bowed heads attested their sense of their loss as statesmen and their personal grief. The train consists of nine cars all deeply, yet tastefully draped. The engine alone shows any other color than black, it having white interwreathed with sable.

All the arrangements appear to have been made with great care and forethought, and the special trains will without doubt conform exactly to the published time-table.

The following is the official list of those invited to accompany the remains. A few of those are not yet on board, but will join at Baltimore and Philadelphia.

First. The relatives and family friends, viz.: Judge David Davis, United States Supreme Court; Hon. C. M. Smith, Hon. N. M. Edwards, both brothers-in-law of Mr. Lincoln, having married sisters of Mr. Lincoln; Gen. J. B. S. Todd, a cousin of Mr. Lincoln; Charles A. Smith, and Ward H. Lamon, Marshal of the District of Columbia.

Second. The Guard of Honor, viz.: Brig.-Gen. E. D. Townsend, Brig.-Gen. Charles Thomas, Brig.-Gen. A. B. Eaton, Brevet Major-Gen. J. G. Barnard, Brig.-Gen. G. G. Ramsay, Brig.-Gen. A. P. Howe, Brig.-Gen. T. C. McCallum, Major-Gen. David Hunter, Brig.-Gen. J. C. Caldwell, Rear Admiral C. H. Davis, Capt. Wm. R. Taylor, U. S. N., Major T. Y. Field, U. S. M. C.

Third. The Quartermaster and Commissary of Subsistence for the escort: Capt. Charles Penrose, ordered to this duty, assisted by three clerks, and instructed to provide for the comfort of the whole party, civil and military.

Fourth. Dr. Charles B. Brown, embalmer; F. T. Sands, undertaker.

Fifth. The Congressional Committee, viz.: Maine, Mr. Pike; New Hampshire, Mr. Rollins; Vermont, Mr. Baxter; Massachusetts, Mr. Hooper; Connecticut, Mr. Dixon; Rhode Island, Mr. Anthony; New York, Mr. Harris; New Jersey, Mr. Newell; Pennsylvania, Mr. Cowan; Maryland, Mr. Phelps; Ohio, Mr. Schenck; Kentucky, Mr. Smith; Indiana, Mr. Julian; Minnesota, Mr. Ramsay; Michigan, Thomas W. Ferry; Illinois, Messrs.

Yates, Washburn, Farnsworth, and Arnold; Iowa, Mr. Harlan; California, Mr. Shannon; Oregon, Mr. Williams; Kansas, Mr. Clark; West Virginia, Mr. Whaley; Nevada, Mr. Nye; Nebraska, Mr. Hitchcock; Colorado, Mr. Bradford; Idaho, Mr. Wallace.

George T. Brown, Sergeant at Arms of the Senate, N. G. Ordway, Sergeant at Arms of the House.

Sixth. Special delegation, appointed from Illinois: Gov. R. G. Oglesby, and staff; Gen. Isham N. Haynie, Adjutant-General of State of Illinois; Col. James H. Bowen, A. D. C; Col. N. H. Hanna, A. D. C.; Col. D. B. James, A. D. C.; Major S. Wait, A. D. C.; Col. E. L. Phillips, A. D. C. and U. S. Marshal, Southern Dist., Ill.; the Hons. Jesse K. Dubois, and J. T. Stuart; Col. John Williams; the Hons. S. H. Melvin, and S. M. Collum; Gen. John A. McClernand; the Hons. Lyman Trumbull, J. S. Vreedenburg, and T. J. Dennis; Lieut-Gov. Wm. Bross; the Hons. F. C. Sherman (Mayor of Chicago), T. A. Hoyne, John Wentworth, and S. S. Hayes; Col. R. M. Hough; the Hons. S. W. Fuller, J. B. Turner, Ives Lawson, C. L. Woodman, George W. Gage, G. H. Roberts, J. Comisky and L. Talcott.

Eighth. The Press. Representing the Associated Press, L. A. Gobright, C. R. Morgan; representing "The New York Tribune," Charles A. Page; representing "The New York Times," L. L. Crounse; representing "The Philadelphia Inquirer," H. H. Painter; representing "The Chicago Tribune" and "The Cincinnati Gazette," Dr. Adonis; representing "The Boston Advertiser," G. B. Woods.

Ninth. The Body Guard, consisting of four commissioned officers and twenty-five sergeants, viz.: Capt. James M. McCainly, Ninth V. R. C.; First Lieut. J. R. Durkee, Seventh V. R. C.; Second Lieut. E. Murphy, Tenth V. R. C.; Second Lieut. E. Hoppey, Twelfth V. R. C: Serg'ts Chester Swinsted, John R. Edwards, Samuel Carpenter, A. C. Cromwell, J. F. Nelson, L. E. Babcock, P. Callagan, A. J. Marshall, W. T. Daly, James Collier, W. H. Durgin, F. T. Smith, George E. Goodrich, A. E. Car, Frank Corey, W. H. Noble, John Karr, John P. Smith, John Hanna, F. D. Forkhead, J. M. Sedgwick, L. W. Lewis, John P. Barry, William H. Wiseman, J. M. Bordan.

Only three of those who accompanied Mr. Lincoln from Springfield to Washington in 1861, now attend his body to his early home — to become his long home. These are Judge Davis, General Hunter, and Marshal Lamon, all personal friends. Mr. Painter of the "Inquirer" represented his paper at that time. Arriving at Baltimore at ten A. M. the procession was already formed, with space left for the hearse and carriages for those on the train, and with little delay moved on.

It is impossible to convey an adequate conception of the number of people who viewed this procession. The whole population of the city must have crowded to the streets along which the cortège was to move. This procession was fully two miles in length, and moved through at least four miles of streets. All this distance the sidewalks were densely packed, the windows crowded. Every house was draped and every countenance sorrowful, many tearful. The colored population — of which there were 30,000 in the city, and the "plain people" seemed most affected — as if it were the crucifixion of another Saviour.

And this in Baltimore, where four years ago they would have stoned him unto death!

I am compelled to close abruptly just as the procession stops at the Baltimore Exchange.

BALTIMORE AND HARRISBURG.

HARRISBURG, PENNSYLVANIA, 11 P. M., April 21, 1865.

PERHAPS there was not another city outside of his own Illinois where Abraham Lincoln was so reverently loved as in Baltimore. Nor is it inexplicable that such should be the case, when it is remembered that Baltimore is now as thoroughly anti-slavery, as any township in New England. New converts are proverbially zealous, and this is a late convert, exorcised of the pro-slavery devil, and quickened into a new life by the might of the anti-slavery gospel. Now, to all men in the South, this dead man stood as the prophet and apostle of this gospel, and was loved and reverenced accordingly. On him rested the benisons of their gratitude, and to him clung all their new-born hopes. And thus, as the embodiment of an idea, as well as the head and front of the great fact of their emancipation, did he come to be Benefactor, Friend, Brother.

This was truest of the plain people and of those that were in bondage. These things, then, account for the mighty thronging to see but the hearse that bore his ashes; account for the tears and the sobs that could not be stayed, and were not ashamed, there were so many weeping together. Let not the reader imagine this an overdrawn picture; it is literally truthful, could not be over-stretched in words. White and black side by side in the rain and the mud, with eyes strained upon that coffin, with eyes running over, and with clasped hands, and with faces all drawn and distorted, or set in marble fixedness. White and black leaned forth from the same windows; the well dressed and the shabby in the same doorway, and there seemed to be no consciousness of any difference of color or disparity in station.

The procession was two miles long, was three hours moving four miles, and a look at the spectators revealed always the same scene. I thought as we passed along that this was one of the good fruits of the National Calamity, this welding in the white heat of a common sympathy and common sorrow of all men into a common brotherhood.

As we would sometimes halt a moment, I could catch the low words of conversation in the throng. There was execration of the murderer. There was eulogy of him that was dead. There were vows that traitors should be banished from the land. Vows that Rebels should never again have place and power. There were demands for justice. There were ejaculations inarticulate in words, but indicative of some great dumb thought too big for utterance, so dumb that maybe it was but an emotion, a feeling, yet to be crystallized into thought and volition. But there were no cries for blood, none of the cries of a mob, nothing unbeseemly, nothing breathing of violence; but all was decorous and peaceful.

One man recalled to another the day four years ago when the Massachusetts soldiers were set upon in those same streets, giving to the country the first martyrs of the Rebellion, as the President was the last. Another spoke of General Butler's occupation of the city, and said but for him "The Rebellion would have succeeded before we got fairly to work." Another said that there had yet been but one man hung for treason, and that was three years ago in New Orleans,— he hoped there would now be some hung for murder.

The City Government entertained the escort informally with dinner at the Eutaw House, — served in twenty-five minutes, that we might leave at the hour set in the time-table, — the carriages whirled us back to where we had left the remains, and the train started for Harrisburg.

Nearly all the farm-houses on the way displayed flags bordered with black, and always the people came down to the road, and stood uncovered as we passed.

At the Pennsylvania State Line Governor Curtin and General Cadwallader and their staffs joined the special train.

At York, where we halted a few minutes, some young ladies were on the platform with a large vase of flowers, which they asked to be permitted to place on the coffin. The vase was perhaps four feet long and two feet wide, and by the arrangement of different-colored flowers, represented the flag.

White and blue violets and red geraniums formed the stripes, blue violets the corner ground, which was starred with white violets, and the whole was entwined by a wreath of orange-blossoms, roses, and various exotics. No more touching thought or beautiful expression of tender sentiment could be imagined. And these young ladies — God bless them — bore the flowers into the hearse-car, and laid them on the coffin, weeping the while as though their hearts would break. One of them embracing the coffin passionately, kissed it, and then they went bowed and sobbing away. The incident affected some of us to tears, and will soon be forgotten by none of us.

Here at York, as elsewhere, there were not wanting the symbols of mourning on the houses, and the evidences of it on the faces of the people.

The train reached Harrisburg at nine o'clock, — arrived in a pouring thunder-storm. It will leave here for Philadelphia at eleven A. M. to-morrow.

IN PHILADELPHIA.

PHILADELPHIA, Sunday, 5 P. M.
April 23, 1865.

ALL that was earthly, except indeed his life and history, and deeds and example, now familiar as household words in all the homes in this great land — all else that was earthly of the President and Honest Man in whom there was no guile, rests to-day in old Independence Hall. Here four years ago, standing on the spot where now rests his cold clay, and speaking of the principle of equal liberty which the deliberations of the Continental Congress, in this same hall, had helped to establish, he said: "I was about to say I would rather be assassinated than surrender it."

To-day thousands look the last time upon his good face, perhaps recall those significant words of self-consecration and prophecy, and think, —

"Here is himself, marr'd, as you see, with traitors, —"

and then go their way sadder and better men. They loved him — is it irreverent to say they loved him because he first loved them? And now

"They would go and kiss his wounds,
And dip their napkins in his sacred blood,
Yea, beg a hair of him for memory,
And, dying, mention it within their wills,
Bequeathing it as a rich legacy
Unto their issue."

It was the love of David and Jonathan, and now is as the sorrow of David over Jonathan slain. They would break out —

"Woe to the hands that shed this costly blood. Over thy wounds do I prophesy;" but they remember how he that is dead had no revenge in his heart, and feel that his shade would look down from the sky, grieved and in anguish, if bare and lawful justice were transcended, or aught done in simple revenge. Only justice, then, is demanded, and it is the traitors' fault if —

"this even-handed justice
Commends the ingredients of their poisoned chalice
To their own lips."

And then the masses cram back the natural cry for vengeance with the thought that the assassination does n't —

"trammel up the consequences and catch
With its surcease success."

Let me recur to Independence Hall. At the head of the coffin, clothed in black drapery, relieved by a profusion of flowers in bouquets, wreaths, crosses, and anchors, is the great bell that ninety years ago burst with the mighty strokes that proclaimed the passage of the Declaration of Independence. It still bears in cut bronze the famous inscription, —

"Proclaim Liberty throughout all the land, unto all the inhabitants thereof. — LEV. xxv. 10."

Then there is the chair in which Hancock sat when presiding over the Continental Congress; the chair he rose from when he stepped to the clerk's desk on the fourth day of July, 1776, to sign his name in bold characters to the Declaration. Around the room are statues and pictures of Washington and others of the fathers. The whole hall is one mass of flags, drapery, and flowers, — flags for patriotism, drapery for mourning, flowers for love, for hope, for all tender and beautiful sentiment, ay, and for the resurrection.

The procession at Harrisburg yesterday morning was large and orderly, and passed through streets thronged with thousands, some of whom had come from hundreds of miles away. There had been special trains from all quarters the day before. The remains had rested in the State House during the night and were exposed to view to a late hour. Governor Curtin and staff, General Cameron, and other distinguished gentlemen came on the funeral train to this city. It halted at Lancaster for Thaddeus Stevens, but he was too unwell to travel. Lancaster is the home of James Buchanan, and his house was visible as we approached the city. No flag, no emblem of mourning, indicating patriotism and sorrow, could be detected on that house, nor, perhaps, was any expected. A thousand times better be Abraham Lincoln, assassinated, than this craven and depraved old man, who outlived his Presidency, and now outlives the respect of all good men. This thought occurred to all, and a shudder ran through our frames as we thought that this hoary-headed man, Booth's moral accomplice, once sat in the highest place of the Republic.

The train reached Philadelphia at half-past four P. M., two hours ahead of the usual schedule time, having started from Harrisburg an hour in advance, and gained another hour on the way. This was in order to secure daylight for the procession here, but by some inefficiency of those in charge here, the gain was of no value, since the procession did not move until more than two hours after our arrival. It was eight o'clock when the hearse reached Independence Hall. Three hundred thousand people packed the streets, and looked down from windows and verandas, and another hundred thousand were in the procession. I give the estimate of the city authorities, and do not think it exaggerated, for there must have been 700,000 in the city yesterday, two thirds of whom must have been present. Broad Street is nearly twice as wide as your Broadway, yet for a mile and a half it was densely peopled from the tops of the houses down to the sidewalks, and then out to the very wheels of the carriages. Walnut, Arch, and Chestnut Streets are as wide as Broadway, but a mile of each was crowded in the same way. Then the throng surged down from each street, crossed from as far as the eye could reach.

I need not try to describe the elaborate, tasteful, costly and universal symbols of mourning on all the houses, for you have the same in New York; nor the inscriptions and bannered mottoes, for you have them too. Not less than twenty times repeated was the divine bard's beautiful characterization of Duncan, so familiar to all of us, and so applicable now: —

> "Besides, this Duncan
> Hath borne his faculties so meek, hath been
> So clear in his great office, that his virtues
> Will plead like angels, trumpet-tongued, against
> The deep damnation of his taking off;
> And pity, like a naked new-born babe,
> Striding the blast, or heaven's cherubim, horsed
> Upon the sightless couriers of the air,
> Shall blow the horrid deed in every eye,
> That tears shall drown the wind."

One wondered where all the flags came from, and all the black cloth, and more, where all the people came from. The countless and various festoons and rosettes about the windows, and the pendent flags, drooping as though with the unwonted weight of the black that bordered their folds. One knew these were the handiwork of the aged matrons, the lovely women, and the beautiful girls who leaned from the windows, as passed mournfully by "the ruins of the noblest man" of our times, — the work of gentle hands, maybe when the eyes were dim with tears, the expression of a grief that was half for other friends fallen in this war, hence all the more a personal woe. God cherish the hearts who thus sought expression for their own sorrows, and so the more tenderly partake of the nation's and make it their own. The pent-up heroism which the trammels of sex kept from the field has melted into gratitude toward those who have gone there, and has embalmed those who fell there.

Not when the Prince of Wales journeying through the country excited the curiosity of tumultuous tens of thousands; not when the Japanese, grotesque and strange, came from afar; not when Henry Clay, he of the silvery tongue, the clear brain, and the true heart, our Lincoln's political father, was borne through the length of the land and through the great cities with funereal pageant, — not on any of these occasions was this, the second city of the continent, ever moved and stirred, and drawn to a common thought and a common action as she is now. That thought is one of mourning, that action, the spontaneous expression of it.

Probably 50,000 will look at the corpse to-day and to-night. As I write, the line is formed back ten squares four deep. This forming in column is not done by soldiers or police, but by the common impulse of order and fairness which is distinctive of our people.

The face of the dead President bears a very natural expression, one familiar to all who saw him often. It is just the hint of a smile, and the look of a benediction. I do not know to what it is attributable, but certainly the face is far more natural, more *his*, than when seen four days ago at Washington.

The special train will certainly reach New York at the hour designated in the published schedule, viz.: ten A. M., Monday.

At the breakfast table this morning the party composing the escort first read the history of Sherman's parley with Johnston. There was the utmost indignation at the terms he would have made, — terms that provided for the surrender of Sherman, not of Johnston. There were present half a dozen governors of States, and five times as many Members of Congress, and all joined in denunciation of Sherman's course, and in approval of the prompt veto put upon it by the new President. "I would n't have believed it of any general in the army," said one. Said another: "He could n't have heard of the murder of the President." "The country won't listen to anything of that sort," said a governor who still carries in his body the bullet that felled him at the head of his division on the field of Shiloh; he was then a major-general. The feeling and the demand of the country are summed up in the two words which first made Grant famous, "Unconditional Surrender."

FROM NEW YORK TO ALBANY.

ALBANY, April 26, 1865, 10 A. M.

As was to be expected the pageant in New York yesterday, as a pageant, was far grander than anything we had before witnessed.

The scenes on Broadway and Fifth Avenue had some features that have not attended the pageants in other cities, and will not in those we are yet to visit. The mourners were on the streets in greater multitudes than could be gathered elsewhere. The architectural magnificence of those streets is not equalled elsewhere on the continent. Perhaps there never has been a procession in the country numbering so many thousands. All told, it was nothing less than sublime, as it surely is an era and historical, — historical as the day the ashes of Napoleon were received from exile to rest forever beneath Vendôme's proud column in the capital of his own France.

But I question whether the wayside villages through which we pass with but a bare slowing of the train, according to their populations, do not exhibit more individual heartfelt and tearful-eyed sorrow than even great New York. It seemed to me in New York that the people leaning from the marble fronts were quite as conscious that they were seen as that they were seeing, that the roofs which had become human bouquets with heads for flowers, were laden with dry-eyed curiosity, and that only a small proportion was wet-eyed mourning. Yet it may be that the emotional contagion — the very carnival of tears, which prevailed in Baltimore and in some of the villages on the way — had unfitted me for appreciating the more ordinary expressions of feeling; it may be that being myself curious only to see, I imagined others were likewise, and do injustice to the order and decorous deportment which marked the mighty million of spectators in your city.

Again I may have fallen into these comparisons from surprise at the unaffected mourning all the way to Albany. Where there was not a habitation in sight hundreds would be gathered on the green banks by the way, and hushed and uncovered as the National funeral car passed by. Or a solitary family had come down to the roadside, had planted there a draped flag, and as we passed the little ones would be held high in the parent arms, perhaps themselves waving tiny flags. Three and four score years hence, when these infants bend with the weight of years, they will still remember Lincoln's funeral, as now here and there an octogenarian will tell you that when a child he saw Washington.

At one place a hundred school-girls, dressed all in white, had come down to the roadside. At another the track was arched high over the cars with tablet flags and drapery, and the inscription " The Nation mourns a Nation's loss." At a third a young lady representing the Goddess of Liberty, or, perhaps the Genius of America, knelt upon a dais, in sorrowing attitude, one hand grasping the flag whose folds, clad in transparent black, fell by her side, while the other rested upon and held fast to a floral anchor. Before her, on the same dais, was a small monument, deeply and darkly clad, inscribed simply "Abraham Lincoln." We saw the figure with but a glance, but that photographed it in our memories. At West Point the train halted, and we found the cadets — boys who may be famous fifty years in the future — drawn up in line, while half-minute guns were fired and bands played mournfully.

After dark, torches at each station lighted up the scene for the throngs who stood by, and bonfires blazed from jutting rocks, around which were grouped weird figures peering down upon us as we whirled through the night.

At Poughkeepsie the train halted twenty minutes for supper, and here we were met by a deputation from the City Government of Albany, who gave each one on board a card like the following: "City of Albany. President Lincoln's Funeral Cortège. Guest's Ticket for Delavan House."

Arriving here at eleven P. M., the hearse was received by the military and the firemen with torches and escorted to the State House, where the body now lies in state.

Governor Fenton will be unable to accompany the funeral train to Buffalo, as has been his intention. The probable adjournment within a few days of the Legislature renders his presence here indispensable.

To UTICA.

UTICA, April 26, 9 P. M.

THE funeral train left Albany at four P. M. The lying in state and the procession there had been marked by all the characteristics which had signalized the same in other cities. The Knickerbockers of Albany as well as the cosmopolites of New York, the Quakers of Philadelphia, the Teutons of Harrisburg, and the emotional children of the South at Baltimore, had manifested in all appropriate forms their common sense of the great bereavement.

Special trains had brought thousands from towns not on the route to swell the population of the city. The remains were looked upon by thousands, and thousands more had not the opportunity. The houses were decorated with fitting emblems and fitting mottoes. The procession was beautifully ordered and very impressive. Governor Fenton and staff were on foot immediately after the escort which left Washington, the latter in open carriages.

At Schenectady, as always before, there was a still multitude with uncovered heads. Carriages that had evidently been driven miles were whirled by each few minutes, industry had ceased its whir in shop and mills, business stood still in offices and stores. The plow was idle in the furrow and the plowman with wife and children had gone to the nearest point on the railroad. A funeral in each house of Central New York would scarcely have added more solemnity to the day.

At Canajoharie, the Palatine Bridge was clad in flags and mourning, and there was firing of guns, tolling of bells, music of bands, and an assembled multitude.

Two women were seen weeping on each other's shoulders, and then one of them fainted and sank to the ground. Both ladies were in deep mourning. When passenger trains were met they were found to be stopped, the passengers out, ranged reverently in line.

A refreshment car accompanied the train, and supper was had at St. Johnsville. The first young ladies of the town, dressed alike in black skirts and white bodices with heavy black rosettes upon the left shoulder, waited upon the guests and were afterward admitted to the hearse car and a view of the coffin. It was a compliment to the guests suggested by respect to the dead.

General Dix, with Colonel M. L. McMahon and others of his staff, will go as far as Buffalo. Generals Batcheller, Harvey, Merritt, and Marvin of Governor Fenton's staff also go to Buffalo. At that place Governor Brough and staff of Ohio will meet the train and attend it to Indianapolis.

The ladies of Little Falls placed fresh flowers upon the coffin. At Herkimer, blazing torches showed the train in a bright light to an immense company, who spoke not a word, but let him pass on in his glory. Multiplied thousands, made weird by torches, wait the train at Utica, with bells tolling and guns firing.

AT BUFFALO.

BUFFALO, N. Y., Thursday, April 27, 1865.

FROM the eastern to the western gate of the great State of New York, whether by day or by night, the people of all the cities and villages, and many from long distances in the adjacent country, have come to the roadside and stood uncovered and silent while passed by the great funeral.

At each station on the way they have sought by every appropriate means to express mourning and patriotism. The thousands of flags bordered with unwonted black, the requiems, and the dirges from bands and hundred-voiced choirs, that made the very air vibrate tributary to human sorrow, the booming of cannon, and the toll, toll, toll, of bells, — these and a great silent multitude met us at every station. After it was dark hundreds of torches flared forth a strange, unnatural day, which gave the scenes a "dim religious light" and solemnity scarcely to be obtained in the rays of the sun. This was the case at Syracuse, where the large depot, hung with a hundred craped flags, lighted by lanterns and torches, and crammed with mourners, where bonfires burned on the streets and improvised lights illuminated the houses, and showed decorations expressive of mourning and of respect and honor for the departed, and cannon and music lent their aid.

So also at Rochester, although the train arrived at half-past three in the morning. Even at that hour 30,000 or 40,000 people had gathered.

A deputation from Buffalo, one of whom was ex-President Fillmore, met the train at Batavia, and tendered to the escort the hospitality of the city. Here there was no procession proper, but a simple escort of the military and the representatives of the city conducted the remains to the hall of the Young Men's Association, where they now lie in state, beneath a black canopy broad and high and most impressive in beauty and solemn effect. As the coffin was borne in, a large choir in a gallery above this canopy, and dimly visible through its black folds of crape, sang a touching requiem. I have seen nothing more fitting at any place on the way.

Of the Congressional delegation only the following named gentlemen are now present with the cortège, namely: Senators Nye, of Nevada, Williams of Oregon, Representatives Washburne, Arnold, and S. M. Cullom of Illinois, Schenck of Ohio, Bailey of Pennsylvania, Newell of New Jersey, Hooper of Massachusetts, Van Horne of New York, Whaley of West Virginia, Phelps of Maryland, Ferry of Michigan, Shannon of California.

The only governors of States now present are Oglesby of Illinois and Stone of Iowa, with their staffs. The Illinois delegation and the military escort are the same that left Washington a week ago.

The news of the killing of Booth and the capture of his accomplice reached here this morning and was received with satisfaction, though all regretted that he could not have been taken alive. This for two reasons: one, that he deserved a worse fate than to die suddenly without torture of soul; second, that he could probably have made valuable revelations in relation to the masters, inciters, and approvers of the plot,—which may not now be readily obtained.

It is remarkable, as it is significant and hopeful, that Sherman's late unaccountable and bad use of power should be so universally and unqualifiedly condemned. I find no one that approves it even by insinuation or implication, while many unsparingly denounce the terms of Lee's surrender. They say that the Rebel leader and all officers of his army of the rank of colonel and over should have been held as prisoners of war; that nothing short of this conforms to the spirit of the legislation by Congress and the proclamations of the late President, which discriminated between the leaders and the rank and file.

Butler's proposition that one of the lessons to be learned from the late murder is that the people of the South are not prepared in the disposition of their hearts for citizenship, was referred to to-day by the chairman of a leading committee in Congress, as altogether true. The President was arranging to guarantee the right of suffrage and a State government to Virginia, when his efforts were answered by the bullet of the assassin sped to his brain under the cry of the motto of that State. "I only want to have a dozen or so hung, but I want to see that many thousands are forever prevented from voting, and excluded from all other privileges of citizenship," said a Border-State Congressman this morning. He but echoed the sentiment of the representative men who compose the civil escort to the prairies of Illinois of the remains of Abraham Lincoln.

FROM BUFFALO WESTWARD.

CLEVELAND, OHIO, April 28, 3 P. M.

BUFFALO was the first city where all who desired to were able to see the face of the martyr. At Philadelphia 20,000 were cut off at two o'clock in the morning from the privilege, for the sake of which they stood patiently in the streets all night; and there was the same disappointment to thousands in Baltimore, New York, and Albany. Whether the arrangements were more perfect in Buffalo, or whether there were fewer people in the city does not appear, but certainly there was no lack of mournful interest, or in some cases morbid curiosity.

Of course business was totally suspended, and insignia of mourning showed from every house. At Fort Erie on the Canada side opposite, from cannon and bells beneath British flags at half-mast, came a response to the guns that fired and the bells that tolled beneath our flag on our side of the river. F. N. Blake, the American consul there, had deeply draped his residence and the consular office, and was waited upon during the day by the leading citizens in token of their sympathy in the affliction of their neighbors.

The city had made provision for entertaining the entire escort; but many were taken to the houses of prominent citizens. Judge Spalding entertained a number of his old associates in Congress, and ex-President Fillmore (who disclaims the charge that he did not spontaneously sympathize with the feeling of the country) likewise tendered his hospitalities.

The journey from Buffalo to Cleveland was like that from Albany to Buffalo. Like the latter, it was made by night, and at each station a multitude awaited the train with flaring torches, the sounds of guns and of bells, and at several, floral offerings were laid by tearful young ladies upon the coffin, which they would fall upon and kiss. Little Willie Lincoln received the same tributes upon his smaller coffin as though they would join in the sorrow felt by the father when the little one died.

The Hon. John Sherman, Governor Brough, ex-Governor Tod, Col. Anson Stager, and General Hooker, with Colonel Lathrop, Colonel Swords, Colonel Simpson, Major McFarley, Major Bannister, and Captain Tayler of his staff, joined the train at Dunkirk. General Hooker will accompany the special trains all the way to Springfield, the whole route being within his department.

The reception ceremonies were very elaborate and well conducted. The procession, which comprised all the organizations civic and military in the city with delegations from other points, stretched in unrivalled beauty and imposing display through say five miles of the beautiful streets of perhaps the most beautiful city in the country. A very appropriate resting-place for the remains, constructed to afford ready ingress and egress and very elaborately decorated, had been built for the occasion in the park close by the statue of Perry, the hero of the naval victory on the lakes.

Despite the falling rain, the entire population were spectators of the cortège, or participated in it, and now in long files move slowly by the catafalque and look upon the good face of the good man. Religious services were first held, conducted by Bishop McIlvaine, and then a hundred or more soldiers from the hospitals marched by the coffin on crutches, followed by all the other soldiers from the hospitals.

In no city where we stopped, nor in any village where we but slackened speed, have been wanting, in all possible symbols of grief and in the tears of the many, the evidences of how deeply the nation takes to heart this murder of our President. To those who have been with the funeral train all the way from Washington, the cumulated effect of such feeling and such demonstration of it is becoming even painful in its weight and strain. The contagion from the multitude keeps all at the same tension of feeling with which they started, or at a greater. Some have sought relief by stopping a day on the way, and others by going ahead for rest at points further west.

Charles L. Wilson, Esq., is here in behalf of Chicago to attend to the wishes of the escort on some points connected with the stay in that city. Those acquainted with the West, those who know how Illinois held in her heart her great son, say that only at Chicago and thence to Springfield will this memorable funeral culminate in demonstrations by the people.

At Albany was this motto, and at least one old Illinois friend of Lincoln's was affected by it to tears:—

"Four years ago, O Illinois! we took from thee and from among thy people an untried man; we return him to thee a Mighty Conqueror! Not thine any more, but the Nation's. Not ours, but the World's. Give him resting-place, O ye prairies. Make room for the ashes of the noblest man of all time."

AT CLEVELAND AND COLUMBUS.

COLUMBUS, OHIO, April 29, 1865.

NOT less than 100,000 people passed through the very beautiful and fitting pavilion provided at Cleveland for the reception of the sacred dust we are bearing westward. Many thought that in no other place had the arrangements been so thoughtfully made, and were so peculiarly appropriate. The population of the city, swelled for the day by perhaps 40,000 from a distance, vied with each other in all sorts of testimonials suitable to the occasion. Fifty private carriages were tendered by their owners for the use of the escort. Two hundred leading citizens, organized into ten reliefs of two hours each, watched by the corpse.

The colored population, including two lodges of "Free and Accepted Masons," and other associations, were in the body of the procession, and passed in their turn through the pavilion. In the evening, Governor Brough, whose residence is in Cleveland, received at his house the Congressional Committee, the Delegation from Illinois, the Military Guard of Honor, and others who accompany the funeral. Altogether, Cleveland, for her beautiful streets, her hospitable citizens, and the funeral honors she paid to Lincoln, has left an enviable impression upon the whole party.

To-day Columbus, the capital of Ohio, has fallen in the mighty funeral procession that, moving the length of the land, from the ocean to the great river, uncovers in mourning the heads of the people of a whole nation. As at Cleveland and elsewhere the population for a hundred miles around has come up in homage and grief for the dead. I see few distinctive features in the tribute of to-day. It is like that in the other city yesterday, and that was like the one in that other city the day before, and the day before that it was still the same. So last night there were the same demonstrations that marked the two previous nights.

By day a procession, a lying in state, with mourning on houses and on countless faces, with the accompaniments of a stately hearse, dirges, minute guns, and tolling of bells. By night a journey night-long, torch-light and a multitude at each station, at many places young ladies with flowers for the coffin, or arrayed and posed to represent sister States mourning for their chief, or a single one in drooping attitude and surrounded by appropriate emblems stands for the Genius of Liberty in sorrow for a martyr to her cause. These are the incidents that attend the way as we go westward.

There is now with us but one representative of all New England, viz., Mr. Hooper, M. C., of Boston. From Washington there is Mayor Wallach, and the Rev. Dr. Gurley; from New Jersey, ex-Governor Newell; from Pennsylvania, Mr. Bailey, M. C.; from Baltimore, Colonel Phelps, M. C.; and there is not one from New York, — from the entire East only those named. Senator Sherman joined the train at Cleveland. This gentleman pointedly condemns the late course of his brother, Major-General Sherman.

We shall be at Indianapolis to-morrow, and at Chicago the two succeeding days. The preparations making for the reception at the latter place are said to be unprecedented. The whole Northwest will pour in there to meet the funeral. They *knew* him.

AT INDIANAPOLIS.

INDIANAPOLIS, INDIANA, April 30, 1865.

THE committee on the part of Congress and the other delegations who attend the remains of the President on their last journey are in more than one sense representative men. They are men who have played prominent parts, and whose careers are not yet exhausted.

Let us look at them. We will walk through the train for that purpose.

This square-set, sturdy, positive-looking man, whose mastiff head is set on a short neck, pushed a little in front of his body, with short-clipped, reddish moustache and hair of the same hue but a little lighter, this man in whom dwells power and positive convictions is Robert C. Schenck, M. C., from Ohio, late Major-General Schenck. He is certainly not a handsome man, but you scan his face with growing respect, which is increased when he, in greeting you, gives you his left hand and you learn that he partially lost the use of his right arm on the battle-field. Able and brave to a fault in the field, in debate strong, terse and sometimes withering, where he sometimes needlessly makes enemies, in private life he is the unstained gentleman; in society, courteous and even elegant.

Near Schenck is E. B. Washburne, M. C., from Illinois, by virtue of longest continuous services the father of the House. The two men have many characteristics in common. The latter is also strong, defiant, opinionated, and denunciatory in debate. Besides, he is the most watchful parliamentarian in the House, and one of the keenest. When Grant was on the point of being relieved from command after Shiloh, Washburne, who is Grant's townsman, by a powerful speech in Congress and by his personal influence with the President procured his retention. A man of stalwart frame, will and enthusiasm, he flings his whole weight into every issue he takes up. I have seen him rise on the floor of Congress like a lion roused, toss back his head like a Bull of Bashan, and beginning with a shout of "Mr. Speaker!" that instantly centred all eyes upon him, bear on and over obstacles that would have dismayed and defeated a less bold man. He is charged with obstinacy and rudeness, and perhaps not altogether without reason. Yet he could illy be spared from Congress. His constituents, at least, seem to think so, since they have returned him seven times in succession, and no man is personally more popular at home than Elihu B. Washburne.

When you are introduced to Mr. Hooper, the member from one of the Boston districts, you see a personification of the "solid men of Boston." A man between middle-aged and elderly, short, heavy, dignified and quiet in manners, close-shaven save a tuft of gray beneath his chin, a kindly, good face and eye that light up with a womanly smile, he has the presence of the cultivated gentleman, and he is the successful financier and able member of the Ways and Means Committee. He is the only member from New England who has continued thus far with the funeral.

Passing into the next car you probably ask who is the tall, massive, handsome man about whom are gathered a dozen friends. Well, that is Governor Oglesby of Illinois, Major-General Oglesby of the army, at home Dick Oglesby, and I have heard him called "glorious old Dick." After the canvass last fall which elected him governor, the opposition charged that "Dick Oglesby's face made him 5,000 votes;" and I think it did, for God never gave a man a more prepossessing face. Entering the war as colonel of a regiment, Donaldson gave him the star of a general, and Shiloh the two stars of a major-general. In the latter battle he was mortally wounded, according to one report, and his body was on the way North, according to another. Obituaries appeared in the papers, and his funeral sermon was preached. But he got well, — to be incapacitated, however, for active service, and to carry while he lives a bullet in his body. His antecedents are those of a man rising by native power from a small farm successively to various official positions, to the command of divisions in the field, and finally to the governorship of his State. He was a lifelong friend and political associate of President Lincoln, whose love and confidence he had in return.

The large, tall, white-haired, yet hale man whom the Governor addresses as "Uncle Jesse," is the Hon. Jesse K. Dubois of Springfield, Illinois, another of President Lincoln's life-time friends. Many years in political life, several times State auditor, and personally known throughout his State, no man has a better name for efficiency and integrity. His hearty Western manner contributes to his success. His friends named him to the President for Secretary of the Interior. The President said to him, "Uncle Jesse, there is no reason why I don't want to appoint you, but there is one why I can't, — you are from the town I live in myself." Whereupon "Uncle Jesse" replied: "Well, Abe, it's all right. If I were President, I don't think I'd give it to *you*, or to any other man from Illinois."

I see you have your eyes upon the slender, dark-complexioned, black-haired, wiry young man, who is just beyond the Governor, smoking a cigar and reading the latest "Tribune." That is the Hon. Shelby M. Cullom, who was last fall elected to Congress from the Springfield, Illinois, district. He is one of the Congressional Committee, and also one of the delegation from Illinois. He is a Springfield lawyer, a native of Illinois, has twice been Speaker of the House of Representatives of the Illinois Legislature, and now goes to Congress, at the age of thirty-four, to represent the district once represented by President Lincoln. It is a notable fact that a remarkable number of men who have since gained national reputations have at one time and another gone to Congress from that Springfield district. First there was Col. John J. Hardin, a man of the order of Henry Clay, a man who at that time disputed with Lincoln the leadership of the Whig party in the State. He fell at Buena Vista leading an Illinois regiment. There were two other Illinois colonels in the Mexican War who died not unknown. One was the late Governor Bissell of Illinois, the other E. D. Baker, who, eloquent senator and chivalric soldier, fell at Ball's Bluff. Again, Douglas first went into Congress from that district. Lincoln's only Congressional term was from that district. Richard Yates, late governor, now senator, Colonel Harris, whom the Lecompton swindle drove from the Democratic party, and Major-General McClernand, were also returned to Congress from that Springfield district. Shelby M. Cullom is a worthy successor to these remarkable men.

There is the Hon. O. M. Hatch, the last eight years Secretary of State of Illinois. He is tall, spare, genial, and approachable, and of the temperament and heart that made him during twenty-five years the bosom friend of Lincoln, who tempted him with the offer of any position at Washington if he would but go there to be near him.

Then of the Illinoisans in this group there are, J. N. Haynie adjutant-general of the State, late brig.-general in the field; the Hon. Ninian W. Edwards, a brother-in-law of the President whose personal appearance is remarkably like Lincoln — men thought them brothers by blood; C. W. Smith, Esq., another brother-in-law of the President; and there are several others who knew him for whom a nation mourns, as a man knows his village neighbors.

You ask which is Governor Stone of Iowa. He is the man yonder, who so resembles Governor Fenton. In New York more than a score addressed him and thought they were speaking to the governor of New York. There is the same tall figure, the same grizzled hair and beard, and both look the governor. Wm. M. Stone has been a lawyer, a district judge, and a colonel in the war; was captured at Shiloh, and held prisoner nearly a year; was wounded at Vicksburg, and before he fully recovered was elected governor of his State, and he is now but thirty-six.

Come this way and I will point you out the Hon. Isaac N. Arnold, who has just concluded a four years' representation in Congress of the Chicago district. In stature he is slight, and of medium height. In manner he is refined, polite, and attentive. His words, terse and clear, show the legal training of his mind, as the thoughtful lines of his face indicate long and hard study and practice of his profession. I believe before he entered Congress he had practised law in Chicago more than twenty years, with enviable success. I know he gave to his duties in Congress the same steady, intense care which marked him in the conduct of a lawyer, and that few members of its last two Congresses have been more assiduously and wisely useful. He introduced, and carried successfully through, the bill prohibiting slavery in the Territories, and he was the first to point out the necessity of re-electing Mr. Lincoln. It was understood that his personal relations have been very intimate with the late President.

The red-bearded, red-haired man engaged in earnest conversation with a group of which he seems to be the oracle, is the Hon. D. L. Phillips, marshal of the Southern District of Illinois, and proprietor of "The Illinois State Journal." Twice a candidate for Congress against John A. Logan,*though his party was in a hopeless minority, he led the forlorn hope with a pluck and skill never surpassed, and has largely contributed to the revolution which swept over that district last fall, when King Kendall, the Union candidate, came in with a handsome majority. Mr.

Phillips is of the Phillips family of Massachusetts, and not very distantly related to Wendell Phillips, whom he resembles in the radicalism of his politics and the force of his diction on the stump.

Another of the Illinois delegation is Col. James H. Bowen of the Governor's staff. He is the head of the Chicago firm of Bowen Brothers, is a successful merchant, an enthusiastic patriot, and a leading citizen of his city. I believe his firm paid tax on an income of about $200,000 last year.

These are hasty sketches of some of the representative men who have been of the funeral cortège from the first. Others must be deferred to another letter.

AT CHICAGO.

CHICAGO, ILLINOIS, May 1, 1865.

THERE has never before been so many people in this city at one time as there are to-day. Only one previous assemblage here can be compared with it; that was five years ago this same month of May, when the national convention of the party of freedom made Abraham Lincoln their candidate for the Presidency. I remember the scenes of that day. Illinois had come up here *en masse* to ask that the man she believed in and loved should be accepted as the nation's chosen one.

Outside of the State he was little known, little honored. Here he was known to all, was idolized by his political associates, and held in no small regard even by political opponents. It has been said that the outside pressure, the clamor of the populace, compelled his selection. Maybe it did, but if so it was the *vox populi*, which is the *vox dei*. Five years have passed, and now, against the clamor of the thousands for their favorite, against the wild tornado of acclaim which shook the sky when it was seen that he had been chosen, against all the unearthly rejoicing of that other day, there is to-day silence for clamor, bowed heads for acclaim, deep sorrow for wild rejoicings, and universal mourning for him who was then and is still their universal friend. New York and other cities, when it was known that Lee had surrendered, and New York and those cities when word came that the President had been murdered contrasted widely as the poles. But Illinois when she saw her Lincoln made President, and now, when she receives his cold ashes, contrasts widely as heaven and hell. And yet she finds some balm for her grief in pride that he in whom they first saw virtue and greatness is now reckoned by the whole nation as greatest and most worthy.

The funeral cortège has retraced the path pursued four years ago, when the President went to the national capital to assume duties he himself felt to be greater than Washington's. Then they would have killed him in Baltimore, where now they lifted up their voices and wept. Then New York accorded him but a cold greeting; now New York makes for him a great funeral, with more real mourners than Cæsar had at Rome, Napoleon at Paris, or Wellington at London.

Then the rural populace knew not or cared not of his coming, or looked with eyes only curious. Now they line the way in uncovered thousands, and their hands have prepared touching tributes to the memory of him for whom their hearts throb sorrowingly as rolls by his funeral car. And as we have come West, where he was first known and first loved, we have found the testimonials more elaborate, more beautiful, as the mourning is more deep, more pathetic. At Cleveland we thought, "Nothing in the expression of sorrow can excel this."

At Columbus we confessed that there the people had worked tributes even more original in design and more complete in the effect. And yesterday at Indianapolis we said to ourselves, "These Hoosiers have exceeded all that has gone before, and there is nothing left for Chicago; she can only copy from the ten cities which have already honored Lincoln dead." We were mistaken, and a suspicion that we were so dawned at Michigan City this morning. This is the most considerable town of Schuyler Colfax's district through which the train passed, and here were himself and many of his constituents in honor of his and their dead friend.

But last night he delivered at Chicago an eloquent and discriminating eulogy of the dead, and he then hurried back to his home. Under his direction there had been built across the track at Michigan City an evergreen dome, tasteful in structure, elaborate in detail, and bearing upon each of the four faces, in letters woven from the arbor-vitæ to the trailing arbutus by the hands of ladies, an appropriate motto. One of them was as follows:

ABRAHAM LINCOLN.
We resign thee to God and History.

Then a number of young ladies, one for each State, dressed in uniform of white with black scarfs, sung hymns and dirges while the train halted for breakfast, which had been provided by the citizens. Here we were met by a committee of one hundred from Chicago. Thence three hours' ride over the prairie and by the side of the lake, which in the distance, where it lay banked up against the horizon, seemed a vast crescent of emerald, and nearer by lay waveless, tideless, and beautiful, and the funeral train stopped a mile and a half from the heart of Chicago, just where the railroad diverges from the shore to pass over the water a mile further on rows of driven piles.

Here Senators Doolittle, Wilkeson, Howe, and Trumbull, and Representatives Wilson of Iowa, and Wentworth of Illinois, joined the escort, and from this point the procession moved. The first notable feature was the structure beneath which stood the hearse, drawn by eight black horses befittingly caparisoned. This structure was an elaborate combination of flags, drapery, flowers, mottoes, and architecture impossible to describe but very beautiful to behold.

The second feature different from other cities was this,— 15,000 children from the public schools marshalled by their teachers; and these were given the first place in the procession after the Citizens' Committee of 100. The procession was four hours passing a given point, and numbered 50,000. A prominent place was accorded the colored citizens and their various organizations.

The exterior of the Court-House, where the remains lie in state is a wonder of artistic decoration, but the interior, with the superb catafalque and decorations of sable cloth, bright flowers, and starry flags, is even more wonderful, more artistic, and more beautiful, while from above mournful music from an invisible choir floats through the dim aisles and falls gently down like incense from "an unseen censer, swung by angel hands."

The "dim religious light," which but partially illumined the coffin and the face of the dead, shines down from the roof of the catafalque through thirty-six star-shaped openings in the black cloth, being a star for each State.

The papers of this city give up their entire space to matter concerning the funeral.

CHICAGO, May 2, 1865.

Yesterday and to-day this city has been the centre where meets the great Northwest, to pay the last tributes of love and honor to the murdered President. I cannot hope to convey to your readers in other sections an adequate conception of the funeral they have made for him here. The emotion that we saw in Baltimore, the multitude and the pageant that we saw in Philadelphia and New York, the elaborate testimonials that awaited his honored dust in cities further west, all these combine and culminate here at Chicago. Large delegations are here from all the cities of the Northwest. Not one in ten will be able to see the face of their slain pride and idolatry. Yes, pride and idolatry; for no less expressive words express the feeling of these demonstrative Western men and women toward Abraham Lincoln. I refrain from copying the inscriptions and describing the decorations, and would only speak of the feeling that is apparent, patent, palpable, that is spontaneous, irrepressible, that is universal yet individual, that is as inconceivable as it is indescribable. Half a million of people in the city, 50,000 in the procession, perfect order, undisturbed solemnity, religious quiet — a funeral that embraces everybody — this is Chicago to-day. Those who have been with the cortège from Washington remark to each other that this is more striking, more beautiful, more mournful, is greater than anything they had met before.

It seems to me that the events of the last few weeks are to give color to those of the next years and years. I mean that they have political significance — that, in the words of one of the mottoes on the way, "Pardon died with Abraham Lincoln," and in the words of another motto, there is soon to be "Banishment to traitors, the suffrage for the negro, and equality before the laws to all." The people are ready for all this, and the politician and the party that stand in the way of this determination will be swept out of sight by the might of resistless majorities. The West and the Northwest, and the Border States of Maryland and Missouri are up to this point to-day, and the rest of the country will not lag far behind. These sentiments as to the drift of popular thought and determination have found expression since we have been West in the conversation of the representative men who accompany the funeral train. Said a senator not hitherto supposed to be very radical: "These people would make John Brown President, if he was alive." Said a second senator, in reply: "Yes, and Wendell Phillips could get more votes in this region than *you* could, notwithstanding you have a clean anti-slavery record." Such, then, is the drift in this section. I but report it; I only say that those who have thought that contrary to the proverb this revolution would go backward, had better gauge the drift of events before they commit themselves. I refer now only to those who try to sound the popular current before they declare themselves, and have no reference to those who have a high standard of conduct. Yet those last will do well to study the effect of the assassination of the President in whom all trusted upon the *animus* of the masses, and consequently upon the terms of pacification of Rebel States which will be acceptable to loyal men, which will be acceptable to those who have borne the heat and burden of the day, have won the day, and then saw their leader fall by the Parthian arrow of a defeated conspiracy.

EN ROUTE FROM CHICAGO TO SPRINGFIELD,
Wednesday, May 3, 1865, 6 A. M.

Nearly all of day before yesterday, all of night before last, and all day yesterday the remains of the President lay in state amid the imposing funeral surroundings in the Court-House at Chicago, and still there was not sufficient time for all who sought the privilege to look upon his face. And when it was night, and the coffin was closed, and young ladies came to place upon it fresh flowers wrought into significant and touching emblems, and the last dirge was being chanted by the unseen choir overhead, and the Guard of Honor and the funeral escorts surrounded the bier, and the coffin was borne upon the shoulders of the veteran sergeants to the hearse in the street, between lines of flaring torches, — even then, when the gates of the public square had been closed an hour, a long, dense column still waited in the vain hope of being admitted.

Taken all in all, Chicago made a deeper impression upon those who had been with the funeral from the first than any one of the ten cities passed through before had done. It was to be expected that such would be the case, yet, seeing how other cities had honored the funeral, there seemed to be no room for more, and the Eastern members of the cortège could not repress surprise when they saw how Chicago and the Northwest came, with one accord, with tears and with offerings, to help bury "this Duncan" who had "been so clear in his great office." The last of these tributes was the escort of torches to the funeral train, showing the cortège as it passed to thousands who were themselves wrapped in darkness.

On board the train now, beside the original escort, are the delegation from Kentucky, headed by Governor Bramlette, the committee of one hundred from Chicago, Lieutenant-Governor Bross, Speaker Colfax, Senator H. S. Lane, and others. At every station of fifty houses during the night, say forty or fifty in all, the train has passed under an elaborate arch; and at nearly all, choirs have stood by the way and sung requiems. The demonstrations at Joliet and Lockport were particularly surprising, for the multitudes gathered at the dead of night. At many places where the train did not even slacken speed, where there seemed to be no dwellings for miles, large companies were assembled, many sitting in the vehicles that had brought them from their homes, — all this in the middle of the night. We have now, at daylight, just passed Bloomington, where had assembled a vast uncovered throng. The passengers, perhaps awakened by the sound of the minute guns, are emerging from the many couches of the seven sleeping-cars of the train. These sleeping-cars are all new, and are most beautifully draped inside as well as outside. They were decorated for the occasion, and tendered to the escort by George M. Pullman, Esq., of Chicago, the manufacturer and owner. This acknowledgment of his courtesy is made at the instance of the various delegations on board.

The vast prairie, stretching away to the horizon in cultivated farms, is a novel sight to many of the party, and there is no little surprise when an Illinoisan remarks: "Now, for the next eight miles we shall be going through the 'Funk' estate, which consists of 37,000 acres in one body, and a number of out-lying farms. Peter Funk, who accumulated the estate, died last winter. He will be remembered for his rough but powerful invective against copperheads in the State Senate two years ago. He used to speak of a body of 4,000 acres of his inclosed grazing land as the "calf-pasture."

There is but time to get a cup of coffee in the forward car before the train will be nearing Springfield.

A RETROSPECT.

SPRINGFIELD, ILLINOIS, May 3, 1865.

HE said, in a few words of impressive farewell addressed to his friends on the 11th of February, 1861, after he had stepped upon the platform of the car which was to bear him away, "I must now leave you,—*for how long I know not.*" Alas, those friends now know just how long. He said too, "I go to assume a task more difficult than that which devolved upon Washington;" and now the whole world, whose central figure he has been from that day to this, must concede that he has acquitted himself of that task like another Washington.

In the mellow air and bright sunlight of this May morning, sweetened by the rain of last night, when those prairies are clothed in flowers and the thickets of wild fruit-trees and blossoming orchards are jubilant with birds, he comes back. His friends and neighbors are here to receive him, not with banners and triumphal music, not with congratulations and grasping of hands, as they had hoped to do, — not so, but in mourning, and his oldest and dearest friends come to meet him to be the pall-bearers at his funeral.

The contrast between that other day and to-day, the contrast between what but for the assassin the day of his return should have been, and what that day actually is, these contrasts force themselves upon the mind and will not be banished from our thoughts.

The train that brought him to his long home, moved slowly into the town, moved slowly through the masses of "plain people" who had come from all the country round about. These people had known him always as the boy struggling for knowledge while he battled with poverty; as the young man who surveyed their lands, and read all night, when perchance he stayed at their humble houses; as the rising young lawyer who pleaded the causes of the poor for "only sweet pity's sake," who upheld the weak against the strong for only justice's sake, and because oppression was hateful to him; as the politician whose continual plea was: "Let us see if this thing be right; if it be right let us have it, but if it be wrong let us put it away from us;" as the State legislator who, with one other, against an intolerant majority dared to file upon the records his protest against slavery; as the Presidential Elector who each four years spoke his convictions in every town in the State, though in a hopeless minority, for conscience' sake, and yet never lost his temper or called bad names; as the candidate for senator who deliberately said, "I will not be double-faced, I will utter the same opinions at both ends of the State, I will not be made Senator by a fraud." And by and by he was made President and went from among them; and they, watching from afar, were proud that one of themselves had become, in virtue and in station, "the foremost man of all this world." And then they saw him accomplish his great task; and now they were seized by a mighty longing to see him once more, and they made him promise that he would come in June; and then they heard of his most horrible murder, and behold he comes in May, but he comes a dead man. Say, have not these people a right to mourn and to refuse to be comforted? Was he not peculiarly their own? and when you and all of us sorrow, shall these not lament?

The train stops, the pall-bearers, those old men, friends of his lang syne, approach. The stillness among all the people is painful; but when the coffin is taken from the car, that stillness is broken by sobs, and these are more painful than the stillness. The coffin is borne to the hearse, the hearse moves slowly, almost tenderly away, followed by the mourners, and the pall-bearers walk by the side. The cortège, more solemn than any that had gone before, reaches the State House where he was wont to speak face to face with his neighbors — where at this hour those neighbors press to behold his face locked in death. All night they will pass by with eyes searching through tears for resemblances and recognition of the features they knew so well. Many will not know the poor, chilled, shrunken features for his, for the beautiful soul that transfigured them into all loveliness no longer illumines this bit of clay, — ay, but it shines at the Right Hand.

The following is the programme of religious services to-morrow, beginning at noon: —

Dead March in Saul; Opening Prayer, Rev. A. Hale; Dirge (composed for the occasion), by G. F. Root; Reading of the Scriptures, Rev. N. W. Miner; Choral, "To Thee, O Lord," St. Paul; President Lincoln's last Inaugural, Rev. A. C. Hubbard; Dirge, by Otto; Funeral Oration, Bishop Simpson; Dirge, by Strotch; Closing Prayer, Rev. Dr. Harkey; Requiem, "Peace, Troubled Soul!" Benediction, Rev. Dr. Gurley.

At the close of this the procession will be formed and pass to Oak Ridge Cemetery one and a half miles due north of the State House, in the receiving vault of which the body will be temporarily placed.

THE CLOSING SCENES AT SPRINGFIELD.

SPRINGFIELD, ILLINOIS, Thursday Morning, May 4, 1865.

SPRINGFIELD has a population of 15,000. It is the best-built small city I have ever seen. The private residences and grounds of the leading citizens indicate an opulence and a tasteful elegance not to be found in many larger towns. It is laid out in wide streets, running with the cardinal points of compass, and covers immense ground for so small a population. The location is upon a black, prairie-soiled plateau, which, in default of a regular pavement, necessitates the building of a plank road along every street. Fifteen years ago the State House (which is located in a public square in the very centre of the city) was considered the finest structure in the West. The Executive Mansion, owned by the State, and occupied by the successive governors — now the home of Governor Oglesby — is certainly the finest gubernatorial residence in the country; spacious, excellent in architecture, and elegantly furnished. Some of the private residences are scarcely less elegant and imposing. That of ex-Governor Mattison is considered the best house in the State.

The importance of the city has consisted mainly in its being the State capital, yet it has a large trade with the surrounding country, and railroads intersect here, which gives communication north and south, east and west. It had been the home of Abraham Lincoln twenty-five years. With his companionable nature and open heart it followed that he was the personal acquaintance and friend of all the men, women, and children in the city, and in all the region about. Besides, Springfield was the political centre of the State, and during twenty years Abraham Lincoln was the acknowledged State leader of a political party. That party, or the one that sprang from it, was finally successful, and rewarded him, not merely with State honors, but with the headship of the nation. Such giants as E. D. Baker, Lyman Trumbull, Richard Yates, S. T. Logan, David Davis, Owen Lovejoy, E. B. Washburne, Wm. H. Bissell,

R. J. Oglesby, J. N. Arnold, and John Wentworth,—all these conceded his right to leadership and cheerfully rallied beneath his standard. And yet more than the political leader he was the popular townsman and good neighbor at his home in Springfield. Springfield, then, is his proper burial-place, and to-day he will be entombed here.

Of course, the town is heavily draped. Even the humblest houses are black with costly cloth. At the house of Mr. Chatterton I noticed a fine specimen of the Washington eagle, splendidly mounted, and holding the flag in its beak, and just beneath it a marble bust of Lincoln, with the motto beneath the whole, "In life ours, in death the country's;" and this is but one of the fifty equally appropriate. Fine taste and money had been spent upon the State House to fit it for the reception of the remains. I won't try to describe it, but will confine myself to the effect of it all. That, whether one looked on as a lover of the æsthetic or in full sympathy as a mourner, whether one scanned it critically or permitted himself to yield to the spell of the place, was all that could have been intended or be desired.

Yesterday and this morning the house where Mr. Lincoln lived fifteen years, and in which he received the deputation, headed by George Ashmun, which came to officially inform him of his nomination for the Presidency, has been the centre of interest to all the strangers in the city. It is situated four or five squares to the southeast of the State House, and is at present the residence of S. Tilton, President of the Great Western Railroad. The house has been often described. You remember that it is an unpretending two-story frame house with a one-story ell, which, the house being on a street corner, fronts another street than the main building. It is, or rather was some years ago, painted a very yellow straw-color, is plainly furnished, and contains but eight rooms altogether. In the small yard are several quite large apple-trees, now in full blossom, and there is some shrubbery. The favorite chair in which he sat and the desk at which he wrote are still there, as are many other of his old personal surroundings. To-day the hundreds of visitors are begging everything available as souvenirs, sprigs from the shrubbery, blossoms from the trees, even palings from the fence for canes.

Up to this morning it had not been finally determined whether the remains would be deposited at Oak Ridge Cemetery or in a vault hastily built on the "Mother Place," which is a fine property of ten acres in the western part of the city, and which the citizens, on hearing of his death, bought (paying $50,000) as a place for his tomb and monument. Preparations were made at each place, but this morning, on the arrival of Captain Robert Lincoln and John G. Nicolay, late private Secretary, from Washington, the question was decided in favor of Oak Ridge, though it is quite possible that the body may finally rest at the "Mother Place."

Last evening Governor Oglesby received at his house the various delegations in the city to the number of say a thousand, and Rev. Dr. O. H. Tiffany, the most noted Chicago pulpit and platform orator, delivered an address at one of the churches on the life and characteristics of Mr. Lincoln, which is to be published.

This morning a large delegation arrived from St Louis headed by General Fiske and Hon. H. T. Blow. At this hour, nine A. M., the relatives and personal friends of the dead have just looked — not spoken — the last lingering farewell of their idol, and the coffin has been forever closed. It is computed that over one million of people have seen his dead face.

What other man in all this tide of time ever had so many come to see him after death had taken him ? A million at one man's funeral !

THE GREAT REVIEW.

WASHINGTON, Wednesday evening,
May 24, 1865.

THE grand review is over. The two days of deserved apotheosis of the two great armies of the Republic have come and gone, and 150,000 veterans have been reviewed, not merely by Grant and Sherman and Meade, but by the people, the grateful millions. Your faithful correspondents have already given you by telegraph the story of the marching in serried columns, the huzzas of the multitude, and the names of commanding officers, from those of corps to those of regiments. I shall only add a few observations, reflections, and recollections.

To civilians looking on, perhaps the most amazing thing was the numbers that marched by. Unused to armies, they sat seven hours yesterday and seven hours to-day, while the men with sabres and the men with bayonets, in close order and at brisk pace, marched past, and still the wonder grew where all the soldiers came from. And yet only one-quarter of the loyal forces now under arms in the country were seen by them. So the dense, swift, long columns were the greatest wonder, because they were dense and swift and long.

The next wonder was that the soldiers seemed so little excited. They tramped along with a certain easy, satisfied, every-day nonchalance that was the perfection of the *nil admirari*. They scarcely looked right or left, and any pride and exultation they did show was grim and bronzed like their faces and their uniforms. There were, however, some exceptions. When a shout of "Hurrah for Massachusetts" would be raised by a group of Bay State spectators, or an enthusiastic Sucker would call for and get rousing cheers for Illinois, as regiments from their respective States passed by, then the rank and file would look eagerly to where the shout came from, and scan each man's face as though hoping to see a familiar one. Again, when a colonel on passing the main pavilion would ask for cheers for the President and General Grant, the imperturbable faces would become transfigured into wild animation and pride, and old rusty caps, grasped by tawny hands and swung high by brawny arms, would circle in the air, while lungs made strong by years in the field, and throats familiar with the whoop of the charge and the cheer of victory, would send up a noise like that of the many waters of many Niagaras. And yet not one in fifty would turn his eyes to see the faces of those they were cheering. Whether the seeming want of curiosity was the result of discipline which commanded "eyes to the front, all," or whether they really did not deign to appear to be curious, I can't say.

There never was so perfectly happy a set of men as those in the main pavilion, — the President and Cabinet, General Grant, and the score or two of other distinguished officers. Not that they grinned and bowed in self-approbativeness, for there was not a bit of that. It was n't self-complacency, but a sort of calm quiet; a settled peace and gratitude seemed to pervade them all. When the crowd would surge up to the stand, at any brief interval in the procession, and demand a sight of their favorites, the President would rise, and bow repeatedly, but say never a word. Grant when called for would but rise for an instant, with lifted hat, and if his face told any story at all it was one of shyness and surprise.

To the stranger in Washington who had never seen the men on that stand, it was well worth while the rushing up as the rear of a division or corps passed, the hurried glance, and the scamper back when the head of the next column approached. There were the President and Cabinet, Sherman, Meade, Hancock, Howard, Slocum, Logan, Hunter, Humphreys, Custer, and fifty others only less famous, — a collection of names that will pass into history among the giants.

Yesterday the favorites among the officers who rode by were clearly Merritt, Custer, Humphreys, Griffin, and Miles. Custer is the Murat of the war, Humphreys has worthily succeeded to the command of Hancock's old corps (the Second), and Griffin to Warren's (the Fifth). It should not and does not detract from the latter that the men raised cheer after cheer for Warren, than whom an officer was never more idolized by his soldiers. It may not be inappropriate to say here that it is understood that Warren stands to-day entirely exonerated from any fault on the day that he was relieved from his corps by Sheridan, and that he and Sheridan are now the best of friends. The statement is confirmed by Warren's late assignment to an important command at the West.

To-day the heroes have been Sherman, Logan, Slocum, and Geary. Howard, having taken charge of the Freedmen's Bureau, and yielded the Army of the Tennessee, did not ride with the troops; but everybody asked for him, and an ovation was waiting for this one-armed hero.

You know before the war Logan was an *awful* Democrat, and in his speeches actually committed himself against "coercion." But when Sumter was fired upon, and his political chief, Douglas, wheeled about and pronounced for coercion, then he, too, began to reconsider. It is said that he wrote to Douglas to know what to do, and that the latter replied, "Raise a regiment, John." Logan did so, and was commissioned colonel by an old political antagonist, Governor Yates. During the first year of the war he remained very much of a Democrat — fought for the Union with slavery. He dates his Abolitionism from the day he entered some Southern city — I think it was Nashville — and found no welcome except from the negroes. Last fall his wife bet a span of mules with General Singleton that her husband would vote for Lincoln — and won them. A few weeks before the election he was given leave of absence, and announced that he would speak; but, desirous of getting at his old political associates, refused to say on which side he would speak. He got a tremendous audience, and pronounced for Lincoln; and then spoke twice each day till election. As the direct result, the political revolution in Southern Illinois was the most remarkable thing in the last campaign.

Yesterday the best horse in the line was Custer's, to-day Geary's. Major-General Geary was Scott's Military Governor of the City of Mexico, has been Mayor of San Francisco, Governor of the Territory of Kansas, and has fought through this war, beginning as coloneL How he sat his horse to-day! — a tall, shining black horse, whose neck was clothed with thunder, whose tail was carried like a banner, whose step bespoke the pride of Lucifer, — a kingdom for *that* horse were not so bad a bargain!

One thing, both yesterday and to-day, never failed to call forth cheers, and that was the old flags, the tattered, torn, stained flags, frayed to shreds, staffs with a few sprays of a lint-like silk, — these were loudly cheered time after time. Sometimes a regiment would show two of these old flags, and alongside it a broad new silken " glory " bearing the names of the battles in which it had participated. One Massachusetts regiment had affixed to an old staff, to which still clung a few shreds of the old flag, a score of bright new streamers, each having the name of one of the battles of the regiment — and was n't *that* cheered !

The Army of the Potomac reviewed yesterday is mainly composed of Eastern troops, while the Army of Georgia (Slocum's), and the Army of Tennessee (Logan's, late Howard's) are mainly Western troops. The exception in the one case consists in a dozen Western regiments scattered through the different divisions. In the latter the exception is the Twentieth Corps (the Eleventh and Twelfth consolidated) which went West under Hooker. Naturally a comparison was provoked in the minds of the spectators between the Eastern and Western troops. It was noted that the Western men had the advantage in physique, were taller men, with fewer boys, and scarcely any foreigners among them, that their marching' step was several inches longer, and that yellow and red beards, and light hair worn long predominated. Officers of the Army of the Potomac conceded that they marched better, that they moved with an elastic, springy, swinging step that does not belong to the Eastern boys, and that their faces were more intelligent, self-reliant, and determined. One could not distinguish officers from men except by their uniforms; the privates and the officers seemed equal in intelligence and manly bearing, and in station when at home. On the other hand, the Eastern troops showed more pure discipline, more drill. There was a marked distinction between the officers and the men in point of culture. The officers were more gaily dressed, and evidently belonged to more elegant, or at least more presuming walks of life than those of the general rank in the Western armies. The Eastern men all wore the close-fitting regulation skull-cap; the Western men the soft slouch hat. The former were exact, prim, stiff; the latter, easy, don't-care, independent, and pioneerish.

It was remarkable to see how the Twentieth Corps, transplanted, as it had been, from the East, had taken on many of the characteristics of their new comrades. They had learned the same swinging stride, exchanged caps for hats, and become military cosmopolites.

Bringing up the rear of each brigade to-day were the jack-mules, heavily laden with the camp fixtures of the commands, and with the plunder of the long march from Atlanta to Washington. Indeed the mules themselves were found on the way. They were led by negroes — also found on the way. Tied to the backs of the mules were a number of big red roosters and fighting-cocks. Crosswise the back of one, with feet in either pannier, was a grave billy goat. Following one brigade, led by negroes, was a pair of small white original jackasses and several cows. These things elicited much merriment and shouting among the thousands looking on, to whom the "bummers" of a large army were a revelation. A half-dozen pickaninnies not ten years old, of both sexes, astride mules, evidently the protégés of regiments, were funny enough.

Commanding a brigade in this corps was Gen. H. A. Barnum, of Syracuse. Your correspondent once wrote that man's obituary —after the seven days' battles. The surgeon reported him dying, and he was left on the field, after having sent his last words to his wife and little boy. However, he came down from Richmond on the first flag-of-truce boat, and lived to fight at Fredericksburg, at Chancellorsville, at Gettysburg, at Lookout Mountain, where he was again wounded, and now to lead a brigade in "Sherman's March to the Sea." You would n't have thought, as you saw him backing a wild horse to-day, receiving the bouquets that were brought him, and bowing acknowledgment to the cheers that greeted him, that he still has an unhealed wound from Malvern Hill, yet such is the case. You could put your whole hand into the raw cavity in his side that still remains, and will never heal; but since he received that wound he stormed Lookout Mountain, and was chosen to go to Washington bearing the thirty-five flags captured there.

Commanding the Third Division of the Fourteenth Corps was Brevet Major-Gen. J. M. Corse, a young man of twenty-eight. Six or eight years ago he was dropped from the roll of cadets at West Point for incompetency, inability to maintain the required rank in his class. But the knowledge of tactics gained in the year or two he was there gave him at the commencement of the war the adjutancy of an Iowa regiment. He couldn't do the mathematics of West Point, nevertheless he was a natural soldier, and, young as he is, has won his present rank by sheer fighting, by sheer *ability* in fighting. When Hood struck Sherman's communications, Corse, with 1,200 men was garrisoning the important point of Altoona. By the inspiration which he infused into his men he beat off half of Hood's army, and was brevetted Major-General for it — but he couldn't get through West Point. His career is a beautiful comment on the assumption and presumption of some of those who do not get through that questionable institution known as "West Point." I never saw General Corse till he rode by to-day, but I think I am correct as to his failure at West Point, as I know I am in regard to his brilliant record in the army.

The Army of the Potomac lacked in this review one of its best corps, — the Sixth, General Wright commanding, since Sedgwick fell. The Sixth was necessarily detained at Danville and vicinity until last week, and left Richmond for this city only yesterday morning. Its absence yesterday is much to be regretted, for no corps has a better record.

And so the last review is over. The war is over. The boys are going home.

"When shall their glory fade?"

THE END.

www.ingramcontent.com/pod-product-compliance
Lightning Source LLC
Chambersburg PA
CBHW051727300426
44115CB00007B/500